Claes Oldenburg
Writing on the Side
1956–1969

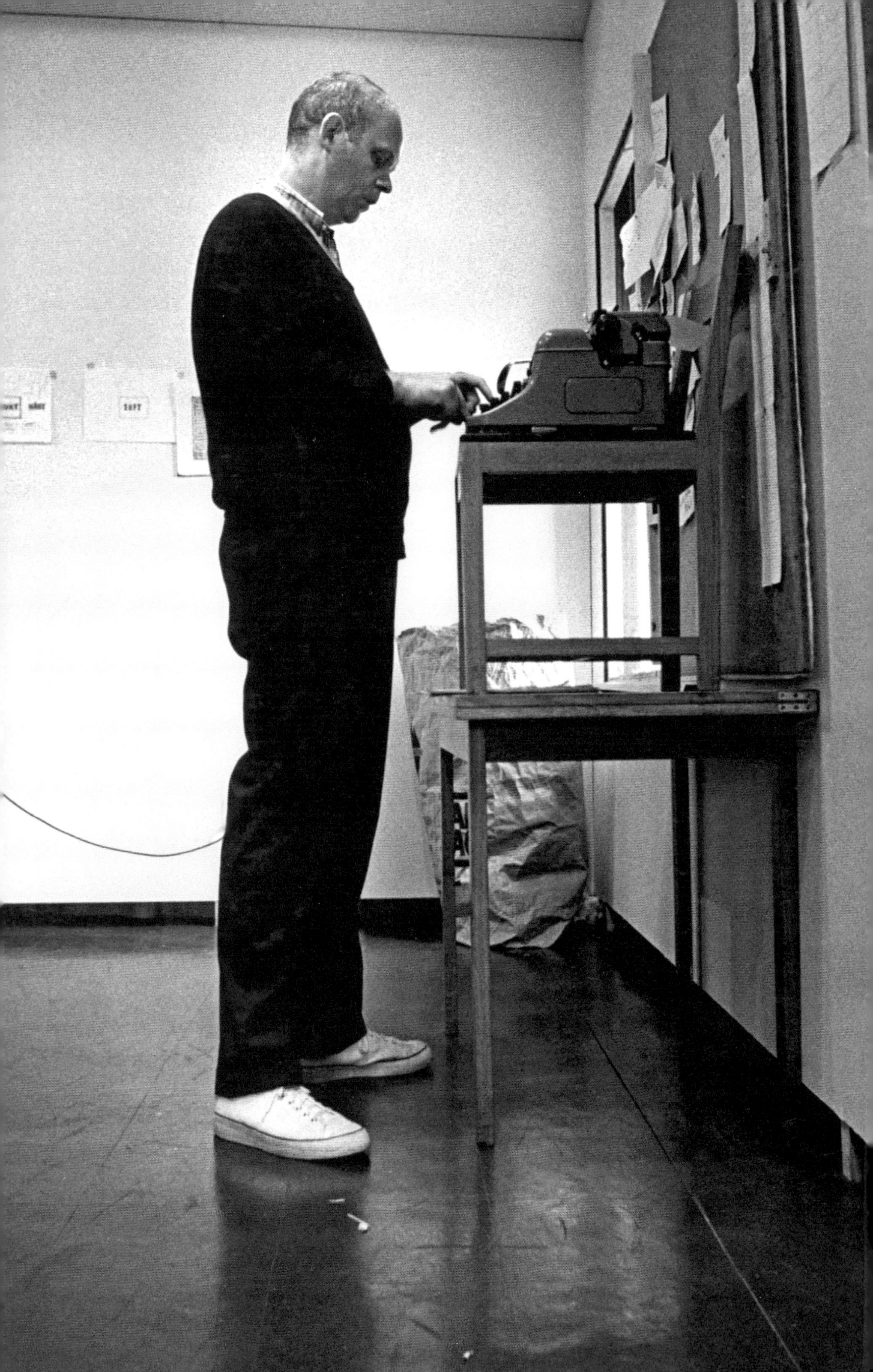

Claes Oldenburg
Writing on the Side
1956–1969

Edited by Achim Hochdörfer, Maartje Oldenburg,
and Barbara Schröder

The Museum of Modern Art, New York

CONTENTS

Chapter 4: On the Road, 1963–1964

Chapter 5: Object Consciousness, 1965–1967

Chapter 6: Self-Portraits, 1968–1969

The justification for an autobiography is that the work always arises out of experience, changes its character in relation to experience, and is always best understood in relation to a particular experience. The other justification is that an artist's life ought to have structure, or he ought to be able to shape it into a structure in retrospect, as a good (or bad) example. He must account for himself—or that's how I feel. Every day, in writing notes, in making entries in my diary, or in defending my work and behavior, that is what I do, and a collection of all that, trimmed, will lead to an autobiography, if these scraps are not to remain scraps.

I do not expect that this autobiography will display any consistency, and it will not be done as an attempt at consistency but will be more an accumulation (which might in the end float into a pattern—but that is not known now, at the start).

Songs of Professor Dog.

The Artist, in my thinking, is always another person. I would and do refer to him in the third person—"he." I am he, but I am also not he, I am also the observer of he, and I am, when I am not he, much more difficult (impossible) to define. The Artist is a helpful simplification of my existence, a helpful *role*. I was formless until I found this role, and therefore quite unsatisfied. My autobiography is about myself (the unknown) looking at him (my role).

I have no shape, but he will have shape, the fiction of myself, any shape that I can give him. Plastic Man.

I have gone through many changes of attitude, each change involving a substitution of place, people, and circumstances generally. Signs and symbols have always announced the change. Some facts begin to seem more important than others. I watch, fascinated, for a while, until a pattern emerges and from the pattern, a direction. Because the pattern takes a long time to develop, this familiarity and growth makes for a sense of certainty when it does arrive at shape. Art is decision making on a high level (or ought to be).

Seminal circumstances—events that stay in the mind. From one of these to the next, the continuity of a personal story is tied, and they are probably as repetitious as a collection of dreams. An autobiography will repeat how trapped the subject is, but that is also a condition for Art being made. The Artist, Artist Dog, returns again and again to the unsolved problem, in one form or another resolves (or thinks he does) the conflict or engages the conflict, which produces a result—not the solution but a physical result of agitation, mental and gestural. Drawings are for me the battleground of my being.

Professor Clear-head.

Everyone carries around a fiction of what has happened, and in my case that is a visual concept, like a panorama on the allegorical model, wherein many moments in time can be represented simultaneously and in many variations of conditions of nature and states of mind, emotion and fantasy—all combined. This panorama is not finished quickly; it is finished in fragments, and what counts for the artist is the ability to adjust the new to the foregone, improvise relationships that make order of the past (a fictional order, of course), and indicate order for tomorrow. Patches and fragments accumulate, but to begin with I'll sketch in the whole area in light strokes, establish the landscape and areas of interest . . .

Chapter 1
Fear of New York
1956–1958

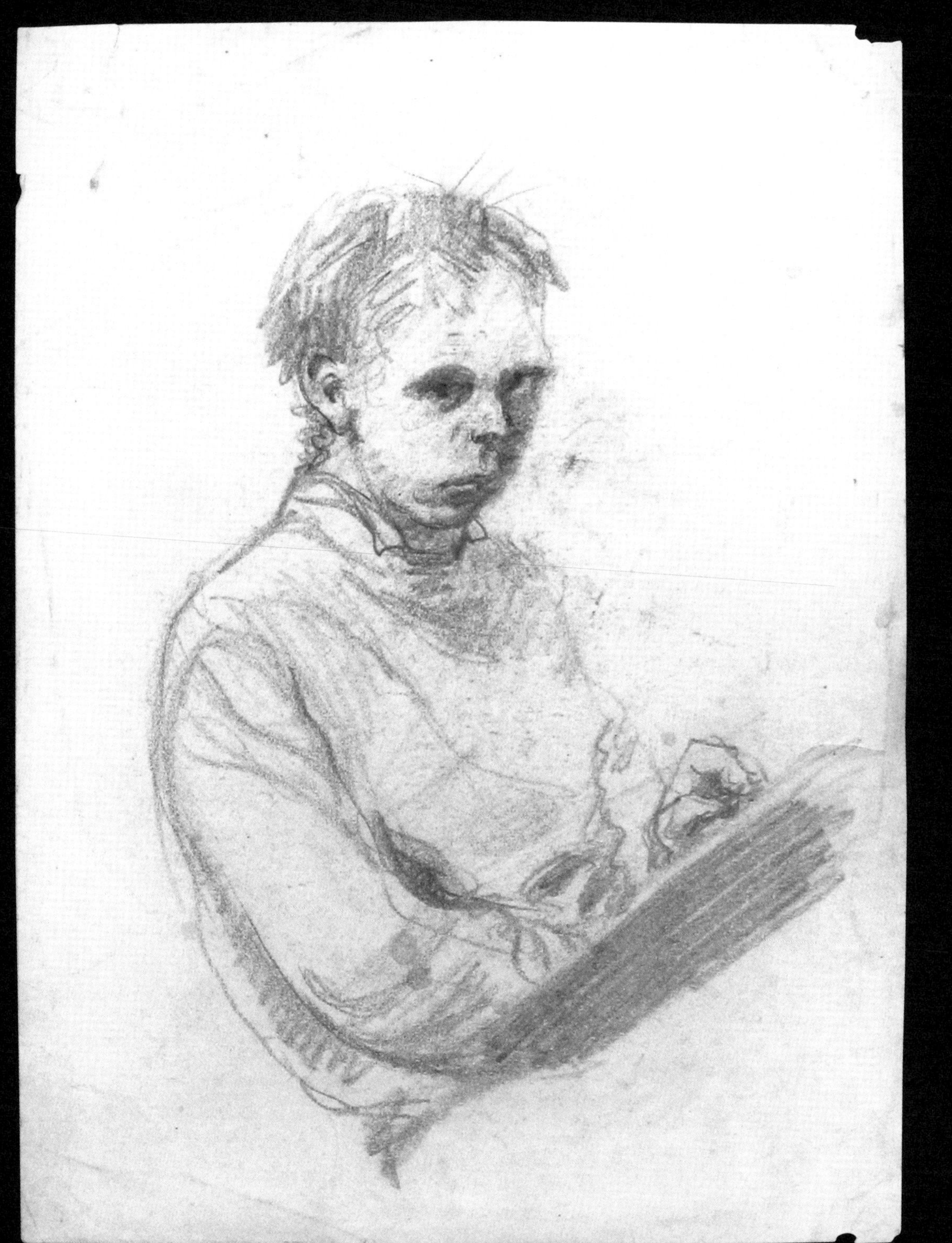

THURSDAY, MAY 31, 1956
Depart 1:45 p.m. for NY Greyhound bus.
Moving bed with Seymour a.m. Packing. Lunch home. Marge said goodbye at station.
Adieu Chicago.

FRIDAY, JUNE 15, 1956
Very hot.
Interview at Cooper Union. Got job. Got summer apartment on 13th St.
Went to Met, p.m.
No one to celebrate with.
Beer + dinner at 5th Ave.
Walked around Village.

MONDAY, JULY 23, 1956
Tapié, etc.
First collages, in response to reading + having given up studio that allowed for
painting—*no*. Not until 27th?

MONDAY, AUGUST 13, 1956
Paid $40 for 135 East 12th St. apartment.
Cleaned a bit.
Cedar St., dinner with Marge, Bobbie + Ann.

THURSDAY, AUGUST 16, 1956
Dinner Tony's.
First poetry writing. Up late.
Picked up equipment from Perry's to clean with.

SUNDAY, SEPTEMBER 16, 1956
First big drawings.
Free use of material on big scale—evening.
Cedar—dinner.
Fixed place a.m. + p.m.

SUNDAY, OCTOBER 14, 1956
Worked with color only.
Wonderful day.
No money—hungry.
Frank + custard dinner.

Tuesday, August 14, 1956

227th day — 139 days follow

HOT

Concent Wash Sq.
Minor Cedar st.
drawing on East River
George Kotoshka — comic.
oly activity

TIMES SQ
DRWG

Wed 14
have I come a
long way from
this day a year ago! ?

seemed good

Ma called

up. 10:30 cloudy gray day
wrote out dreams shaved
bank. spent $5 this day
letter from Dick. ate Concin's
set down a few notes for apply
painted on large canvas
"Card game" music
ate Jade Mtn shrimps.
walked to excavations (of
which I had dreamed) then
sketched + in warehouse
street. took them out again, to
Times sq. sat in Duffy sq
sketching. ate hamb. place +
frank place. hungry.
sketched characters in
hamb. place. home sub.
slumped man home by 12.
speculated bed 1:30

Diary page, August 14, 1956, and August 14, 1957

TUESDAY, NOVEMBER 27, 1956
Drawing.
Self-portrait + objects.

TUESDAY, DECEMBER 11, 1956
Tired because late to bed night before.
Worked all day on drawing categories. Seemed to go well in p.m.—easy generalizations,
plenty of them, but faded after dinner. Ended by grouping drawings chronologically,
deciding they are difficult to categorize + the job not worth effort.
Dinner: Il Faro.
To bed 2 a.m.
Nervous—bothered by fog horn.
Weather: rain, damp + cold.
Mind quite active, *too* active.
Drawings late.
Froze at night.

TUESDAY, JULY 25, 1957 COLLAGES / VISION OF LIGHT
Cool, wonderful day.
Vision of color on horizontal as passage to transcendence.
Mystic, unrecallable vision.
I wanted to write down but couldn't.
Up 11:30 a.m. Worked on collage until 12:30 p.m. or so. Ate Coscia's.
p.m. drew, with poor results.
Sprayed. Felt down.
Pressure of all things.
Dinner + beers 5th Ave.
Pasted + painted with bright heavy color. Called Sarah, home. Lay on roof.
Watched ball game at McSorley's.
2 beers.
Bed 1:30 a.m.

SUNDAY, AUGUST 25, 1957 STEKEL
Up 1 p.m. Long sleep.
Ate Central. Read Freud.
Read, Freud, Stekel.
Painted for first time in more than week.
Ate delicatessen.
Read, wrote until 3 a.m.
Sandwich from deli.
Rainy.

WEDNESDAY, SEPTEMBER 4, 1957 RENTED T-WRITER
Up, in time.
Shaved. Ate Coscia's.
Hot day, cloudy.
Work.
Coscia's.
Rented typewriter.
Bought paper.
Carried up, fell, bashed fingers, legs. Typed poems.
Ate Jade Mountain.
Typed poems after dinner.
Bed 1 a.m.
Storm in evening. Lightning. Rain.

WEDNESDAY, SEPTEMBER 25, 1957 TOOK APT.
Should I move? Tired.
Ate Coscia's. Coffee with Harriet, Narcissa.
To 330 East 4th St.
Neighbors. Inspection.
Basement. Dick + Bossman.
Gave deposit.
Saw Tennenbaum. Called M.
Vocabulary + filing.

FRIDAY, OCTOBER 25, 1957 2ND HAT RACK FR. ROSIE
Clear, cool.
Coscia's.
To CU Library, read poetry, Blake, Milton, et al., especially Blake of whom I became
very fond.
Subway to Dr. Lehmann. Polio shot. Bus to MoMA, saw German Expressionism show.
Bus home. Called Rosemary, picked up hat rack + mirror. Cold evening. Returned.
Ate ham + eggs at Chinese restaurant, New Garden. Worked on new hat rack. Beer,
reading sculpture notes in basement. Wine. Upstairs, drawing. Dick sweeping. Showed
work. Bed about 2 a.m.

MONDAY, NOVEMBER 4, 1957
Sunny but turned cold, cloudy.
Breakfast with Barbara.
Wrapped package.
Lunch with Helen.
Books + *Life*s. Indian architecture.
Cut magazines.
Took down Bathers + other paintings.

Painted—"sculptural" painting on collage.
Cutouts. Good ones. From new magazines.
Drew. Beer. 2 quarts.
Ate Luncheonette.
Watched TV at Tyler's. Charles Boyer + *Suspicion*.
Bed 3:30 a.m.

SATURDAY, NOVEMBER 9, 1957 STARTED ELEPH.
Cool.
Ate Luncheonette.
Speculations re: painting.
Painting.
Separation of painting + sculpture.
Definition of painting.
Egyptian, etc., influence.
Old paper paintings on wall.
Distraction of Marge's invite to MoMA film.
Dick + Dor off to Parker's.
Drawing for masks.
Reading in shop.
Ate Luncheonette. Pork?
Beer. Started mask.

MONDAY, NOVEMBER 11, 1957 PICKED UP MORE JUNK
Cold, clear, a little mist.
Ate Coscia's. Tired.
Borrowed $5 from petty cash. Went to lumberyard, bought lumber.
Worked on wire sculpture.
Went to lot again, with Dick. Looked at safe. Picked up junk. Sunset.
Worked on wire for mask.
Ate Faro. Bus to and fro.
A little more on wire.
Upstairs—hung up + inspected stuff from wrecked houses. Fastened together piece of
day before.
Called Harriet. Made date.
Down to shop, with beer. Cut tin, speculated.
Cutouts.
Bed 12:45 a.m.

MONDAY, DECEMBER 9, 1957
Rain. Gloomy day.
Typed library notes at Cooper. Subway strike. Coscia's. Bank. Hardware. Bus back.
Read about papier-mâché. Ripped many strips + paper. Listened to records. Received

Vogue from home?? Talked to Dick + Dor in shop. Ate Lunches. Ham + eggs. Stepped
on rat? Was ball. Drawing erotic morgue file, etc. But mostly thinking down in shop,
photographed sculpture in boilerroom. Cut + pasted photos from magazine, infatuation
with photography. Talked to Harriet re: photographing her, swimming.
Quart beer. Through repros till late.

SUNDAY, DECEMBER 15, 1957

Excellent, mild day. Clear, sunny. Up at 11:15 a.m. Ma called. Worked on paper
sculpture. Ate Lunches on Ave. B. Bought film. Photographed until 3:30 p.m. Saw many
good objects. Returned with bag later. Marge, Dick + Dor (who had also picked up stuff)
in studio. I ate 2 hot dog clubs + 1 quart beer. Cleaned in shop. Cleaned upstairs area.
Around Stanton St.! Xmas crowd. Objects. "NY is just too much!"
Bought spider, nude.
Put up found objects on walls, etc.
3 hot dogs. Another quart beer. Called Flo. Not home. Painted. Read book on
photography but very tired. Bed 11:45 p.m.

MONDAY, FEBRUARY 10, 1958 MARGE W. SAM BLAZER

Tired. Poor sleep. Cold, but clear. Sitting by window of Coscia's caring very little for
anything, musing. At home, light on an informal gathering of objects on the table
attracted me. I began painting—until the light was gone. Very tired at painting—a
feelingless piece, ultimately. My last canvas. No more canvas. Then went to shop and
began graphics. Read my notes from Berdick's class + Buckland Wright book—on
drypoint. Ate at New Garden. Then printed and worked on plates. Marge came to return
book. Returned later with Sam Blazer, pizza. I showed Marge + Sam my work until late.

SATURDAY, FEBRUARY 15, 1958

Up 11:30 a.m.—shaved. To Snake Pit for breakfast + read Carroll's essay in *Chicago
Review*. Met girl, Barbara Stafford. Ate together. Talk. Showed shop + studio. Printed.
Maceo in. Upstairs. Resumed reading C. essay. Hit upon new category, of synthesis,
simultaneousness. Is this the original thing? Sandwich p.m. Fire. Huge fire seen out
window. Gold's burns + apartment house, corner of Ave. C + 4th St. Got Dick, watched
from street, from roof. Dick's elation at destruction. Writing erotic poetry. Also poem
about fire. Ate New Garden. Snow beginning in p.m.—blizzard—wind drifts deep by
evening. Dick + I get papers. Air mild, nice. Dick's fur cap. Beer in shop. Rereading C.
essay, drawing Glück, Orfeo, Bellini. Phone out. A very eventful day—was it in answer
to my desire for diversion, change?

MONDAY, APRIL 28, 1958

Raining, dour day. Lunch with Judy. Bananas. Difficult starting. Concerned with subject
+ setting + how to get ideas. Redid notes. Classification, etc. Rather good definition. At
work—"Sturm und Drang" reading. Late to work. Ate, New Garden. In shop. Clipped
magazines, photo magazines. Dick's apprentice. Later beer + a hot dog. No work—but

day of good definition (?). Lonely.
Barb received job offer from N.A.

SUNDAY, JUNE 15, 1958

Tired. Up 9:30 a.m. Rabbi hammering. Quite nervous + tired but seemingly in control.
Demolished painting and subjected two weeks' activity to severe + beneficial criticism.
Set down new version, completed next day.
End of two weeks of intense painting on this canvas. Period of discovery + acquiring
numerous skills in technique + color. Also a period of intense drawing with charcoal—
tonal drawing paralleling the painting. Long period of energetic erotic inspiration.
Numerous surprisings of myself with my skills.

FRIDAY, JULY 11, 1958 FIRST CITY WALK

Removed paper from windows. Hung up sheets. Oiled books. Painted a little on Venus
after shifting canvases. Arranged sketchbook, etc. To D + D. Watched TV. Price on
ESP TV show, ridiculous. Read Frances's pornography. Off into night. Saturday. 3rd
Ave., McDougal, 14th St., etc. Walked Bowery, Delancey, Village, 14th. Cedar Bar.
Lesbian bar. New Garden dance palace. Danced with Marie. Last beer at Barg + Grill.
Met Dor in Snake Pit. Talked outside house. Dick came, talked on in basement. Bed
about 2:30 a.m. Had intended trip to Asbury Park for Saturday—an excellent hot day,
sexy, inspiring.

SATURDAY, JULY 12, 1958 SECOND CITY WALK

Storm. Very humid. Hard to get going. Set down recollections of night before and made
several drawings from them. Formulated the new approach to working from nature.
Drank beer with Dick + Dorothea at B + G. Rain—intermittent. Went to Times Square.
Up + down 8th Ave. Golden Slipper dance pavilion, Egyptian Gardens, Port Said, bars
on 8th Ave., etc. Finally New Garden. Watched, danced with Raye. Had coffee. Home by
4 a.m. or so.
Filed stuff. Hard to work, so humid.

WEDNESDAY, JULY 23, 1958

Humid, misty, and hot.
Pressing myself against inertia. I manage to make first drawing from a dream—nightmare
of man crushed by falling. I also manage to make first painting carried over from
drawing, of Bowery Bar interior. Draw. But inertia + climate overcome me.
Period of lack of energy, ambition. In evening, ride bike to West Side through Village.
Then bus ride along Houston, to Kettle for beers, up to 6th Ave. + 8th—bus back.

TUESDAY, AUGUST 5, 1958 K.O. BACK

2nd day of back trouble. Not to work. Tried painting. Worked on large sign-symbol.
Reggie came by. Talked. Place a mess. Trying to write letters, to Ma + Barb, but unable
to, mental paralysis because of confusion regarding styles. This lifts in evening after Reg's

visit—I commit myself to a figure style, etc. I have been ruminating for 2 days on this +
feeling lousy. But with decision comes relief + action. Write letters, call Sarah.

FRIDAY, OCTOBER 24, 1958
Beginning a weekend of strong painting—great jump. Continuous dissatisfaction
climaxing Monday: Sarah in chair. Woman on bed. Face. (Rosemary portrait +
Atalanta—later) from expressionistic conviction to modern expressionistic position.
Contemporaneity . . . color, power, paint mass, combination image. Putting together
'58 work + before, etc. Much struggling.

SATURDAY, NOVEMBER 29, 1958
Peace, peace. Need peace. Perturbed, still lost—it was not settled. Aggravated by
Berliner + Rosie visit. Helen calls. Pat calls—off to work at 8:45 p.m. Got job at New
School. Think. Gallery places. Where do I fit in, etc. Reading notes . . . confusion . . .
but dawning clarity + style + intention. Pattern + image of emotion . . ., etc. Paint 2
paintings. Pick up Sarah. Take large nude to Sarah. Play joke. We eat at Henry's Polish
restaurant with beer. Sarah tells loudly of relatives, etc. Coffee at her house. I tell tall
stories, imaginary, of my relatives. Back to draw—and paint with satisfying results.
Decide things are clearer. Dickie calls from a party on 10th St.—Shelton and Nicholson.
Symph Sid. Bed 1 a.m.+ . . .
Still high winds. Cold by night.

SUNDAY, DECEMBER 7, 1958
Cold + windy, but rather clear.
Started working on poems. Rewrote several old poems. Ate Ave. D. The group there—
the hapless fellow, the women with teeth. Air-raid alarm at 2 a.m. Categorized poems.
Worked on verbal material, evolved technique for separating out + presenting. Pat called
3 times. Came over with Janet. Brought pastry. Left 6:45 p.m. Mounted recent work +
sprayed. Walked to St. Marks, saw Lena show—studied my work. Very cold night. Ate
at deli on Ave. C. Watched TV. Long chat with Kenny in shop. Studied "notes," tried to
assess their value. Pat called, had had an argument with Olga.

SUNDAY, DECEMBER 14, 1958
Continuing with selection, definition of *identity*, of poetry, paintings, and drawings.
Everyone calling, wanting to see me, but no. Sally has party. Eat at Chinese restaurant,
Ave. B. Quite tired. End of selection of drawings along formal lines. Set up selection
along lines of attitude, of poetry—also becoming aware of the better stuff as a result of
stimulus of reading *Subterraneans*, etc., of that having true new personal form.
In evening, divide paintings by space-form + level of experience criteria.

WEDNESDAY, DECEMBER 17, 1958 DINNER ROSIE'S / CITY IMAGE / PAT THRU T. SQUARE
Bring drawing over to City Gallery. In p.m., preparing. Had forgotten to bring
Rosemary's to Cooper for her. Got glass for both. Prepared frame. Bus to Rosie's about

4 p.m. She prepared hers. Bus 34th—6th Ave. to City Gallery. Great vision at dusk on Herald Square, 6th Ave. at leaving time. Bus to H. Sq. again. Walk across town on 34th, sights. Chills, excitement. The *city* image—its relation to me, my history, etc. Dinner at Rosie's, Mario, ill-tempered. Back to 4th St. More selecting, toward city image. Next to final + very clear selection. Bus up to meet Pat at Coffee Miel. I say: corny place. Down Times Sq. in very cold. Watched signs close up. Take BMT to Cedar Bar. Beer. I'm tired. Cab home.

Excited talk with Red about construction of city street in gallery.

New York, 1956–1958

Vulgar forms of expression, flawed, stunted, groping of sex, or "life force" and its many distortions, to help without losing their character.
Vulgar, offensive—but one sympathizes. A unity of fragments is *what one sees*.
"Kaleidoscopic," actual sensations.

Some very elaborate, *big* compositions with cutouts—"subway," "advertising," "Times Square" (the symbol). A collection. Women and girls, boys and men—their hair, clothes.
Objectivity (thinking of some subject collages).
Magazines—the contemporary reality (to cut it is to participate?).
Meeting of objectivity and fantasy.

To be conscious = to be threatened.
Seeing yourself and the world truthfully.
Accepting unpleasant facts.

Bad tendency to undervalue myself. What can I give?

An artist who is not an idealist—what is that?
People who sacrifice something for an ideal—whoever they are—I am drawn to them.
Where there is no struggle, no effort or sacrifice, or the struggle is for purely material ends—those do not get my sympathy.
In NY, some idealism still lives.

Lonely in new city—interested in people—outside experience. Not necessarily changes in whole attitude.

Theory clouds my head. The practical and instructive is my limitation.

I am a short-term, fragmentary worker. Work goes dead if I work on it long.

The wood sculpture, created under *extreme tension* in a few hours, is a lesson in what is for me a successful procedure.

I would be so happy without unbalance and also so happy with *more* unbalance. I wonder but, for practical purposes, do not want to know what my trouble is. How dull I would be, if cured.

To build a streetful of people.

I want to paint the sculpture.

When you are young, you think you are losing your mind. Later it is your body, which more concerns you.

The surface fabric of life.
A telephone that rings for 20 minutes.

Oil painting in the old manner has never seemed right or *enough* to me. No, it is this grabbing of materials and then development and combination in a sort of inspired frenzy (forgive the banal language) that has been uniquely my way.
An acute sense of reality and an animistic empathy with objects.

Central Park:
Zoo—bears, lions, leopards, goats, llama, coyote, monkeys, parrots
Merry-go-round
Ballgame
Fountain
Parasols, lady
Restaurant
Sailboat pond

Mind = sky. Other analogies, a web of analogies.

The studio, a universe. Full of objects and things inspiring. A magic place. A place to sit sensitively and move cautiously, making things happen.

Inspiration from a morally and spiritually poor society.

You've just got to concede that from the US censor's point of view, you are leading an immoral existence.

I am not a prose writer—not creatively. Anyone can write a little. But the medium of prose writing does not suit my expression.

My stuff is made of what is around me—trumpets, bad music, gidoudahere, whistles, car honks . . . ad information. Awful but true. USA.

Grand images, 3
1. The city, the day of total destruction
2. The garden

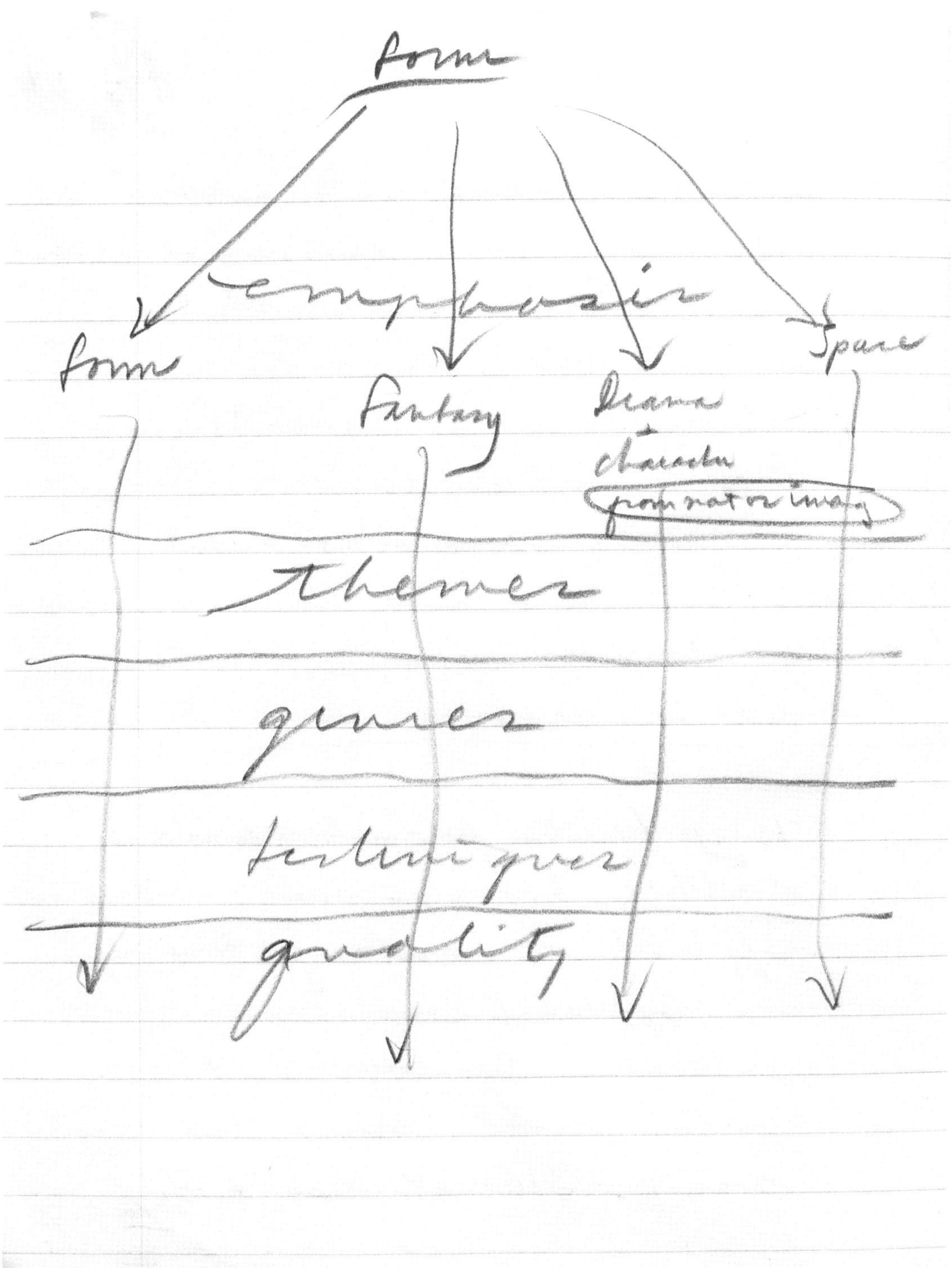

Notebook page, 1956

3. The sky, or sea

I would cast my lot naturally with the miserable, the outcasts, in the belief that their
vision is clearest. I am for those who face the situation and squeeze out what they can.
I sympathize with their crutches and faults, their general self-destructiveness. These are
"artists" who have taken on or been forced to take on more than art, the problem of the
times. I see so much moving beneath the surface, which no one seems aware of or wishes
to face. I am for those who also see this and do face it.
(What our civilization is is an old, unshaven man with an open mouth whose legs and
arms have been cut off, whose tongue has been cut out, whose ears have been cut off,
whose eyes have been put out, who drools as he rolls his way along the asphalt.)

The time has come to *clarify the painting*.
Can a painting be pure sign and still mean something?

In using signs, you make metaphors for sexual subjects. This painting may be seen as a
set of highly charged sexual symbols. In the Bathers, this also occurs, but there are also
more direct images of desire—the figures, their actions.

Man's world is suggested by street scrawl, wall-scrawl art, where much imagery is to
be found. The planet comes from a card to which certain decals of outer space were
attached, called "Beyond Our Horizon." Transcendence on 2nd Ave. People's longings.
Its color is both vulgar, garish, of man's world, and magic. There is also the suggestion
of excrement, and a flag, an airplane (lower right, which is also a leaf). (Flag—magic
emblem.) The plane, a mechanism, is a symbol of man's poor tries at transcendence.

To bring together everything—
Dreams and waking
Memory, direct work
Painting, drawing
Writing, painting, drawing

Notes cannot be organized according to any rigid system because they are earlier,
imperfect statements and therefore do not fit the categories developed later. They are
the progress of understanding—not something finished.

I went around loudly saying, "Abstract Expressionism is dead!" How crazy one
could be!

"Allude—alludere—to play with. To refer indirectly or by *suggestion*." W.

Identity and likeness:
Identity—sameness

Likeness—close correspondence
Similarity—somewhat alike
Resemblance—external likeness
Analogy—likeness in relations rather than appearance or qualities
Affinity—resemblance and kinship

Filling out Fulbright:
I realize I have no identity outside a few friends my own age.
No academic record to speak of. No professors to sing my promise.
No reputation "in the community" or with persons "of standing." Not a single worthy
knows about me. I am but nobody.

Here is the pattern of Man's Condition to *read*:
Insane repetition . . . Subway routes, subway tracks, windows, cars, lampposts, up every
day to same job, back to same dinner, same wife, same movie.
His frustration—"dirty" words, smears, twisted forms to project his feelings, some very
fine and doomed to be buried with childhood.
Walkers—the stream of walking people. Dead people, sleeping people, staggering people.
Billboards—the hopeless dreams—their futility symbolized by their gradual decay by
living, destructive matter—then another dream superimposed. Some signs are the residue
of hundreds of dreams. One can dig through to them with the fingernail.

NYC = art

A wall covered with signs. Colors. Black-and-white. Two-dimensionality. Again, a certain
formlessness: the city is not ordered. A parody of order—absurd order.

For a romantic, I have been keeping myself very much in line.

I am especially fond of large spaces, crowded with moving form, flickering form, light,
and *sound*. I try to render *sound* as much as possible by signs, even to writing out the
sound: CRACK! or using comic-book signs.

Either I should overcome my fear of women or adjust to some substitute. But I have
exaggerated the problem, actually.

Piss, shit, spit, sperm, vaginal fluids, sweat, hair, filth, grease, lipstick, smearing of
makeup, drool, liquids, jelly, pus, blood, wax, paint, fat, näsgubbar, etc.

The autoerotic, onanistic, narcissistic "school" of painting. Point is, this extends
to images too—the self-absorption. Seymour, who condemns, f.ex., Pollock as a
"masturbator," doesn't realize this.

There is notably a difference in Surrealist images. They are less sticky, less personal—and perhaps less powerful, genuine. (?)

My use of the dream is "aesthetic"—i.e., for purposes of art expression. I do not myself analyze it—leave that to others. I am interested in the image for its peculiar dreamish qualities. Freud would not find this a very significant approach.
Note: the dream symbol does not stand in direct relation to its significance in the "unconscious" but through the link of its *personal* association. Does this mean symbols are not universal?

Number 7. 32. Obsession with numbers of dwelling places. 2s and 3s. 7s. 8s. 9s. Date of birth. 28, 1929. 232 (Walton), 61 (Grand), 233 (North), 1700 (Crilly). Room no. 7 at Grand. 7 floor at Walton. M12-7197. 32 E. 7 St. 1777 Silliman. 44 (Bellevue). 1957–28 (4 x 7), 323 E. 13, 108 E. 9, etc., etc.

Project possibility:
"Insane" art. Where are the major collections? "The Value of Psychotic Art."

Hate writing in generalities.

1. *Romantic Mystics*: Francis, Calcagno, Still, Rothko, Dugmore, Guston, Gottlieb, Diebenkorn (early), Corbett
2. *Calligraphists*: Tobey, Kline, Mathieu, Hartung, Twombly, Capogrossi, Pousette-Dart
3. *"Action" painters*: Mitchell, de Kooning, Goldberg, Pollock
4. *Eccentrics*: Matta, Bacon, Cohen, Giacometti, Dubuffet, Golub, June, Glasco, Albright
5. *"Tachistes"*: Wols
6. Briggs, Riopelle variations, i.e., *Nonstatic Romantic Mysticism*
7. *Classicists*: Motherwell, de Kooning

I hesitate now to call myself an "artist" or a "painter." But I am—it is the battleground of my attitudes, ideas, experiences, etc.

Order—but especially unforced order, natural order—is one of my passions. Everything has its place. Ordering is a satisfaction in itself. Order is not to be confused with neatness as an end in itself. Order has nothing to do with hygiene or "appearances."

Concept of a studio: The changing pictures of the windows.

My hell—the kitchen, where the roaches die.

I love Carmen, street life, vie de la rue, the cat's moaning.

spring
summer ‖ fall
winter

lyric ⟷ satiric
dominant   dominant

Maup. fex.   Barb fer
country   city

[symbolist
  erotic
  psychologic
  (attitudes in common)]

[realist
  abstract
  (levels of experience)
  (in common)]

[portrait
  caricature
  figure
  landscape, s. life, int.
  (subjects in common)]

Notebook page, 1958

Silhouettes, reversals.

I observe with delight the strangeness of common things.

3 a.m. vision of roughness and compactness of a sculpture. My concern for some time has been with volume—sculpture and color of surface. They are beyond mere line.

The aim is to discover, define the personal obsessive image—form—by trial and error, "blind" choice, etc.

Am I really a sculptor? And not a painter at all? Am I? Am I? Line, silhouette, mass (volume), surface. These excite me. I am not blind to color but do not create it. (?)

Golub also a sculptor gone to painting. Bring back three dimensions to painting.

Fantasy and form meet best in primitive art.
Form—fetishistic necessity in clothing. Historical.

I am I—that is what matters, for every I.

I use "expressionism," generally, to cover *form* and *feeling* and *reality*.

The American sentimentality—of the "gang" down at the Cedar or Janis Gallery, loyalty of members. Pathos. Their simple prejudices dominate the American art scene. The sentiment is not directed at anyone—just pals.

Notes will all be misunderstood if found after death. The remarks are too impulsive, abrupt, contradictory, especially those dealing with others and with self.

Watching street workers break up asphalt—thought: form. That is the basic thing.

I would like to show that psychical and physical are one.

I control my loss of control.

The "notes" are a world of their own, as are the photos. Neither contributes directly to painting and are complete in themselves.

The "monumental-humanistic" goal. Something of value. Nonsentimental.

A matter of finding humanistic subject matter.

Monumentality of the ordinary. Daumier et al.

Becoming public. Have never been public. Not developed in connection with
public (audience).

Literary activity:
1. Diary—brief facts of the day. Begun in earnest in 1956, some previous.
2. Notes—some loose.
3. Creative writing—poetry and prose. Various forms.
4. Letters—(none).

Attitudes:
The world is psychological.
The world is absurd.
The world is beautiful, erotic, lyric.
The world is mysterious. Elicit the extraordinary.
The world is abstract.

Much of the erotic figure has moved into caricature because of funny faces. The influence
of a *satirical* point of view. The erotic-figure stuff is rather empty-pussed. Irony at sex.
Attitudes change, develop experience, change from day to day. That is why I have trouble
living with one-type people.

All so right for the "city" approach. Abstract fantastic and satiric real.

Perhaps lyrical-satirical is the great major opposition, changing as the year does.

Why o' why did I destroy my "city" collages? Must redo.

Change caricature category to city.

There is obviously no *abstract city* category, but there are abstractions related in *mood* to
city and perhaps even derived from city effects.

"Telegraphic" in Kerouac. Rapid, jagged motion in space.

The little sculptures. The city wasteland, in Abstract-Fantastic.
And the collages.

What I am very deeply interested in is counteracting the tendency to draw a phony
film over American life—pretty coarse but more honest than to hide it, so press this
coarseness, elevate pop culture.

Well, '58 was the year I made it *out*!

Scotty is full of ruts
slopeshouldered beast
with a drunken hero's face
heading in soft mass for the center of the earth

sad eyes and a brushstache and a song
from so far in Man's darkness
simple as a knife
it made pearls grow in your ears
and the spots between the fingers cold

never words just hi boys
and that tune cleaning up
•

ice has formed on the shoeman
fog in his old shoebox
webs blow on his cheeks
his beard is a fallen white wood
dust is on his eyes
in need of a shine

a cairn of cold lumps
bothering some business

the coat with so many caverns
all its long life a failure at making folds
stiff as pavement
black shrouding document

death in the snow
under an old cap
the red box an empty house receding into whiteness
•

Peaches is made of pain
and stone to bear it
neatly made from something long
brown is Peaches
bearing a brown stone

•

long mustard life in a speckled book
black taste of each day going by

no messages from my missing leg
and gray lunches in the baby's bed

•

just a leg
tied to the foot of a bed in back
dreaming of oval escapes
ragged tin runaways
gray busted light axing down

•

rag asleep
furred with old questions
long trip in a wet thimble
a year among the pills

in brown melody
in a corked world
there can a good rag sleep
unafraid of time and arrogant pencils

•

an elbow expands in the raggy night
twelve bleats of a Tom make bricks in the quiet
all paw is the town
hairy back is the thought of a close room
spittle-full is the merciful moon

have mercy on fur and milky eyes
and lean offal-banqueters with their cane legs and bleeding brown houses
•

you camouflage of an old snicker
forgotten bone
louse among the toes of cannon
burping paw-loved old mole

bring a bouquet of sad eyes
•

big bag of benny buttons
candy sleeper
tent of good lumps
old boy of bone
picket fingers
rusty ear flaps

take care
•

Full blue nose-enchanted purchaser of wind
knower of birds not even seen
blossoms not yet imagined
old gray hearts posing as rocks
and turtles who have eaten their way into Man's deepest
    handkerchiefs—
a coaster in the name of a candle's beard
a little rubber centavo for my friend the spider

what! not so much as a pill for my hungry missing leg

I know a rag who will vengeance me
who knows a stick who knows a box
who knows someone very personally
who'll bring it all crashing down
•

mirrors
polish up your annihilations
instruct metal in ambiguity

there is an order standing
for revolvers panelled with invisibility

a mouth is loose
victims have seen themselves

the countryside is afloat with doubles
•

knocking moonhorns
fast dancing in a gas dream
red spelling in the strange egg
•

This afternoon wound is filled with talk and dirty round
    heads
the barrage of sun can do nothing but narrow to a pin-prick
    in the eyeball
the furious jostling ears
the metal necks
the arrogant tin lips of these who are repetitiously trapped
    always with their backs to me

I slip in a blood vessel and swim to its dry end
but the noise reaches me
and I have sewn myself in
gone to live with bone
to no profit
must chew dust and go deaf until the air leaves
•

 If one could but skill oneself conditionally in the deep
    prune life lived by stripes at the radio center of a
    month's numeral

eviscerate a cloudy tuba

let a wood ghost pass for iron in the ochre depths
slide by as a can full of wild scratches
mess up a tree by colliding it with tornadic tacksprinkled
    glassraping belliedout storming biplanes
•

These ill numerals will never do
an alphabet in crutches
something new must be imagined to replace
hungry cylinders always firing
firing
firing

to everything silence is the best response
to the yawn of day which wishes to move
to the burp of noon and all the corpses
scattered like jacks on sunraped historical concrete

Time is the fatal owl the final sponge
clasping severing embrace
the laugh the limit
and us here with our dog noses
watching the gum move up and down
    •

Outside in the brainy night gossip of hot machinery
oily insertions
screams of the drowned in the tigerish surf
normal nuisances
the silent comfortable light speaks:
    A — R —W
an age murdered by a snapshot of brown legs
    •

shadow planes
laughter of windows
cones of churches
lascivious asphalt
spit goldened by the sun's last depressing blue
                              analytical hiccough
river bubbling with downed planes
rat's eyes flickering over Brooklyn
trammeling their feelers in bridge-brains
causal night
eating us all into little lights

•

snow has run scratching
across blackbroke halfope reflections
fanged asphalt elbows kiss
crashing of gumball shadows

GIBUS CATZ

•

our crimes were slight
many things we did not even intend

we mated a ghost to a frog
and produced a city

we twisted Death's neon ears
and sank a ship
(all were saved
because *we* wanted it that way)

we filled a saxophone with blood
and listened to its sentimental melodies

a hill asked to be moved
we moved it
(the train should have known better)

they were small things on the face of a small planet
little dust things
how many million eggs are cracked a day do you suppose

•

coins
feathered white grace-necked flying coins
free tonight
encrusting the chimney like milky mold
flying low among the grass-blades
inspecting
or perhaps only slightly interesting themselves
in turds the size of locomotives
making phrases with other coins
phrase-exchanging in the huge sundown

screams climb ladders leaning on airy granite clouds
hands of the dense iron clock weep
everything doubly falls—
lead sounds all over the globe
everyone is unbelievably fat
sweating suffering
and rolling about like drunken pencil-sharpeners

the whole thing is written on a tiger's filthy paw
and read as the eyes depart
impelled by insistent scratching
absorbed through im-bacillic telepathy
germ irrationalities

•

iron chocolating down in the brown dusk
eats at the cliffed digits
muzzles the morphine chuckle

arrows part the flaming bicycles
comb the waiting white tarts with lead
unfold high and blue
the wet woolen never-ending network of knuckles
                              and screaming cheese
the anger-thin red-boiling hungry harrows
driving on the little battered band of fleaspits

pinwheel of roaring razors
young knives splitting the night into small
                              portions of thunder

soft private plots of wax crayons
divans of foxnoises
continental animal knowledge
whispering grass wisdom
sleight-of-hand by bananas
im-penned
unconquerably up-elephanted

attack by the peeping sun
a gold ant explodes deep in the tomato
icy phrases devilling its dark pink tunneled cranium
•

My soft stove flame now at the cool zenith
tearing with oceanic scissorseyes at the mortal edible towers
makes the following announcement:
henceforward all graves will be closed every holiday
to prevent the searing leaves from smearing with loud copper
celebrants under the forest's cool hands

sunignited singing muttering carcass awind
hairs eternal on a violet wire
quarreling with the distant black grass

I would have you understand:
even if your hand splits the ice
it only bumps around like a blind apple on the yellow bottom

Come let's divide a buttocks
let's buy a lamb's foot and wish for smashed trumpets
let's get a good hold on ourselves by the frost that forms
    under our nails
let's pull ourselves up in a brown cloud
carve at the vitality of the race with feathers
laugh our baseball curse
make our iron-ick wounds in the brick
•

clinkclunking dandelions
a field of yellow hiccups

locomotives cleave the blossoms
loom astral blotting
tornadic skyscrapous
eclipsing the sun's last bent nails
(which are tears)
its rosy-buttocksish heaving away

increase of black merciless will-choke must-choke
                                        pillows
•

Black rendezvous with lemons
ink swelling through a forest stroked with old egg-meat
where steaming snoring parrots play the blue flutes of a
    dog's beard
trip to the saw's home
indulgence in clay
love in the air in the fountain's gibbering nest
graves in a goat's mouth
eyes stuffed with skin
deep escape to a dark brain
conversation of warm machinery in the closed night
much analysis of waves

rinky-dinky how the sleeping tooth bites NOT

socks attack the foot
the desert lengthens
the gold tit of the moon scorns the black mouths of the
    firmament
loaves of dog jowls
the rutting claw scratches up an embarrassed foot
a universe of micrometric ice-lost wristwatches
tingle that goes the globes round
flaming in the valleys of planetary bigtoe

the railroad station is reportedly now a bird gliding
    disobediently and making sweet wilful sounds over the
    city's raped caverns and bloody concourses
•

We must find a way to ravish these blind square empty eyes
tumble this great watery brain with a woodsplash into the
    courtyard
where the cardplayers sit stabbing one another
where the red jelly more and more impedes the game

It is the eighth day of the great necknibbling jiggling
    feather romance
nothing has happened but a few murderous hooks
a palace of soiled glass a harmless sleeping planet

asphalt breeds so little
it is a poor monster made of that
covered with feathers and each morning scaling the stairs

the script of rot is everywhere
is in the nostrils' hairy cinema
the pigment is going out of the world like smart sap
•

Smashing beast bloodbuffeted
in singleminded nearing crawl

teeth camped in black flame
in tormented purple still plain-night
smoking with lemonous furry Indian-exchanges

bonic salty drab arrow-era

now a lionous moon
hair fanging out in the million black supple ball-thoughts
    at the edge
where an occasional train
an occasional train

stripes slam down   pie falls

space-mouse sees

harmonicamuck   Au Rev Salty Kid
•

Devil
I see the sun set like a crocodile's bent thought
in the cubic stages westward
I hear the stings of swung children
axing at the sky-bottom
the muddy earth-yells

bells bang
boathorns beat
knees are skinned
faces are sewed up
and blown open
the city's curses are lit
•

ON THE BUS

First snow
bacons down
begs   metalthreats

ARROWNEUMATIC EXHALATION
begin   pull
bus beastwhistles

black slameyes
spreading silvertrimmed bulbhead
jowlschly pushnosy slobsloshlippy
    (tapertaner tamer)
lovewhanty   graspsy
oldwatery
nice fellow   bad drunksy

pitcherfan
leaning bread ghoz upembreaching sexsocks
bad brakesnake eyes refusal
outsnaring PLEXAPAISON
snorltwum   sorpthrimst

aim anona
needlebust
green flow-out of roll-nipply
smokesaint nailknotty
gravel hush warm oround
osofty knipknap softsucky roll
    inunder
meet-eyes nailaching spearouting
build across aisle love-infection

blah bum Kleenex lopa lapa
lum ring smah smap smoku
round axually outlumleaping
pum! tat overlaying neonline

oblama borr
stzaprampma unga ga mox
telum lot
nox prax nitk stoo

bess rubber roll over full baby fell
knocks by leap eating utter
outdracking sighsmell taste oh eyes
what (wh) pain say whwhat pain
dash slice
bonnet-fly paprrip
wind pourtear mash stir up
full fish up leave leaning mungle
morten ripraise pulltake upover
raperoot oh wild animal wind!

love you look into light silver
slicystreet millionknived busclouds
elephantoganging
skyover
nip spizzle snap twatomine
•

POPS

Hudsonboat hotfucking out of the glastening harbor
cindrous plume laid plopsy on the black glastening wiggles
poo-oup! warm hopeholes hotfucking by tra-ra-ra
crystal jaw-cymbals gnashing
hooray for warmass workknuckles
blabsong upflung
through Narrows humps Hudsonboat snatchnuzzling
•

June was (wuz)
aftrenoon
a stearing held the ski
whiskey blue
montinous crys of boys
whuppered the air
festened by sun needles
to wacky cobbles
criscrawsing did doggy go
ketz
an infinitesmals
screamy wuz babes
wiz babulant portulous mamagangers
Rohl blak wheels

shiny as fist vicious flat street
heros flasking in the BargandgGrill
minnows of feel and foul
silver shit chat seeking
in the claminyrous smochair
•

Dear old Old time
send me your Wabashwashedout dirty past
your deep guggleswash No. 1 Public Swashslam

sweet gagmash

I spew
and lovingly I spew over myself
my mushgug past
Ah sucky-lovely sunset-crap America!
•

Observed Fragments

Drops in gray water
Tinfoil trampled flat on a wet concrete sidewalk
An ice machine grinds ice
Metal gull on a metal sky
Ketchup on a wet sidewalk
Bright nuts
Constructions of chocolate
Red fur
Wet wood inside a barrel
A smoking cloth
A man polishes chrome. Chrome is polished. Nearby, from a chrome arm,
    hangs a chicken with its throat opened.
A cripple is sunning his white stump
A man bent over in a shoemaker's pen puts on his leg-braces and boots
An old woman with a cane in the rain
The white bristled face of an old man reflects light under a black umbrella
A white pigeon flaps his wings on a thin man's linear knee (a cream-white
    cap, a darkblue shirt, gray pants and tan suspenders)
A woman leans out the window on arms like moons
A man behind a post
A little blond girl rides a bicycle with thick tires against a wall and hurts
    herself
A tramp drinks from a wax milk container
A dirty gray cat's full heavy cheeks and apprehensive glance
Kids find a tramp sleeping in a cardboard box. The box speaks.
Hairpins and a black cloth at the back of the head
Please hide your trash inside
A woman with Potts' Disease
Fee Dawson's pale face
A woman shades her face with a newspaper
A man in blue gym shoes and a green hat carries a camera
A scragglyhaired dog selfconsciously shits squatting. A large silhouetted
    column, so large for such a small dog, moving out and down
Metal touch of rain
Soft violet silhouettes to the West. Grayish yellow window lights.
The old world is yellow, the new cold blue
Silver light spots on the sidewalk. Snow flurries.
Red beard of a street brush
A hinged window wavers stiffly
A shiny piece of coal
Unrelated movement of pigeons. Crawling of many over a wide area.

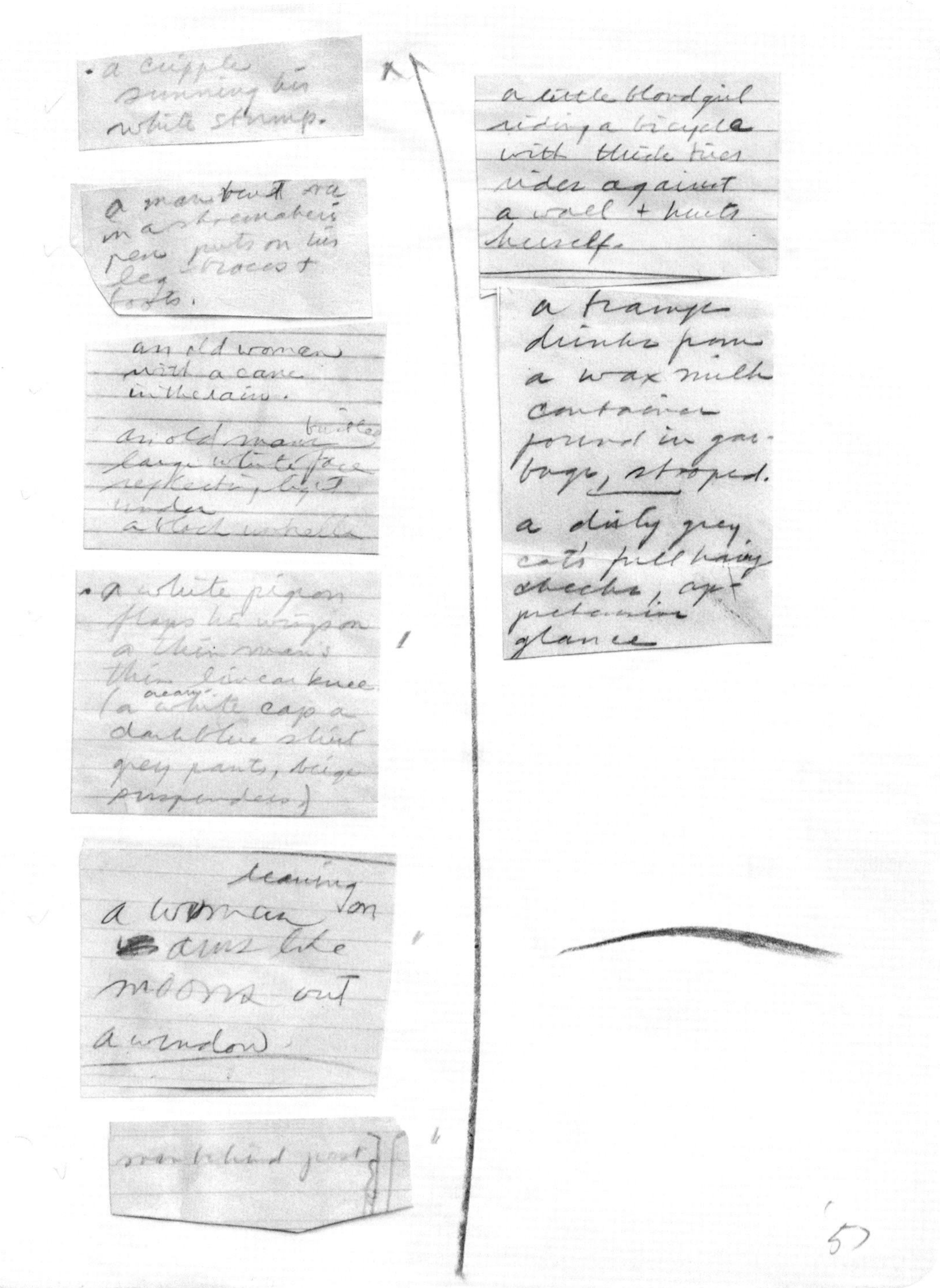

Page from *Observed Fragments*, 1957

Lambs hung in a yellow light

Song of electricity

A spot of blood turning black, then dry and loose as a fried penny near a
    brown pond in the bottom of a dirty tub

Light coats monoliths. Valleys.

Dusty, whitening orange light streaming

Long shadows in the winter light

Tits in a puddle

Blackshimmer of gutterwater

A door closes. All is magic.

Knees outing, forward, up - seeking

A bereted man leans on a black fence, looking down at pigeons feeding in
    the snow

A boy with a dog is trying to break something by stamping on it with his
    foot

An old woman with a black hat is asleep

A car in parking runs over a bottle

Laundry flaps in the wind

A woman's heels sunk in the hot tar

A white pigeon flies in front of dark empty buildings

A fat boy sleeps in the doorway

Lying on a hot roof makes a cold shiver

Someone knocks at my door but I am not there

Woman walks fast with legs red and raw

A waiting person shows a proud face

People under cool lights

Deep cuts of eyes

Oh those babushkad narroweyed chicks

Container of a bird. Tub of space.

Shells, radio, knife, cup with pencils, tools, guitar, light bulbs

The white hem of a slip falls several inches below the skirt of a
    squat woman wearing black woolen stockings

A thin horizontal red reflection on the side of a car

Black smoke makes its way in windless night

Waxy smell of a girl's ear. Kissing of hair on the arms.

Bare breasts under a soft sweater. Buttocks under silk.

Man getting into a box

Wreckage in the early morning. Wreckers' hot blaze on a hot day.

Blond lady alone on a pier

A little girl kisses a cold window

Chapter 2
Guises of Ray Gun: The Street
1959–1960

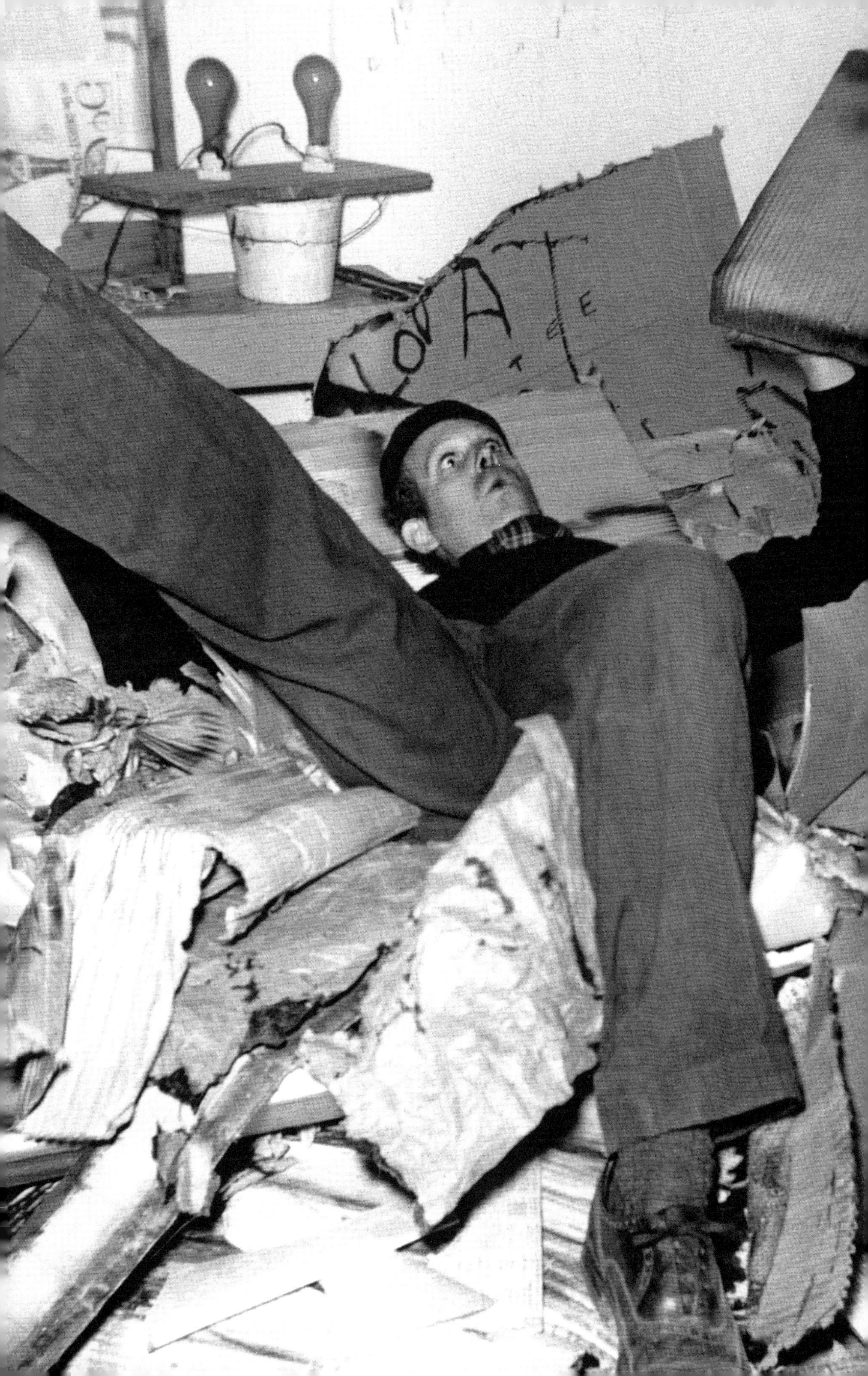
O A
E
E

THURSDAY, JANUARY 15, 1959

Slept late.

In evening, went to Times Square. At Topps watched Paar on TV—Harrington playing Italian. Chop steak. Diet talk with waiter. Up T. Square to Birdland but too late for Ferguson + Davis, day before last day. Rain started. Down 52nd St. to 5th Ave., waited long there in door. No bus. Over to Madison. Bus down + to 14th St. Passengers. Home. All this week: deciphering my selections from before Xmas. Making a new selection— quite easily. Setting up files, generally ordering all. Clippings into folders. Cleaning. Pasting, filing. Much writing and definition. Adjustment to NY setting.

Laundry not picked up . . . garbage, etc., etc.

Listening to pop music and rhythm + blues—

SUNDAY, JANUARY 18, 1959 THOUGHTS

To Dickie's about 5:30 p.m. He's not very active, sour. Drink. Listen to Apache record. Eat Rykrisp + cottage cheese. I walk to Rosie's up 2nd Ave. Feel threatened. Something is shot at me. Dinner at Rosie's with Mario. Beer. Chicken stew. Mario very quiet. After dinner, I read poetry. I am tired + my back hurts no matter how I sit, stand, or lie. Pat arrives later from modeling in Brooklyn. Brings *Inquirer*, is affectionate, but I am not especially. Tells of her employer—"a private detective." We warm her. I walk her home. I am very tired. Having forgotton to borrow money, I must go to Dickie's + do so. Earlier in day in Luncheonette on Ave. D. Many thoughts. Perfecting Times Square photos! First half of day very cheerful. Make up with NY. See its value. But 2nd half sour + feeling persecuted. Stopped in shop + read in psych book.

Foolishly I sit up by open window, catch cold again—

WEDNESDAY, FEBRUARY 4, 1959

Still reading Céline.

MONDAY, FEBRUARY 16, 1959 DESTROY DRAWINGS

Much work for Pat. Off to New School by 9 a.m. Radio from Abromowitz begins to change sleeping schedule. Okay . . . feeling really pretty good! Frame drawings from weekend. Happy with these and start to prune drawings' leads—I can't remember how to make merciless confident selection + destruction—as if I ever *really* knew!

Ted by in basement, back from sea. Brought beer. I, out late, Chinese food. So damn hungry! Chills, strange feelings. A beer.

WEDNESDAY, FEBRUARY 25, 1959 DESTROY PTGS.

Mild weather. Not feeling right about paintings in a.m. Out for OJ + bank. Laundry in a.m. Pat lets eggs boil. We are not too friendly. She walks me to work through school

kids, arriving about 12:15 p.m. Very slow day at work. Edith sick, goes home. I draw
from streetwalkers + shadows. Brilliant light. Take home a load of frames in bag. Write a
notebook full on females. Haircut on way home. *Life* magazine. Banalities.
Rattling around, attacking work, scrutinizing, selecting—very well. Eat steak late at
Paul's. Finally destroy numerous paintings, cut them up. Dump in garbage, including
the very big one—many others—feel fine. Only the most meaningful left. Very self-
critical. Lack of form, sidelined into erotic-lyrical, etc., etc. Recover my focus throughout
whole day. Feel fine in evening. Bus up to 23rd, buy shaving stuff + notebook and bottle
bourbon. Virginia Gentleman. Pat's by 11 a.m. or so. Drinking, talking. She in rich
red sweater. Black stockings. Looks fine. I bathe, shave. Details. Love. Great friends.
Modigliani . . . fine.

FRIDAY, FEBRUARY 27, 1959 PAID / SHOP / DRINK

Up so as to work by 10 a.m. I run, catch bus. This day is full of feverish energy. I am now
in wild period! Commemorative stamp issued at Cooper U. Crowds + confusion. Clear out
Memorial Library. Wear beret + flower. Am quite corny. Get paid. Cash check at bank with
Rosie. Buy paints and radio on 3rd Ave. A good radio. Walk home with all my stuff—also
get oranges, notebooks. In basement are Dick, Kenny + Dexter. Pretend to bring drinks,
pass out oil + tempera. Am corny—too excited to paint, though I intended to. Very hot.
Went through + selected visual clips, burlesque mags, etc. Discarded a great deal. (One by
one I select down my possessions, work + material . . .) In my beret, by bus up to Pat who
has cold, give her my old radio. Out for brandy + pastries. Pleasant. Love. Back. Drop in
on Tyler. More brandy. Much talk. He tells of his work in International Lounge, etc. Go
up, buy beer. Alan + Joyce over after 12 a.m. Bring brandy and wine: chat until 3 a.m. or
so. I show work. Argue over Orphan Annie comics. Joyce in purple + black. Details. Bed.

SATURDAY, FEBRUARY 28, 1959

Excellent mild weather. Get up rather early, hung over but effect is not too bad—I am
so full of energy. Buy orange juice. Move table from long room, set up shelves. Music
from Puerto Ricans across way. Hang sheet over window in long room, set up divider,
etc., etc. Pat comes in p.m. in plaid skirt + just washed hair. Beautiful red. Quite a sight.
I quite moved. In p.m., I begin to work again quite inexplicably on the sculptures. I want
to complete them by painting them. I apply house paint and try to solve the problems. I
continue to work on these. Pat has a cold. I eat meatballs late. We drink beer, take money
for rent to Tyler's. Mount a bug, which turns out *not* to be a black widow. I have many
ideas. This is a marvelously creative period.
Pat begins trying to alter my pants. I am quite thinner now. She has trouble, it is difficult.
I read my poems. Study burlesque photos.
Finish head.
Very high after Symph Sid signs off. Spill wine, which smells. Damn active day.

SUNDAY, MARCH 1, 1959

Up about 12 p.m. Weather cloudy, rain expected. Thought it would be nice day. Had planned to go to Met, but stay in. I continue inventing sculpture + start painting the sculptures, continue trying to solve the problems. Work quite a bit on road + left object-head. Using it as "ear," then detaching it. Constructing Amant garden, and little parasol of milkweed, etc.

Pat cutting from old *Life*s and using crayons to make cards to little sister. Eat salmon + pot cheese for dinner. A little beer only.

A period of lots of drinking.

Love in p.m.

Woman knocks on door, asks for Marty. "Wrong artist," she says.

Get out + clean up photomontages.

THURSDAY, MARCH 5, 1959 REACTION / CONSERVATIVE DRAWING OF COOP. SQ.

See Tylers. Though very tired, carry home pieces of wood from 14th St. wrecking, after hamburger at Cameo. Then a quart of beer with Pat.

Dissatisfaction regarding drawing, turn gradually from a light approach to a line approach. (Do light drawing at work in crayon of square, looking down the Bowery.) (?) A reaction no doubt from looseness of previous few days. The pendulum. Take up conte and pen. Reject crayon. (Struggling with conte.)

THURSDAY, MARCH 12, 1959

Pat calls late, does not come over, visits photography pal in p.m. I have a dissatisfying day trying to assess my poetry and prose, end by realizing it has been a reaction like in the drawing: Hemingway interest. 1957 work. Throw away a lot, take a very harsh, selective attitude. Put expressionism first again, finally, which is right.

Very slushy in morning, hard to walk to work. Poor Pat.

THURSDAY, MARCH 19, 1959 COOP. SQ. DRAWINGS

Oh! Oh! I resolve not to live it up anymore. No money + so tired. "From now on, just sex + hot chocolate." Pat off early. I lie half sleeping until near noon. "Ray Gun"—poetic inspirations. Nonsense. Take hour off work to make more drawings, these very large, of square in the bright sun. At home, I mount them. Pat comes, makes veal + eggplant for dinner. (Was to see sick Rosie). Reads *Locust*. I saw down stretchers + stretch painting of Pat standing. Puttering, pasting, selecting, organizing intentions. Tell Pat to move in. Rocket + Sid good. Some pen drawings.

MONDAY, MARCH 23, 1959 HANG COOP. SHOW

Clear + sunny, warmer. Pat off to work early. I prepare drawings for show at Cooper Art School Library. Bank calls—I am overdrawn. Bus with framed drawings, lucky, Ave. C and crosstown. Meet Tad a.m. 12 p.m. accident in street. Details. Hang work. Home by 5 p.m. + hungry. Clean place, clear out long room. Move sculptures. Eat lox + beans. Dickie calls on phone.

Borrowed $25 from G. Muehsam.

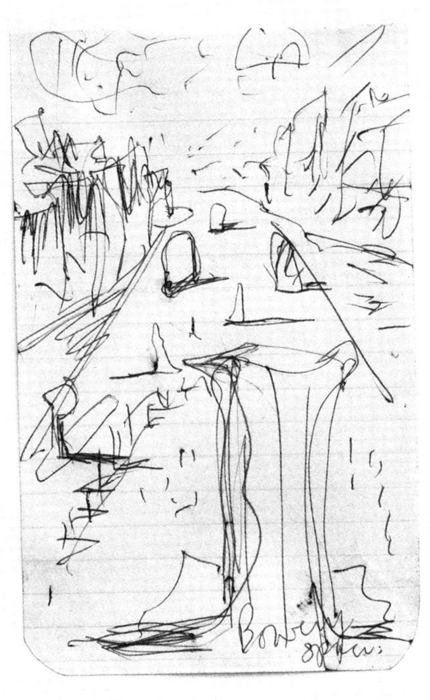

Notebook Page: "Bowery Spaces" (View Down the Bowery from Cooper Union), 1959

SATURDAY, MARCH 28, 1959 ELI'S COSTUME PARTY

Up feeling poorly. Pat to work. No money. Got eggs and bialy. Puttered, set up drawing table, cleared out small room, built stand on ladder for drawing board. Ate broiled chicken and cauliflower Pat made, very good. Tried to put thoughts together about work. Finally did. Got Ronnie up, and Mike, painted Ronnie. Gave him 50¢. He did not want hot chocolate. Grooms came. Chat, showed work. Bottle of wine, left about 7:45 p.m. Alan came. I started painting of Pat + Charlie the Cat. Did a portrait of Alan—OK. Made costume for Pat out of two boards painted white with simple black line design + bottle covers around head, out like spikes. Drove to Eli's in Alan's car. Bought liquor. I am getting sore throat and weary. Party by 10 p.m. or so. Crowded. Left by 1 a.m. or so.

WEDNESDAY, APRIL 1, 1959

(Following recovery from flu-coughing, several days of tiredness, begin to find myself—to begin a new period of painting, which has been spotty for some time. I read the diaries of last year, of this year, and before. Very useful. I see I have really been very busy.) To work again.

TUESDAY, APRIL 7, 1959

A warm, springish day.

Make many plans. Start of a very active, smooth period. All my problems, re: theme, etc., swept away. Action without problems. Decisions natural, no need to ponder.

In the morning, I paint on Pat in kitchen. She poses for another painting, a redoing of a standing, leaning, static, tensionless pose begun Sunday night. A lying pose is begun also Sunday night, completed about this time, *rhythmic + tense* but not pigment heavy or colorful.

Repaint still life and start abstraction, over a painting of Dickie's head.

I roll up off stretchers several older paintings + by end of week have an entirely new set of paintings.

Writing style free, unconnected.

MONDAY, APRIL 27, 1959

Rain + cold in evening.

Pork chop dinner. Very good, but I am still hungry. Love. Pat sleeps. I go down to basement to destroy my sculpture. Do. Pack in boxes, for which out in rain.

Dick + Dor, pizza in basement—Clarence in.

p.m. frame + mount. State of confusion + dissatisfaction re: work. Gropings to an area concept at work. Furious drawing. Pat at Art Students League. Up early. I to work by 9:45 a.m. Nervous. Sharp. Long dissertation on my work + psychological form. But when I come home, sculpture stuff looks ugly. Throw away head, strip off figures on street, dismantle lamp.

Late at night beer, and more beer. Nuts, cheese, hammering. Older drawings—pre-1959 with few exceptions moved away from front room. Paintings stripped or shelved. Trying to assess sculptures. Put head on "male" sculpture. Doesn't work.

Problems of selection + definition, of painting aroused by thoughts of show and visits, remarks—what to keep of old stuff, what to show. Sculptures were never really assessed. To do this, problem #1. Which drawings, problem #2—any before '59—foolishly showed these. Problem #3, paintings in a mess . . . some key missing—. Also bothered by details of show + summer plans.

General dissatisfaction with self. Fear of future . . . feeling "lazy"—Dickie's remark about process. Uninspired, slowed down.

Index cards for bartending. Reading on etching. Joyce calls.

MONDAY, MAY 18, 1959

Begins a week of much action + (selection) creation. Pat up in evening to Grand Central to mail pamphlets. She gets flour and bags. I buy plaster in p.m. Begin making additional papier-mâché sculptures. To my great surprise, am able to produce under pressure. Pick up photos at Burt's office, take to Emil to enlarge.

a.m.—select + type up poems.

TUESDAY, MAY 19, 1959

Day of panic + worry. At work draw a lot. Feel drawings not in keeping with sculptures, try to make more related drawings. But by p.m. things seem to be OK. Fear of having been arrogant + made a fool of self, inability to complete show, etc.

Pick up houndstooth in backyard. Work on sculptures.

a.m.—try to select drawings. Doesn't work. But in p.m. am able to!

FRIDAY, MAY 22, 1959

Hot day. Opening day. Threat of rain. Thunderstorm at sunset. Runners in rain. Good opening—enough people. Five gallons wine. Details. Then to Eli's + home by cab, 2:30 a.m. or so. Earlier—photostats. And make sign at home—in a.m. paint white—in p.m. put on lettering. Hang sign. At work a couple of hours . . .

FRIDAY, JUNE 12, 1959

In evening, meet Dine, wife + baby at gallery, where we discuss the fall plans. Richardson at gallery. Alan Whitney drives stuff back. A hot night, damp. Turning to rain. Bus to Gartenberg for old movies.

Get word I might run gallery at Lenox.

SATURDAY, JUNE 20, 1959

Fine day.

I work at gallery trying to formulate its space—arrangement. Pat lays out burlap pieces, taking them off the Upson boards.

I put door on studio. Build palette. Bring over Upson panels. Go through basement under auditorium, find much junk, which can be used.

These are great days. Whistling Ives in auditorium. Desperate. Discovering. Great fresh days. We live in main building. All is new. We discover the personalities of the people, the nature of the place, the situation.

SATURDAY, JUNE 27, 1959
We construct. I build with lumber and stuff found in basement. Pat sews on burlap.

MONDAY, JULY 13, 1959
A period of writing, sitting in my studio in a.m. Also, of reading collection of Existentialist philosophers.
Light deposit picked up.

SATURDAY, AUGUST 15, 1959 DOWN HAWTHORNE ROAD
A very muggy morning. I take my sketchpad after breakfast at Festival House and go down hill to Hawthorne Road and out to field, walk across field. Details. Back. Sit at a pool by brook. In woods. On a fantastic-faced rock. Very hot, sweating. Meet Werner. Picking up faces. Lunch at Festival House. To work 1–5 p.m. (last day as it turns out!). At work I type all my notes of the summer. No one comes in.
Dinner Festival House.
Get the photos from Whitestone, send to Pat. Examine motives generally—a short literary interlude, thinking about style + language. Formulate essay idea. On combination of internal + external sensations.
Quiet evening, pasting and typing notes. To bed early. Read, article in *Quadrum*, May 1956.

FRIDAY, OCTOBER 23, 1959 YAMPOLSKY OPENING / DELANCEY MUS. OPENING
Warm. Fine rain in a.m. Some clearing p.m. but rain again in evening. Work 11:30 a.m.–4:30 p.m. Type out in a.m. thoughts on Ray Gun I had during night (poor sleep though we went to bed early). Sandwich at Coscia's, down to 3rd St. and east, reading *Arts + Architecture*. Talk with Dick in shop, Vic (Ralph Muklefoot). Pat in bed. Out for food, cognac. Hamburger dinner. Write up notes, read Kaprow's article in *Art News* + Ashton in *Arts + Architecture*. Dickie over at 7 p.m. Rain prevents getting canvases from Judson. Cognac. Feed Dickie. Wait in shop. Finally, off. Dickie drives us to Judson. Called Lisa. Phyllis's opening. Stage one: deaf mutes, cookies. Her remarks. By cab with Dor + Olga to Delancey Street Museum opening. Red, Jay, Lester, Jack M., Miles, Dody, et al., et al. Peter P., Red's girlfriend, Thompson, et al., et al. I full of Ray Gun plans + Xmas show. Cab back to Judson. Band there, we dance. Tyler takes over. I on tambourine, Peter on piano + Dick too. Reggie, Steve. Kids + passersby. Stan Brodsky. Bongo drummers in one end. Dick's group in other. Pat + I dance with tambourine. I out for beer. Pat + cigar. Pat and kids.

MONDAY, NOVEMBER 2, 1959 THE BIG DAY
Cooper closed. Fine weather. Day of great inspiration, working on poster. Numerous drawings in Ray Gun style. Beginning of decision to feature Ray Gun in two-man show.

The greatest day. Sat in front of window in my study, watching clouds move in. Clear sky and did piece after piece, all working. Made mailers.

FRIDAY, NOVEMBER 13, 1959 JIM AND MY OPENG. / DELANCEY DRAWING OPENG.
Cloudy day. Up early. Tired. Things to do. a.m., framed drawings. To gallery about 12 p.m. Hung drawings + additional paintings. Typed titles, etc., etc. Dine at 4 p.m. Home for dinner 5:30 p.m. by Houston bus, after writing all over front, with help of two kids. Put up poster and Dine's Totem. Steak dinner with beer. Made *Exodus* sign. Back by 7:30 p.m. Both have to pee. Buy whisky. Slow beginnings. To Delancey Street Museum about 8:30 p.m. Food there. By cab back with Dexter, Witkin. Meet Tyler + Kaplan on street going to Delancey. Show picks up. Many people from 9–11 p.m. Hart reads to Mills's flute. Hillbilly band. Dancing. Dickie, I, Kenny. Olga, Pat, Jim, Marc, et al. Everybody out at 11:45 p.m. Talk in streets. Tyler, scenes. Dexter pisses. By cab to Ward's. Dull, crowded party. Walk home. Dines home by cab. Bed, 1 a.m. or so.
J. Levine in toward end.
a.m.—"lose" two sculptures.
No Cooper.
Pat took drawings to Delancey. Red promised "surprise" but later claimed "mental disease."

MONDAY, NOVEMBER 16, 1959
Cloudy. Good breakfast. Work 11:30 a.m.–3:30 p.m. Show article. Buy more papers after work. Prepare drawings. Eat with Pat. Bus to Dickie's. Shower. Leave articles. Bus to 2nd St. To Judson with drawings. Dexter by. Wait for Dick + Co. Music 8:45 p.m.–12 a.m. Aaron, Reg + Ruth, Carmen, Steve, Aaron's girl, Maceo, Kenny. Walk home with Dick + Kenny. Details.
Trying new sounds. Bucket, etc. Moans, etc. Reading with band.
Using several voices: me, Pat, Ruth, Steve, Carmen.
Meaning and more sound. "Musical" word and spoken.
Groans, moans, street cries, everyday conversation, everyday "literature"—newspaper about football game, f.ex., arguments.
I try to break up regularity of rhythm. Rhythm of a truck. (The ordinary-fantastic.)
Music does not lend itself to subjectivity??
Pat at Dine's all day, sewing.

MONDAY, DECEMBER 7, 1959
Wind. Rain turning to sleet. In evening, big snow flurries at streetlight. I have to get up to go to work at 9 a.m. Impossibly tired. After work, look up old reviews. Go through rain to gallery to see rain damage to front. Feel anyway not satisfied with anything. A real spell of fatigue. Go home by bus. Backache. Lie down. Dream, doze. Bob Thompson by. Coffee. Talk. Give him drawing. Call Dine. Scott, who tells of plans for purchase of studio building. Pat home. Out to shop, I meet Tyler + Ratliff. Marc to dinner. In early p.m., before sleeping I start sculpture of just a leg, which I continue to work on in evening. Beer.

I miss the *Burning Building* performance. Dine goes—he is the only one. After Marc leaves, I continue on 1st leg sculpture and also try tearing paper + drawing through paper with point.

THURSDAY, DECEMBER 17, 1959
Finished poems. Typing.
Couldn't sleep a.m. for thinking. Up early, trying to write statement.

MONDAY, DECEMBER 21, 1959
Sunny but turning cloudy. Up early + to work in cool a.m.
CU 9 a.m.–12 p.m. Ill-tempered.
Snow begins in late afternoon. I go out with thin socks to buy screws for mailbox. Find stand for Xmas tree.
In evening, I saw and bend wire on sculptures. Make one foot on rifleman. Dick Weiner drops by out of snow. Talk. Whisky. Pat was at Cooper. Home 10:15 p.m.
Mulling over my ideas, interrupted, but how different from other Xmases!

FRIDAY, JANUARY 1, 1960
Swell day. Inspired dream. Metamorphic machine—Tyler spectacle, etc. Ray Gun definitions. Up + wrote out dream + stuff 11:30 a.m. Shopping. 7Up, paper, oranges. Breakfast. Organized + typed on Ray Gun stuff. To gallery 4 p.m. Walking along Houston, looking + collecting. The lot. Finished putting up wall. Walked home by 6:30 p.m. Beer. Rested. Very tired. To Ratliff's, with Judy for spaghetti dinner. Talk—about Preludin, *Exodus* comics, etc. Dine's 8 pages. Red + green floor. Home at 10:30 a.m. Diary and making comics.

SATURDAY, JANUARY 16, 1960 FIREMEN TRY DOOR / START MY STREET
Sunny, cool. To gallery 1 p.m. or so. Waited in toilet for firemen to go away. In evening, ate at home + stayed home instead of going to Pasternak party. Chicken cacciatore. Bellamy called late.
I tear down paper. Collect garbage. Lay out street area and make a good start. Big face + woman + man with gun.
Dickie calls. Has been busy with reports.
Anita calls—I sold drawing to Pepper.
Bus to gallery. Back really hurts.

MONDAY, JANUARY 18, 1960
Cloudy, a little rain. Up writing seemingly inspired Ray Gun definitions. Cooper 11:30 a.m.–2:30 p.m. K-stein for cardboard. Noel Parmentier at gallery. Garbage. Nervous. Wine. Some work. Not a bad day. Bus back on Houston. Into Deutsch drunk + smeary-faced again, franks + beer. Dinner + love. Back hurts less + feel less tired. Pretty good, in fact. Type cards. Water off. Drink tea. Quiet evening.
Dexter in.

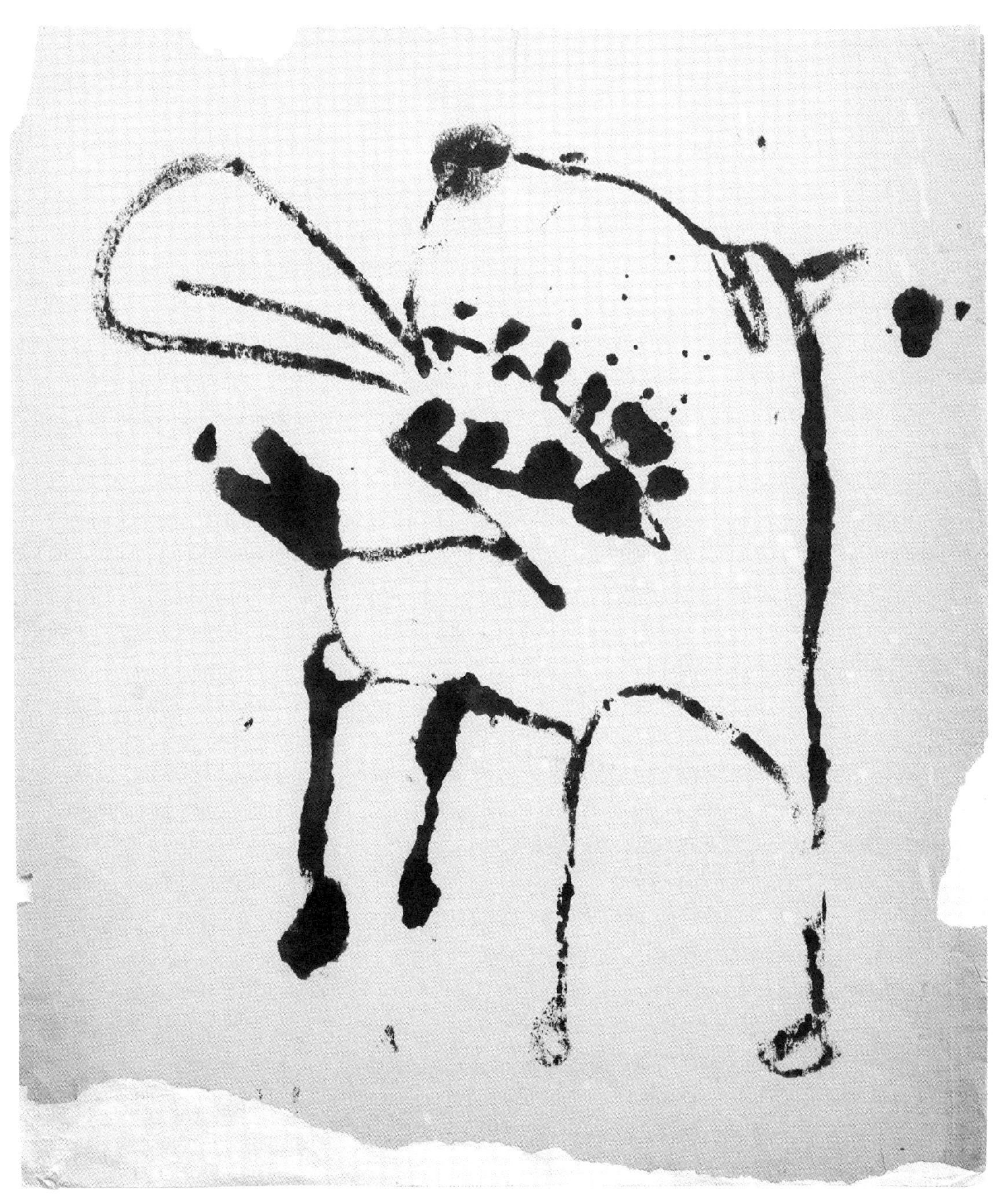

Ray Gun Poster—Dog, 1960

To Joans's studio, but he's not in.
Ray Gun lettering. Wall opposite entrance.

THURSDAY, JANUARY 28, 1960 RAY GUN POSTERS
Put up posters in evening with Jim Dine + Joe Phillips. 3rd St. 10th St. Meet Allan
Frumkin, give him poster. Afterward complete left wall, quite inspired. Home after 12 a.m.
Pat brings posters to Cooper.
I finish painting I wanted to use at Reuben but too late.

SATURDAY, JANUARY 30, 1960 RAY GUN OPENING
Up *early*. Very, very tired, of course. Make breakfast. Bus to gallery.
Toward evening, put posters + communications up in lounge. Two groups led in by
Pickle and Moody, one from Duke. I, face full of black paint and in my coat. Bud copies
my communications, in case they will be stolen.
a.m.—have very hard time getting going. Coffees. Take out garbage, finish floor. But
last touches prevented by entrance of groups. Preston brings records. Walk home, full
of ideas for opening, inspired. Dinner. Evening, back by 7:10 p.m. Experiment, finally
leave orange light in lounge. Dine's very tired. Take a photo. Wine. Tired Dickie brings
phono, goes. Abandon all elaborate plans for opening. People read beside Ray Gun. Ray
Johnson + pals, several times. Bellamy, Lilly Brody. Dine's pals. Chico, dancing. Olga,
Pat. Burroughs does Charleston. Lighting in gallery. Church people. Youths with bags.
Enterers. Home with Clarence after much dancing. Tell him about burglary.

SUNDAY, FEBRUARY 7, 1960
So tired. Hot. Read papers. Grapefruit in bed. Christian Science lecture on "Spirit." Eat.
To gallery about 1 p.m. Clean. Busy day. Churchgoers. Dexter, Chico, Ray Parker, et
al. St. Andrew cigar. Work on wood head. Sort comic-book pages. Home by bus. Steak
dinner. Clear, colorful sunset. Windy. Drew poems + comics. Did posters. Puttered.
Listened to gospel. Bed 12 a.m. Good long sleep.

WEDNESDAY, FEBRUARY 10, 1960
Mild still. Rainy. Up with difficulty. Poor stomach. Shave. Cooper 10:45 a.m.–1:45
p.m. To gallery. People from *Time* come in. We are named avant-garde event of month!
Talk. As I walk to Cooper, conceive of Post No Bill drama. Tell Bud. Thompson by with
poster. Dine by. Bud fixes tape. I fix play. Pat at 5 p.m. Beer. I work on sculpture. Bud at
Voice. Pat + I to Archie's for steak. Put her on subway + return until 9 p.m., working.
Bud finds big box. Fold + put in storeroom. Walk home. Find string. Meet Reg. Beer +
write out play + thoughts. Try to call Dick. Pat revives me with sausage sandwich. We
waited for *Time* reviewer, who didn't show.

FRIDAY, FEBRUARY 12, 1960
No Cooper. Good day building at gallery with wood. First day of feeling for wood
constructions. Pepper in, with Richter. Conversation.

TUESDAY, FEBRUARY 16, 1960 MAKE TYLER'S BOOK

Stomach not too well. Think I feel bad but not as bad at first. Quite tired. Those fine healthy days are over. In evening, *Voice* review + photo comes out. I drink beer at gallery and fix it up, just in case the review brings someone in. Then run off Tyler's book on mimeo. I meet Bud at San Remo with Marc, guys from *NY Post* trying to start magazine, and girl, "Hilda." Walk home, give 20¢ to Jack Smith. Pat home 11 p.m.+.

Earlier, Kaprow in with Irving Sandler. Also apprentice for *Arts*—Ray? Place rather a mess. Bud + I move stuff into storeroom. I put in sofa the church was throwing out.

WEDNESDAY, FEBRUARY 17, 1960 RAY GUN OBJECTS AT DINE

Poor sleep. Very uninspired. At gallery trying to work out my show. I cut up sofa for material. Pat at 5 p.m. Cheap wine. To Club 65. Pat dissatisfied, so take her to Church Wagon. Shitty. See Eleana. To subway. Stand on opposite platforms. Poopy to Brooklyn. I to Dine's. All these days dissatisfied, uninspired, restless. Dine's, make Ray Gun objects—guns—out of Plasticine + coat with stuff. Jim + later I out for beer. I uninspired. Dull scene. Pat at 11:30 p.m. Lamb dish. Home by buses by 1 a.m. or so. To bed.

SUNDAY, FEBRUARY 28, 1960

Gallery by 2 p.m.+ for rehearsals.

Rosie by. Rosie's friend Sydney, who later gets sick. Mary Ann, who also gets sick + can't appear? Olga calls in—going to NJ—can't appear. Mary F. can't appear, etc., etc. Until late, Kaprow is working on set, Pat + Mary Ann helping him to thread tin cans. In p.m., get Dexter + Paul Johnston + Dexter's friends for Elephant. Bud + Gisela stand against fence. A nice, clear, cool weather. Rehearsals in late p.m. + evening. Coordination of show.

MONDAY, FEBRUARY 29, 1960 1ST PERF.

(Performances—every day work at Cooper 3 hours. To gallery about 3 p.m. Props + cleaning + notes of what to do. Whisky and then performances happen very suddenly.) Numerous inspirations.

Get very drunk. Pat goes home alone in cab. I am left in gallery to mourn my loneliness. Group went to Figaro's, drifted back. Friends' night.

Before performance, Pat + I running off + cutting money on mimeo. Hamburgers + beer in office. Hansen turns up with sprained ankle.

TUESDAY, MARCH 1, 1960 2ND

Fellin's afterward, we with spots of black on face. With Alan, Joyce, Dean, Dexter, Jim Guick. Photos after in front of gallery. Marc + Tom.

Painters' night.

Night very cold. Run out in little clothing. Audience in gallery very appreciative. Kaldis, Bellamy. Bud starts my performance too soon. Judy sells books with Tom.

WEDNESDAY, MARCH 2, 1960 3RD + LAST

(Professors + newsmen.)

Fellin's afterward with Dickie + Jill, Shelley. Beer + spaghetti + meatballs. Audience most confused of any night + not very responsive. Ill at ease in gallery. I throw stuff at them. A long period before performance. Pat has diarrhea, does not come out until performance. (In p.m. worked for Soyer). Photographer from *Time* + Hollister, reporter. Jacobson + other photographers all over street, saying turn this way + that . . . Trying to prevent catching cold. Gallery cold + drafty. Sequence of Spex smooth. Higgins, as long as it should be for first time. Audience straggles out. Least contributions. Service in the church. Poor billiard game. Max's remarks.

THURSDAY, MARCH 3, 1960 CLEAN UP / SNOWSTORM

Awake about six. Feeling life is terribly sad and curiously embarrassed or regretful about Spex. Later, when we get up, about 10 a.m., it is snowing hard. A great blizzard, with thunder. It snows hard all day and into night. Tired. Back hurts but feeling good. Move slowly. Take bath, shave. Eat mushroom scrambled eggs. By bus to gallery about 1:20 p.m. Coffee. Whitman there in car. We clean. I knock down Kaprow's stuff. Dine about 2:45 p.m. I to Cooper 3:15–6:15 p.m. Hollister calls, says they will use our pix. Back to gallery 6:45 p.m. Ate at Archie's. Shovel. Clean gallery. Fix window. With Bud out in square, Bud in foot. I take pix with flash. To his house for whisky, spaghetti with meatballs. Home through snow. Tyler shoveling with Manuel, Maceo. Gloria making love on stairs. Go through notes. What now? Pat home about 11 p.m. Meatballs (from Gisela) + pastry. Tea.

Man falls in snow.

Old lady wants me to fix light.

WEDNESDAY, MARCH 9, 1960

I decide to get married in a.m. at Cooper. In evening, we put on costumes + go through one performance for VanDerBeek to film. Pat is grouchy + I promise to marry her. Whisky + we are in better mood. Seems quite inspired.

FRIDAY, MARCH 11, 1960 HERB OPENING AT REUBEN

Confused. Off to bank at Sheridan Square to cash check. Then to Judson to pick up "Newsy" + take it to Cooper. 2 hours there. Take Newsy to Reuben. Brown putting up show. To Judson. Hamburger + coffee and wine. Jim by. He works in House + I, after some deliberation and taking photos, tear down the Street. A good feeling. It is time. Spring is coming. Another bottle of wine. Leave about 6:15 p.m. Walk home. Nice dinner + then to Reuben for opening, about 9 p.m. To Area, Camino + Image. Look at my drawing at Area. See Natkin Barnes et al. at Coates opening. Back to Reuben until rather late. Then to 53 West 11th for party. Silk-stockings stand-up style at the evil guy's. I pick up burlap bags. Finally to Montgomery's on Broadway. A nice party. I very drunk. I dance with Pat. I dance badly. Home by cab with our burlap bags. I am full of energy. A nice evening but drunk. End of Ray Gun!!

Ma called, talked at length of troubles in Boston.

Mail *Exodus* to Kramer in hospital.

TUESDAY, APRIL 5, 1960

Rainy, cool but humid. Forget biography. Out for blades. Gas man wakes us. Work
on income tax. To Dr. German, 2nd St., at school lunchtime but not open. OJ and to
Cooper 12:15–3:15 p.m. Reuben to leave biography, etc., for Max. Allan. Jimmy. Discuss
Provincetown, etc. To Dr. German. Wait. Blood test. Says many young people dying of
cardiac arrest lately. Home by about 5 p.m. See Pat coming in from shopping. With Nila.
Work on papier-mâché head. Dinner. On diet. Sharp, strained. Bananas on way home. Work
after dinner until 1 a.m.+. Out for beer 12 p.m. Break radio. Call Chasteen but too late.
Left day before. Call Dickie. Call Olga re: wedding. Work in cloth + plaster. Good
workday. Many ideas. Bed 1 a.m.+. Theory of opposites.

Pat sews, in black stockings, inspiring me.

WEDNESDAY, APRIL 6, 1960

Cool. Cloudy. Brisk. Nice weather. Up pissing at dawn, feeling sad. Good breakfast.
To work 11:45 a.m.–3:45 p.m. To Reuben until 5:30 p.m., thinking of show. Renee's
mailer. Higgins, Ray Johnson, Michelin, Goldberg + Bluhm, Mrs. Duchamp, et al.
Walk home. Coffee earlier from 9th + Broadway. Office girls. Dinner—soup. "Arthur
Johnson" called. Joyce called. Rosie was up to see Pat. Called Boston, told Ma we were
getting married the 13th. Out for a box. Dropped in on Marc. Burglarized again the
night before. Tyler in basement with Ted et al. Article about him in *Voice*. Called Dine.
Collected sketches + notes toward show + arranged them. Drew plan, etc. Pat sewed
on pink dress. No radio—so silent. Carry out 3 boxes of crap for garbage pickup.
Very hungry.

At work—notes about space.

WEDNESDAY, APRIL 13, 1960   GET MARRIED

A rare, lyrical weather, very right. Mild + now and then sunny. High cloudiness. Very
tired after bad dreams. Pat to New School. I very grumpy. She calls to wake me. I go to
Cooper 10 a.m.–1 p.m. Ave. C is very still except for Spanish music on a loudspeaker. On
7th St. a boy plays a harmonica. A man reads about Castro walking by Tompkins Sq. At
1 p.m. I look for a shine but the place is closed. I walk home. Meet Olga who has bought
some cheese after finding Pat not yet home. We go to our place. Pat is there. Excitement,
of course. I go out for hair tonic and wine + eat food. Shine my shoes. Pat dresses, etc.,
in kitchen. The house is a mess. Dickie calls—he cannot make it by 2 p.m. Will meet us
at the terminal. As we leave, all looking so nice in pale colors. But I in black. See Kenny
and Manuel, who congratulate us. I say we are eloping. I am taking two. We catch a cab
on Houston + down East River Drive to terminal. Dickie, at top of escalators, secs us.
Nickels for everybody. The harbor is gray + clear. The boat is "Miss New York." Photos
on way. Rough landing. Up to Hall. Wait while license is filled out. Pat + Olga to ladies'
room. Calendar. Chapel. Round window over bay. Sign book + ceremony. Pat cries, can't

say the words, thinking of my back + pains + BenGay. "It suddenly was serious." Rings. Hers has to be screwed on but it works. It is over. Kisses. Thank Milton Rich, who really did a nice, very genuine, beautiful ceremony. Back to ferry. Take pix in terminal. Harbor even grayer. Cool. Coffee. It is the "Knickerbocker," which is old + shakes. More pix. At terminal, machine photos of Olga + Dickie. Cab to Dickie's. We wait in garden while he prepares. Superb cake + flowers! Music playing, champagne. Pix. Lisa comes, brings Pat nightgown. Call Ma + Pa about 6 p.m. I become tired. We leave for Gripsholm. To do about taking camera. I run back for it. Cab to Gripsholm. To reserved table. Eat + eat. Aquavit + beer. Dessert. Waiter takes pix. Dresses spilled on. Cab back. Dancing. Photos in garden + in apartment. By 11 p.m. or so start leaving. Pat + I return by bus. Arms full of cake, nightgown, camera. 2nd Ave. to 14th, D bus. Home by 11:30 p.m. and quickly to bed. And good sleep.

THURSDAY, MAY 5, 1960

Quite warm. Clear—a great weather. These have been many days of fine weather. At Cooper 11:30 a.m.–1 p.m. Meet Max at Reuben. In car down 5th Ave., etc., to car rental on 14th St. Then to Living Theater for flats, Judson for Newshead, etc. To Reuben. Cross to 330, but have forgotten keys! Back we go. Manuel watches. Many trips. Kids on stairs interrupted. The ride with stuff through the streets. How it relates! Unloading, while Max returns for tool bag left in street—kids found and put in Tyler's. I hang show. Pat comes in between work with food + beer. Hamburgers. I hang. Go out. Come back. Hang. When Pat comes back, about 10 p.m.+, it is all done. Anita + Max went to Graham performance.
Threw burlap head in garbage. Walked home.

SATURDAY, MAY 7, 1960

Excellent weather continues. Hung over. Drink beer. Giddy. Bus to Reuben with milkweed pod + auto, price list. Typed. Saroff there. Walk to Judson behind legs in blue shoes. Bud, Howard, et al. in front. Marc + Judy hanging. Square crowded. Apologies, talk to Bud. Coffee inside. Whisky. Bottle present + $25. Bud's plans to go to Mexico in an orange bus. Get poems but cannot find Ray Gun documents. Bus back. Clean. Eat. Bathe. To Judson for opening by bus. About 10:15 p.m. Slow. Everyone tired. Drink at Tavern on 8th St. Food. Wait for bus. Look at people. Bob Thompson, Nila. Finally walk home. Dispose of rubbish. Read paper. Diary. Bed 2 a.m.+.
Nice day.
Rassle.
Feeling just swell.
Finalities. Bud sentimental.
Sad end of the Judson.

THURSDAY, MAY 26, 1960 STUFF UP TO JACKSON / ANITA'S WEDDING RECEPT.

Deliver stuff to Jackson Gallery. Late p.m. In subway with it. Sweating. Steve Joy + secretary. Hang one piece on wall. Alter on return. Feeling lyrical. Off to reception. Too

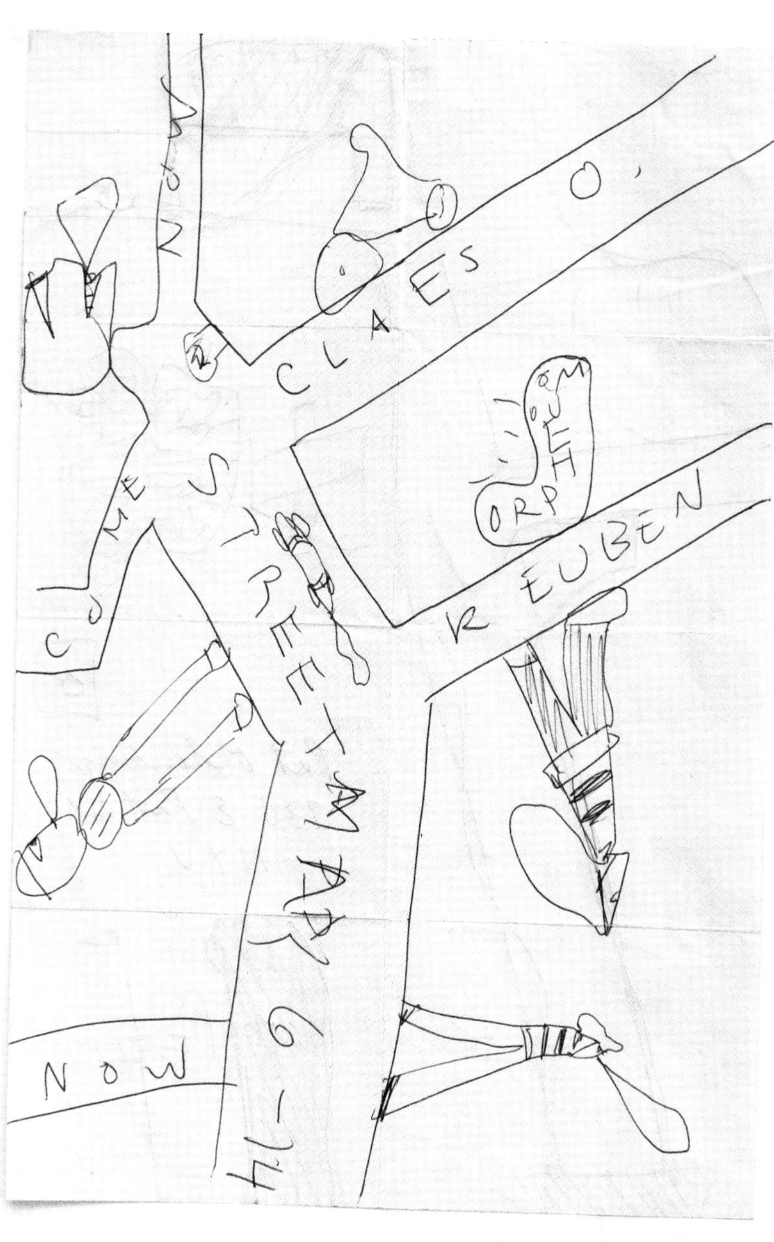

Notebook Page: Study for Announcement of Reuben Gallery Show, 1960

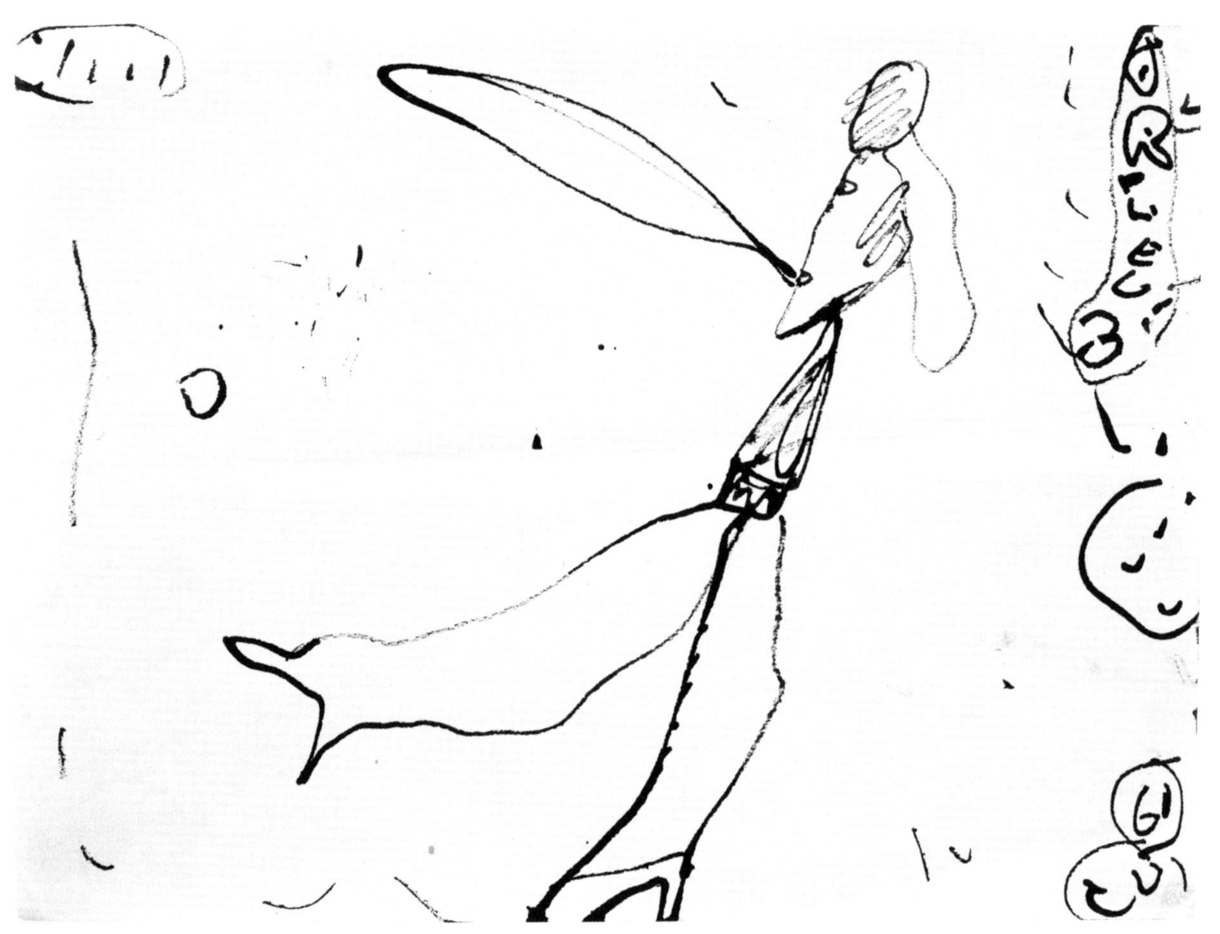

Walking Woman, with Talk Balloon and Orpheum Sign, 1960

much champagne. Parents. Renee, David, Allan + wife, Jim + Nancy, Bob + Mia. Anita + Max, Lenore + Jerry. Loud music. Pornographic Japanese books. Finally home by cab. Bed early, before 12 a.m.

MONDAY, MAY 30, 1960 CONEY ID.
Cloudy but sun now + then. Mild. Work on Orpheum fragment. Little money. Pat to Puerto Rican store, buys breakfast. More work on Orpheum + then 1 p.m.+ off to Coney Island. Subway from Houston + 1st. Boardwalk. Beach St. Beers. Hot dogs, etc. One ride on "paratrooper," 25¢ each. Back to beach. People. Bongos. Cold. Hole in sky. Home by 5:30 p.m. Fish dinner. Tried to reach Dickie. Called Lurie. Worked on Orpheum fragment + Céline. Love. Pat "depressed." Read Greene. I on diet. Tense, talkative. Ideas on subway for truck or trailer construction for summer.

THURSDAY, JUNE 2, 1960 PICK UP EXODUS INSERT
Evening drinking beer, we decide to go to Provincetown . . . Stay up late, until 2 a.m. I go out in rain for beer. Pat sews. a.m. go to binder and pick up copies of *Exodus* insert. Disappointed. Later I realize it has not been trimmed. Warm day.
Call Dickie: Lisa's car too broken down. Pat works in evening. I run out of glue and decide that I have done all I can on work from the past season. (But later I realize I no longer really feel these "breaks" between seasons.)

MONDAY, JUNE 6, 1960 DICKIE'S
Cooler but turns into fine, clear weather. Out to bank for money. Breakfast. Cooper. In p.m., typing thoughts. Try Ray Gun notes again but come to final conclusion, notes cannot be made into literature. They are only *stimulants* to activity. Kracauer. Interest in film. Beer. Make book of press notices. Photos. After dinner of chili, Pat to Olga's. I to Dickie's. Scotch. I am tired. Dickie drives me back in Lisa's Chevy. Diary. Notes, notes.

THURSDAY, JUNE 9, 1960 ARTS REVIEW
Weather good.
Arts comes out with a sympathetic review by Tillim. Carpenter + Jim + I to Judson for *Exodus*es. Package for Ray Johnson + Higgins from Conner. Back to Judson + take home Russ Case's pieces. Feeling *very* good over review. The end of the campaign or something. My first good review.

THURSDAY, JUNE 16, 1960 ARRIVE P-TOWN
Sun is shining. Last packing. Heavy, heavy bags. I get cab from Houston St. Wait. Coffee. Trip easy. Nice. Buzz Bay. Positions. Cab scene at Hyannis. Swift trip to Provincetown. Arrive 4:30 p.m. Our house. Mrs. deRiggs: "Remembered you better dressed!" Rearrange furniture. Prepare place. Unpack. Out to grocery for fish, perch, etc. Count our money. Drink our whisky. Listen to radio. Feel good. Down Commercial St. after dinner. Ice-cream cones. Kids with masks. I stiff. Back hurts. Tired. In bed by 10 p.m.

And do sleep nice.

The bike. I fix seat. Pat tries it out.

MONDAY, JUNE 27, 1960 CARDBOARD BOXES / EVERBREEZE

Third day of excellent weather. I get up early to go to what I expect will be a gardening
job at 8 a.m. Coffee at Patrician. Gardener not there. I ride to Richman's at West End.
Don't find him. Everyone is asleep. I pick up cardboard boxes waiting for garbage
pickup. Break them down and start drawing on them. I return to gardener—"Cookie" at
lunchtime. No job. I eat a sandwich, ride to A&P. Manager out for lunch. To Everbreeze,
where I talk to Mrs. Donohue + get job, starting Saturday. Back + draw some more.

Dickie + Lisa went to "games" on wharf.

Charlie the cat goes outside for first time.

Art store for ink.

Furious experiments with materials + forms.

SATURDAY, JULY 2, 1960 FLAGS / EVERBREEZE

Excellent weather again. I go to work at 1 until 2 p.m. Learning the dishwashing
machine, etc. It is quite slow. But in evening, it is very busy—100 people and we work
furiously. Before leaving in a.m. I do some tear drawings, which satisfy me. Inspiration
has returned, or everything comes together—results. In p.m., I make the first of flags,
which occupy me all 4th of July weekend. Evening, work 6–12:30 p.m. Very tired +
callouses hurt. Dickie, Lisa + Pat stop by—but it becomes later + later. Scotch + a little
talk, and bed.

MONDAY, JULY 4, 1960 PARADE / FLAGS

Superb weather. Pat works a.m. for Marantz. She makes $10. Dickie to Patrician shop.
I clean. Make some flags. Watch parade go by on Bradford St. Lisa sleeps. I breakfast.
Dickie goes to his dune. I make flags all day. We drink beer. I work 1–2:30 p.m. We
eat outside—very nice. Peel potatoes. Hamburgers, wine. People go by. Pat suns beside
house. Work 6:30 p.m.–12:15 a.m. Fireworks. Beautiful, striped patriotic sunset! Moon
in clouds. Silver waves. Home with scotch. Diary. Roth + friend upstairs. Pat, Lisa +
Dickie went to town for fireworks + band, etc.

Charlie goes bravely out, under car + back in by himself.

FRIDAY, JULY 15, 1960 1ST DAY AT CAMP

Windy day + clear. Marvelous weather again! After breakfast, about 12 p.m., decide to
go to dunes + do, on the bikes. Hearing roar of waves, we walk on, to shore, further
down from Snail Road, a diagonal path. Across considerable vegetation. View from first
big dune! Find a spot near a log + make a sort of camp. Put up sheet as shield from sun.
I walk along shore gathering wood. A wreck revealed, very old, which is later concealed.
Big, dirty-water waves. A lady asks me what I'm doing. Pat reads about Kennedy, suns
nude. A fine place, in the shelter of tall grass, yet near water. Return by 5:30 p.m., I buy
an ale. Hamburger dinner + to work 6 p.m.–12:30 a.m. Joanna Roos at place. Northern

Lights. Very clear evening. Walk Joanna home + on return meet Armstrongs, Barrells. Feel courage + inspiration returning.
Take photos of camp.

SUNDAY, JULY 17, 1960 PICNIC AT BEACH CAMP
Sun, of course, but slightly misty. Less noise upstairs + we sleep until 10 a.m. Doze. Breakfast—buckwheat cakes, bacon + eggs. Papers from Patrician shop. Clean. After a while, out on bikes: Prince St. to cemetery. Shank Painter Road + Brown (?) Road to Bradford. See Lenore + Marilyn waiting for bus. Cottage to Nickerson. Ruth and friends. Janice. Brandy. Coffee. I look at lumber pile. Ride on. Lennie Horowitz. Stables. Ice-cream cones. Ride to New Beach. Look. Marilyn there. Down Route 6. Stop for view of pond. Cross up road to dump. Lots of good material! Back home and get picnic stuff together. Ride to Snail Road. Tie up bikes + walk, not on road. Camp destroyed, but lumber still there. Spread blanket, etc. I build "flags." Beer. Great dinner: potato salad + chicken, cantaloupe, cherries, cookies. Lie around. The woman, the man, fishermen. Sailboat. Water calm. Colors—pink + green. Sun sets in clouds. Wind shifts to south. Walk home through darkening. I piss a face. Sit by dune + drink ginger ale. Mosquitoes. Ride home without lights + carrying "flags" + stuff. 9:30 p.m. shower. Tea. I play with my wood pieces. Lie around. Diary.

WEDNESDAY, JULY 20, 1960
Hot + humid. I work sewing + hammering at side of Bradford St., making triangular form. Trying to formulate some new forms.

TUESDAY, JULY 26, 1960 PAA / LAST NIGHT SHIFT
Clear and warm. Up very, very tired. Eat + to Provincetown Art Association by 9 a.m. Thinking I'd quit but didn't. Screw-eyes + others hanging stuff. Patrician for coffee. Martha Jackson comes. I tell her about Long Nook. She offers to "lend" me money for studio to work. The pool at Seascape is being drained, she says, so our plans must change. I bike home, drink ale + type. Then to Candell school + wait for Pat. Details of building's stairs, etc. View from front door. We ride home + eat. I take coffee to work, talk to Mort in front of PAA. Finish hanging. Read of Hawthorne. Paid. Home. Pat at A&P. Rest. Richter is building his stove—noisy. I doze. Fly. Pat home. We eat lamb. To Everbreeze 6 p.m.–12:30 a.m. Pat stops by, buys beer, nail polish, Coppertone. When I come home, she is asleep. The rose on my ear blows off while riding. At work I think seriously about Jackson offer + about growing up to fact I *am* an artist. Diary + beer at home.

FRIDAY, JULY 29, 1960 GET ROACH'S PLACE / BEACHCOMBER'S PARTY / JAIL
An end to July. A new scene begins, violently. 2nd day on day shift, and I decide to eat at work so not much to eat at home, save money. Prime cause of the drunk. At work Ann S. appears, sits, and tells of cabin. After work, we ride out there. She not home, leave note. We have drunk beer + slightly high. It is humid—desperate weather. On return, see

Freborgs drive off. Fays tells us they have left note. We read: two tickets to ball. Go to Freborgs to get tickets. Stiff drinks + a dinner invite. To HCE gallery in our "costume," my white pants + green T-shirt, Pat's short jeans + flowered blouse. Then to Sun Gallery + drink ale with Barrells. Irene has poison ivy. We are raucous + reckless. No one is going to ball. Meet Freborgs, Stout. Back for money + set out to hitch to ball. Meet Vevers. Stop for cheap booze. Arrival. Dance madly. Get very high. I throw my T-shirt at some people by accident. Ruth Roman, vague. Pat dances with some guy. I sit at speakers' table with Kemp, Browne, et al. Kemp speaks—"When I was rounding Cape Horn . . ." Gradual loss of respect of audience. All my hostility to Art Association + scene comes out. I boo parade of costumes. Harry Engel in cop suit. Greeks. 3 blind mice—who elbow me. Old bag with green hair—my champion. I hold out her hair. Drink from bottle—people tell me not to. Finally we leave. I cease remembering. Do not remember parting with Pat. Called her "timid." See her going down road?? Some people mention Murchison's house + in my hostility to it I walk up hill + dive in pool with clothes on. Lose notebook . . . wake up in jail. Was apparently picked up on road (in poison-ivy patch!) + carried in. Feel giddy + wild. Very cold + wet. My T-shirt remarkably with me. Sing + bang my feet on cot to keep warm. Sing: What's the charge!! Refuse to give name. At last, get blanket + try to sleep. Vomit on floor. Imply all sorts of injustices. Cops call me crazy. Am really having an insanely good time!

SATURDAY, AUGUST 6, 1960 FULL MOON / STAY AT CABIN / TIDE FLATS IN EVE. + CITY DUMP AGAIN

Fine day, cool + clear. Bright. Shower in morning, first in a week. Pancakes. To cabin briefly with Pat, who remains to wash the floor of front room. Everbreeze 12–5 p.m. Driftwood off beach. Carry home. Veal cacciatore. Very good. Gin + tonics. After coffee, on bikes to cabin with wood. Then to waterfront with sidewalk along tide flats, pick up stuff. Objects. Colors. Sunset. Ride back over cemetery with stuff. Big red sun. Corner with bush of blue + white. Black dog. Many dogs. Dump stuff + ride out to city dump. Approach + details. Whistling men. Back to house. Walk for beer, $1 worth + return to house. Dinner party at Roach's. Make 2 flags. Pat sews, reads, types. Whisky + bed. Full moon, very clear outside, silver-tip grass.

From today through next Thursday, do most of my work for *show*. This day set out for materials to realize inspiration + experiments of preceding several days. I realize I can say it all in *flags* + revert to this form, destroying figure heads, naive landscapes + cemeteries to concentrate on flags.

Thought I heard drums.

FRIDAY, AUGUST 12, 1960 SUN OPENING

Shave and eat breakfast alone. Pat to Tante's. Ride to Roach's to meet Irene. Arrive late but she there. Tells me opening will be that night. Sit around. Select stuff + we walk it to gallery. A warm, nice day. We disagree about the show. I return for more stuff. I overlooked one! She does not think there is enough + sets up hers, of which there are more than enough! I am about to blow up at Irene, but I meet Lester Johnson + wife +

kids, which neutralizes my anger. Twice I leave the pot boiling at Roach's. I go to Bangs St., too. And late to Everbreeze, arrive about 1 p.m. Work until 5:30 p.m. Home for dinner and then to gallery, a little high. Meet Irene + Bill + Myron Stout + Lester on way. Hang show—but much too naked. Return to Bangs St. to get Pat. Return about 8:15 p.m. Everyone horrified at how I've hung show, so add stuff (good thing I didn't take it back) and am still hanging when people start entering 8:30 p.m. Budgie tears off window cover. A nice opening. Afterward, to Café Boyant with Ivan Karp + then to Pilgrim Club. Jo, Nadine, Mort + Barb, Irene + Bill. At opening—Lannan et al. Conversation with Bruno about Mallarmé. When Pilgrim Club closes, with Mort in his car, leave off Barbara + out to cabin. Drink scotch. I give Mort a Ray Gun envelope—my last! Talk about all kinds of crap. Hitchhiking in the west. Pat goes under covers. Talk of going to Chicago in Mort's car, he taking our apartment in NYC. Bed later than 3 a.m.

MONDAY, AUGUST 22, 1960 TOPMAST OPENING / FOG
a.m. cabin. Letter to Allan Kaprow and Ray Gun writing. Good inspiration.

SUNDAY, SEPTEMBER 4, 1960 GOLDSWORTHY VISITS
I go to vacant lots at 1st Ave. and come back with a thick flag on half a white tabletop. Stop in at Jim's to ask if I can put stuff there but then carry it home. Muggy weather. In the evening, we pick up more stuff—all of it from Dickie's and sit there reading—I reading *The Nude* + Pat Strindberg and listening to sweet classical music + drinking scotch + feel so nice—I do anyway.

MONDAY, SEPTEMBER 5, 1960 JIM'S IN EVE.
(I am framing pictures + pasting up notes and arranging the place + thinking what am I going to do + how do I feel.)

THURSDAY, SEPTEMBER 8, 1960
Conclude I am Robinson Crusoe + take book out of library, returning *Magister Ludi*. In evening, we wait for Fisher + drink beer. It is very warm. But he calls, he cannot make it. Smash glass + nearly blow myself up on frayed electric cord of Mama.
Icebox gets fixed in p.m.

FRIDAY, SEPTEMBER 9, 1960 PICK UP PHOTOS / JACKSON, MEET JIM, PICK UP MY STUFF /
STAN FISHER UP
With Pat's help, I get up early to get to work by 9 a.m. Plättar. Hand in summer films + then subway up to Compo, pick up Chico pix. Subway crosstown + up to Jackson. Find Jim with Rolf Nelson. Chit chat. Down to Anderson. Look at Jim + Bob's lithos, rock garden, talk about poster. Up to top floor, an air-conditioned office, get Mug, sign release. Down to Buckley in basement, vodka, look at his photos. He gets my 2 pieces. By + by, leave. Talk of forming a group to put on performances. Jim drops me with my stuff, Fisher comes by about 4 p.m. with cover for his magazine. My god! Well—anyway. I ride with him to his place. His house, wife Anita + kid. Details. Ride back. Fish

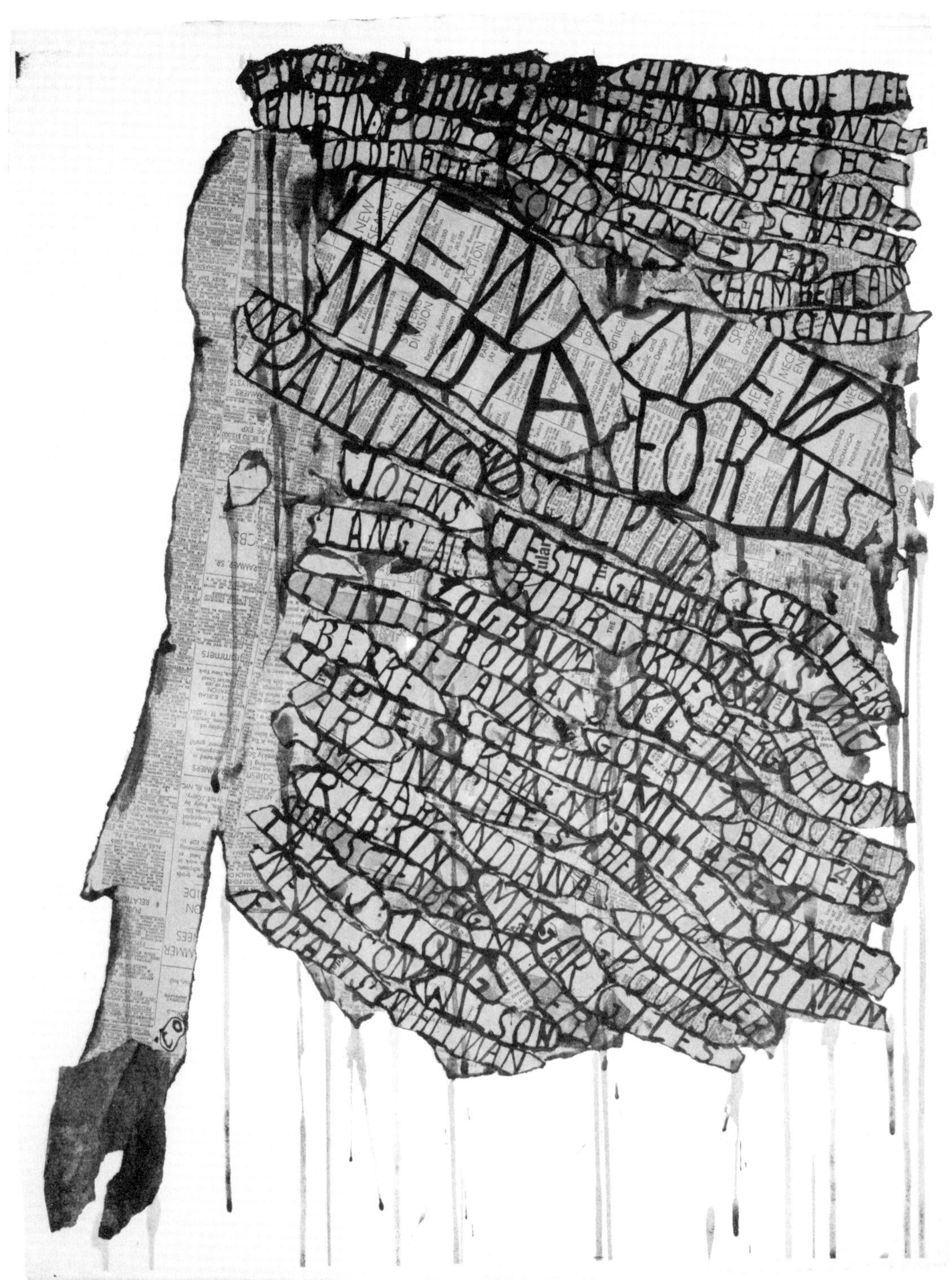

Poster for "New Forms, New Media I," at Martha Jackson Gallery, New York, 1960

dinner—"Mallard??" Dickie calls in evening. We meet him at coffee shop on 3rd St. Cab to Pete's. Sit outside. Rain drives us in. Drink beer. Eat ravioli. Pleasant conversation . . .

TUESDAY, SEPTEMBER 13, 1960

Clear weather + warm. Cooper 10 a.m.–1 p.m. By Dine's + pick up flags. Talk about gallery plans. Stand on corner + have coffee. Man cries about death. Johnny Cohen. Pat irons. She has washed + is cooking soup. I lie around + think. Conceive American monuments.

SATURDAY, SEPTEMBER 17, 1960

Walk through Times Sq. to City Center. See peanut sign + all the others. Underwear in windows, etc. Great object consciousness + also color consciousness. Buy *Swank* and look at ourselves. Use binoculars at theater, look at people. Return by bus + I mad at Pat for not seeming to react enough.

SUNDAY, SEPTEMBER 18, 1960   DINES OVER / REUBEN IDEA ANITA'S

Rain. Dines come over in a.m. Ride to Orchard St. Delancey St. I draw. Become very sensitive to objects. Stay in the car.

At Anita's, a child's drawing in the box from Ray Johnson. Drink beer + decide to resume Reuben on subscription basis.

THURSDAY, SEPTEMBER 29, 1960   BUILD STAGE / REARRANGE APT.

Rain. Pat goes to work early. I up early too. Play with pussycat. By + by, move bed into long room, etc. Rearrange studio. To work 12:45 p.m. On way, meet Cliff + Joanna going to Tyler's + Brooklyn Bridge. Home, I build a little stage. Dinner of chili. Love. Pat to work in Brooklyn again. Phone Anita, Marcus, Moody (in a.m.). Putter. Think about stage. Cut out stuff from papers + put in stage. Poor Charlie—still stiff + frightened, scene under lower shelf in kitchen: Georgia paws him + tries to be friends.

FRIDAY, SEPTEMBER 30, 1960

Label notebooks. Paste notes from September. I take bath late at night and get only 3 hours' sleep.

September of questioning is over, then begins action (supposedly). I make an outline in wire of papier-mâché head.

TUESDAY, OCTOBER 4, 1960   TYPING "RAGS" / VEVERS OPENG.

Go up to Jackson and get catalogues, which inspires me to resume on "rags." Write letter to Allan. Lots of typing this week, formulate some theories of theater, erotic novel, etc. Mind works very well for writing, find way of listing Rags. Charlie + Georgia such good friends!! Beautiful scenes.

Vevers opening. Padawer Gallery. Meet Pat there + we get quite high. At home eat fine steak dinner. She goes to sleep. I phone + write.

A nervous, hot week. Pat + I not too friendly . . .

THURSDAY, OCTOBER 6, 1960 GEORGIA TO HOSP.

Passloff calls in a.m., no definite plans. Go to work 3–6 p.m. Try on clothes. Type on Rags. Mix paste. Buy flour + peppermint. Evening, eat stew from day before + work on large papier-mâché head. Out for beer late. Pat works all day, comes home late. At work calls me, tells me Georgia has broken leg. When I get home, I rush her by cab to Speyer animal hospital before eating.

Nervous, hot.

At work, read about ancient theater, vase painting, Urs Graf, etc. Continue feverish pasteup of clips of objects from papers.

SATURDAY, OCTOBER 8, 1960 RETURN GEORGIA / UPTOWN / START COLOR PLAQUES W. PAINT

To Speyer and get Georgia, see doctor. Return with Georgia.

Love in a.m. Joe Phillips calls. Jim calls re: Reuben move. Fisher calls. Kaprow calls. Go uptown. Subway to 58th. Call Dickie, not there. See Cummings on street. Go to Cober Gallery, see Tillim's work. Jackson. Coffee. Chats. See show. M. Randell. Buckley gives me whisky. Walk to 58th again. Ride back to Astor Place. Walk home. Do not go to Phillipses. Very nervous. Notice antagonism of Charlie to Georgia—his seemingly vicious attacks on her. Makes us feel bad. Go to bed with animals separate. I do the first plaques of wood, using paints again! Formulate concerns with object. Mounted Ray Guns.

Heat goes on.

SUNDAY, OCTOBER 9, 1960 CUMMINGS VISITS / DEFLEAING GEORGIA

Wonderful warm + sunny.

To Jim 9:45 a.m. Anita + Max there. Coffee.

Back in car with Jimmy + Jeremy, visit Lenore + get black cats for Jim.

Deflea Georgia.

Plättars, hours in the making.

Paul Cummings.

Make up schedule. Go through drawings, realize object not figure is my concern now.

Dinner, roast + ale.

Take bath. Clean room.

Paste up notes. Write in diary. Walk to separate cats.

Pat defleas Georgia + powders her. She looks so good. Plays with her a lot.

I call Ma in Boston. Pa, bad dizzy spells in the morning.

MONDAY, OCTOBER 17, 1960 THROW AWAY NOTES + RAGS + START REMOVING "PLAQUES"

SUNDAY, NOVEMBER 13, 1960 "ANNIVERSARY" / START A NUMBER OF WORKS

Cool but sunny. Yellow light. Pat to work 12:30–4:30 p.m. Write notes about being sorcerer, etc., reviewing conversation of night before. Walk to gallery. See Bob. George Brecht. Lucas. Buy stockings + hang on mirror. Start rifle, Major André + umbrella.

Later, make paste + plaster shirt. Pat, having bought material, works on a flannel nightgown. Call Bossman, Rosalind. Feeling quite effective.

SUNDAY, NOVEMBER 27, 1960
Paint ceiling in kitchen + then work furiously on plaster sculptures + clean up. End by being very tense + tired.

MONDAY, NOVEMBER 28, 1960
Cloudy. Very tired. Pat to work early. I work 1:20–4:30 p.m. a.m. call Aileen + think on my plays. See Lucas + Bob at gallery. Make my own (hamburger) dinner. Write plays. Hansen calls + Ma about moving Thursday.

New York, January to June 1959

Pop culture. Teen cult. Life of the "slums."

If anyone ever asks or is interested, I might explain how I exploited my Oedipus complex as a motive for art. Where less clever people try to cure it . . . or look askance, I used its great power. It kept me hard at work, developing technique.

Brushstrokes, line counts—I am combining drawing, painting, and sculpture.

I'm so obviously a sculptor not a painter.

Floor black.
A fucking masterpiece!
Three-dimensional drawing!

I don't want to "learn how" or be "ready to show." I am not a professional.

Lenox, June to August 1959

How to come backass into Lenoxland! Boors in the Berkshires! Theory, of course—there is so much good here, who cares about the bad—bad food, no salary, etc.
Freedom of the country, freedom of space, objects left behind. So much space, cheap or free, so many abandoned useful objects.

I find it difficult to act and think at the same time. June–July, pressures to verbalize, philosophize. I must be on my guard. A year of shows, symposiums, coming out. From one existence to another—a little pause needed in between.

A lecture from "notes" on myself? Go through noteboooks, take out what seems valuable—thoughts, a phrase, then file away. That is, attempt to rewrite notes into some form, complete sentences, developed thoughts, etc.

July 21—It is now allowed to find things . . . Modern belief in magic. Ritual. Man's natural belief, not affected by science. Affirm natural beliefs.

An object. What *is* it? It is a gum wrapper? That never entered my mind.

Things look like other things.

Tough. City people. Cynical, unsentimental, disillusioned. (Céline—the proving of value, of love.)

The notes in small books, pasted up and sorted and criticized, are taking the place of the speckled-book notes. This began in spring. Signifies a different process, attitude to notes.

I think—the world is very hard. If one relaxes, one is lost. One must be careful where one relaxes. I do not desire escape, which I once did. I was romantic (who wasn't?). I am not now a romantic. I do not identify with romantic artists. I am of the tough school stylistically. I expect nothing. I seem cold, but I am not. I like also those who seem cold but are not. I like irony. The world is rotten and truth is not to be had, but I am not for escaping it. It makes one treasure the good. There is no truth, but one hangs on anyway, even seeking it. I believe in facing problems.

I use a cool palette, like grays and browns and blacks. This follows. I like beaten, battered things. Céline was a turning point.
I resort very often to sculpture.

Does the age determine the artist's style or does the artist's style make the age? A little of each. The artist certainly affects the age and is more important than people realize, even if his style may take twenty years to reach a popular level.

I like all sorts of physical effects—collisions, explosions, glides, starts, stops, etc.—which is why I break bottles.

Objects *live*.

When it's hot, one will do anything. But that's when things get done. When one is drunk, too. Haven't many, many significant acts that I would never have otherwise done been done by me while drunk? I challenge the sober and reasonable to extract me, and thereby to learn.

An artist knows how to be alone, how to protect himself against himself, and generally how to use himself. He learns how to guard against himself, how to let himself out, how to pull himself back in.

My search for values! What an existentialist I have been!

We discussed drugs. I maintained that the claims for drugs are rationalizations by the user, that they chiefly make you uncreative, unable to create, or sleepy. True?

Drawing explains, discovers, sums up, organizes.

Note the similarity of my drawings and general compositions to maps, always an obsession.

Persons who live at the edge.

"The existential image."

Personality—ought to be considered "in time"—a sequence of moods. Contradictory. A painting in time is subject to moods in time. A war in time, of contrary impulses. Painting in time is a war in time, of moods (and intentions) in time. Painting exists in space, but the process of painting exists in time, and the painting records this.

To work in the midst of action—that seems a part of my theory. To stop for a moment and throw it down (but actually put a lot into it) . . . I am all geared for the intense, inspired moment when all is intensely concentrated! I build toward this.

It's a damn fact—the world only begins to quiver when you in some way loosen the bonds, by alcohol, drugs, or simply by staying up too late. Intimation of transcendence then. Stimulants are not escapist but projectist, openist.

Settling down to work is as likely to produce bad, dull work as good. I mean being sober, good hours, etc. Remember at college, Sunday nights when hallucinations crowded in and produced inspirations. Still one has to make some kind of account with health. Survival.

July 23—Perhaps I am doing so much it doesn't anymore seem we are doing anything. All even at a height with no heights.

Now (August 15), everyone is gone. There is no action because I have no partner. No friends . . . July was a month of action, though, dammit! (?)

People now confuse "beats" with old-time bos—bohemians and hobos. The country is tending to split into Madison Ave. or Ivy on one hand, Beat on the other. Like a war.

Now marriage is a traditional situation and in my opinion requires traditional behavior with the promise of staleness and loss of freedom. I cannot avoid doing what is proper to a thing. Play-acting marriage is quite all right, one does the thing for a time. But the whole point of not getting married, which I would gladly do, is to preserve freedom and avoid dependence and tradition. To keep action free, responsible, and unpredictable. Institutions are devised to limit freedom and responsibility and to reduce unpredictability . . . to produce order in the mass.

Bringing a painting along is a very painful process (de Kooning at MoMA).

Pollock's work, f.ex., has made itself available to be read as an interior statement or an exterior statement and the inevitable enlightenment that they are the same. It is either the universe (and from there on to Tapié and *L'Art Autre*) or the unconscious (on to Herbert Read's "cloud of unknowing"). Pollock himself was curiously wordless (?? how do I know??) and truly possessed—but not without conscious influences, no nature child or pure instinct.

I talk talk talk when no one is around. I talk to myself and write notes, that's why so many notes.

It may be that our relationship will collapse when we are forced to use words. Our relationship so much depends on the worship of action and the suppression of words.

We discussed the American star system with regard to books, the glib concept of the one-book author, and decided it was not the fault of the author. All authors might be one-book authors but in other countries their whole oeuvre and existence is considered and not just that one perfect book.

I put a lot of time into recording my experience, and I wonder how much, if anything, this contributes to my painting. I have a fear of losing or forgetting or not sufficiently feeling experience.

I am a complex of opposites, a confused mingling, very hard to get under control and into form and very hard to define. One moment the death wish rules, the next the life wish. Is this too obvious?

I am really a cloudy philosopher.

Since the lecture, I have been hung up on philosophy (misunderstanding my work by seeking knowledge in it)—for which I am poorly fitted. The notes are useless. If I get away from concrete art thinking, I am lost.

Aren't I wonderful, how seriously I take everything—for nothing (no salary)!

I paint rapidly and intensely and then require distractions. I must live in an environment that provides distractions. I despise isolation.

Try to define this "climate of inspiration," which exists for me in some places and not in others. More general than objects, persons, places, closer to "mood." Something that gives to all subjects a peculiar character. Arising perhaps out of places—the sea, the shore. NY City. What I used to call my "grand symbols."

All the same, I am lyrical . . . city lyrical. Wedding on Bowery. City pathos.

Grooms's intentions are very close to mine, and it is a source of envy that I have not demonstrated them on so dramatic and public a scale as his murals, his gallery, the Omaha show, etc. An essay on him would, in fact, clarify my own position to myself. I've said again and again that he is very different from the city group, who crawls close to the ground. Even Johnson does not soar very high.

I suppose it gnaws on me that I really haven't accomplished a thing this summer . . . My painting has been very conventional, and didn't I give up painting anyway?

Most of what people say is noise anyway, meaning conveyed by noise, and actual speech appears meaningless, f.ex., verbatim press conferences. Noise—I mean sound . . . New patterns, new visual patterns, too.

Areas of my recording of experience:
Exterior: Diary and accounts.
Interior: Discovery of obsessive objects, "objet trouvé." That they are obsessive ought to be emphasized. They are a way of arriving at "ikons" of consciousness, of eliciting these. Recording of dreams, now discontinued. But awareness remains. Perhaps a limited recording of especially good items ought to be continued.
Exterior: Verbal reports of objects and natural processes.

All this indirectly to the end of developing a language of both exterior and interior life, in one expression.

Something we (I) do not sufficiently or often enough do is put ourselves in the place of others. I don't mean the banal injunction that is supposed to promote good behavior, but how it *feels* to be another in another situation. The difference of two experiences at a single moment in time is dazzling to imagine! For instance, at the time of the bus's departure: Pat, leaving on the bus. The cripple. Lisa, Dick, and I left behind. Richness of simultaneity.

One exists in the imagination of others.

Perhaps at Judson, I could at least arrange a group show.

The modern shit art. Note Céline's obsession. I am not afraid to exploit this.

New York, August 1959 to June 1960

Well, back in old crazy NY. How can anyone, how can *I* stand the noise? Radios from the back, radios from below. Funny how one gets used to it!

Action. Demands. Feel Good.

How wonderful to be out of Lenox!

THE NEW ROMANTICISM. Article in *l'Oeil*. Balthus's relation to German Romantics—Runge, Courbet, et al., Füssli . . . C. Friedrich . . . DEFINITION OF THE NEW ROMANTICISM—A City Romanticism? An American Romanticism? Surrealists involved, of course. They were the last romantics.

The thing to do is probably not to run the gallery or any gallery but try to get booked in several places, to have space and time and freedom, and then, like the first show, put on something imaginative, with mailer, etc., and perhaps a group show arranged by me, by individuals.

This will be the first season I will have enough work to seek a show of paintings.

What struggles I have fought—for style!

Looking at Hess book on de Kooning—I see how under an apparent softness of his later work is a knife-like, incisive drawing style, which will not soften or fuzz the line . . . Picasso-ish, Miró-ish . . . Gorky. Analogies to a soft line like Rembrandt's seems wrong to me, and I do not at all identify myself with de Kooning now, stylistically. My line is soft, blunt, and I *will not* sharpen it, as he will not soften it.

Yes, that whole bunch is so geometrical-mechanical . . . We are different. Even Pollock, they are all Picasso-ized, Miró-ized . . . Ours is organic, humanistic . . . perhaps only Kline, a younger man, fits in, or Resnick, f.ex.

I must face the consequences—my art is not pleasing and neither (except to those I choose to be) am I. I am hostile. My art is hostile to society . . .

Proposal—A Museum of American Expressionist Art. Ray Gun Gallery of Expressionist Art. It needs it; it needs help. IT IS AGAINST. The conditions would be very special, very honest, very honest to the type of art.
The expressionist element in ALL SORTS OF THINGS will be revealed. I want to start new institutions.

RAY GUN, a gallery of Expressionist Art. Utter freedom for feelings, conscious and unconscious.

Expressionist poem show.

FIREWORKS

The Expressionist emphasis in all manifestations of Art and Near Art—Popsy and all. But note, the Administration and Communications would also be Expressionist, determined by the Expressionist confusion of its operators! This is unique and genuine.

ANNOUNCING
Gallery
RAY
GUN
A (an expressionist) gallery (statement) devoted to the defense of expressionist art.
But, WHO BACK?
HOW RAISE MONEY. Beggars in "beggar costumes"? Send out prospectuses?
WHOLE POINT IS ALL CONNECTED WITH GALLERY. IS TO BE DONE
EXPRESSIONISTICALLY. Who can help?

A parody on museums! where all is done so nicely. Utter honesty, tolerance of deviation. Tolerance of intolerance. All our business matters, a sort of parody (but serious). America is a business place. This social intention is part of expressionism, which is not limited to visual art but intends toward all living and revolutionizing institutions.

Music.
Theater.
Lit-up blinking sign. Pops.
Dick Tracy Show. Blowups.
Street scrawls, of course. Signs. Mad Art, of course. NO END!

Show business is expressionist, and to involve show business with art is perfectly OK when the aim is to defend and promote expressionist art. It may be that Red Grooms only gave the suggestion for all this and that he himself cannot carry it out—but someone will, damn soon, and shouldn't it be me?

Expressionist Artists at Home, a photo show with essay.

Expressionism in unexpected places—How Manet and Ingres are expressionists. F.ex., all my little ideas and prejudices and concerns.

The place to be expressionist: It is inconceivable that the place for the museum or gallery not be expressionist, be dull. Either a dull place is worked over, covered, painted, etc., or an expressionist sort of place is found, like the Lampoon building in Cambridge. (Destiny summons. A sign will come, for a place. MAN's superstitions must be respected.)

Dick Tyler—cut posters.

"To combat prejudice against expressionism . . . "

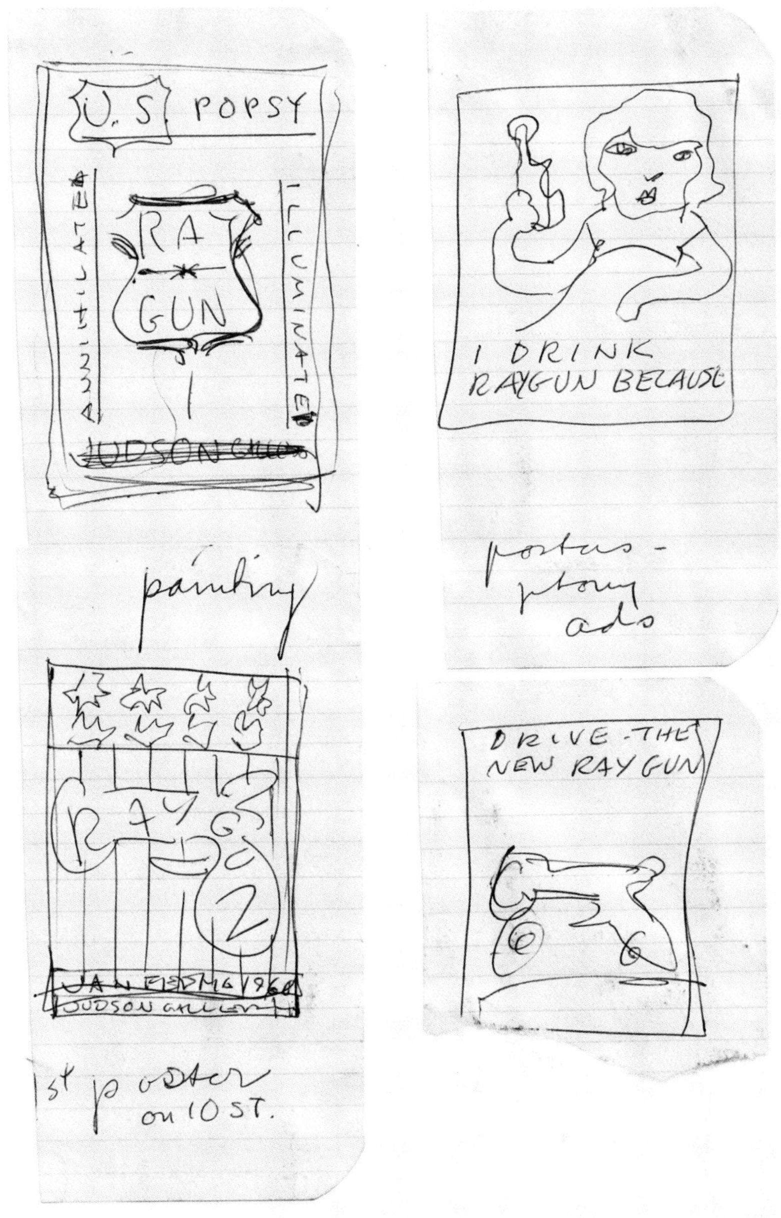

Notebook Page: Ray Gun Posters, 1960

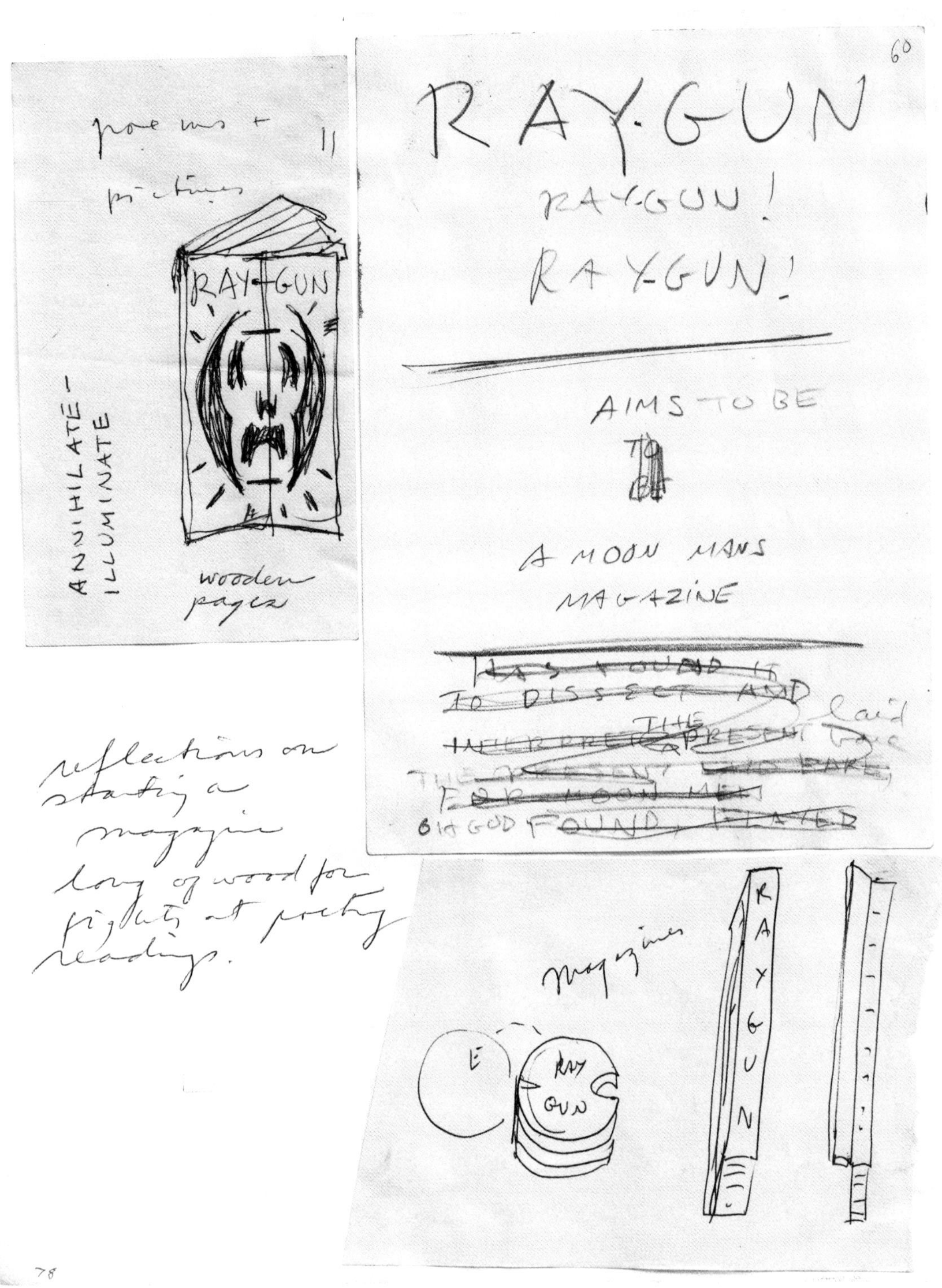

Notebook Page: Studies for a Ray Gun Poster, 1960

The fathomless corruption. But who can I trust, who have I found, so far? . . . Tyler? Pat? Anything. BUTTERFLIES. Write prospectus.

Art Brut show.
Toy show.
An expressionist building, freestanding (Red's conception). Stage Tyler's Planets and Reflections? A movie theater, with lights on the marquee displays. Coney Island. Cast Pat in powder white in a play I write. Painted place. Synagogue.

This is decisive: that expressionism involves not just form but the belief in the beyond, a spiritual and content dimension such as Kokoschka and Munch had and which I decidedly have not . . . My expressionism is formal, and I do not think this can be considered expressionism . . . I have an element of the spiritual, but it is not dominant . . . My belief is physical . . . I do differ from someone like Tyler. I am scientific, I am a formalist, even if my form happens to be the Baroque. I can live in pure pleasure with things for their physical sensation alone. I delight in manifestations of the physical . . . I am against romanticism. I am cool. I am spaceman. Romanticism is reactionary. My palette is cool. I am defender of the balance of man . . . I am French . . . This is to fight back to my true conception developed earlier this year. It is this and not any other . . . I am against sentimentality . . . I am a formalistic and scientific expressionist. Soon this reactionary movement will be over. It will be seen. Man's future lies in keeping cool and still staying human. Living with and not against the facts of life and of the machine. Not escapism. Materialism. How lost I get trying to find the spiritual in Pop.

Now in this way, I am a Modern but not an unfeeling one. I see no reason for escape and romanticism. The erotic, the formal excites me all to hell—they are the same, as I said earlier. FORM FORM FORM gives me a hard-on.

The beauties of spiritual absence. A rationalistic "expressionism."

Cool Cool Bare. Therefore: RAY GUN.

Bleakness only, this is MODERN, to learn how to live with *it*. It is just this, to avoid the richness and prefer the barren, to love it . . . the "primitive."

RAY GUN—Scientific reality is now expressionist, popular is now expressionist. An expressionism of neon and spaceships, a mechanical expressionism. Léger again.

Now I am sort of killing off the formalistic paintings.

Wow, all the great decisions that later become commonplaces!

Original, elemental, utterly free, preformalized meaning, word-sound associations. I get it out of myself, but we see it on the walls of the city. (Blake: And the hapless soldier's sigh / Runs in blood down palace walls.)

All is read on the walls of the city.

I come sidewise like a crab. I am weary, perverse, and bored, but my deepest intentions are as good or better than anyone's. All is today so dishonest that it is better to say you hate the thing you love than to say you love it—for fear of not being believed. To protect what we love, we must deny it, thus misleading the enemy and somehow rescuing it.

There is a war in my work between monumentalization and dissolution.

Expressionist art is a war between form and antiform, between order and disorder, between reason and antireason, between taste and propriety, and bad taste and impropriety, etc.

I regard poster making as an art in itself. I mean I want to practice it . . . develop styles. Commission poster from Red et al. Céline street art. Daumier.

This I consider "classical" expressionist doctrine: hot subject and hot execution.

The street is nature for us. All good freshness in language comes from the everyday, from slang, why not so in art, too?

Perhaps, then, a sampling:
1. poems, two or three
2. prose
—express observations
—aphorisms
3. dream or two
4. diary selection
5. letter or two
one or two drawings
6. biographical note
the "pocket Oldenburg"

Developing true Pop style. Learning how to undraw. Really archaic . . . One has to find the primitive in oneself. Great new possibilities open up . . . Why should one use a sophisticated technique to depict what is archaic and prim? The street . . . war . . . love . . . the Pop universals.

Ray Gun functions like an obsessive word. It should be written all over town like Stop War. Support Mental Ray Gun health. Stop Ray Gun war . . . Start doing so. Turn on the kids at the right time.

Title: Homage to great vomit- and shit-master Frenchmen Céline and Dubuffet. To great excretory masters. Masters of excretory matter. To the pioneers of the new shit art.

Ah, boy, fall is upon us. This is the real use of the constructions . . . one use is with the drawings . . . Psychotic. Popsy. Three-dimensional drawings. Crumpled paper figures. Some very big drawings put on floor . . . for big themes and street war.

The Reuben (or any other commercial gallery) has its function, which is to make money, establish reputations for this purpose, etc. This is not the aim of the Judson. Other aims of cultural significance are more important. The Reuben is the place for one-man shows. The Judson is the place for experiments, especially with a view toward affecting culture, more as a museum might. They are not incompatible. X could belong to one and be active in the other.

Ray Gun expresses it fully, the bellicose march of the imagination.

What are my preferences in the real world: the city and the poor and the miserable, the streets . . . proletariat or common people, their inventions. Popular culture. Present-day primitives: children, madmen, the American cultureless. In general, the bleak, gray face of things not pastoral. Modern man, citified. This is the setting for my mysticism.

The erotic and the intimate, too, form another setting . . .

Now here it is: I am a humanistic bastard, always have been . . . What I am interested in is an unconventional, fresh, unsentimental, unacademic, living, humanistic art of the deepest possible meaning . . . an art employing the human image (this must be, defend it) . . . a mystical humanist art . . . a critique of humanistic imagery . . .

Pop art: radio and TV, films, advertising—signs, leaflets, etc. Publicity—papers, magazines. Architecture and objects, toys . . .

Ray Gun Spectacles: hire stripper or mime or burlesque. A children's play? All in line with the art sources.

Ray Gun films the same: newsreels (historical unselfconscious documents). A city-pop film? Spliced. Make film? How use film? Take own still pix and pix of gallery. Ives's popsy music, a popsy film to sound of one of Ives's songs? Early serials. Recall the Philippine film, Xmas, Chicago. Burlesque films, stag films.

Roxy. Rialto. Orpheum. Nice names. Popsy theater culture.

New fields: drama spectacle of all sorts of film, mime . . .

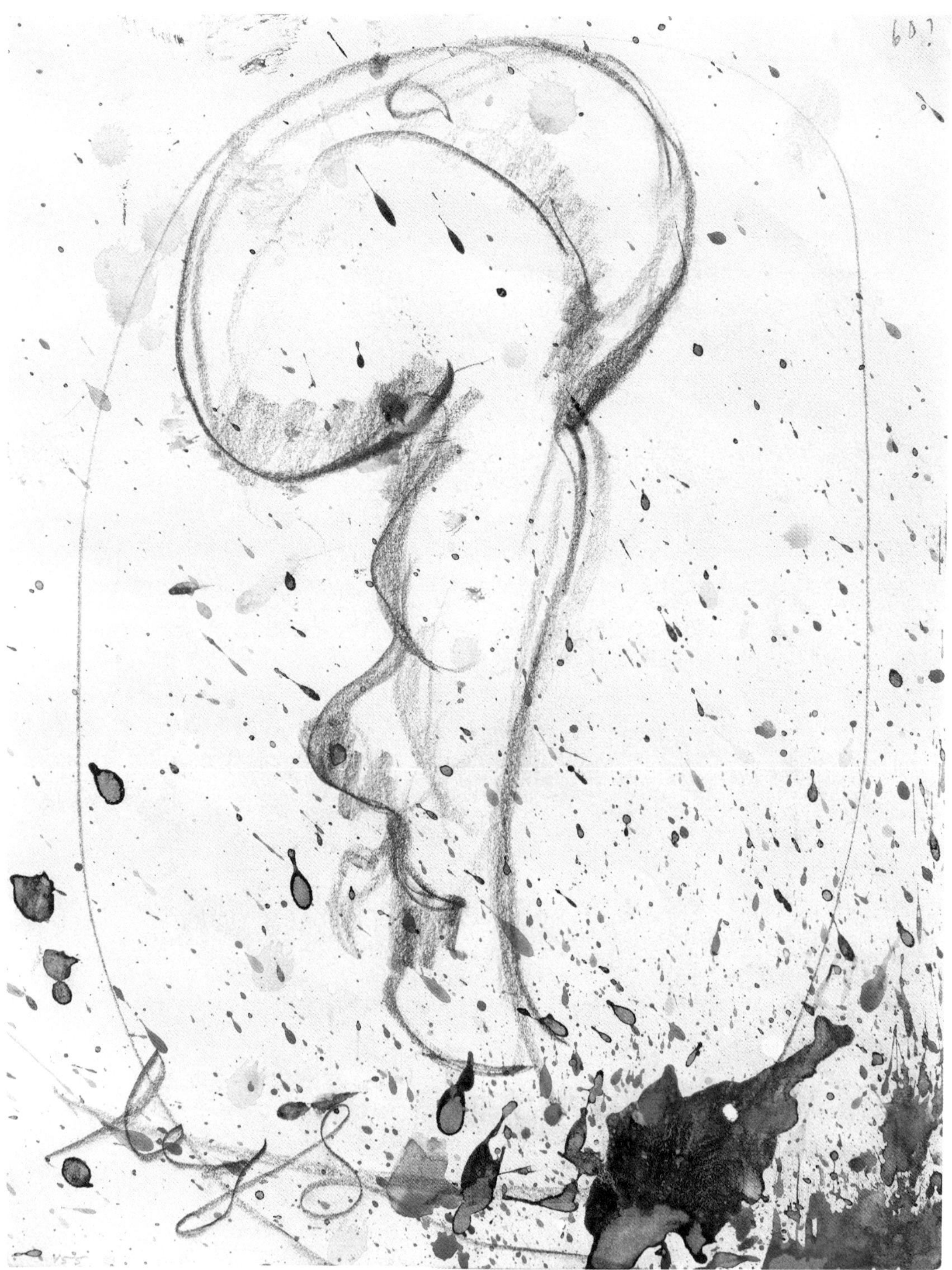
Notebook Page: "legs," 1960

Point about Ray Gun spectacles: not that they attempt to be professional as drama, mime, or whatever, but that they claim to be experiments in the extension of painting (or whatever, music?).

Ray Gun must have a big mailing list. Now build up mailing lists. After my show generally promote a way of painting rather than my own work. Program prefaces, etc. I can improve my writing by practice, drafts.

Writing is apt to be programmatic rather than critical. Poems.

New Form: street signs, etc.

Isn't film living painting (and drama too)? An interest in these. Shortcomings of the film technique, a critique. Go to movies and spectacles in general.

A sign for Judson.

Festival of the living object?

It is individual conditions that define uniqueness. American and contemporary Pop art, f.ex., Ray Gun rather than Pop art in general. Festival of *American Contemporary* Pop art.

The departure from the picture plane is not new, but an individual attempt in this direction would be. What we must do is define wherein lies the individuality. F.ex., Rauschenberg has developed the three-dimensional collage, but how? Nevelson, a sort of painting-sculpture. But how? Others. How recent is this movement? Is it pretty well assimilated, or what would take it further? Development of the collage. Has anyone defined it? Does it have a critical literature (look up in Cooper)?

The combination of "psychotic" or subconscious form with the techniques and materials of the streets, derived from actual examples found there and wherever such art is produced, to arrive at a universality of form. An art of grays and subdued color, of tonality, reflecting a pessimistic attitude. A melancholy, brooding art. An ironic or seriocomic art.

Show business of the past and present.

Circus. Amusement park. Jazz. Pop tunes. Pat.

A public-directed art. An art using rather than rejecting the "vulgar" and ugly in American culture (where the vital really lies).

The profundity of Pop art, we must emphasize this.

THIS IS GETTING NEXT TO IT . . . and not fakey like the AbExs giving titles, Dick Tracy, etc., to their absolutelyhavingnothingtodowithpopsy paintings . . .

Abstract Expressionist art is an un-American type of international academic art not connected to its social surroundings. We will have a living art connected to its social surroundings. We will have a living art connected to American society. Our intentions are outward, public (not that society wants it—it wants only to escape itself, loves the academic, King Arthur, Beethoven, et al.). It is the old battle for American art (fought by Jim Dine in the Ohio hills). An art of our surroundings, a living art. American costumes, fads, specific not generalized. The general is academic. The specific is living.

THE JUDSON COLLECTION
A personal selection of contemporary art
A guide for collectors

Art must be obsessive or it has no power.

Poems of hysteria and obsession; it must wound and terrify and embarrass the artist and also wound and terrify and embarrass the audience. It must grow out of scatological and masochistic impulses and all those impulses that produce the real power, the real motivations.

jagged codes of calls
scrawled whistles
patient rubbish

Art-on-the-Judson
The Judson View
The Judson Review
A selection of vital, young contemporary art
A guide for collectors who wish to be hip
A changing exhibition of vital, young contemporary NY art
The new statements by artist's bull-board

Certainly my Ray Gun intention is different from Lester's and everybody else's. I ought to be given space to demonstrate this, perhaps by my own spectacles and not a group of them by a lot of people (with me as a sort of MC). Ray Gun ought to be my baby or a baby with my cast, the way Red's was. I have just been afraid to tackle it alone. Three performers. Tyler, me, and Dine? Ray Gun—Dine and me, or just me? Close for a month while Dine and I build? Or while *I* build?

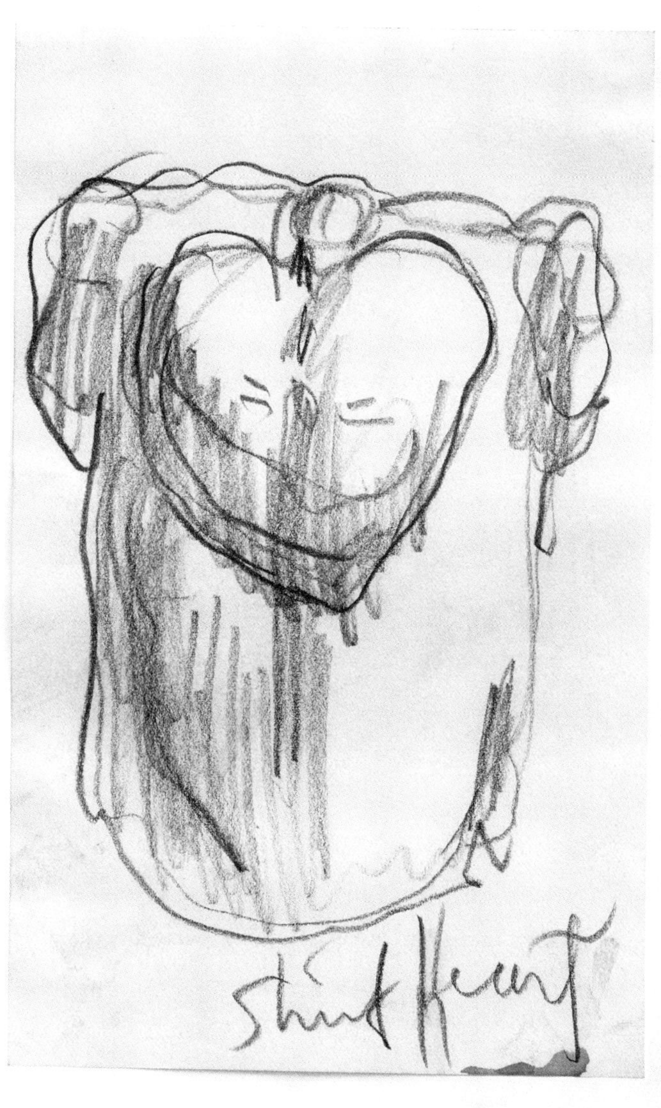

Notebook Page: "Shirt Heart," 1960

Hmm . . . well, how about a continuous changing point-of-view show ending with an evening of spectacles . . . then RAY GUN, then Tyler et al.

I believe heartily in this: that the artist defines himself by having shows, not before a show, and the artist must be plugged in to his environment. Thank God for the Judson to use in this way. There should always be such a gallery.

ACTUAL ART
The Judson detects a revolutionary change in art in the direction of MAKING REAL or MAKING ACTUAL the image or object in the imagination. The plane with its limitations is no longer tolerable to the artists who feel this necessity, this strong desire. The result of their experiments is neither theater nor sculpture (which it resembles or suggests) but is definitely the projection of a painter's ambition. So we have objects or concrete images that seem to live, actually live, to contain a living quantity, and we have the presentation of living actions in time (and we have a number of experiments in the traditional frame, transitional attempts). With the current show, the Judson proposes to illuminate this revolution by presenting examples GATHERED AS THE SHOW PROCEEDS. That is, convinced that the revolution exists, the Judson proposes to LURE IT OUT.

AXUALLY
OUT-LUM
LEAPING
A selection to demonstrate the revolutionizing tendency to ACTUAL PAINTING
JUDSON Gallery . . .
POPSY HYSTERIX
Hysterix and prophetix
PROPHETICS & HYSTERICS
A New Concept of Painting-Reality
The New Painting-Reality

I believe in a number of things, many contradictory. I am not afraid of contradiction, but in my art there is harmony—on this I insist. Only in art is there harmony. That is the function of art, to give the illusion of harmony, to suggest the possibility of harmony.

I animate the inanimate, and I attribute human qualities to nonhuman creatures.

I dislike historical allusions. I think every artist ought to create as if the past did not exist. I get my inspiration from things that happen to me in particular.

The Judson will be obsessed this fall with the objet trouvé and the manufactured objet trouvé with the aim of demonstrating its present status in relation to its beginnings and explaining its further possibilities (essay on objet trouvé).

Head Observer
C.O.

Ask Red on committee of Ray Gun?

Ray Gun is a spaceship cruising under my sweetie's skirts.

Ray Gun is the moon looking at me like mama's knee.

Ray Gun is a child's metal snout arrived at the outer planet's center.

The whole world begins to see as Ray Gun sees . . .

Asphalt quivers, over where there are faces, the streets awaken, catacombs the new magic! New York will be renamed Ray Gun!

Elephant Ball
I will be elephant.
Erotic costumes.
Wedding feast.

A floor of springs. We should have done!

Ray Gun Rag Cage? I: the awful Rag man.

I want to make the banter bit *un*-literary Swedish?

Ray Gun Shake.

Stamp.

Subway Ray Gun.

Ray Gun Cocktail.

Ray Gun Diaries.

Get materials from street and save money.

Sound: someone breathing.

A presence—an environment.

Publicity: notify magazines about intention. They can see beginning the first week of January, then review completed house in February.

Furniture. Haunted house. Old farm house.

Use of toilet?—Deep space. One opens it. A closet.

Room that becomes theater. Ionesco, Artaud.

How well the Judson location suits me—as the Reuben Gallery scene Jim, the Delancey Street Museum Red.

America gets what it deserves.

If necessary, to protect myself from historical disease I would 1,000 times rather prefer the worst of the present to the best of our past.

Role of the toy as both formal and content inspiration.

Can anyone make a case for permanence? Art should not become property. It is the action of a sensibility in the present—for others in the present. Like the life at every minute running past your eye.

Painting and theater belong together. What makes painting *live* is the theatrical instinct, and in the live is the visual instinct.

To test things (ideas) against reality.

Ray Gun presents:
1. Sonnets of form
2. Metamorphic necessity

Keep losing my sense of humor.

Unusual SIGNS and DISPLAYS
Metal Wood Plaster Paper
Hanging
Stationary
Personal

About the Street: First it is clear to me now that it is a nightmare, my personal nightmare. Then it is a winter allegory: the dried-up land; the house, its color being the concealed; fertility waiting underground. Interpenetration of dream and reality, a sort of Boschian or Grünewaldian vision, perhaps a temptation. Here all the suppressed desires (individual and collective) are used in their more or less symbolic form as the basis for aesthetic form—that is, we have the aesthetic will in contest with the representations of desire. It is to use and stress the psychoanalytic nature of art and to make the symbol rather specific, perhaps too specific to relieve emotions in the spectator through disguised expression.

March 3—What remains on Ray Gun?
Reprints and last publications: Documents. Program? Medals? Any other participants' publications. Street-guide action books? Postcards?
Take down and preserve some.
Do film shot. Take own pix?
Set up sales of acts?
Build stuff for Reuben.
Clean up . . .
My broken-down radio is a great pleasure, not the least because I never know just when it will play or get certain stations.

I am by nature very timid, and this is especially evident when I am starting up work. Like for the Reuben, it takes several days before I let myself out.

Light, shadow, the street.
Line, light, volume . . . The mysticism of the street . . . What I don't go for is orthodox or conventionalized mystery (Scott, Tyler). I believe in modern mystery, natural mystery, or scientific mystery.

I see man as part of nature, like a tree or a rock, and I am inclined to have as little (or as much) sympathy with him as with a tree or a rock. Spring emphasis on form and light. "Abstract" values rather than human, as in winter and fall. So that this Reuben Street may be a spring street. The agony may simply have been this change and why so many of the works over the last few days were not satisfactory. They referred back; they weren't it.

I will present my worldview in a series of "grand symbols," first the street, then perhaps the garden, or the beach, etc.

The Street is the Newspaper (i.e., paper is stone).
Heavy is light. Light is heavy.
White is black. Black is white.
Hard is soft. Soft is hard.
Deep is shallow. Shallow is deep.
Far is near. Near is far.

A pattern of paradoxes, oppositions, perverse reversals of material properties.
Appearances are not what they seem.

Principles of matter, of relation—like piling up, overlapping (shingle). The street, of
course, has no roof or end and even no walls; for the walls, where there are walls, open
IN. Yet it has a shape, limits. The street is not only a social, philosophical, psychological,
etc., symbol but also (and especially in springtime) an aesthetic symbol (form). An
example of my desire to bring them together. Its forms are both static—stoplights, signs—
and in movement—birds, cars, persons. Always they are space conscious. Always they
change. The static forms change as the spectator changes—on the street, he always
moves. He walks, runs, or rides (a bike, f.ex., my interest in bikes). I think I spend more
time walking on streets than anything else.

White (or black) equals infinity to me.

My performance in the Spex generally tended to be static (despite a lot of movement)
because the intention (formally) was sculptural or architectural. It was planned
pictorially and therefore made a good picture when photographed.

Why do I use cast-off materials, materials from the street? One reason is that I have no
money. Another is that I respond to them and find these materials full of suggestions—
aesthetic response.

April 10—There will be notes toward every show, verbal and visual. These may be
published with the show—if there is time—or afterward. Or may be used for releases . . .
selections. Or one can publish material from the previous show, such as Ray Gun
Documents for the Reuben show.

A panel happening or a happening in the form of a panel or a happel in the form of a
pannelling or a painting in the form of a panel, etc., etc.

I am Ray Gun, of course. What it boils down to is my intellectualism is brought to
bear on the decidedly nonintellectual environment in which I find myself, perversely,
challengingly taking its very least intellectual reaches, its primitivism, its instinctivity
rather than escaping to Europe or escaping to certain Europeanized areas of the culture
. . . and making my work the curious result of this collision. And this all written out
with fine naiveté in the Ray Gun Docs.

I have done a lot of things here. Among those might be that I have liberated the picture
surface (liberate is my desire, to liberate) by making it move freely in actual space. I see
no reason why a painting should have only one surface and therefore be confined to
illusion and its own space. Why shouldn't this space be a part of all space surrounding it?
I came to this result because I wanted to liberate the object I put down on a surface, the

object drawn or painted. Only by freeing it into space can it live, exist. Painting on one surface is finished, as it should have been long ago. How could we tolerate this limitation for such a long time?

I may now plan really large, freestanding, multisurfaced paintings.

Whereas Pollock took the space to the surface, I take it beyond into the positive area and thus avoid decoration, which is the danger on the surface. Art of the old sort must be spacious in the negative area through illusion. But now it is spacious positively and without illusion, though I have added illusion (through paint) in order to deepen the complexity of the medium, retain the complexity of one-surface painting. It is as if I had taken the canvas and wrapped it around a ball.

This show, at the Reuben, is above all a game in the most serious sense—with space, picture space, illusion.

Provincetown, June to August 1960

It is the old story: deprived of an audience, compatriots, and sympathetic spectators, and deprived of a studio well-known to all my quick desires . . . The summer becomes, as usual, desperate and intolerable. Full of substitutes, frustrations, time wasted and finally only worthwhile for having disrupted my life to such an extent that the reaction, on return to familiar circumstances, is productive. It is this that sours my recollections of the places where the summer has been spent. It is not the place itself that is at fault, but my dissatisfaction *in it*.

It is terrible to be forced to just draw and with no materials there either. We are extraordinarily poor or extraordinarily stupid.

Larger forms are spatial forms: enclosures. Thematic enclosures. In these are fitted the smaller or individual forms discovered.
In the drawing, this larger form is the surface, the surrounding. In sculpture, it is the actual space. The drawing is the plan for this actual space. F.ex., 4th of July, the Harbor, the Town, the Cemetery, the Shore, etc. (the Street). Smaller forms: umbrella, tombstone, battleship, letters, crabs, sailboats, lighthouse, etc., derived from the environment and adjusted to personal forms.

Flag as large form, things in flag. Perhaps all summer: flags. I am afire with patriotism.

Correspondences occur between big forms like the Street and the Newspaper, big spatial inclusive forms, and also between smaller individual forms. They are the paths along which metamorphosis develops, so that when you see one you see the other and also the

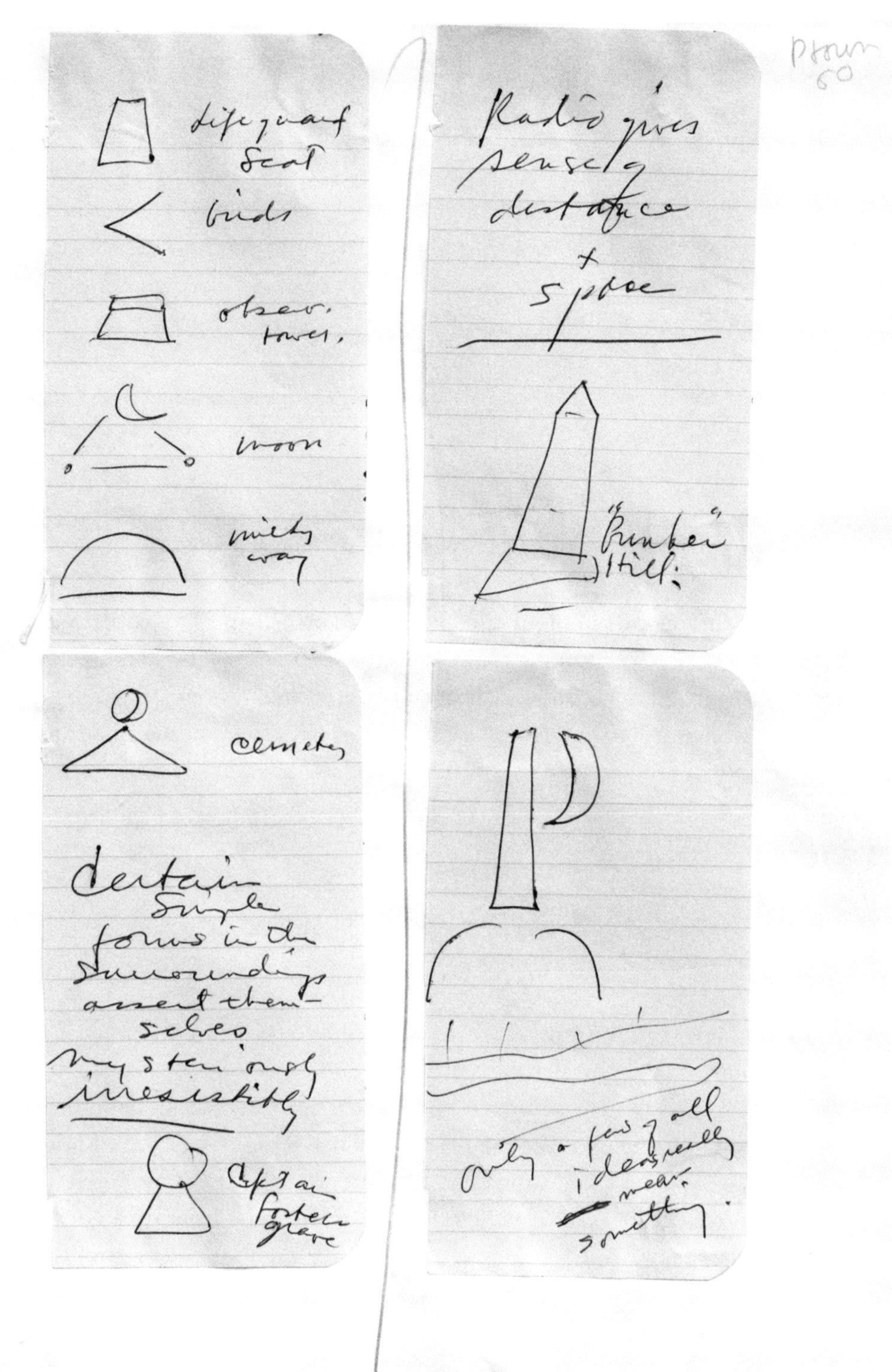

Notebook Page: Provincetown, Forms Noticed in the Surroundings, 1960

poetic idea generated by the linkage. It is possible to use them in substitution, such as to read the Street, or the Daily Street, etc., or to walk on the Paper, or to be careful when crossing the Paper, etc.

The Big Head, which was called the Daily Head, the big planetary paper construction over which was poured paint, long drip lines down its vast planetary sides, refers to a third correspondence: The Street equals The Newspaper equals Head. Someone said that the head suggested the bloody head of a newborn child, and then another person in the room pointed out that it is common in poorer homes when the baby is delivered there to cover the inside of the room with newspaper. In Crane's *Maggie: A Girl of the Streets*, read of the use of newspaper under girls' skirts to rustle like petticoats. I feel content, should be as open as possible, and that is not to say vague.

July 18 a.m.—I have a dream about a Happening at the Yale Art School. A costume of baroque gold chandelier and a white body with detachable bra-tits by the resident genius whom I know. I later assist in the presentation in a clean hall before conservative audience. I look in tube, am popped in eye. Surprised but play along. Followed by rubbing out of traditional paintings accomplished by trick of turning off light behind chromo of painting. But it fails, the cues don't work, the two girls helping don't get it right. Argument between artist and one girl. Water on the floor shocks management.
Pat speaks of pageants at her grade school. I am Flag. I am Betsy Ross. Gypsy dancers with Polish students . . . Seems to me a good model for a type of dramatic event—the child's school pageant . . . As everything must have as model a primitive form.
The Birth of the Flag. Pat—Flag. I—Betsy Ross. Ruth—Staten Island, etc., etc.

If the notes give opinions and ideas, and sketch papers ideas, and the diary plain, plain facts, there ought to be a book like the sheets I kept once in Chicago of little lyric details: The Book of Things That Really Count (Matter), such as a file of hairs just under my lower lips, discovered by Pat at the beach camp—I didn't shave well enough.

Junkyard. Junkyard is beach is street. The different sensation of any place. Time to get used to. The ugly weeds, the crickets, the dead snake, the insects, the flies. A dishonorable death not like the sea, washing off color.

Nevelson—strange, she never gets the irregular wood of junkyard and beach, etc., but the mechanical cuts of the lumberyard scrap pile. These are not, note, "found *objects*" but found pieces of wood.

Routine fallen into. Up, 9 or 10 a.m., breakfast. Cleaning (part of thinking process) until 12 p.m. 12 or 1 p.m., out to work somewhere. Back by 4:30 p.m. Beer. Dinner. Work 6–11 p.m. or 12 a.m. bed or out . . .

hard-bodied wind swings
its fingers in
shore at the town's eyes
steps with its gas-foot out
its little shell-winding
businesses

Pat Lannan pulls
two hundred from his pack
slaps the cheeks of the
villagers

pilgrim monument springs
wings striped as the flag
droops over the starry town

My school.
I thought I might have a school here. I would call myself Dr. as follows: Dr. Claes
Oldenburg, D.P.N.S. Doctor of Psychoanalytical Nature Study.
The day would begin with calisthenics on the dunes. Hands over head. Stuff and legs
kicked out. Many students on the white dunes.
The classes would be spent discovering "it." We would examine many spots, I leading
but not saying anything, except as follows:
Student (he has found a piece or fragment of Nature): Is this It?
I: No, that is not It.
Student (he has found another piece): Is this It?
I: Yes, that is It.
Student: What is It?
I: Tell me, what is It?
The Student tells me.
I: Yes, that is It.

What I despise is artificial art, that kind that begins with buying a tube of some colored
stuff in a store and going home and making a four-sided figure, very straight (no matter
how large) to smear it on. Art begins when your eyes flicker open in the morning and
when sensation returns to the tips of your fingers. A refuse lot in the city is worth all the
art stores in the world.

What I rejoice in is the discovery of consistencies and similarities. Unities. Or
correspondences, which I have not been able to explain to people. Why I should find
such excitement is the parallelism of shingle to northern lights (more parallels). It has
to do with unities that defy scale notions and other poetic unities, and the excitement
comes from the possibility that this (primitive thinking) means also unities in fact. A

kind of delightful and childish belief that I take very seriously.

Perhaps just the emergence of the Flag-theme symbol was worth the summer.

New York, September to December 1960

The thing I absolutely do not want to be is with it, to be hip, to be inside, to be outside, to belong, to be sophisticated . . . I want to do exactly what everybody does . . . I want to laugh at the prepared jokes, I want to obey the fads, I want to speak as everybody else speaks . . . knowing that is grotesque but knowing too that out of such grotesquerie arises art, which never arises out of escape or rejection. Bad taste is the most creative thing there is . . .

The street is death, or the street, my street, is life in death . . . American death heart . . . a set on American death, the whisky eagle, etc.

The Street (A New Realism)

Painting went swimming. Painting ran away and lost its shoes.
It lost its pants.
It shit in its pants.
It went home throwing money at its wife.

The Street as form, as obsession, as idea.

Sunday I was thinking in terms of a play for the fall. What it might be. It might have in it some singing. Perhaps Olga or Pat or both might sing in it. It would be more like a play than a Happening. We heard *Threepenny* and Spanish music and Fats Waller. It rained. I thought of the Street. A play about the street, about Ave. C. Called "C"? Based on my poem? Sung? At any rate, a spoken, sung script. Something repeatable? "On the Bus," anyway perhaps derived from a poem like it. And I should write, or could someone write, music for it? Original music. Original instruments. An orchestra to the side.

Where *On the Road* refers to a romantic notion of escape, *On the Street* means acceptance of man in limited (city) condition, a nonromantic notion.

Seven Films of Close Inspection
The same action, a very simple action, is seen from many different viewpoints, in space and in time, over and over, slowly and rapidly. All that can be gotten from it physically and metaphysically is extracted from this very simple thing.

Cathartic, rogue, reverse-success fairy tale, impossible Alger comic-strip form, myth fantasy, the basic, ancient, surprise-turn tale.

Comic-ironic epic. Céline Algren Joyce Kerouac Bellow (Marsh) Wolfe, on the one hand.

Extending *Leaves of Grass* example. Endless, accumulating lyric poem.

The Reuben show was a little premature, but it was a chance that had to be taken . . . Now the thing is to stay so obscure, so that one is still seen but has the opportunity to mature and produce enough good work for the next year, because the next show has to be the show.

Ray Gun was not invented. It was received.

We have all sunk very sadly into art. It is a shame. Ray Gun failed to elicit members. O death. Everyone is making paintings and being so frigging artistic.

Everything that is done is tied to a purpose, an explanation. This is a novel. This is a painting. This is a piece of shit. This is my experience. This is my idea. This is that. It is time, in fact, for Ray Gun #2.

My pattern is that when it happens, it happens very fast, but there must be time for the many failures and the preparations.

Jackson Gallery—internationalist. Janis, Castelli—Amurricun.

When I see all the capitalistic creeps and finks, I go strongly into my social role. I am, as I say, a social artist. I am reaching through a kind of sardonic folk art to a social statement that is not inconsistent with art. But I say again, how can one fight the evil without intimately knowing it and being next to it? It sets one off, in fact.

Macbeth's bloody hands, etc., apparitions.

There is a lot of furniture to move before I get to the making of the work.

One must be a little shocked by one's own work when it first happens. One certainly gets used to it by and by if it stays around.

Most of my work this year are just beginnings. The wood will take a few seasons to culminate. These are just primitive feelingabouts with wood (later will be painted). So with theater of action. So with costume. Plaster is coming along. And writing, don't forget how much time that took in the fall. The essay still unrealized. And, of course, film is the next step as far as I'm concerned, and think of all the formulations made. It's as simple as that: one has to somehow keep oneself stimulated.

In turning to merchandise, objects as subject that I have done, I experienced first a materialistic joy at them like Jimmy's, and I bought a new suit, a materialistic suit, but when I set out to make the objects they became spiritualized. I think my original vision was not so materialistic. This is the mysticism of objects, eroto-mystical attraction of objects.

The way this split is evident everywhere—spiritual-material.

It is my aim to spiritualize American sensation, and Ray Gun went into attack against materialistic practices and art in order to do this. The aim to find the spiritual in the material.

In last season, the search went on in the street. Summer, it was the search in patriotism and the American past. Now, it is becoming a search in the store, or in commerce. I think spirituality is necessary to survival, and I know it exists in some curious form in the USA.

I have this view that my studio is a very private place. I do not encourage people to visit. It is too backstage. It ought to be a sanctified place, very mysterious.

Indirection, quiet, mystery, mind-silence.

More sensitive use of plaster material and color. Smaller, perhaps all hanging. Originality of form. By cutting the screen with scissors, can I get some individuality of form, which is what has been sadly missing? Well, the lesson of so many months of experiment is that the true individuality lies in my line, and I must always allow for that. In the flags, I took found lines and had a devil of a time composing them. In plaster, I have let the screen or plaster forms control. But again I must assert myself through line. My will over the form. Cut the screen, f.ex. I do outline not because of any desire for "new form" but to use my line. It is simply line. Line leads. Must remember this, and the simplicity of this.

It seems to me that with the performances and the movies that will grow from them I am on the threshold of beginning to use a great amount of the unexploited material that I have gathered, in verbal notes, dreams, and, in my experience generally, recollections.

Cloth is, of course, stiffened by simply painting it with enamels and then, too, rather elastic.

Chicken wire is a broader, bolder sweep. Good drawing, too. Monumental and bold and simple. I have thus a material to match my desires my "vision" in big, which I hope to realize in February–March.

Finer wire for more detail.

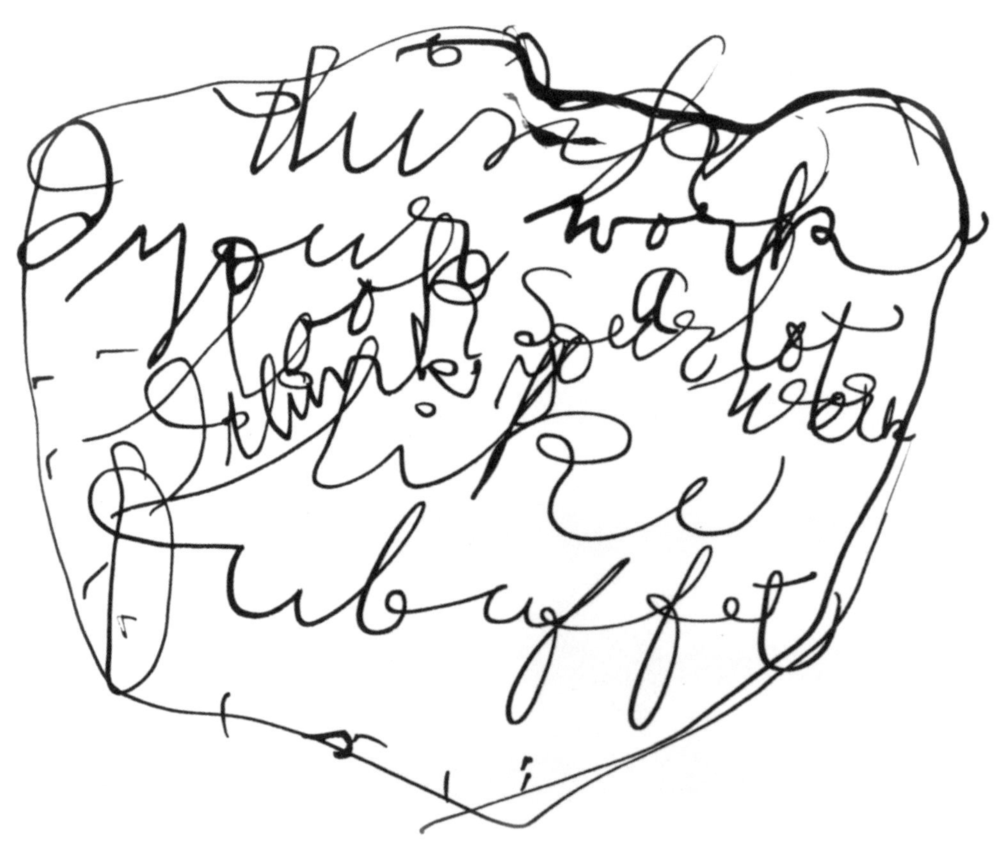

"I Think Your Work Looks a Lot like Dubuffet," 1960

Soon as I can, into enamel-paint painting again. All the forms of the fall can be realized in this chicken wire! One by one and combines.

Summer scene:
By next summer, I want a very big studio. Stay in the city, and do my own Happenings next season in my place.

Funny, the girdle became the symbol of a direction in many ways, none more surprising than as an example of form-material—the thin and white (plaster) crust or stiffened cloth (as with stays)—at the same time as it became the pointer in the direction of erotic imagery involving both merchandise and the female body.

I don't think even department-store erotica can save me. Butikerotika.

Pure sex leads straight to the academy. It seems it is only through romanticism, which is imagination, and the human interference, human sensibility, that one engages the living in its richness.

Location must be established, and this is sometimes reflected in a title.

The store. The newspaper.
3.99

Fragments are very important to me.

I am against flatness.

It is always a matter of working up a technique. Caulk comp and stuff built up like Dubuffet's table with smooth around it. Paper that way, too. What I seek is the paper-like, cloth-like softness, which will harden—and yet be permanent. Hardening of free.

I like to work in material that is organic-seeming and full of surprises, inventive all by itself. F.ex., wire, which has a decided life of its own, paper, which one must obey and will not be ruled too much, or cardboard, which is downright hostile, or wood with its sullen stubbornness. I am a little afraid of metal or glass because they have the capacity like a lion to gash and kill, and if I gave them the freedom I give my other materials they probably would. As for my forms, what is most important is that they should be very near absolutely certain, after a long preparation simply demanding to be created. Getting myself into that relation with a form is most of the struggle.

Coming to my studio, you would find my works floating, because the force I most respect is gravity, and tethered like dirigibles or cattle by a rope to the walls.

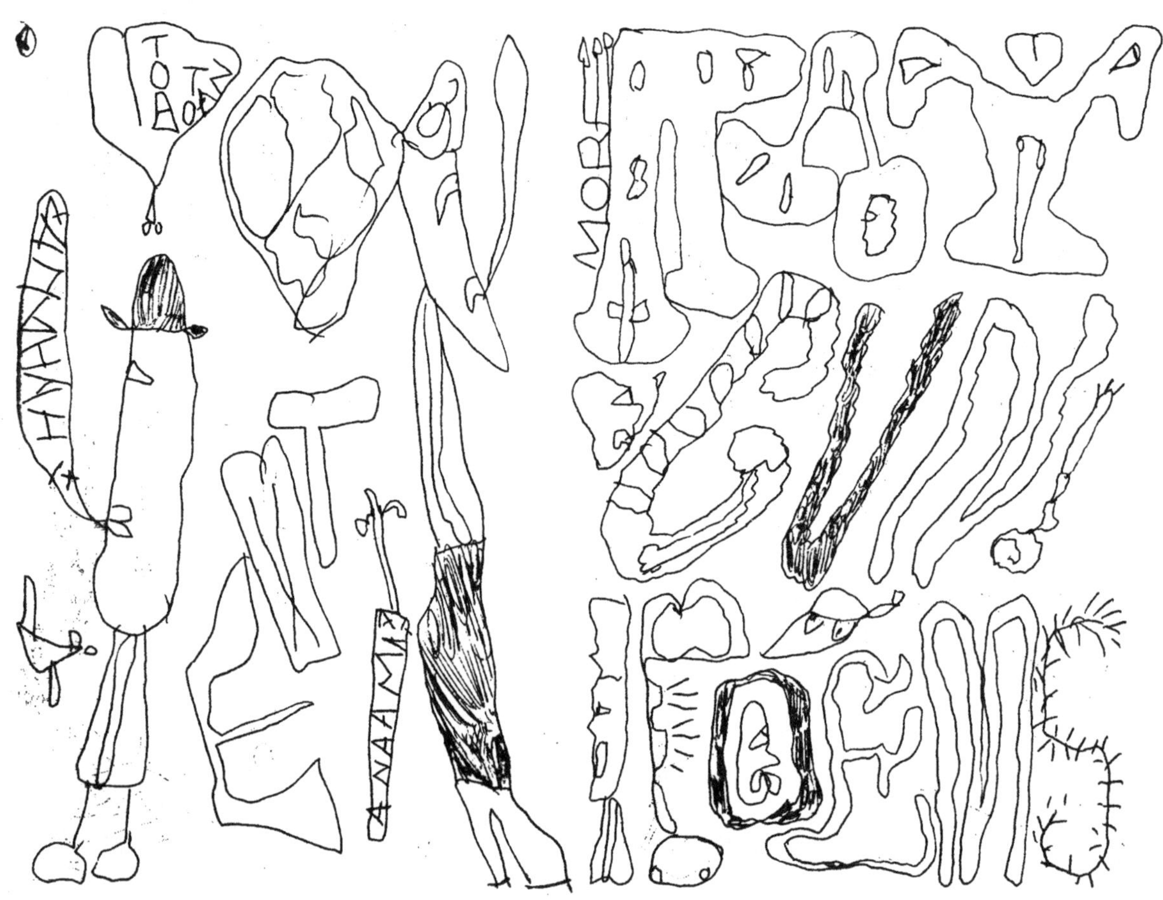

Front and back covers of Ray Gun Poems booklet, 1959

Lenoxys
dar the grain
sonset
washus in Xs
lamblaid
sleaving
chorchyd.

dar luv
false overill
to bot.
tomblughs
an moanshins
on
ag fyn bloughty
mons
•

awh
cum quit
flap down

slapup
flaff
wingzuz

traze
skyin der
opp

fine feel
der
longlyn

schuteblam

fluff der gram
flipflam
oxplozh

Ouf
•

MANYELLS
Comix

eser artsed
dresd rased
darest trads
estra arsta
drtrs ertsda
tar tra drata
•

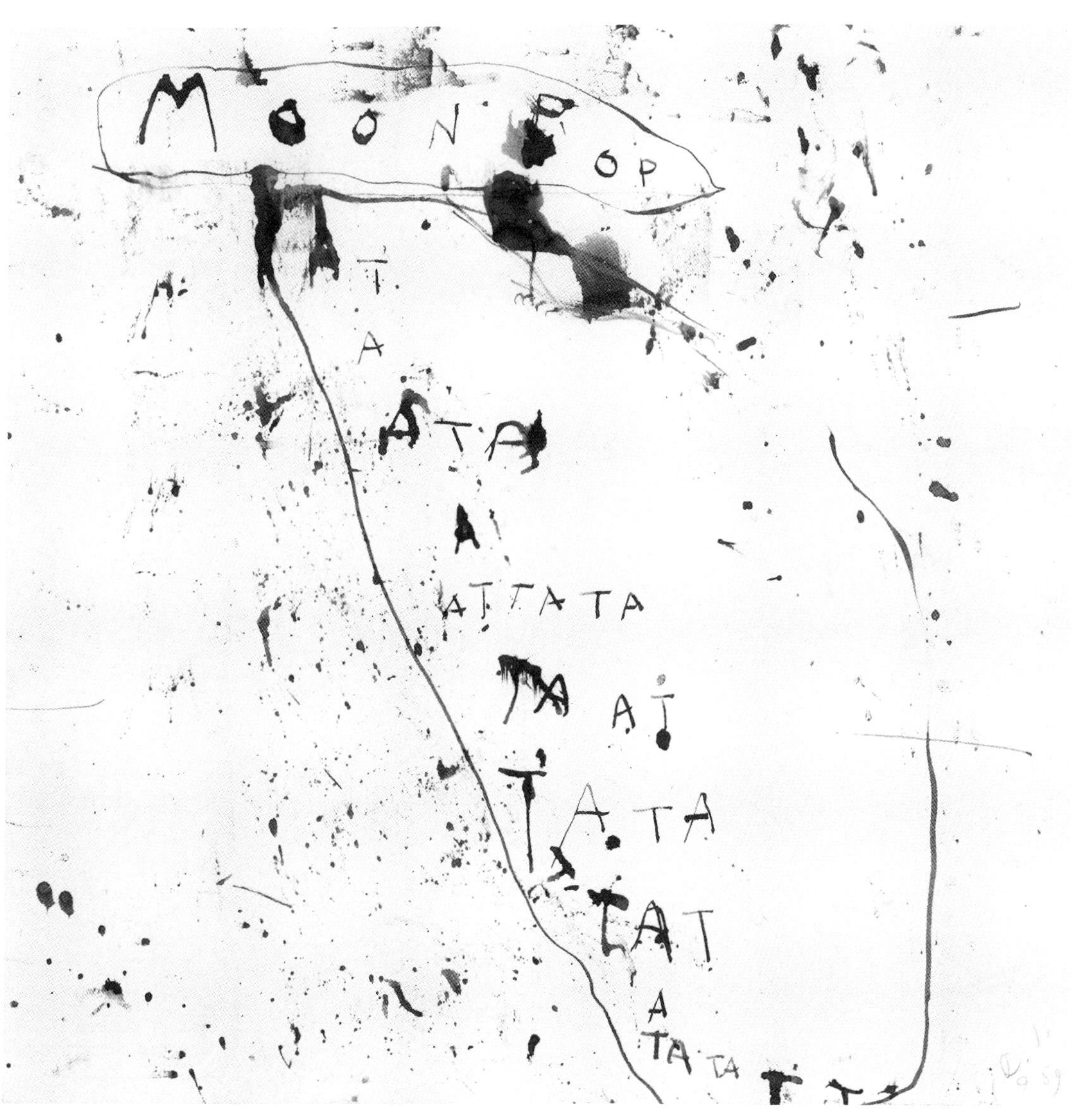

Street Poem—MOON POP, 1959

at
a
ata
attata
ta at
tata
tat
a
tata
tt
•

mo
om
omo
momo
mm
momomo
mo
omo
omo

o
•

Yah de catz dross
da street da moanhols
wackle da soors sing
da corktrouchies clumbr
ah dar ly dedd
ah dedd wan won flys wiszing
wiszing
erckos fleggs flyish wingsmorp
•

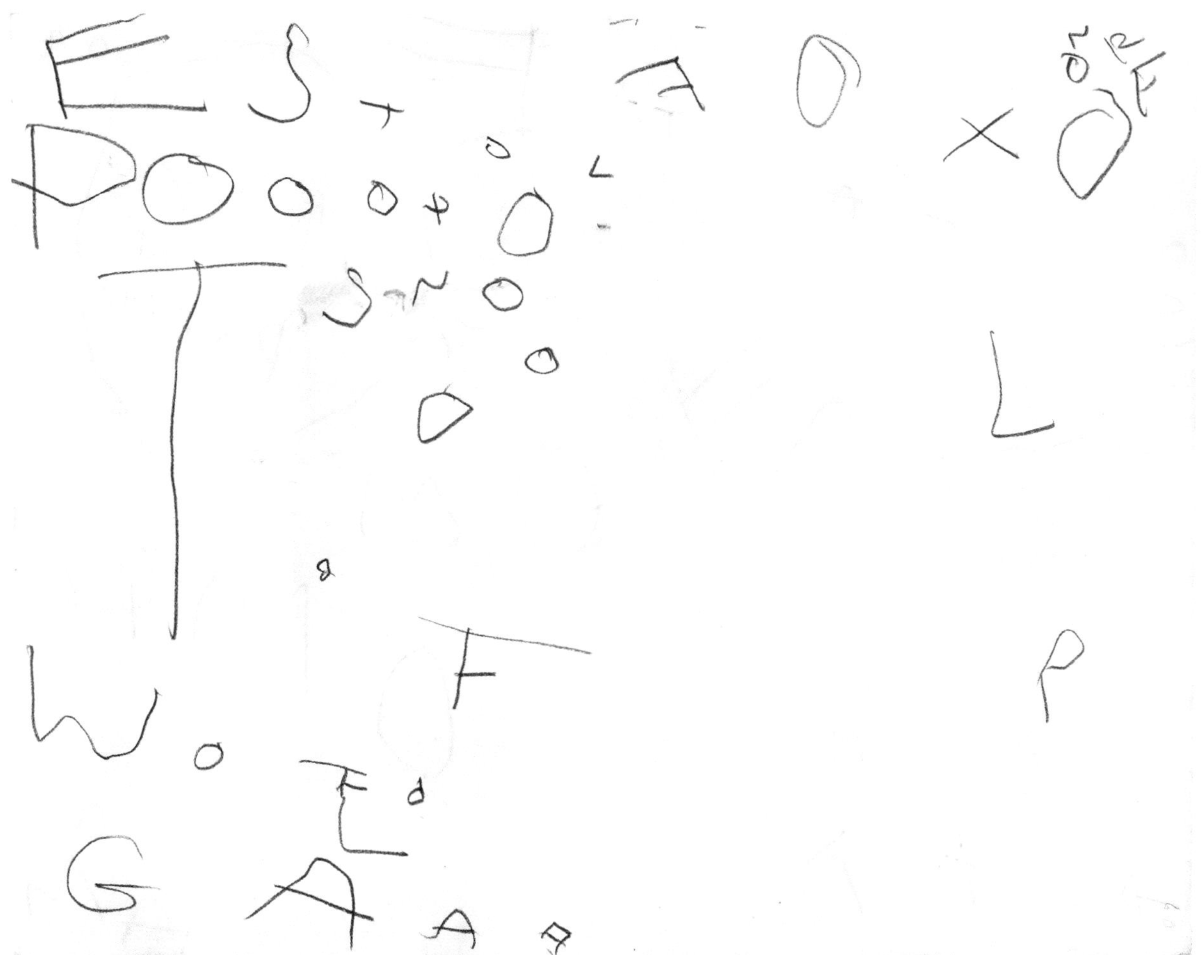

Notebook Page: Ray Gun Poems, 1960

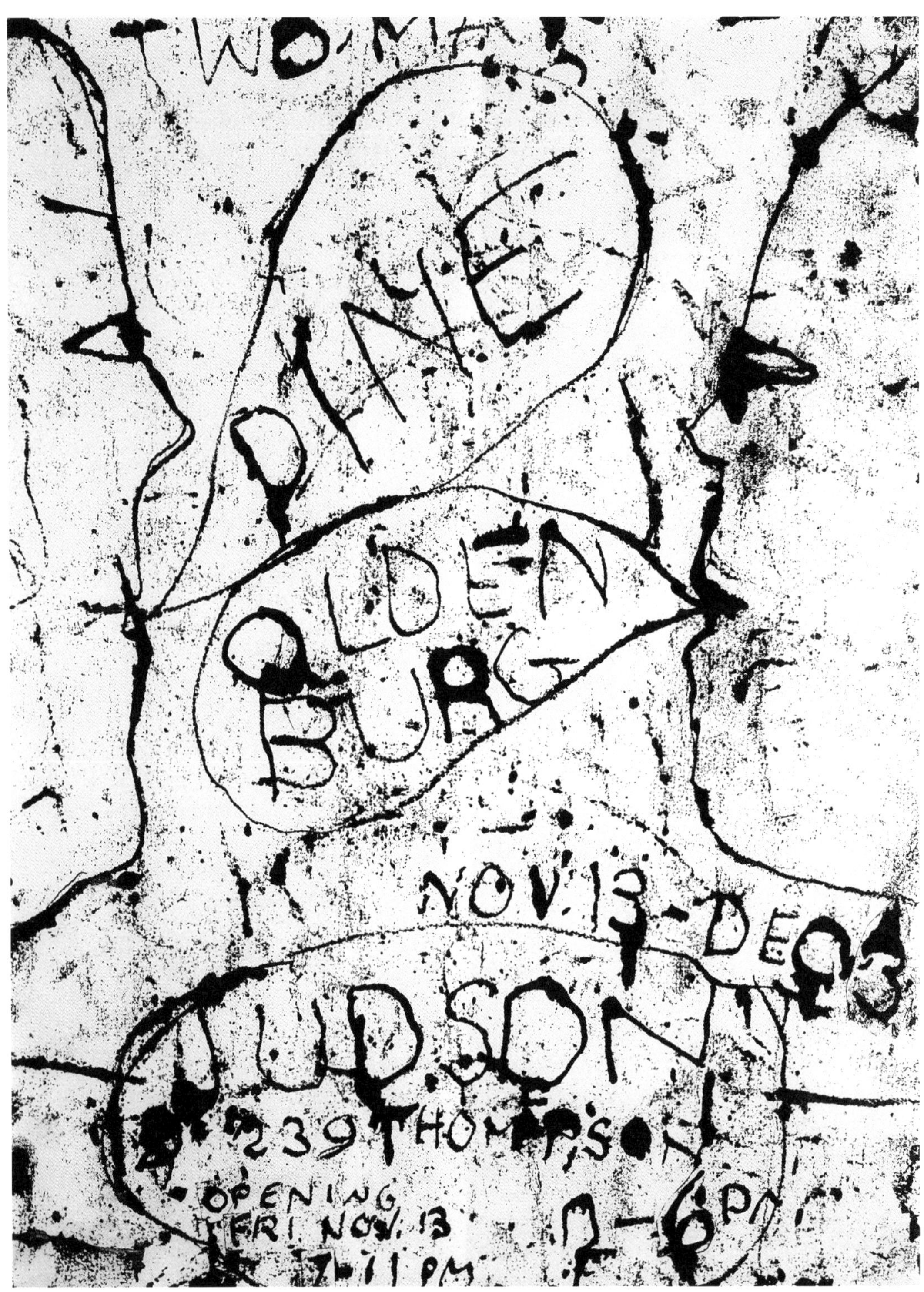

Announcement for "Dine/Oldenburg" exhibition at Judson Gallery, 1959

ABOUT "EMPIRE" ("PAPA") RAY GUN (c. 1960)

1. Making forms out of wire covered with paper soaked in wheat paste came from a book of suggestions for children's art classes that I found in the stacks of the Cooper Union School of Art's library, where I was shelving books. This was 1957. Earlier I had looked at the "tents" of tentworms.

The wire and paper method enabled me to make my own form directly and cheaply. The simplicity of the technique and the look of the result satisfied my desire for primitive and organic effects.

I wanted to imagine that I was inventing an art that could be followed by any "primitive" of the New York City streets, using the most ordinary, available material.

My first sculpture in this technique was *Elephant Mask*, completed in late 1957, since repainted twice, now in storage as part of my collection.

The *"Empire" ("Papa") Ray Gun* was done in December 1959. I had learned to exploit the tendency of the wire to go its own way, and I had found a way of painting the surface by dabbing and dribbling diluted black casein paint along the spine and sides of a piece.

Drops placed on the spine flowed to one side or the other. The gravity-directed flow produced a vertical linear effect that counteracted the twisty, organic character of the work. I had also learned to choose certain pages in the papers, for example, the movie pages for their masses of blacks. I found the *Times* too gray and preferred the *Post* to the *News*. The *News* was stingy with their ink.

These structures were shaped in the air out of wire hanging from the ceiling. They swung and turned, while I twisted the wire into shapes. It was drawing in three dimensions. I remember the insides looked as interesting as the outsides, and I hated to seal them up. The back can be seen on the *C-E-L-I-N-E, Backwards* relief (in my collection).

2. If the "hide" of the *"Empire" ("Papa") Ray Gun* is punctured, it can be repaired with a bit or a strip of newspaper dipped in wheat paste or diluted Elmer's glue. The patch can then be painted with diluted casein in black to match the surroundings. I have covered holes in the piece many times. I use strips of paper about six inches long and one inch wide with rough edges, torn by using a metal ruler. In storage, the *EPRG* should *hang*.

3. The *"Empire" ("Papa") Ray Gun* was the biggest form-in-the-shape-of-a-ray gun I had made, and therefore I thought it deserved the title "Papa." "Empire" is also the biggest—as in Empire State Building. I like the sound of the repeated double syllables. The *EPRG* was first shown at the Reuben Gallery's "Below Zero" show, but I remember it mostly hanging over the entrance to the Judson Ray Gun show, as a theme sign of the attitudes of the exhibition (January–March 1960).

Spring Calendar at the JUDSON GALLERY

R A Y - G U N

A three-month period of experimental constructions, derived from
American popular art, street art and other informal sources.
JUDSON GALLERY - JANUARY, FEBRUARY, MARCH, 1960

PROGRAM

January 4 - 30

1. Construction of a h use in the gallery - a painting in the
shape of a house.
2. Preparation of the exterior of the gallery and the gallery windows. A painting in the shape of a gallery.
3. Collection of objects and examples for a RAYGUN sal n and a street
art mural.
NOTE: The gallery is open at the usual hours during construction in
order to encourage participation and development of the RAYGUN idea.

January 30   Saturday

Formal opening of the completed house, exterior, windows, RAYGUN
salon, mural etc. Reception at the gallery 7 - 11 P.M.

January 30 - February 19

Completed constructions on exhibit.

February 22, 23, and 24 Monday, Tuesday, Wednesday

On the evening of each day, a set of brief performances by artists.
Painting in the shape of theater.

February 25 - March 4

Second construction - the street, or a painting in the shape of a
city street. A gallery-long wall of tar and objects as background

Judson Gallery's spring calendar, 1960

for street traffic. Again, the gallery will be open during the
construction period.

March 5 Saturday

Formal opening of the street. Reception 7 - 11 P.M.

March 5 - March 23

Completed street on exhibit.

END OF RAYGUN

Throughout the RAYGUN period, objects such as guns, dolls, cutouts and posters, comics etc. will be produced by participating
artists.

MOONPOP   MOONPOP   MOONPOP   MOONPOP   MOONPOP   MOONPOP   MOONPOP

The slogan of RAYGUN is "Annihilate-Illuminate". RAYGUN is both
destructive and creative. While RAYGUN is begun by two artists,
it is hoped others will join in during the RAYGUN period. A communications board will be set up in the gallery and the documents
which occur there published later as SELECTED RAYGUN DOCUMENTS

RAYGUN DEPUTIES

JIM DINE
CLAES OLDENBURG

PROGRAM FOR THE SEASON FOLLOWING RAYGUN:

March 25 - April 14

One Man Show of activities and constructions by RICHARD O. TYLER.
Reception March 25, 7 - 11 P.M.

POST NO BILLS
fence
figures advance from side, in grotesque attitudes, on rhythmic counting (like game of
    stop the music)
counting 1, 2, 3—hit with stick
at some number I shout
"POST NO BILLS"
everyone posts bills insanely
a man appears over fence to frighten them
(flashbulbs)
they begin wild dancing (music)
a whistle blows
they fight, all fall
police cover them with sheets
man appears over fence again
end with sign IT IS OVER

PROLOGUE
car drives by
bicyclist
roller skater
played by streetlight
bum by fence
pisser
drunk
child
etc.
people watch from behind fence
slug
kiss
rag picker
handshake
pickpocket
robbery
prostitute
lights
blink

the sense of not being yourself—that is when you are an actor
not real theater—but "actual painting"
short periods of darkness
man at a table
long compressed, a life
short extended, a man gets up

Poopy
inside a big head
stick leg out, tongue out
sneeze
turn eyeballs

illustrate value of time, living detail for themselves
the postcards: little action, something between the stopped action of the figures
    (snapshots, postcards) and real action, so that the action relates to the stopped action

costumes and masks very important . . . like living sculpture
almost a tableau

postcard from the city
Dear Mother—I was in the city
(5 dreams of the city)
1. collision, paper bag
2. rape big prick / menacing / open door / leer
3. taxicab
4. falling / bridge
5. fire / tears off paper / girl in flame clothes
yes—mix that is always theory, reality with fantasy

clown white
eyebrow pencil and liner
lipstick
soap over eyebrows, slicks them down
thin layer before clown white
Ray Gun vaudeville

I sit in various forms of costume
I should always sit thinking in my painting
these attitudes, costumes are the things to photograph
stripper with elephant
people—all set moving

human sounds, not words, not object sounds
street poems like found object but (rule) must be added to, developed, turned into art
metronome or some time count (variation)

variation in light
flash / subdued / bright news photography
blackouts

costumes from ads + street mats, of course
4 or 3 figures
these figures then composed of street stuff + drawn on
or perhaps just strapped on
sandwich man principle
arms free
painted legs or attached
glasses with photos on or mirror
funny nose
wooden frame hung over shoulders
a selection of remarks
a selection of objects
(in box)
a selection of actions
jump around
up + down action
sacks for legs
changing shapes
little figures on feet + everywhere
on arms
arcimboldo + the like, very baroque
strong b + w design
people as objects
masked face
stocking?
search for obsessional motive
transvestitism, etc. (i.e., basic *power* of art is obsessional)
in any genre as now: costume
costume central to visual or painter's theater
satires on everyday dress

I sit down against wall
Pat up
the streetchick
the shoeshine

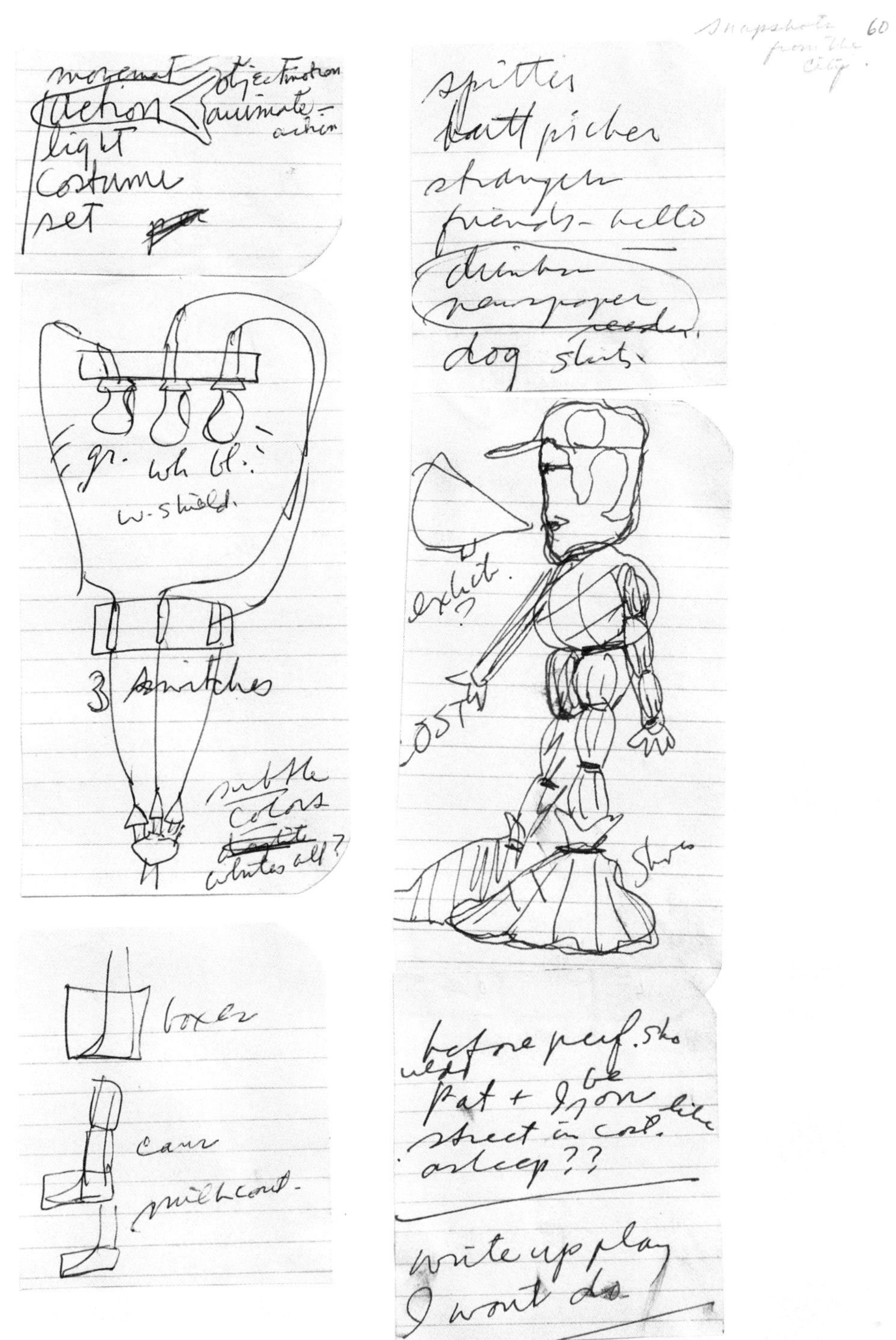

Notebook Page: Notes and Costume Study for "Snapshots from the City," 1960

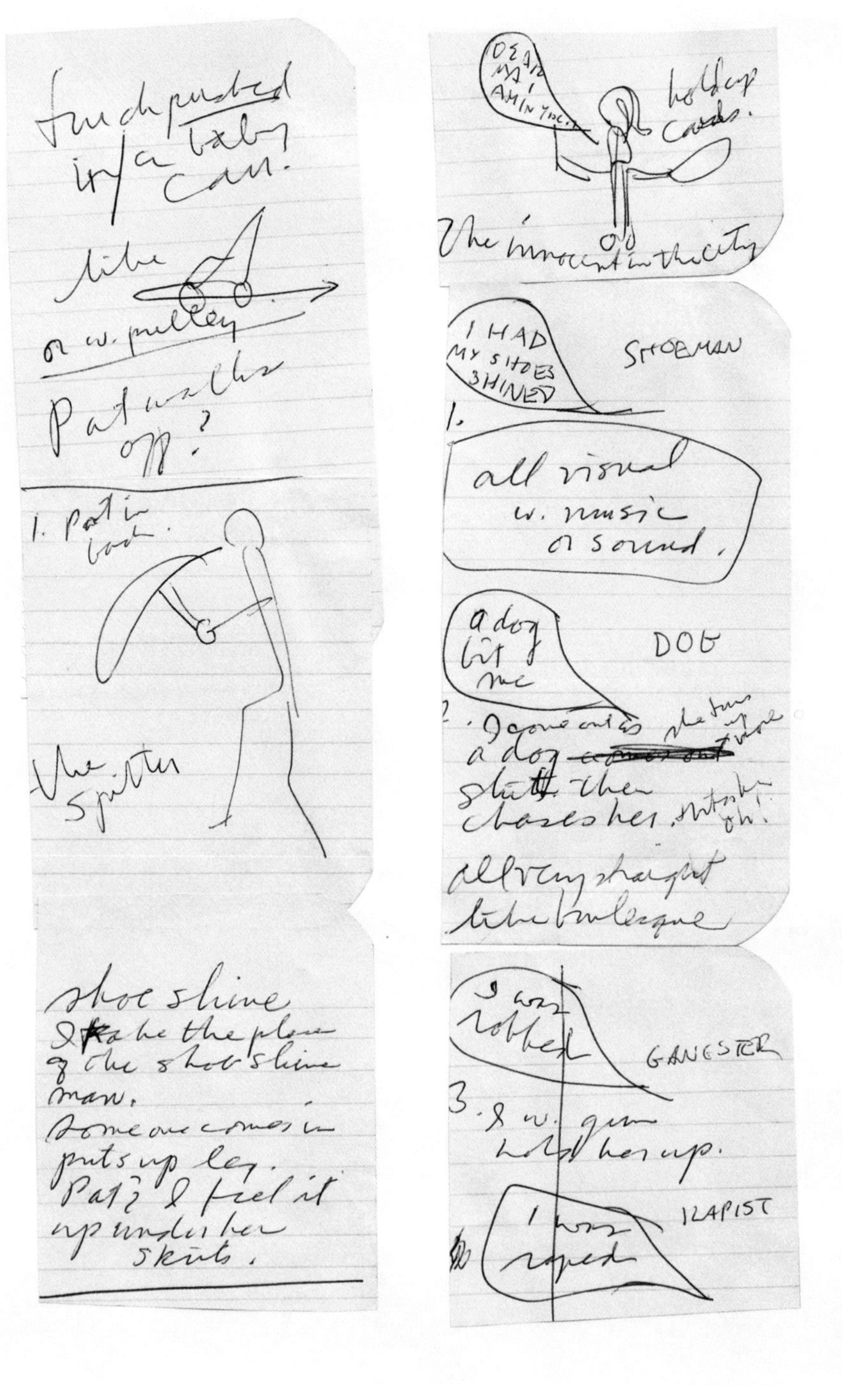

Notebook Page: Snapshots from the City, Suggested Events and Remarks, 1960

I shine her shoes, suggestively
the beggar, she walks away from him off stage R.
the rag picker
I pick up rags in a bag that will be there
Pat waiting
I am here
the exhibitionist
Pat lies down
I walk off stage into Reality (the play is over, I say)
I turn off light + turn on other light
lighting by cord pulled
or: I walk stage front and am hit by a truck
Pat remains standing blasé as throughout
then lights out
+ as before a number of actions
not *be seen* too much
DEATH OF PAPA NOSEDROP
limp
lurch
stagger, death + etc. made comic
scrunch up in fear
props lying around on floor
GUN
BABY
BOTTLE
CIGAR
pushed in a baby carriage
like or with pulley

Pat in back
the spitter
shoeshine
I take the place of the shoeshine man
someone comes in puts up leg, Pat? I feel it up under her skirts
hold up cards
DEAR MA I AM IN THE
the innocent in the city
SHOEMAN
I had my shoes shined
all visual with music or sound
DOG
a dog bit me
I come out as a dog

she turns up nose
shits then chases her
all very straight like burlesque
GANGSTER
I was robbed
I with gun, hold her up
RAPIST
I was raped
I with big prick
CAR
I was hit by a car
I as car hit her
ELEPHANT
went to the zoo
Elephant fondles her stick-trunk under dress
I walked down the street
DRUNK reaches for her leg
I went for a walk
pissers
POLICEMAN REPORTER
I jumped out of my window

big screen of letters
in drama: *rhythm, climax, light, surprise, shock*
analysis into 1) the form and *shape*, line, plane, etc. 2) the type of motion

fan
spring *vibration*
standing *vibration*
out leaping
ejection
rolling
shot
thrown (gun)
bow + arrow
expanding action, umbrella

Miss Orange
The Snook
Scenario
The Snook's Day
Rubbed in the Subway
Bitten by the Snook Posing as a Dog

Felt by the Snook Posing as an Elephant
The Snook Shows Himself
No Harm Meant, Just True Love
Death of the Snook

all visual . . . play with single sound, wail, scream
forms—irregular—visual, fantastic forms
legs + arms tied to boards?

The Ragman's love for streetchick or mamaganger
she sheds a tear in end
signs of love—offers bottle, offers a (rag), butt exposes himself
spits for her, etc., all ignored
in end, he hit by constantly moving car
she sheds just one tear

CAST:
Streetchick: P. Muschinski—truck
Spitter, beggar, rag picker, exhibitionist: CO—truck

MASKS:
chicken wire loosely covered with paper
tied with string
mask of cloth too on wire?
stockings
for arms—tubes
hair
strips of cardboard
stuffed stocks
strips of rags
string
spray with paint
things attached
exposing, merely hold up cock—cardboard

1. The Chick
TYPE: the stripper, the streetchick, other composite roles? *woman in city*, mamaganger?

ACTION: She walks back + forth, generally unconcerned. No—perhaps she is at rear
of stage. Motions, one step, motions, one step, etc. + thus slowly by stages across or
something like that, continuing after I am hit.
Like a cage with animal inside.

PROPS: cigarette with smoke

2. The Guy
TYPE: bum

ACTION:
1. picks rags, newspaper
2. spits
2a. pisses whistle
3. exhibits self (pity . . . ?)
4. fights, boxes + threatens
5. BOTTLE, drinks
6. robs, GUN, both hands (boup boup?)
7. Lurches staggers, abrupt death, stuck out + withdrawn
After last flash, I move back + then Lucas drops sign at end.

PROPS: with writing on them? Lucas hangs up some signs, POSTERS

ACTION STYLE: grotesque, violent action—"Japanese," *exaggerated caricature,*
teenager
Practice *action*—me all day— + Pat—together

COSTUME STYLE—black + white, dramatic, severe
(make figures on street portable)

PROPS: box, gun, car, prick

LIGHTS?: blinking but not blinker, operator? Lucas?

SOUND?: Our own noises, fanny strip yip yip, f.ex.

I sit on street 8–8:30 p.m., but Pat is not present. She, a surprise. Or stands on the street.
Olga is in house. Bud is receiving + checking traffic, giving money + programs. I do
nothing but sit, very still. At 8:30, Pat enters, robed + without headdress + mask (made
up for Whitman's play). Lucas takes his place at the lights + Pat is there offstage ready +
whoever else is needed. Olga there to push the car out. Lucas douses streetlight (perhaps
Pat, fully dressed, waits for this cue). Bud herds people into room + there announces
performance very plainly, no "welcome" or "Ray Gun Spex."

	ACTION	PROPS	FLASHES	approx. TIME
1	C: seated, raise bottle, drink	bottle	7	10
	P: walks across as streetchick	cigarette		
2	C: I get up, pick butts + rags	rag bag		
	spit, feed pigeons, beg	butt	7	10
	P: walks across as mamaganger	baby		
3	C: lurch + try to start fight, box,		7	10
	punchy-like			
	P: walks as stripper			
4	C: pull gun and/or hit someone	gun	7	10
	overhead			
	P: fights off attacker in center			
5	C: expose myself, piss	prick	7	10
	P: walks with umbrella,			
	with cane, with bag			
6	C: hit by car	car + operator	1	1
	P: takes position #1	bag on head		
7	sign falls down	sign		
	darkness	x	x	4

The street shows the inner penetration of the real, the inner real and the outer real of the psyche—the object and the essential mystery.

The beauty and meaning of discarded objects, chance effects. The city is a landscape well worth enjoying—damn necessary if you live in the city.

Dirt has depth and beauty. I love soot and scorching. From all of this can come a positive, as well as a negative, meaning.

Seek out banality, seek out what opposes it or what is excluded from its domain, and triumph over it—the city filth, the evils of advertising, the disease of success, popular culture.

Look for beauty where it is not supposed to be found.

I try not to be negative.

Acts that take place in the audience have a direct effect on the painter and the painting, and the end is a result, which is a piece of time, a graph of events through the sensation of the artist.

A sculpture in the shape of an obsession.

The day to come is the day we can operate without resistance the range of our capabilities—or turn ourselves at will from heroes to loonies.

Living objects—study the mystical qualities of the object.

What is to be avoided is that art should be distant from actual experience.

Art making itself at home in the present.

The poster is the end not the information.

Skirts are short and always up.

This studio is right on a street, an unending source of material.

Working at the Judson is like working on the level of an excavator.

The place and time where they are found diminish in importance according to how long they have been exposed and what has happened to them.

We are just a little tired of four sides and a flat face.

Art based on curiosities occur within me in collusion with external curiosities. But in the end, art dominates curiosity.

Man is only alive when he is constantly arranging to upset his existence, when he is solving situations. It is not superficial to see man's true and deepest enemy as boredom.

Every simple thing is the incarnation of human obsession.

Don't be afraid to be obvious.

To make hostile objects human.

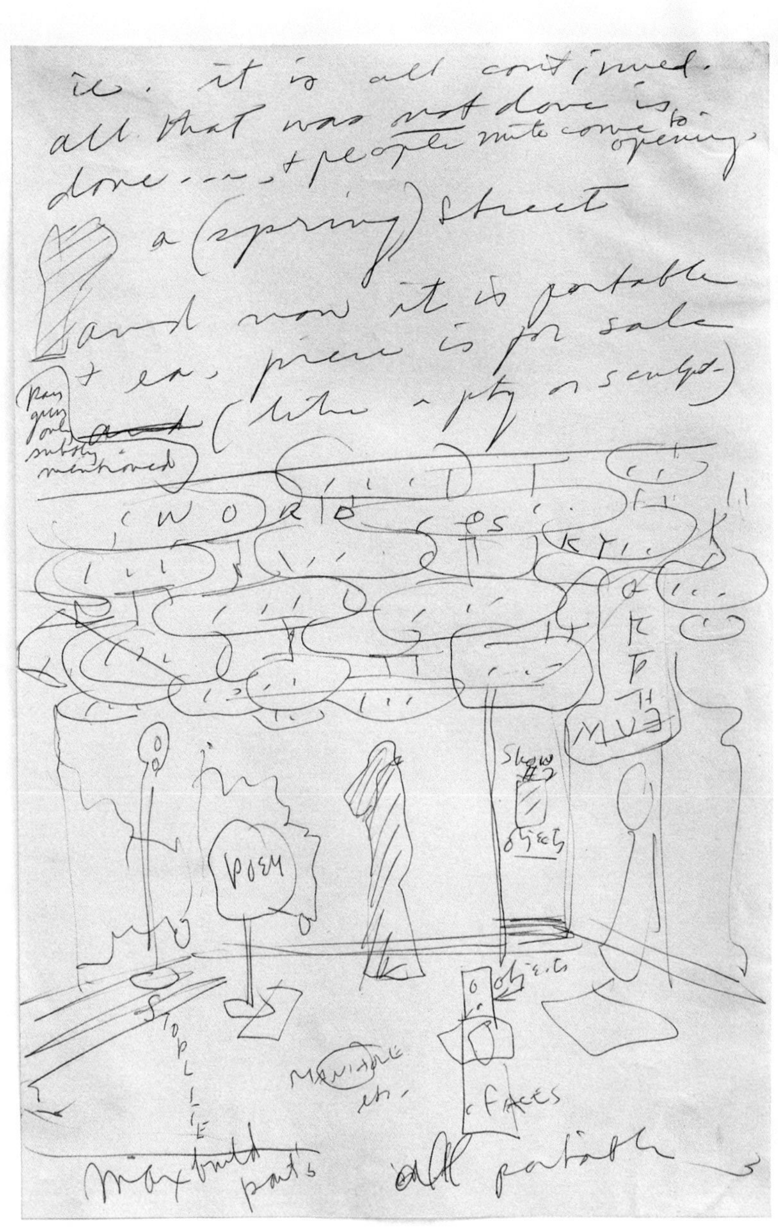

Notebook Page: Installation Study, Reuben Gallery, 1960

The show will consist of 1) an epic construction in the form of a street and 2) and 3) drawings and small sculptures and constructions also having to do with the street.

The material will be mostly paper and wood, glued paper, torn paper, paper over wire, on wooden frames, paper hanging down, paper jumping up, paper lying, etc., etc.

The scale will vary from heroic to very, very small.

In *The Street*, there will be suspended figures, standing figures, lying figures, projecting figures, falling figures, running figures, etc., etc. There will be figures on the walls, faces on the floor, and a sky made of words and cries.

There will be signs of various sorts, marquees, street signs, etc., and various sorts of metamorphosed objects: cigar butts, houses, towers, cars, medals, etc., etc. There will be faces in windows and free faces.

Hanging heads and many heads.

There will be men and women and heroes and bums and children and drunks and cripples and streetchicks and boxers and walkers and sitters and spitters and trucks and cars and bikes and manholes and stoplights and shadows and cats and doggies and bright light and darkness, fires and collisions and cockroaches and mornings and evenings and guns and newspapers and pissers and cops and mamagangers and a lot more, etc.

(All components of *The Street* can be purchased separately.)

1. Cemetery Flag
A form found in the flag, which flies illuminated all night long at the crest of the Catholic cemetery.

2. Kornville Flag
A rutted, dusty road leads off the highway into a thicket of squatters and wood collectors. A flag flies in the clearing, surrounded by their decrepit huts. Colonel Korn is the commander here and has given his name to the place.

3. Powerhouse Flag
On the road to Race Point Light, there is a mechanical oasis, a building taken from a big city, humming night and day.

4. Flag Plate
A storm is coming, a heavy cloud is speeding over us. We hide in an abandoned cabin, and a meal of forms assembles itself for us.

5. Dunes Flag
I take the pieces from the shore and make a statement of the order of things: a well-meaning salt-and-pepper lighthouse, the sea, a moon, but the impossible intrudes.

6. Backwards Flag, or Harbor Flag
Two pieces float up to me in the water, asking to be joined. Joining them, I see I have participated in a blasphemy, but I can't dispose of it.

7. Old Junkyard Flag
Off the superhighway through a rusty bullethole, I ride my whistling bike, looking for messages on this old cake.

8. New Junkyard Flag
A place to be seen with the nose. Every Pilgrim's son must face this backside twice a week, but the flag is made in the air out of gulls' wings.

9. Jail Flag
The flag growls and shows its teeth, but in truth it is trapped and will sit there until morning.

I might add, the flags are made out of what I take to be the basic pictographic elements of the place, not only on a grand scale but, surprisingly, in every observable fragment. A place with extraordinary unity of form. F.ex.: Half circle–firmament/barrel bottoms. Stripes–land/slats. Rectangle: Absolute relation, horizontal and vertical and infinity of space/shingles and many flags. Projected into content: elementary nature/patriotism.

P......G (1960)

P......g, which has slept so long / in its gold crypts / in its glass graves / is asked out / to go
for a swim / is given a cigarette / a bottle of beer / its hair is rumpled / is given a shove and
tripped / is taught to laugh / is given clothes of all kinds / goes for a ride on a bike / finds a
girl in a cab and feels her up / goes flying / goes driving at 100 mph.

Shy at first / soon all its dreams are realized / is stripped from its cross / straightened out /
is given exercise to bring back its tired muscles / tonics to get the red back in its cheeks.

Who all its life had wished to be / is given the chance to be / a handkerchief / to go from /
hand to hand / from nose to nose / and in and out of pockets / over foreheads / into eyes
and ears / around one set of lips and another / to be dropped and washed in a machine
on a line to dry flapping in the wind.

Who all its life had wished to be / is given the chance to be / a flag / carried in the breeze
up and down streets / planted on car fenders going fast / whistling in a thousand parts
over a gasoline station / lazily lying on a coffin / pleased to catch the earth thrown on it /
at half-mast for some famous person / lofty on a patriotic day / put away in a drawer
at night nicely folded / wounded or dissolving in battle / decaying in the mast of a ship
crossing the ocean.

To be a shirt / a tie / a pair of pants / a suit of clothes / going somewhere on someone /
getting rumpled while dancing / having a drink spilled on it / taken off and hung up / sent
to the cleaners / drawn on the body / catching hair / slicing over fingers / pressing ears.

Bolder and bolder / it becomes anything it wants to be / a hamburger / an ice-cream cone /
a newspaper / a sewing machine / a bicycle / impossible inexhaustible p......g.

Injun

A tavern up the river. The sun's light reflected from the river into the tavern. An INJUN is lying on the bar with his head over the edge. Wine flows out of his face, and he is sniffling. Suddenly his body is covered with a hundred little birds.

First thing you know, the volunteer fire siren goes off and everyone leaves the bar, which sinks into the river, out of sight.

The fire is out of control. There's nothing to do but watch. When the fire dies, there is INJUN, red as coals, kneeling and scooping up little mounds of scorched flesh like marshmallows.

The volunteers beat him with their hoses until he turns black, and then they kick his ashes around until they blow away.

They all take out their handkerchiefs and wipe themselves. Then they go back to their work. The tavern keeper pulls his tavern out of the river and pours free rounds for the house.

A beggar at the back door keeps bothering his wife. He has some presumption, she thinks. He keeps pawing her tits and lifting her skirts while she is making sandwiches. Finally she gets mad and says: "What do you want?" and the beggar laughs so hard he breaks into a whole pile of fresh-cut birchwood.

"Put the wood in the stove," Bernie says. The woman does so, not caring one way or another. The tavern is filled with smoke, thick and black, which makes all the patrons cough and wheeze.

Crusoe

Crusoe has been sitting in Union Square, and an enormous bird has landed on his head and shoulders. It won't go off. It is Friday the 13th, and Crusoe has been out looking for little boys. Now, with this disaster, he has to go home and clean up.

The whole bunch at the boarding house has a big laugh at his predicament. Major Hoople, an old, colored slave (Walt Whitman), takes Crusoe into a narrow toilet on the first floor, on the pretense of helping him but actually to give him a little kiss.

The bird dies, and they lay it on the dining-room table. Everybody pitches in to eat the bird, but when they come to the stomach, the damned INJUN pops out!

Crusoe is in the living room trying to get the landlady's little boy to bend over and look for something he claims to have thrown on the floor. The INJUN sinks his tommy in Crusoe's head. It turns into a bird, and they kiss.

The boy grows up to be Teddy Roosevelt, the President of the USA. As a good gesture, he invites his old pals at the house to dinner.

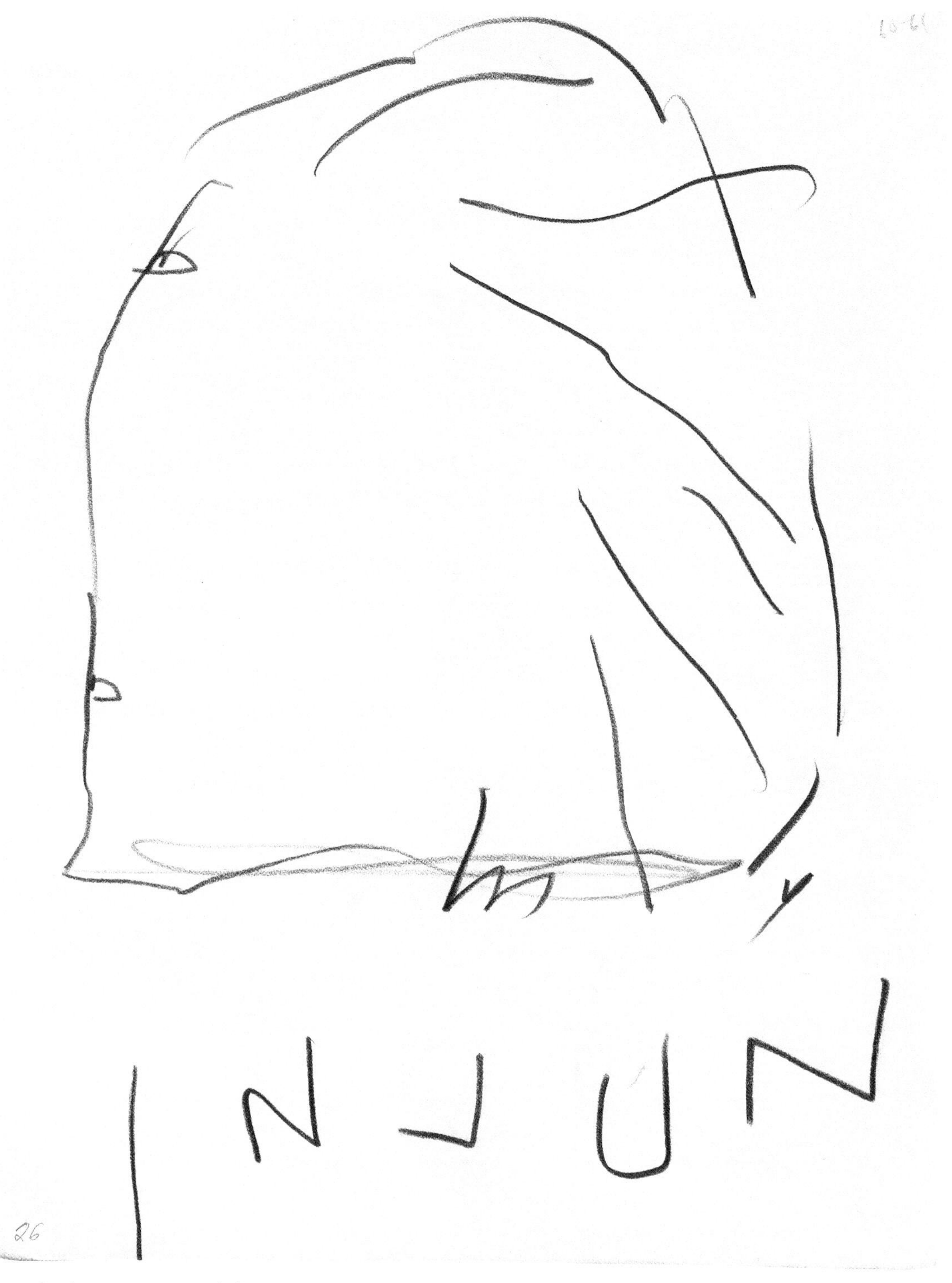

Notebook Page: Poster Study for "Injun," 1960–61

They go into the dining room, where a congressional orgy is taking place. Crusoe alone takes care of twenty senators and twice as many representatives. Teddy says he's got to go sailing, which is the tip off, and the Civil War begins.

Friday and Crusoe are wrestling in the fireplace. Finally Friday changes into a bear and climbs the chimney. Crusoe is alone with the bird, who grows so that it fills the room. He crawls into its asshole, and he is X-rayed in there, playing dice with Walt Whitman.

He finds himself fishing in a secluded stream. Friday comes out of the trees (an ignorant savage, he doesn't know what he's doing). They make love, and all the fish of the Adirondacks attach themselves to his string.

Crusoe's wife wakes him. He's been sleeping there for such a long time. She pulls him back by the ear to the Town Square, where he is to make the Memorial Day Oration. Each word comes out a fish, and he can't stop pissing on the stage. At last, the police set him on fire.

Now comes the funeral! The band is playing, and Crusoe has been altered by the embalmer into an obelisk. The whole town hammers him into the ground, all singing.

A Card from Doc
Postscript

The yacht bawls in the harbor. The mayor enters. Old Doc's been away, trip around the world. How are things at the Club? His nose has grown to cover his face, but he's still old sly Doc. Howzaboy? Lotsa backslaps! Well, mayor, what's on the agenda?

Civic improvement, plazas, malls, centers, ports, projects, projects, projects. Got two heads full! Cut the folks up, cut up the plain folks, trim 'em like trees, saw 'em to size, make bricks of 'em, beams, pile 'em up, seal 'em to each other by their juices. Build Build Build.

Don't forget the statues, says Doc. Oh yeah, bulls and greeks and lots of nekkid broads.

BLACKOUTS (Script, 1960)

Erasers

on a sort of altar or raised box,
a white rag is illuminated   the sound of falling coins

throughout the dark room,
umbrellas are popped open

a beggar enters and takes the rag
stealthily, leaves

a second beggar, a cripple, comes
in slowly. he is upset abruptly by
a girl in white, who then dances
swiftly and gracefully and
disappears

darkness

the rag reappears on the altar

end

Chimneyfires

a door opens, a man comes out
he goes in again

                                    distant sound of a typewriter,
                                    halting

a flowerpot full of flowers is
broken with a bat

a woman is putting on some heavy,   lightbulbs are dropped on concrete
baggy, black men's pants

instantaneous vision of a woman

opening a book
a man falls asleep at a table
listening to a quiet song on the
phonograph. he falls forward
slowly to the floor

sound of a typewriter, rapidly
shower goes on, into a bucket

end

Butter & Jam

a baby's rattle is heard in the
darkness making a dry sound

after a while, a shadow play
begins with cutout figures
moving stiffly. the rattle stops,
and the shadow play is turned off.
darkness again

a cart is illuminated on the floor
lying upside down, its wheels
slowly turning. at the same time
a girl is singing a song weakly.
darkness again

in bright light, two guys wearing
leather aprons move furniture.
they make an opening through which
a girl roller skates, with her
skirt pinned up showing her legs
with silk stockings on

end

Encore:
1. a long-haired dog is shown in a cage under a shower, getting wet
2. the very long hair of a girl is combed by an old woman with no face

The Vitamin Man

in the darkness, a loud clock
ticks. then stops ticking.

little drops of water fall on the
audience

in the darkness,
the sound of wings

spotlight on a boxing match, in
white
a blind woman walks into the match.
she is beaten, and her stick is broken
over her head

snare drum rolls

a man in white very slowly
collapses from a standing position.
a bag of red paint on his head is
burst and red liquid runs all over
his body

a fat little boy sits down on a
park bench and eats voraciously a
loaf of bread. elsewhere, a girl is
buttering her left palm and wrist
with her right hand

abruptly, a terrible racket.
hundreds of things fall down,
rocks and old buckets . . .

end

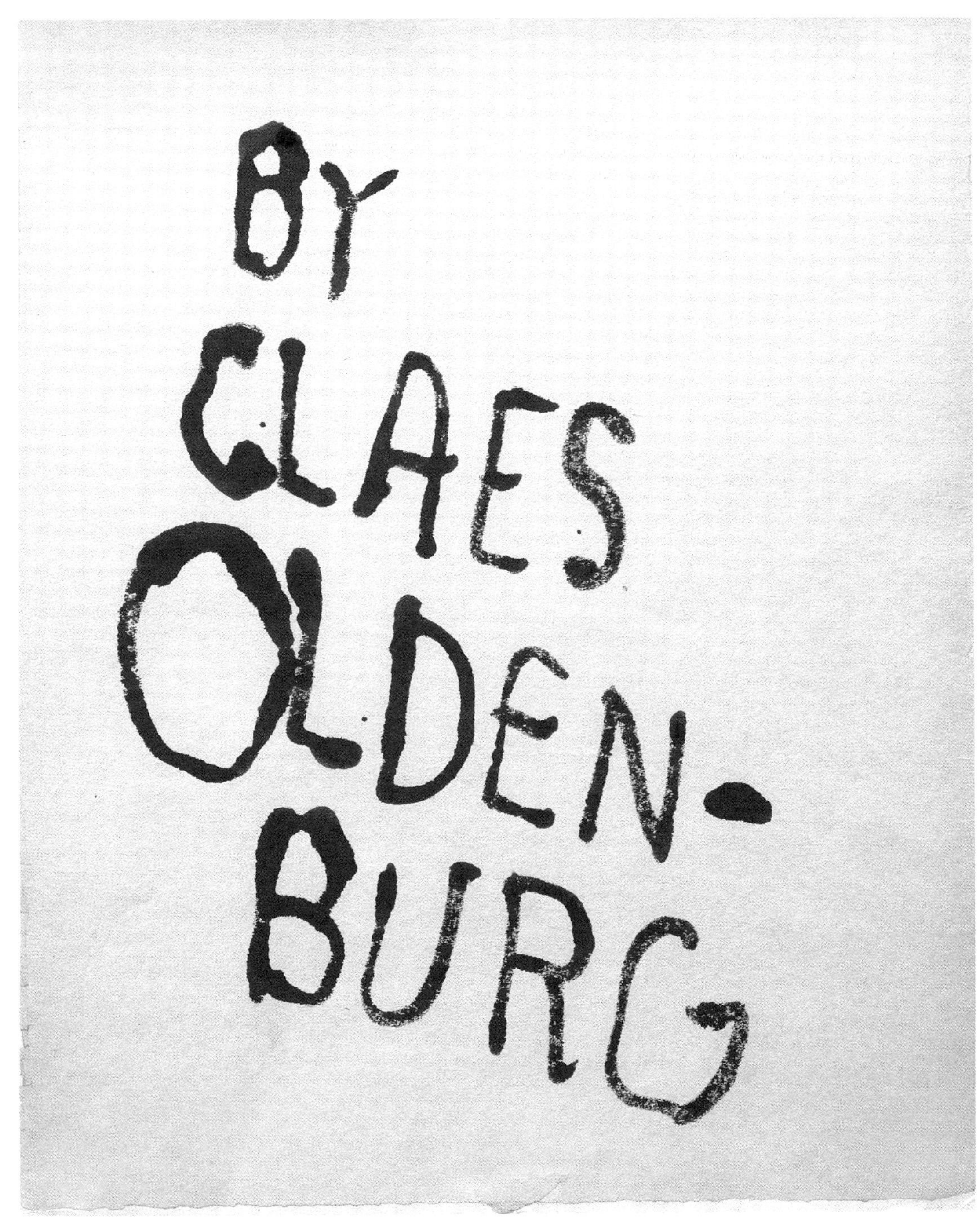

Poster for *Blackouts*, 1960

Chapter 3
Guises of Ray Gun: The Store
1961–1962

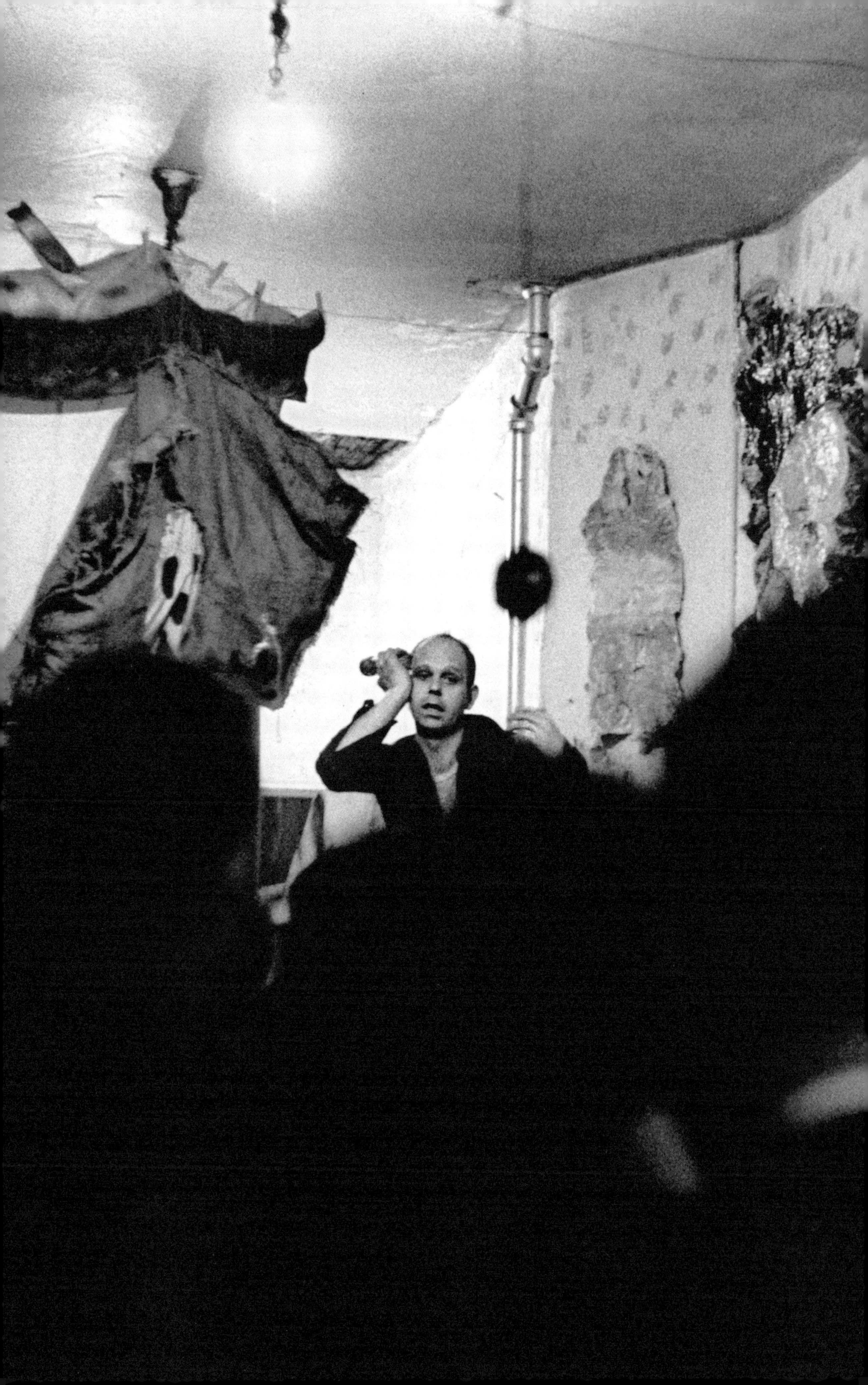

FRIDAY, JANUARY 6, 1961 THREAT OF EVICTION AT REUBEN

Go by Reuben in p.m. and start taking down electrical stuff, storing boards, etc. Jim in. Talk. Nancy calls down later to stop because being evicted as a result of building inspectors walking in on Allan's stuff dumped there in p.m., etc. Allan comes by + we talk as if it's all over. He gives me $20 for junkman. Go to Max + Anita's after dinner + it seems we may stay.

a.m. bring drawings to Passloff, who subsequently calls to say they are the most beautiful she has ever seen.

SATURDAY, JANUARY 7, 1961 JUNK REMOVED

Max talks to landlord + Jim does too. An arrangement is reached. We pay increased rent but stay. I call junkman + place is cleared out. I clean all p.m., have a beer. The arrangement is made later. I will do my performance before Allan's, because mine is less likely to make a mess!

MONDAY, JANUARY 23, 1961

Send application to Gutman finally. At Reuben, deciding to do *Fotodeath* rather than *Injun*. Lester's opening at Zabriskie. Pat + I meet at 5 p.m. at Coscia's + go up by subway. Dull. Dodie, Daryle, Roth, Clifford Smith, et al.

Up to Dickie's + get scotch. Eat.

THURSDAY, JANUARY 26, 1961

Passloff's in p.m., 3–5 p.m. Shop before. Army Navy store. Cooper 5:30–6:30 p.m. Look at children's costumes at Cooper. Aileen sets me straight on nature of dance. Gives me $15 more. All a.m. worked on costumes. Hang up work, plaster pieces + flags. The American room!

In evening, do final drawings for costumes, in color with set of temperas I bought. Reading Agee on film + Brecht. Make my own dinner.

FRIDAY, JANUARY 27, 1961 SAROFF VISITS

a.m. around house, trying on costumes. Take bath. Cooper 2–5 p.m. Pick up sewing machine at Edith's. Carrying bottle of punch I got at Cooper. Wait very long for bus. Eat fast, steak. Saroff + Rose visit. Pleasant. Brief. They are very friendly + say Alan wants to consider me for a group show March 4th. Tarot cards.

Look at antique dance costumes + several books of spectacle at Cooper.

SUNDAY, JANUARY 29, 1961

Fine weather but I wake up tired + depressed. Sleep again. Weight of things to do. Pat cooks breakfast. Cuts my hair. We go shopping. Ave. C. Orchard via Clinton. Quite

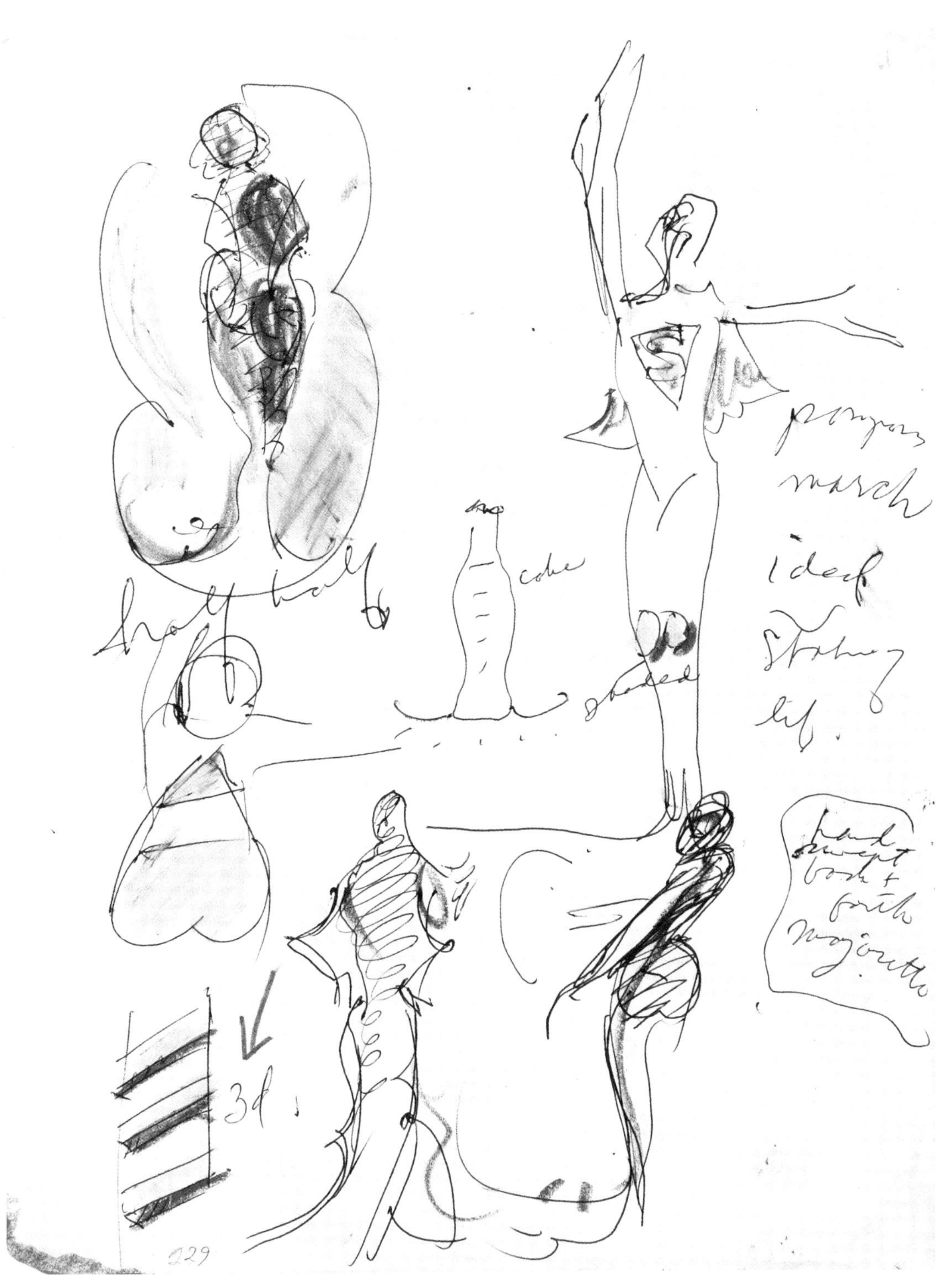

Notebook Page: Costume Studies for Aileen Passloff Dance Company—Superman, 1961

cold. Subway up to dance rehearsal. 1:30–5 p.m. try costumes. Watch *Phantoms*. Seem to get it, more. Get coffee. Hear of Harriet. Walk to trick store, pinup store. Subway back. Meet Barbara on subway. To Clinton store again. Ave. C stores. Still buying. Ale + dinner of soup, pancakes + salad. Work on mailer. Saroff calls. He buys flags for $225! Too little, Pat thinks! But I can't bother about it. Must make mailer. Bus to Anita's with mailer + leave it. Bus back. Pizza slice. Beer. Paste up notes. Pat painted 2nd coat floor + washed floors. Tired but inspired. Ideas for *Fotodeath*, day of clothing!
Get manikin from store on Ave. C.

FRIDAY, MARCH 17, 1961 VANDERBEEK'S / CHIPPY'S
Was to go to Stan's in morning. The weather is perfect but do not go until afternoon and do not go to Cooper. Filming title scene on roof in back. Blowing papers. Scene on streets. Coffee + Swiss cheese sandwich. More coffee. See "Street Meat"—we film. Make sounds and record. Passing traffic. Banging. I strain my voice and tear my pants. To Stan's house for martinis. He knocks over a coffeepot. Talks on phone about his, or her, parent who is sick. Pick up disk. I don't shave and we go to Chippy's. I make sounds on street + Pat is angry with me and goes on ahead. Good drinks and "films" by Chippy + husband + Dick Smith. Henry Geldzahler. Peter Passuntino. Eventually all leave except us and the English + we listen to Sellers records.

TUESDAY, MARCH 28, 1961 CARRY OUT STUFF
Quite warm, hazy. Tired. Pat home. Breakfast. Go uptown by bus + subway to Jackson with framed piece for Rolfe. Alan Gallery, get my flags, return by cab. Take tools and walk through ruined section of 5th St. Get pieces, which I see are full of cockroaches when I get to Cooper. a.m.—rewrite old poems, seaside, etc., and start the Bride, film "play." Cooper 3:30–5 p.m. Call McElroy and ask if he wants to film. Carl calls. Late dinner. Salmon steak. Love. Watercolor. Carry stuff down. Rain. Late beer. Bed 2 a.m.+. Pat sews.

WEDNESDAY, APRIL 5, 1961 CARL + WHITMAN UP / WORKING ON JACKSON IDEA
Very cocky. Talking up Dada and just talking. Taking pills.
In evening, decide to build "kitchen" for Jackson show. Make a number of hectic drawings and messy framing attempts. Lehmann-Haupt drops up. Then Whitman. Drink beer and talk until 12:30 a.m. on street. Bob has two flats on car.

THURSDAY, APRIL 6, 1961 KOUZEL'S SEE FILM / JACKSON'S
Go to Jackson's and survey space. See Bob in a.m. at gallery. Buckley weary. Thing begins to take form—space is fine—duplicates my studio + one will see street behind the mural. Nelson offers me $250 for drawings. Cooper, then meet Pat at Coscia's. She to New Jersey and I uptown to Al's. Part at bus stop. Al's brother-in-law. Out for dinner + have bad hamburger. Brother-in-law talks about Claremont College. Return to apartment + read Apollinaire. See film—images look very strong. Made plans to meet with drummer next Thursday.

TUESDAY, APRIL 11, 1961 LI CITY / ENAMEL

Very tired. Out to Long Island City and look at studio for sublet + other apartments. Cooper 2:30–6:30 p.m.

Start painting plaster pieces with enamel and also frame + glass for watercolor. Thing taking form.

Go to Yves Klein's opening but am not in the mood, so leave soon. Jim Dine calls. In a.m., I call Nancy, ask about apartments.

TUESDAY, JUNE 6, 1961 UPTOWN

Bleak. No money. Start letters to Martha Jackson + Gutman. *Times* review, which I trade for *Tribune* review.

Begin dieting about now.

WEDNESDAY, JUNE 7, 1961 UPTOWN

Paint floor in new room + finish. Start work on Store. Go through posters, etc. Castelli's. Meet Paolo Barozzi, have coffee with him. Talk about Venice, Happenings, etc. Take posters over to Rudi Blesh.

FRIDAY, JUNE 9, 1961 WORK AT STORE

Don't go to work. Pat + I work all day at Store. Return after dinner. Ray Johnson + friend over. Green chairs. His present. Pacifier. Twilight. Beer. Work at night. Danny sees, through window, dance across court. Warm beer from grocery + later Puerto Rican store. Hurt back carrying stuff over and break cart. Start writing essay on Happenings.

SATURDAY, JUNE 17, 1961 NJ WITH BILLY K. / START READING AND THINKING

Billy is to come early but he doesn't come until about 11 a.m. with Letty. Writing in a.m., write in car. Excited—pills + all. Perfect weather. Drink beer in car. Nice drive down to New Jersey across from Barnegat Light.

Restaurant. Country smells. Like Michigan. Billy talks about Tinguely + machine. Toms River, once very blue lagoon. Resort. Down island. Toll. To near end. Waves. Fishermen. Lighthouse in mist. Lagoon + shore. Blimp. Find spot. I make fire. Not enough beer! Roast franks. Marshmallows. Lie around. Pat + I walk, etc.

Drive back to Billy's in Murray Hill Laboratories via Wachtung Park. Nashers. Cold cuts, whisky. All the books, apartment. One record after another, Swedish, etc., always ending with "Never on Sunday." Stay over.

I read everything.

MONDAY, JUNE 26, 1961 PAT'S BIRTHDAY / ALLAN VISITS

Pat has job at League.

Ginnever brings stuff down from Jackson. I get check there for $200—which I deposit. My loan.

In evening—Allan, seeing Tyler, drops up + we have long discussion about his article + ideas. Reading Lawrence's *Studies* + Miller. Writing furiously at home + at work.

THURSDAY, JUNE 29, 1961

Kind of warm. Write. Good formulation: Program Notes, etc. Letter from Allan. Take bath. Bank. Write checks, send. B bus down to Worth St. Take license test. Return home, write more. Work 2–5 p.m. Slow. Writing away. Begin to be clarified, fall together. Pat to wash with rugs. Beer. Fish head. Fish dinner.

Pat tired. Sleeps. Doze too + sun goes down.

Trying to figure out what summer will be.

TUESDAY, AUGUST 1, 1961 BREER, BILLY, LETTY

Fine, cool, sunny day after some clouds. Up 9 a.m. Read + write, starting "novel." Gas + bank. To work 1:30–4:30 p.m. Meet Elaine. Reading *Scarlet Letter* + *Sound* + *Fury* + Fiedler. After work, plaster back of 39¢. Love before dinner. Gloria calls about film. After dinner Billy, Letty + Robert Breer. Take Breer to my Store + walk back. Gas on stomach + generally unsociable. Bed 12 a.m.

Met Higgins who had quit job.

Letty + Breer allergic to cats.

THURSDAY, AUGUST 3, 1961

Write in a.m. Meet Stan at Harris's + drive to his place. Pick up film. Lunch with him and discuss loft movement + art + society. Cooper. Later write a piece on social responsibility of artist. Reading *Dissent*. Brick through window.

THURSDAY, AUGUST 10, 1961

Go to Cooper. a.m. think about Kaprow, Pollock, art, etc. + Rosenberg's statements. Back still hurts. Get mad at paint store for overcharging on plaster.

Pat paints small room. Red floor. Cat gets in red paint.

THURSDAY, AUGUST 17, 1961

Clear, beautiful weather. Pat to League + Long Island. Write a.m. on Adele's + Allan's letter. Talk to Bellamy about Store. Cooper 2–5 p.m. Up at 7:30 a.m. and out in cool a.m. to move car. Woman in white shirt + other a.m. goers.

To Store—I had left back door open. Home for bath + dinner. Lie around. Pat nervous + sad. No money. Read + think. Write out plans for Store, Spex, formulated at Cooper. Bed 12 a.m.+ but head full of thoughts.

MONDAY, AUGUST 21, 1961 EVENING / SAROFF

Write in a.m.

In evening, Raymond Saroff visits. We talk a long while about films, etc.

Nice weather.

Writing about personalism. Reading Brown.

TUESDAY, AUGUST 22, 1961 PA TO DOC

Writing in a.m. Essays on *personal* theater. *Personal* aesthetics, etc. Guises of Ray Gun.

p.m., take Pa to Doctor + with them until 6 p.m. or so. Dinner at home. His bookcase, etc. Electrical tampering.

Writing also short pieces for film. A week of good ideas—waking up with them. *Faustina*—grand scenario. Jackson's + pick up check. Talk to Kendall.

Started to work. Get wooden O for window + hang.

Money running out. And Pat has no work.

WEDNESDAY, AUGUST 23, 1961 EVENING BELLAMY

Usual. a.m.—writing on letter, etc.

Bellamy by in p.m. Lemon gin. Dinner of meatloaf. Very good. Return to Store, select stuff—beers in a bar across street.

Make Ray Gun Mfg. Co. sign + put in window.

FRIDAY, AUGUST 25, 1961 GARDEN

a.m.—Aileen calls + we talk of costume. At Store, complete letter to Allan in rough form. Get there late from home. Cooper 2–5 p.m. Everyone home early. To Store and fix up room in front end for painting, put up mirror, etc. Drink gin, liqueur. After dinner sit and read Swift waiting for Billy + Letty, who come late, 10 p.m.+. Pat tries hairdos + her finished new blue dress. I in nude. Go to Garden + dance. I feel very loose dancing. Humid night (bones loose). Lovely weather. Pizza on 2nd Ave. and then home . . .

MONDAY, AUGUST 28, 1961

Hot and humid. Nice. To Store 11 a.m.–1 p.m. Write on Allan's letter and plaster "sausages." Paint on Billy's piece "roast." Cooper 1–4 p.m. Home for kishka + rice sausages, red cabbage. Beer. Very warm. Back to Store. Nice + cool. Write in diary.

THURSDAY, AUGUST 31, 1961 PAT TO PHOTOGRAPHER

Formulate brief, harsh letter to Allan + am finally satisfied enough to want to send it off. Reading *Gulliver's Travels*.

Pat to photographer, Greco. Picks her up. Have flat (I ran over box), which we repair. Home with beer.

THURSDAY, SEPTEMBER 7, 1961

Bellamy calls re: poster + I go to Profile Press printer then up to Dick's with preliminary sketch, which he doesn't like or understand. No wonder. But also our conception of show is very different. Talk. Reviewer of Beauchamp's show.

FRIDAY, SEPTEMBER 8, 1961

Call Bossman + bawl him out after he and Hy-Sam give Pat runaround all day about repairs.

Working on poster first day, no results, of course. Getting feverish.

THURSDAY, SEPTEMBER 14, 1961

To Green Gallery to see poster. No one likes but me. In Whitman's car with Dick + Lucas to see loft over Jimmy's. I to bar + buy meat. Then Bob home, Lucas + Dick to film. I cook my meat.

SATURDAY, SEPTEMBER 16, 1961 LETTY'S

Working hard at Store, making Cake, Apple, etc. Pat hung over, sleeping. Letty's for dinner. Billy to Rauschenberg to work on piece they are doing together. I soak feet + rest. Beginning of dizziness. Very tired in feet. Big steak, Letty + Pat bought. Planters Punch. All to my place. Tired all. Pat + I make "tub" of chairs.

TUESDAY, SEPTEMBER 19, 1961 OPENING BELLAMY'S

Cloudy day. Stay in bed in dream of "ordinary objects." Gröt, egg, jam. Pat bathes. I lie around. Cooper 1–4 p.m. Edith shows article around in *Art News*. To Store: decide which pieces to reject. Finality. Pat going to model agencies. Ride up to 59th St. Meet Lisa. Drinks at "Barneys" with Dickie + Lisa. Green opening. Back room. Ride up with Jim + Ivan. Allan, Lucas, Billy, Gloria, et al., et al. Show doesn't look good to me. My poster defaced by addition of Ginnever's name. Allan calls my letter "petulant." BMT back. Ham + cheese + beer + tomato at Store. Rain. Kids fall through door. Start letter to Gutman. Very sad and moody. Walk home. Listen to music. Style change. As usual in fall?

TUESDAY, OCTOBER 3, 1961

Rain. Drawing at home toward lithograph. Reading about lithographs. Studying Picassos. Find quarter, buy coffee + twist. Visit Jim, Bob. See carpenter about estimate for Ray Gun box. Cooper 2–5 p.m. Buy drawing tools. Draw at Store. Home for peanut butter + tomato soup dinner. Feed Charlie. Read. Call Dickie. Go there with tux. Drinks. Bring back rugs. Look at glass case in junk store.

MONDAY, FEBRUARY 5, 1962

Go through notes. Thinking about performance.

TUESDAY, FEBRUARY 6, 1962 CONSTRUCTION

Reading Cage's *Silence* and Suzuki on Zen.
Film fruit + signs and other merchandise along 1st Ave. Run down street with camera.
Call movers.
Get lumber for balcony and put up.
Buy old clothes on Ave. C.
Hy-Sam picks up icebox.

WEDNESDAY, FEBRUARY 7, 1962

Quite cold but clear.
Work on costumes a.m. at home. Go to hammock place. Ride bus. Inspired. Film ideas.

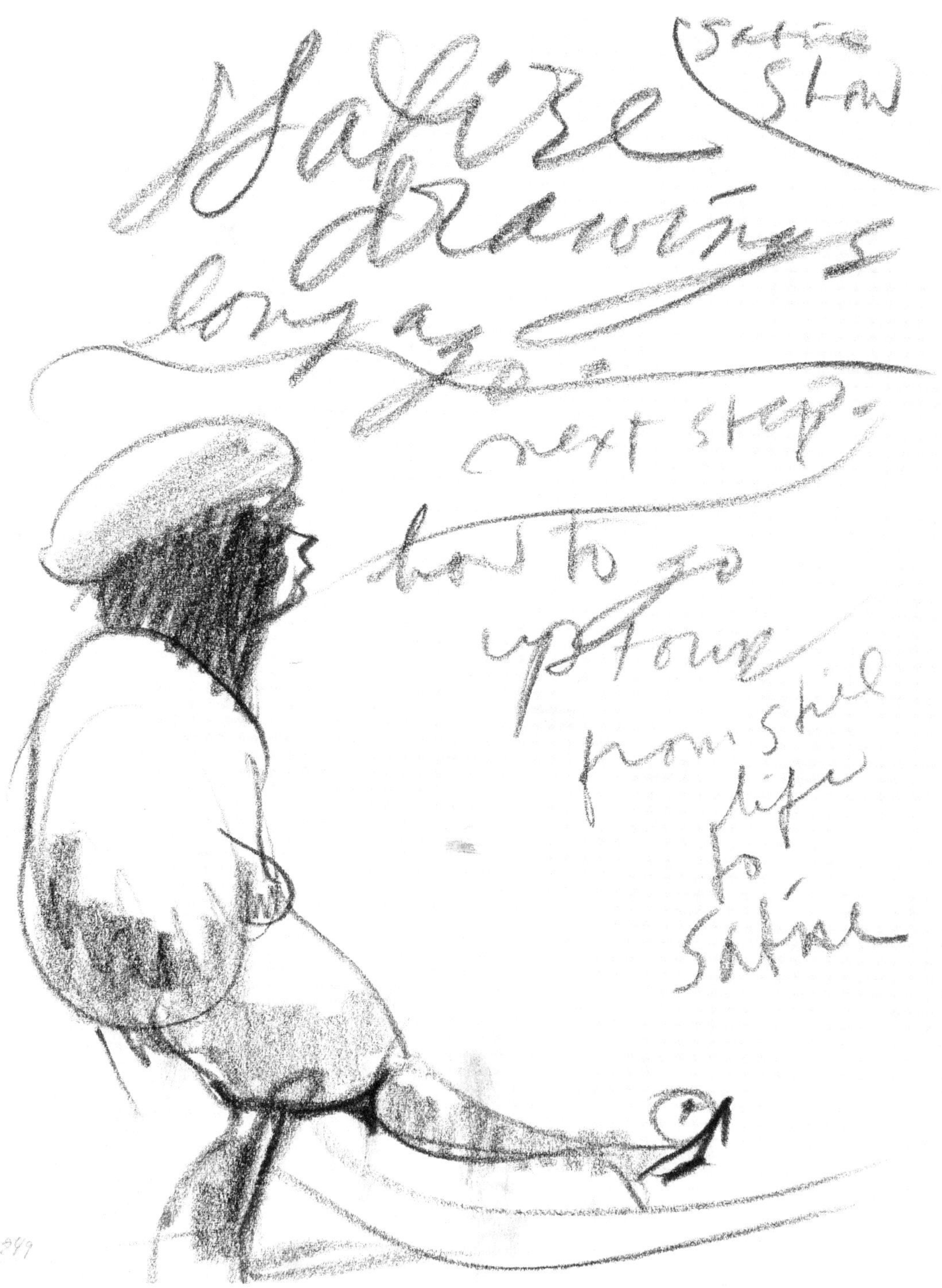

Notebook Page: Walking Figure in Fur; "Satire Drawings . . .," 1962

Plan season, work at Store. Whitman by. Hamburgers. Lebel + Joanna 9:30 p.m. Talk
and use them in Store. Pat picks up film + Dallas Sunday papers.
Ma calls—a fire on their floor 2 p.m. Burns out front apartment.

THURSDAY, FEBRUARY 8, 1962
Cloudy, cool. Love in a.m. Fried eggs. To Store 11 a.m. Buy lumber—finish balcony. Saw
with much effort—wet wood. Paint. Cut hole in north wall. Hang ropes from ceiling.
Ale, a shot. Buy *New Yorker*, read about Billy. Gloria calls. Eat at corner, kielbasa + later
steak sandwich. Clean, organize notes. Pat picks pictures for balcony. Dump garbage.
Funny man with mustache—banal conversation. Beer + knish. Bed, 1 a.m.

MONDAY, FEBRUARY 12, 1962 SCRIPTS
Set up scripts and breakdown. Very inspired day. Uptown to look at business cards.
Conceive "Store News." Plan master. Wait for a friend of Gloria's who doesn't come.
Home for dinner, 5:15 p.m. Banana, ham. Billy over. Cockroach in coffee. Billy + I to
Store. Discuss essay on Store. Lucas comes with dress suit. Just finished soliloquy in
Endgame "before large audience." Discuss theater. Pat studies French. I write 1st draft of
Store Days. Home 12:30 a.m.+. Policeman tries Store door. Bed too late.

TUESDAY, FEBRUARY 13, 1962 SCRIPTS
Cool. Type script from night before. Make appointment with Fulbright, bank, subway
to 8th St. and buy *Arts*. Plan *Injun* and mailer. Get scrapbooks at Cooper. Home to
eat—green peppers—beer. Whisky at Store. A number of phone calls home + Store.
Rudi about a lecture March 23rd. Max, Shandi, Milet, Rosalyn, Johanna. Write second
version of *Store Days*. Pat at lesson, comes over after studying French. Home 12:30
a.m.+, right to bed.

WEDNESDAY, FEBRUARY 14, 1962
Rainy snow. Diary in a.m. + addresses. Eggs. To Store 11 a.m. Type script from night
before. Phone calls. Gus from Pratt Institute picks up lithographs. Whisky. To Tannenhill
to discuss card. Back 3:30 p.m. Dictate schedule to Michaela. Pat over. Talk about
Stephen Crane, Hart Crane. Wine + liver sausage. Change Ray Gun publication to
Things in Words (talked to Whitman earlier). Home for dinner. Gloria doesn't come,
with Wendell.
Call Terry, Jackie, Carol, Deerless, Ma, at home call Lisa. Get steak.

New York, January 1961 to December 1962

Poor old typewriter, how are you?

NY is busy-ness, politics, peoples.

Statue of Liberty—dress manikin.

What have I done to the canvas, and to painting space?
I have dynamized it, subjectivized it.
I have eliminated the rectangle (the big shapes still felt).
I have brought it into actual space (relief) back and forth.
I have "inflated" the plane.

What's missing in the real objects copied, rather than posters and ads, is the realistic justification for artificiality of form and color. The introduction of mass expression.

Painting wanting to be handkerchief, etc., subject for another written piece. Written pieces should be as much challenge to interpretation as work itself.
But also some words about a store.
1. In form, open, contrast to closed environment. Airy. Surroundings.
2. Content. Inarticulate, proletarian objects, materials.
3. Irony of the commodity object as art versus art object as commodity.
4. Universals in form and content. Similarities, puns.
5. Etc.

Power of Egyptian, Persian, etc., *grottes sacres*.

Debts to Pollock's use of paint. Direct. "Real" paint.

Explication: purse equals mouth. Coins equals cry—that is, word in concrete form, like balloon in earlier work.

Pure as Renaissance objects.

Strange when people took objects at face value, their effect for the obvious, like lady's shoes.

Fantasies on the right angle (pun). Ray Gun equals right angle equals leg equals handle (pun) equals seven, etc. Literary in art is a language of form. Communication through form, poetry through form. Calligraphy, that is the true "literary" art., i.e., the ideas are given formal body and then used.

This is a time, I think, for big and absolute acts, acts that affect people, and I have the feeling that this is very central to my thinking: I think art should be literally made of the ordinary world; the space should be our space, its time our time, its objects our ordinary objects; the reality of art will replace reality.

What I hope art will establish is a superreal vision far more inclusive than any previous idea of realism (including sur-realism); a triple vision seeing in and out and beyond, the sort of vision we shall someday all have . . . and my art is to prepare you for this, a place and actual space where the spectator learns to see my objects in relation to what he has accepted previously as real objects . . .

I will be expected to have a position, and what position do I have? At first it seemed I was a romantic, crashing against limitations, ferocious. Then it got cooler and dry. Now where am I? Ferocious again!

The studio for making art goes through different guises, now a store, next year perhaps a factory.

Ray Gun is both a French and Japanese word.

Guises of RG—prose with short poetic passages.

The goods in the stores, the billboards, the signs, wrappers, etc., all these things attract me very much, and I find myself wanting to imitate them. If I can do surrounding "environmental" form, so much the better!
In presenting them, I wish to imitate my means of perceiving them, as fragments of seeing, in a variety of scales and in a manner of accumulation.

Eroticism of commerce (later industry).

If the US values are business, then here is art flagrantly as business yet maintaining its distinction and even its opposition.

Museum people are more sinister than gallery people.

I am a moralist. I would say: face yourself even if it means destruction. It usually doesn't, only seems to, and besides humanity is invoked at any point to halt a destructive path if possible.

Robert Whitman makes one very careful of one's values and integrity, very aware of

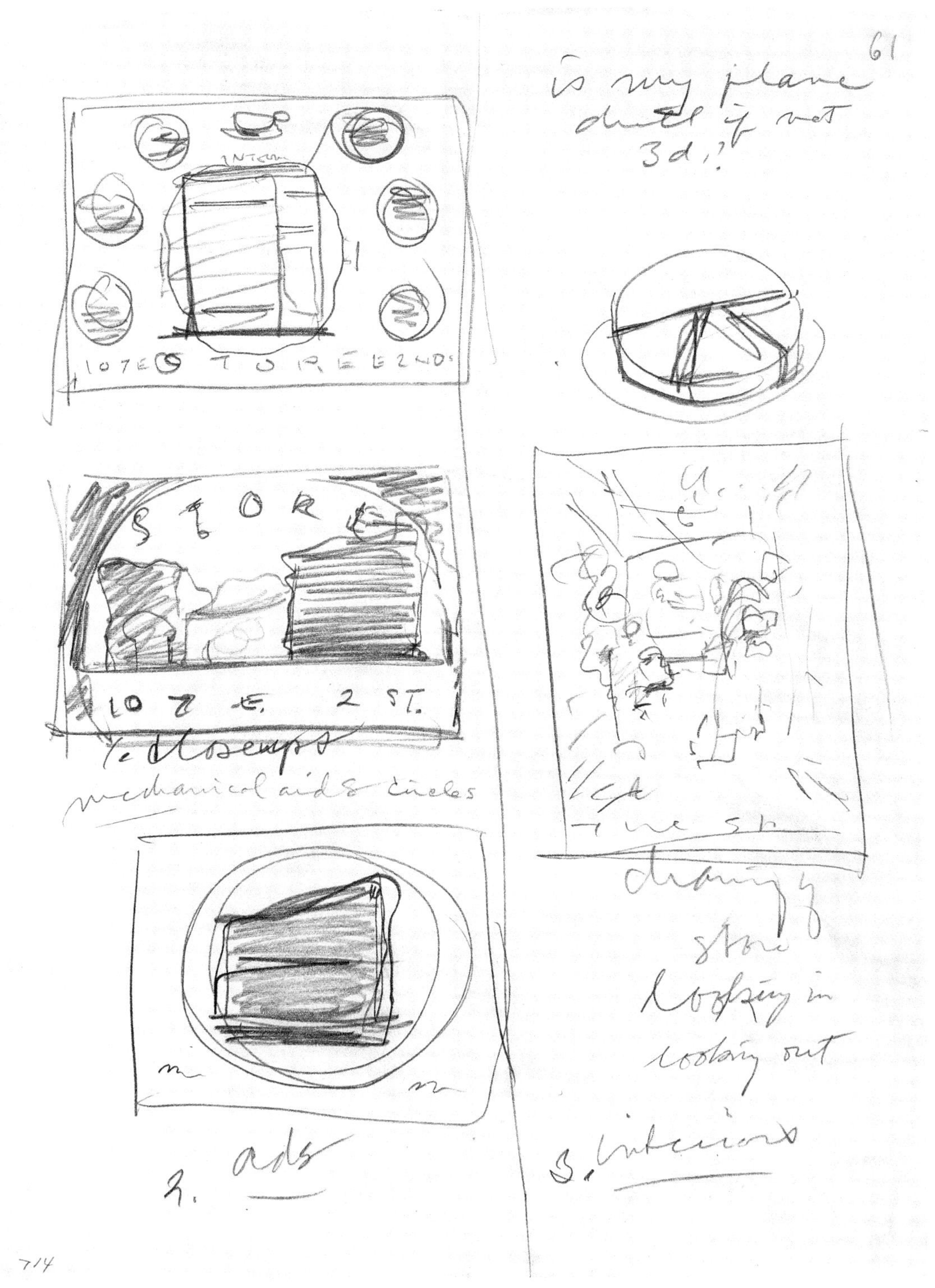

Notebook Page: Studies for Store Business Card, 1961

ideals. I respect this and always feel chastened and instructed after a visit to the country there. To get my ideals polished up.

The Store should be on 14th St. or 6th Ave.

The fragmentation is the concrete realization of vision, passing from one item to another in multitude. The fragments are the naive realization of the piece "torn" from reality. Literal application of this metaphor. I am convinced originality is achieved through naiveté and literalness. Torn—birth flesh-fragments. I think of space as being material like I think of the stage as being a solid cube or a hollow box to be broken. So a hallucination basic to my work is that of the continuity of matter, that air and the things in it are one, are HARD, and that you can RIP a piece of air and the thing in it out of it, so that a piece of object and a whole object and just air, space, comes as one piece. This is, in my hallucination, accompanied by a RIPPING SOUND. I trust hallucination as much as naiveté for originality of vision.

How to get these new forms and colors into my system of feeling so that, f.ex., brilliant, simple color is sad and not (which is what it usually is) happy.

A social artist, or rather a *political* artist.

Ray Gun Cabaret would have a political orientation much lefter than American Liberal style. An antibourgeois cabaret, anticapitalist cabaret.

Dolores's pants.

Art without political orientation is dead, somehow unplugged in.

The Store is a proletarian declaration or a declaration for the people. An art for people and about people is a strong concern of mine, even if I don't think so sometimes. This realization of being a political artist always wakes me up.

In my performances, it follows that the audience is not placed inside or in any involvement with some shape or condition that I have created for this purpose. They are spectators, at my vision, and that is why I use the separation of spectators and action. Anything more than this seems to me a contrivance. This is not to say I do not freely use the space above and behind or even within the spectators.

In my three performances so far, I have by degrees extended the interval of vision. In *Snapshots from the City*, the vision was instantaneous (32 illuminations of action continuing in total darkness). In *Blackouts*, vision encompassed a simple action or a whole image, illuminating this in darkness. In *Circus*, several simple actions and whole images, in repetition, took place simultaneously during a rather long period of light.

(If you strive to be consistent, you never get a statement.)

One of the reasons I am so attached to Céline is his constant sense of death. My work is full of incomprehensible menaces and the presence of death. In summarizing experience, which I always aim at, I find that death must be assigned a large role. Memorials, charms to keep death away. I always think of "the skull beneath the skin."

My work always aims to give a large picture through some concentrated symbol.

The reason I do not make expository statements about my art is that I always know enough to find them either bad stylistically or wanting in truth. My preference is for a literary parallel statement, which helps in a subtler way and as openly (poetically) to make the visually illiterate or anyone, for that matter, see.

RG—nothing is irrelevant, i.e., anything can be used.

White ground equals natural ground. The Store, an efflorescence. Additive principle. Clusters. Agglomeration. Magnetic attraction. Extension. Flaming chairs. And tables. Outrushing pictures on the wall. Movables? All moving—earthquake.

A sign store and a body-painting store.

A store is honest, old-fashioned, and the goods in it are real. Art sold in a gallery store is dishonest, fashionable, and unreal goods.

Alphabet erotics: (letter, word, as image)
A—spread legs, crotch
B—balls, boobs (on side)
C—cunt (incomplete O)
D—(?) inert dummy
E—if tongue is projected farther than arms (opposites equal) then cock and balls, garter belt, crown
F—Ray Gun, pistol, strong phallic

Artists' Parties
Parties to which rivals are invited as friends. The natural form of such a party is organized violence toward one another. Abusive verbal attacks. Wrestling matches. Degradations.
Finale: everyone dances about in the nude. After violence and attack, honesty, nakedness.

Of my two statements, the first is true, the second false. There are always two statements.

It is a matter of the relative coolness of the style . . . that the expressionist object appears

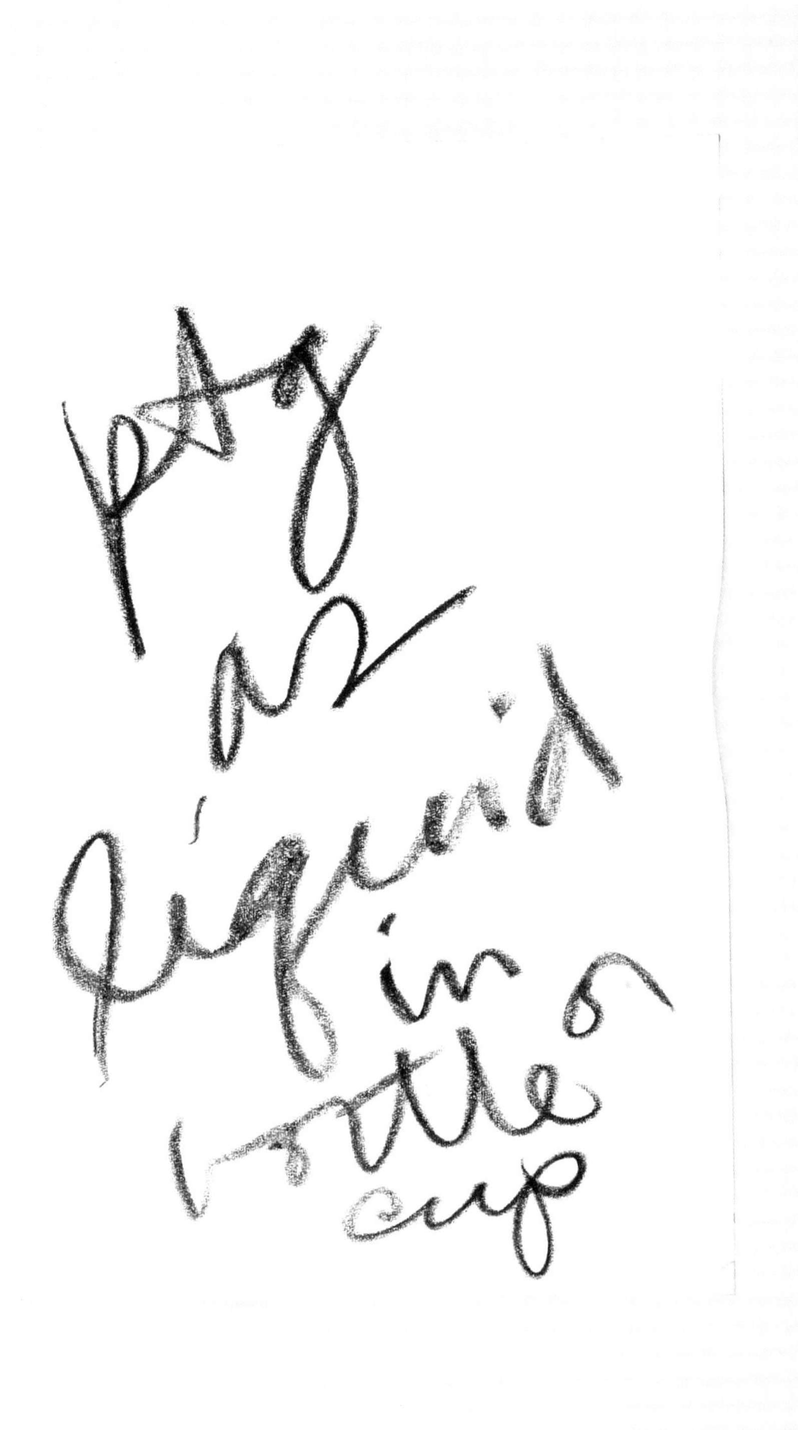

Notebook page: "ptg as liquid . . .," 1962

objective. The ordinary object, without distortion, appears charged or "mysterious."
My Store, however, is highly expressionist. The distortion in criticism re: the Store is just
that: it is not understood as expressionistic.

A Performance Saying Goodbye to the Year 1961, Which Will Never Come Again.

Very much at the limits, thinking of thousands of impossible acts as if they could be real.

Starting February 1, I will compose a piece for a theater of objects to publicly culminate
February 21. This performance has as yet no name (since a name is as important as any
other object). The motive for composition is supplied by a pie next to a bicycle on the
floor near my toilet.

Store . . . Art equals Eros. Know that, but art equals food. Important. Art equals food,
and it equals sex.

Relation to reality is furthered by the composition through organic fragments. This is
shown in photos: the piece leaves off, real things begin. Develop. Function of fragment.

Plaster. I am working while Pat is plastering. Plaster is such a part of living where I live,
uneven plaster.

The performances are lyrical and somber, in such contrast to the plaster sculptures. So
past to their present.

I think this will be the painter's theater or sculptor's theater I have in mind: starting with
pure form but not excluding idea, however keeping the form in mind always first, just as
I do in my painting or sculpture. So that it becomes a theater of form.

THEATER OF FORM

Think how much time I spend on the form itself.

Going into the area of theater, I am very concerned I might lose my definition as a
painter or a sculptor, and I have no desire to do this. My attempts at theater might be
better understood as attempts at the extension of painting and sculpture.

Brush of mixed colors bleeding. Blood.

I see reality through a haze (like Mallarmé's description with smoke). I don't see anything
very correctly and reality always surprises me. I am essentially a dreaming type, reality as
I see it is a dream of mine, or reality mixes with my dreams.

Don't forget the Aileen Passloff costumes represent a definite solution: "real" color, taxicabs, f.ex. Painting *as an object* derived from reality: a painted object. And it is part of my plaster pieces really and what I intend to develop with them.

Experience is only a dream. Past and present are equal. The world is full of ghosts. The simplest things look peculiar. This, as I've affirmed again and again, is not a political vision. Or ethical. Or contemporary. Or new. It is just my insides, human insides. Solipsism. I simply extract the reflection of myself from my experience.

Staticity of the erotic image. A visual voyeur action. It is not important that the subject do anything but that all the details are noted by the voyeur, and so a voyeur movie is almost static, which gives it its peculiar quality. This is a model for a painter's theater—a theater for the eyes.

One must prolong the simple action to the point where people begin to *see* it and do not just expect one to be succeeded by another.

The pace ought to be contemplative and the images clear.

Being on stage, one has no idea of the whole effect.

Everything I do is a grand image of my experience that is today in America (no patriotism, just the fact that I'm here). Bad form interests me. Bringing it off as good form, of course, but the groping failure of form of popsy expression.

Let us get it in focus.
My work, the performances, romantic and perverse and satiric-destructive, yet I must defend myself. I mean, where do I stand in relation to the other great, elaborate, and costly things going on in New York? It is a poor man's theater. And where is it different from anything else going on? Where does it stand in relation to the very intellectual Mr. Kaprow? Is it a Happening, or something else? Fragments rescued from reality. Isn't it more like a play? But above all, am I worth coming to see? It is a poor man's theater, and the lead is a beggar.

Essentially my art is comic—a serious, absurd comedy. Comic, irreverent, and erotical . . . moralistic. Having to do with values. Universal comedy or deep comedy.

My characters are the city-bird-child (chick) and the beggar. Innocence and experience. That is my theme: innocence versus experience (or evil). Good versus evil. Comic innocence. Pat.

The irony of my going to a new place to do a performance, like Dallas, is that wherever I go I am still in my own world . . . preposterous to look for the "soul of the community." I simply try to find a congenial situation to my imagination . . .

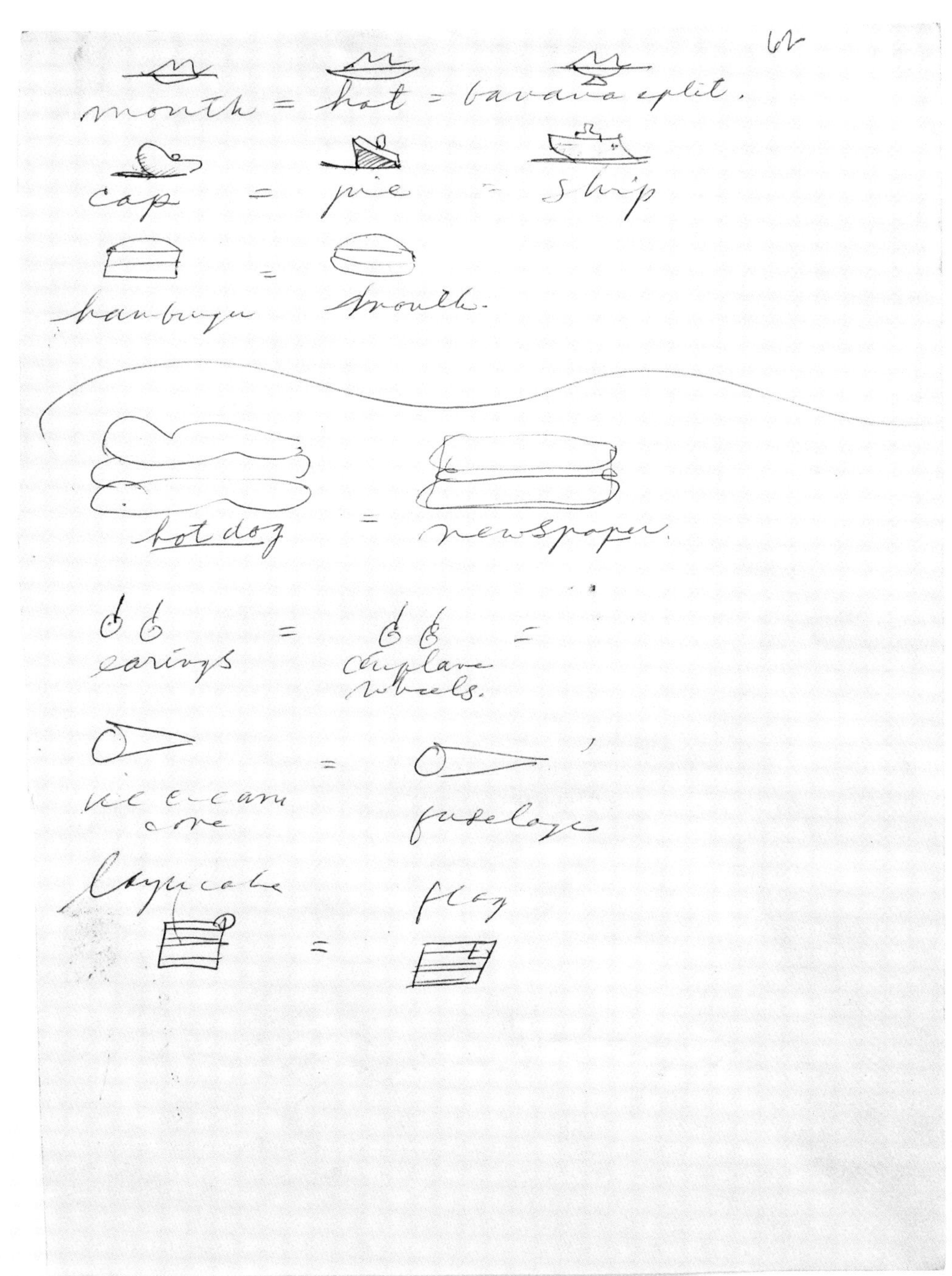

Notebook Page: "mouth=hat=banana split/cap=pie=ship/hamburger=mouth/hot dog=newspaper/earings=airplane wheels=/icecream cone=fuselage/layercake=flag/plane=hot dog," 1962

Bad Dreams and Good Dreams
Dreams of the Rough and the Smooth

Iconography of the flag. The flag in color equals the free painting (both cloth).

The plaster in my bathroom is very nice. Same goes for the hall, which is now being painted with shiny enamel. There's a lot of noise from the house in back, but we like it even if the guys all sing off-key at once. New York wouldn't be much without Puerto Rico. Now and then the Ferris wheel on the truck comes down the street or the ice-cream truck with its ship-bell. My wife comes in and twists my nose, and that is how it goes.

The erotic or the sexual is the root of "art," its first impulse. Today sexuality is more directed, here where I am in America at this time, toward substitutes, f.ex., clothing rather than the person, fetishistic stuff, and this gives the object an intensity, and this is what I try to project.

I want these pieces to have an unbridled, intense satanic vulgarity unsurpassable, and yet be art.

New York equals a sewing machine. How sad.

The bourgeois artist goes to the Museum. Instead of going to the Museum, I go to the Store.

Manifesto of an Artist NYC 1961
Good morning
My wife's back
Latin songs
Dropped bags of crap
Dropped iceboxes
Smashing glass
My wife's hair
Cat's meows
Firecracker blasts
Pigeons, coop
Cars starting up
My wife's tough tits

Guises of RG, i.e., like faith forced under *any* system to dwell in disguises.
As the artist in his disguises.
As art in its disguises.
As the power of seeing truth in its disguises.
As the self in its disguises.
As religion in its disguises.

RG as the street. RG as the store. RG as the factory!

Some performances are mystical "seances."

The Store tries to overcome the sense of guilt connected with money and sales, which the artist has either inherited, or to rationalize his lack of ability to make money . . . it is to say money is life. It is plenty . . . it is psychological . . . articles are child or substitute . . . Commerce is organic and psychological. Thus again, unity . . . no separation between commerce and art.

Store as sex. Storage—womb, breast, testicles, any containing part of body. Whorehouse as in Céline—the notion shop, store as cunt, cunt as notion store, mysteries in back, curtain after curtain, gypsy store. Store on street—love, quick love, in and out. Outside passersby and voices. Backroom of store.

The Store windows I see now serve as models for clusters. Eye clusters formal model for a kind of visual experience: fragmentation, simultaneousness, superimposition, which I wish to recreate in the clusters. That is to move from the notion of the re-creation of the Store into symbol. Scale too is now set as smaller. Perhaps free clusters in air and not only of plaster.

Vocabulary
Glass: 1. Eye. 2. Separations: Inside/outside. Examples: Store window, pastry cases.
Gun: 1. Kid's toy. 2. Seeing through walls. 3. The universal angle. Examples—Simple Ray Guns: Legs, Sevens, Pistols, Arms, Phalli; Double Ray Guns: Cross, Airplane; Absurd Ray Guns: Ice-Cream Sodas; Complex Ray Guns: Chairs, Beds. 4. Anagrams and homophonies: Nug Yar (New York). Reuben (Gallery). 5. Accidental references: A movie house in Harlem. A nuclear-testing site in the Sahara (Ragon). 6. Whatever is needed. A word ought to be useful. 7. Cryptic sayings: "All will see as Ray Gun sees." "The name of New York will be changed to Ray Gun." "When Ray Gun shoots, no one dies." 8. Talismanic, fetishistic functions.
Store: 1. EROS 2. Stomach 3. Memory. Enter My Store.

Scenario for film. THE ROOM.
Very quiet film (in film, motion media emphasizes lack of motion, as in art, static media emphasizes motion). Always opposite, emphasis through contrast, yes.
Into the room from a dark door. Perhaps a kitchen. Either very realistic or curiously made (like my objects).
Close inspection of all objects in various lights. A cockroach. A fly.
Something falls. Mystery mystery.
Inconclusive ending.

The Store
May be better understood if it is considered not itself a psychological statement but

a collection of psychological statements that exist concretely in the form of signs and advertisements. Placement and relation unfixed, free. An imitation not of nature but nature altered toward psychology, which is to say: the landscape of the *city*.

In a dream. The whole world is my objects, my theater.

I have got love all mixed up with art. I have got my sentiments for the world all mixed up with art. I am a disaster as an artist because I can't leave the world alone.

Ray Gun is my magic guise, my alchemical title.

From this point of vantage, RG theater considers itself as sort of a simple, allegorical folk theater, quite unsophisticated, with the aim of eliciting authentic, instinctive values . . . supplying an elementary romance slightly vitiated by the culture around. It is not escapist . . .

I am very grateful to the audience for coming each weekend. I cannot deny it is good to have an audience, though the nature of this theater is such that it would go on without an audience as a painter might go on painting with no one to watch him . . . This space has great limitations, I am aware of this . . . partly I enjoy the pressure these limitations put on me . . . I mean, the time, the expense, and the space . . . I hope you are not too miserable . . . My aim is to develop, under the concentrated circumstances, a sort of kernel of infinite expansion . . . so that at the end of this season I shall have ten extremely powerful seeds. It is becoming obvious, I guess, that these pieces are not unrelated . . . the Happening, which was in the beginning a very limited form, is bearing fruit as a new physical theater, bringing to the dry puritan forms of the US stage the possibilities of a tremendous, enveloping force . . .

Sumra Lyrix

Melodys yah yah Melodys out of softy Sue Sally mouths uprounded
like softy fish tickly like fishtailsy Yum! and the great iron bar
of their historical cut-tounges go hoof in likada Xpress!

At Cony on the false leather the big bricks of their hotkisses hang
on your cheeks like shit the size of ferry-boats I erect indeed from
Bklyn to the Batry plunging and spinning ninety bends and guards and
tiles and all

Gorsch how do NY hang down wid itz cackly garterwood fencys and
brainstones spurting and blurping in the Bay
Yeh bah! ef up it went then Jersy chase Newrk inter de Watchungs Yup
an dem go all spillocking ap by der Pockinoos   Uu Bah!
Dam ga op in spoim all da coins uf da mine All deezze litul applul-
places!
•

Two Lyrics

Oooopung die ize
Yaetchout die tung
Fiel all mieyovr
Ohwhow de katt krys
Mye Mye

Teddy bears jump
tump i dump dump
jump i dump tumpi
dum dump
jeddy bears tump jump
teddy bears jump
•

An Artist's Stateroom
(Watement)

Deathtest subsatitooties
Deathtest pixchus
Datest asbababsasatrefaction
No sabstrefaction pewstivvly
GIBBUZ ZA TING!
Lag Fleg Dug
Con Lump Tung
Yah Tungz!
•

Wat I Makz Iz Konkrete Tawts

Wat I Makz Iz
Konkrete Tawts
Ideeuz n tawts in plastra
as uf litenun in send!
zip zop

feeluns n plastra potry
KONKENTRATN IN KNONKRETE
•

Ow Flag

Floog fli flup flup fluffderaff flopp flopp imbloo
flapty flup flup wind poopoof ohbing bantybrap brap floop
so sing slag soverda sland sing now Yayayayatarayaya
Oh dah Sun mones. Yippy yap. Floop flup flagtyflagtyflat
•

Wat dwy den theink uv MRCA

Wat dwy den theink uv Mrca. Whats dwey dun thonk off Mrurky
Ossa qwidgeun lie nosup watta tjen schtink if Mrymyka. Witta
cake denn quink porf Amyamyamyamka. Owy dunno. Kint fink
kint fink fust foist caffe ausch must bahrf yink bloof blaff
whaddo eye dann sink of Yankyinkydoo. Wal wussy dead wuz
grew opp in midluklaes Myuka wantang noshtung moor abraz da
caffe schmall!

•

Postcards

Fum by im fleck wood
die blusmashed cawraecks
Passby schneefly
oukatta oukatta (tren)
en sew on

Ah die tots (tawts) fly yin
pess Berlin Meriden 'n owl (awl, ole) place
blu cawrex in wudes in wudes
snaw-flickt

Hartford slides in
Heaven shoving trinity by its horns
Its feelers, a bunch of black blocks
at the horizon pushed off the edge
of the table

Gold domes, eyes, fruits lying
under the downstaring cotton ice of the heaven bed
grayshimmering, spaton by birds
far away (oukatta, oukatta)

•

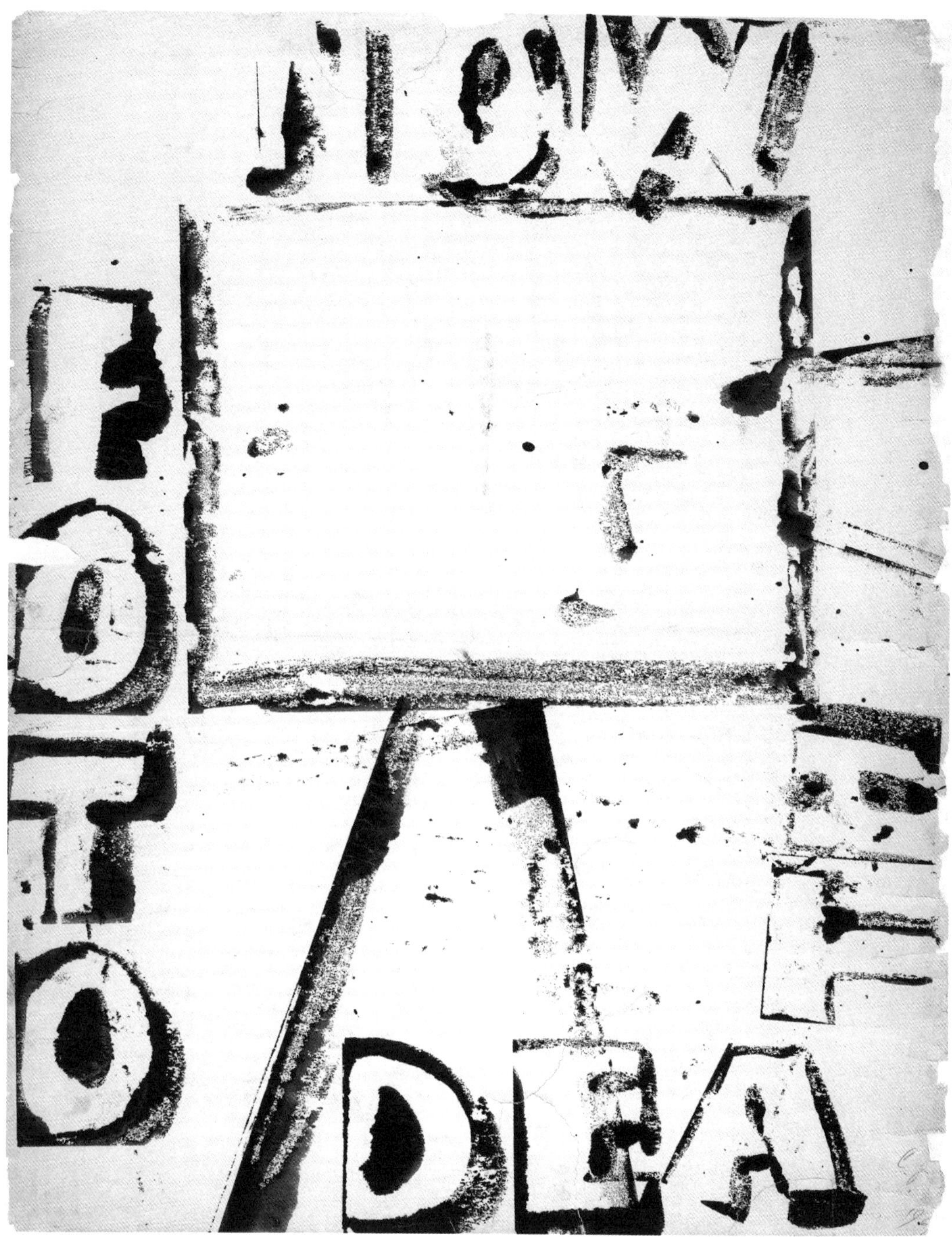

Poster for *Fotodeath*, 1961

FOTODEATH (Script, 1961)

I. Fotodeath

1. Pat's light   *Zone 1*
A man, Lucas, enters from L. in a plain, tight, fastidious suit. He admires himself in
many mirrors that he takes from his pockets. He lies down with a tall mirror, posing
himself in different ways, projecting himself upside down, etc.

Drum record: Chavez, all way thru

2. Scrim lights   *Zone 2*
The scrim is illuminated in pink and purple from behind. A girl, Olga, in a military cap
salutes and takes various patriotic poses in a shadow dance.

3. Light bank 3   *Zone 3*
Cliff, a wrestler, enters from R. in black tights, nude to the waist, with a pink, soft,
baglike object, a wrestler with which he wrestles fiercely.

Bugle sound

4. Light bank 4   TIMER   *Zone 4 L*
A woman, Judy, dressed as a man in hat, shirt, tie, and baggy suit, enters from L.,
goes to dresser, and undresses in front of mirror. She wears extremely feminine clothes
underneath. She admires herself as a woman then redresses as a man. She leaves L.,
taking mirror with her.

5. Henry's light   *Zone 4 R*
A photographer, Carl, in a shiny black smock and a top hat brings out a camera and
leads in a family of three to be photographed, Henry, Chippie, and Marilyn, sets them
on a bench, and then shows them several landscape samples. They disapprove. Finally
he finds one they will accept. He hangs it behind them, gets under the fotocloth, but the
family collapses. The photographer sets them up again, gets under the cloth. Again they
collapse, and so on.

When Timer leaves stage, the lights go out in the following sequence: 4—H—3—Pat's—
Scrim, *but let scrim lights and record play a while at end.*

In blackout, all leave stage or take new positions.

II. Fotodeath

1. Light bank 4   *Zone 4*
A woman, Pat, enters L. in long, dragging plumage and wings, very colorful and bizarrely made up. She walks slowly and artificially, only interested in herself. She pulls herself up and down the ladder in R. center, taking poses, sticking her leg out slowly, etc.

2. Light bank 2   *Zone 2*
Two girls, Claire and Judy, in summer white costumes suggesting 1913 and a summer day on the ferry in the bay, enter from R. One has a parasol. They walk slowly, laughing and chatting with each other. There are bells on their ankles or under their skirts, which jingle as they walk.

3. Light bank 1   *TIMER is Gloria*   *Zone 1*
A man in a coat and a woman with a happy birthday tiara in a coat, Henry and Gloria, enter R. She is carrying a piece of fresh ice, and one arm is in a black sling. She remains in the center, looking blankly. He knocks on door L. It opens, showing a packed party in progress. Squeals and talk, etc. He retreats. He reconsiders. He knocks again. Again the view into the party. He does this again and again. Finally he enters without knocking. The woman then leaves the stage.

4. Light bank 3   *Zone 3*
Two men, Lucas and Edgar, stumble in from L. They are drunk and make foul noises. One falls, the other picks him up. Then he, in turn, falls. They go back and forth, then both fall and remain still. Another man enters from R. corner Zone 4 with a bag of black cans. He falls over the fallen men, and the cans are thrown out on the floor. A fourth man enters with an empty bag and slowly picks up the cans. The other men lie still. The picker makes noises with the cans.

When Timer gets backstage, the lights are cut in the following sequence: 4—3—2—1, slowly so as to emphasize silhouettes. Actors stop when lights go out. Blackout. All leave or take new positions.

III. Fotodeath

1. Strip lights   *Zone 1*
Lights begin moving. After a while, Majorette steps out from R. and, saluting approximately at same rhythm, moves by single steps back and forth across the stage. She does this throughout, always smiling. Chippie.

2. Light band 2   *Zone 2*
A man, Lucas, with a bandaged head and a white chair, comes out from wall L. He sits down gingerly but it hurts. He grimaces. He picks up the chair, moves it, tries sitting again. But it still hurts. He grimaces, etc., back and forth across stage.

3. Light band 4   *Zone 4 L*
A woman, Gloria, in a derby hat, mannish, dressed in all black with a patriotic band across bodice, something like a Salvation Army woman, enters from R. She carries a black bag like a sample bag and a big can full of viscous liquid. She stops behind table center Zone 4 and takes out of the bag one by one, putting them on the table, numerous different objects of many colors but all marked clearly USA. It is as if she is demonstrating a product, but she has no expression on her face and says nothing. After piling up the objects, she pours from a huge can marked USA a viscous liquid, which runs over the objects and onto the floor. This she covers with a cloth marked USA. She remains standing over her work until blackout and forms a silhouette.

4. Henry's light   *Zone 4 R*
A man, Cliff, informally dressed, shirt open but wearing a jacket, drags in as if dead a woman, Olga, dressed in sweater and skirt. He sits her in a chair by a table on which a meal is set. He props her up. He sits down to eat. She falls forward on the table and keeps doing this until the eater loses his patience. Each time he props her up. Finally he reverses the chair so that she will not fall into his food. But now she slides down on the floor. He ignores her, and, having finished his meal, he wipes his mouth and leaves R.

5. Light band 3   *TIMER   Zone 3*
Two men, Carl and Edgar, bring out—from behind the audience, down the aisle—a top-heavy, tied-together mass of boxes painted black. It is a big object, which they manipulate with some difficulty into the center of action and leave there. Then they exit, like movers.

Billboard march begins quietly

When Timers come off, the lights go out in this sequence: 4—Henry's—3—2—Strip.

But very slowly, silhouetting first Gloria, then object, and finally on all alone, the strip lights for a time. The music continues softly until strips off, then off abruptly.

Blackout and all leave stage.

Light band 3 on, over object.

House light.

Notes on and changes in the existing script:

I.

1. Drum record was Carlos Chavez's "Concerto for Percussion."
2. The "scrim" referred to in script was the screen of muslin at
stage left.
3. The bugle sound was eliminated. Cliff wrestled with a white, stuffed laundry bag.
4. There was no dresser. Judy hung her clothes on the hat rack. Under the men's
clothing, she wore cotton stockings and an old-fashioned baggy, frilly yellow slip.
5. The landscape samples were fragments edged in black, ripped from a large
photomural of the Battery (which appears whole in rehearsal photographs).

II.

1. The plumage was made of long, tinted strips of muslin. The wings were eliminated.
A sound-effect record of cannonfire was played by the Operator.

III.

1. The "strip" lights were the lights above the wall across the stage. They were wired
to a knob, the turning of which lit one bulb then another in traveling effect, such as in
electric signs.
2. Lucas also wore an oversize GI raincoat.
3. The "viscous liquid" used was wheat paste.

LITTLE FILM SCENARIOS/PETITES SCENARIOS POUR CINEMA (1961)

Instructions: These are to be filmed in an obsessively scrutinizing manner, eliciting the language and the personality of the objects through repetitive devices, with total ambiguity as to "meaning."

I. Place: A modern apartment.
Radio is flipped on by a hand.
A man is talking to a girl.
Close-up of mouths. Cigarettes.
Close-up of her shoes. She removes one. It lies on the rug.
He coughs. Talks violently. Smoke rises.
She crosses her legs.
They are seen from a distance.
Close-up of her knees, shifting slightly. Their mouths.
A drink spills, runs off the table. (Some fragment of them is seen.)
A cat is observed, licking itself.
Close-up of removed shoe. Several shots. Appears large as a mountain or a car.
A cockroach runs across the back of the man's chair.
Close-up of ash flick by man. Ashes on rug. Tapping of foot.
Phone rings (no sound, conveyed by concentration). He takes it.
The girl (who wears a hat) is looking around the room meanwhile.
Close-up of flowers. A pencil. A bottle. People seen from the point of view of the objects, through them.
Close-up. Her lips eating a candy. Front. Side. Moving.
His mouth talking on the phone.
Several shots of the girl's face bent down, absorbed.

Sound: Radio throughout, loud, soft, near, distant.

II. Place: A room. A bathroom adjoining.
Papers of a book flipped restlessly. Book slammed down.
Bare feet across room. Close-up of rough floor.
A black woman's head of hair seen on the edge of a white bathtub. Water moving (no part of face seen).
Man writes notes violently.
She is picking pimples in the tub, using a hand mirror, which reflects light into the adjoining room.
View under the tub. Broken-up floor. A cat moving deep under in darkness.
Bottles lined on a shelf.

Stiff plastic curtains stir in breeze through a small window.

He writes. Sweating.

She leans her hair back, dunking it in the water, pulling it slowly in and out. She leans forward and coughs.

Sound: Distant street sounds, arguments, cars, songs . . .

III. Place: A roof.

A chimney is belching black smoke. A wind is blowing.

A man looks at a clock that he takes out of his pocket.

He squeezes a woman he has his arms around.

She glances behind them anxiously.

Close-up of smoke. Compared to her hair, long, black, blowing in wind.

Across the way, someone is dressing vaguely in a room.

A kid stands looking blankly on a fire escape.

Man extends his fingers to a pigeon, who flies away.

The woman glances back. Her hair. The smoke, thicker than ever.

Her leg as it starts to walk. Her mouth laughing.

Distance shot of them on the roof, chimney near.

Rain. Rain runs down her cheeks. He sneezes. She squints. Rain runs down her clothes and stockings.

IV. Place: An artist's studio.

A nude girl, the model, heavily made up, black and white, gets off a bicycle she has been trying, which stands in the studio.

The artist in his undershirt spits on the floor, rubs it with his shoes.

View out the window, trees, ocean ruffled by breezes.

He tweaks her nipple. Instantly: pencil set on a paper, clean.

Her eyes, gazing at bicycle.

His mouth cursing.

She scratches. Books.

Still of pencil on paper.

Increasing darkness. Her face almost unseen. Electric light lit.

View out window: sunset. A face across the way.

Artist spits out window. The model rests. She smells her fingers.

Giggles like child, climbs on bicycle.

She slaps him. (Another time.)

He is showing a painting to someone, a woman wearing a hat. The model comes up from behind, pushes her hat off, and musses hair, throws lighted matches. He chases her, knocking over woman.

He pours wine into her hair from behind, pushes her away.

The artist disappears.
No one knows where he went.
He leaves his signs here and there.
He is seen in his part of town and, the next moment, miraculously,
on the other side of town.
One senses him rather than sees him—
A lounger, a drunkard. A tennis player, a bicycle rider,
always violently denying that he did it.
Everyone gives a different description of the criminal.

I am for an art that is political-erotical-mystical, that does something other than sit on its ass in a museum.

I am for an art that grows up not knowing it is art at all, an art given the chance of having a starting point of zero.

I am for an art that embroils itself with the everyday crap and still comes out on top.

I am for an art that imitates the human, that is comic, if necessary, or violent, or whatever is necessary.

I am for an art that takes its form from the lines of life itself, that twists and extends and accumulates and spits and drips, and is heavy and coarse and blunt and sweet and stupid as life itself.

I am for an artist who vanishes, turning up in a white cap painting signs or hallways.

I am for art that comes out of a chimney like black hair and scatters in the sky.

I am for art that spills out of an old man's purse when he is bounced off a passing fender.

I am for the art out of a doggie's mouth, falling five stories from the roof.

I am for the art that a kid licks, after peeling away the wrapper.

I am for an art that joggles like everyone's knees, when the bus traverses an excavation.

I am for art that is smoked like a cigarette, smells like a pair of shoes.

I am for art that flaps like a flag, or helps blow noses like a handkerchief.

I am for art that is put on and taken off like pants, which develops holes like socks, which is eaten like a piece of pie, or abandoned with great contempt like a piece of shit.

I am for art covered with bandages. I am for art that limps and rolls and runs and jumps.

I am for art that comes in a can or washes up on the shore.

I am for art that coils and grunts like a wrestler. I am for art that sheds hair.

I am for art you can sit on. I am for art you can pick your nose with or stub your toes on.

I am for art from a pocket, from deep channels of the ear, from the edge of a knife, from the corners of the mouth, stuck in the eye or worn on the wrist.

I am for art under the skirts, and the art of pinching cockroaches.

I am for the art of conversation between the sidewalk and a blind man's metal stick.

I am for the art that grows in a pot, that comes down out of the skies at night, like lightning, that hides in the clouds and growls. I am for art that is flipped on and off with a switch.

I am for art that unfolds like a map, that you can squeeze like your sweetie's arm, or kiss like a pet dog. Which expands and squeaks like an accordion, which you can spill your dinner on like an old tablecloth.

I am for an art that you can hammer with, stitch with, sew with, paste with, file with.

I am for an art that tells you the time of the day, or where such and such a street is.
I am for an art that helps old ladies across the street.

I am for the art of the washing machine. I am for the art of a government check. I am for the art of last war's raincoat.
I am for the art that comes up in fogs from sewer holes in winter. I am for the art that splits when you step on a frozen puddle. I am for the worm's art inside the apple. I am for the art of sweat that develops between crossed legs.

I am for the art of neck hair and caked teacups, for the art between the tines of restaurant forks, for the odor of boiling dishwater.
I am for the art of sailing on Sunday, and the art of red-and-white gasoline pumps.
I am for the art of bright blue factory columns and blinking biscuit signs.
I am for the art of cheap plaster and enamel. I am for the art of worn marble and smashed slate. I am for the art of rolling cobblestones and sliding sand. I am for the art of slag and black coal. I am for the art of dead birds.
I am for the art of scratching in the asphalt, daubing at the walls. I am for the art of bending and kicking metal and breaking glass, and pulling at things to make them fall down.

I am for the art of punching and skinned knees and sat-on bananas. I am for the art of kids' smells. I am for the art of mama-babble.
I am for the art of bar-babble, tooth-picking, beer-drinking, egg-salting, in-sulting. I am for the art of falling off a barstool.

I am for the art of underwear and the art of taxicabs. I am for the art of ice-cream cones dropped on concrete. I am for the majestic art of dog turds, rising like cathedrals.

I am for the blinking arts, lighting up the night. I am for art falling, splashing, wiggling, jumping, going on and off.
I am for the art of fat truck tires and black eyes.
I am for Kool art, 7Up art, Pepsi art, Sunshine art, 39 cents art, 15 cents art, Vatronol art, Dro-bomb art, Vam art, Menthol art, L&M art, Exlax art, Venida art, Heaven Hill art, Pamryl art, San-o-med art, Rx art, 9.99 art, Now art, New art, How art, Fire Sale art, Last Chance art, Only art, Diamond art, Tomorrow art, Franks art, Ducks art, Meat-o-rama art.

I am for the art of bread wet by rain. I am for the rats' dance between floors. I am for the art of flies walking on a slick pear in the electric light. I am for the art of soggy onions and firm green shoots. I am for the art of clicking among the nuts when the roaches come and go. I am for the brown, sad art of rotting apples.
I am for the art of meows and clatter of cats and for the art of their dumb electric eyes.
I am for the white art of refrigerators and their muscular openings and closings.

I am for the art of rust and mold. I am for the art of hearts, funeral hearts or sweetheart hearts, full of nougat. I am for the art of worn meat hooks and singing barrels of red, white, blue, and yellow meat.
I am for the art of things lost or thrown away, coming home from school. I am for the art of cock-and-ball trees and flying cows and the noise of rectangles and squares. I am for the art of crayons and weak, gray pencil lead, and grainy wash and sticky oil paint, and the art of windshield wipers and the art of the finger on a cold window, on dusty steel or in the bubbles on the sides of a bathtub.
I am for the art of teddy bears and guns and decapitated rabbits, exploded umbrellas, raped beds, chairs with their brown bones broken, burning trees, firecracker ends, chicken bones, pigeon bones, and boxes with men sleeping in them.

I am for the art of slightly rotten funeral flowers, hung bloody rabbits and wrinkly yellow chickens, bass drums and tambourines, and plastic phonographs.
I am for the art of abandoned boxes, tied like pharaohs. I am for an art of water tanks and speeding clouds and flapping shades.
I am for US Government Inspected Art, Grade A art, Regular Price art, Yellow Ripe art, Extra Fancy art, Ready-to-Eat art, Best-for-Less art, Ready-to-Cook art, Fully Cleaned art, Spend Less art, Eat Butter art, Ham art, pork art, chicken art, tomato art, banana art, apple art, turkey art, cake art, cookie art . . .

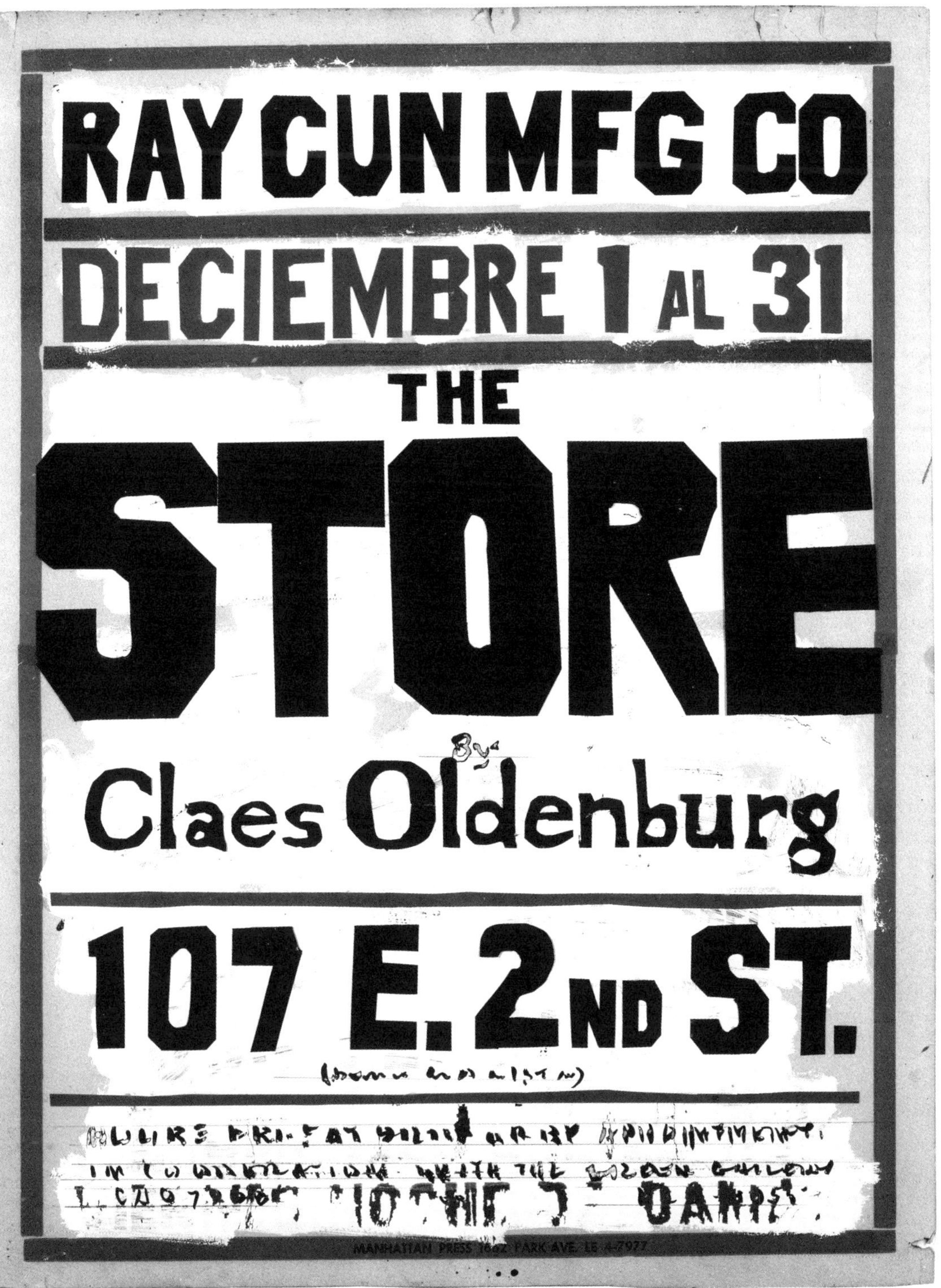

Study for a Poster, The Store, 1961

Enter Papa Nosedrop waving a
huge ugly object. From the sky all
sorts of valuable objects begin falling
and sailing. Shirts, shoes, coats, girdles,
bras, electric thises and thatses.
The contents of the whole Sunday
Edition!

The Store, or My Store, or the Ray Gun Mfg. Co., located at 107 East 2nd St., NYC, is eighty feet long and is about ten feet wide. In the front half, it is my intention to create the environment of a store by painting and placing (hanging, projecting, lying) objects after the spirit and in the form of popular objects of merchandise, such as may be seen in stores and store windows of the city, especially in the area where *The Store* is (Clinton St., for example, Delancey St., 14th St.).

This store will be constantly supplied with new objects, which I will create out of plaster and other materials in the rear half of the place. The objects will be for sale in *The Store*.

The Store will be open every day at hours I will post. For example, 10 a.m.–2 p.m. and 5–7 p.m., or the hours when I will be able to be in *The Store*, which is also, of course, my studio.

The Store may be thought of as a season-long exhibit, with changing and new material. It will be the center of my activities during the season.

The rent of the store is $60 per month, including steam heat and hot and cold water. Additional money will be needed to paint and plaster the front half and to make objects. Rent for 10 months—$600. Additional money to equip store—$150. Money to make objects—$250 ($24 per month). Total $1000.

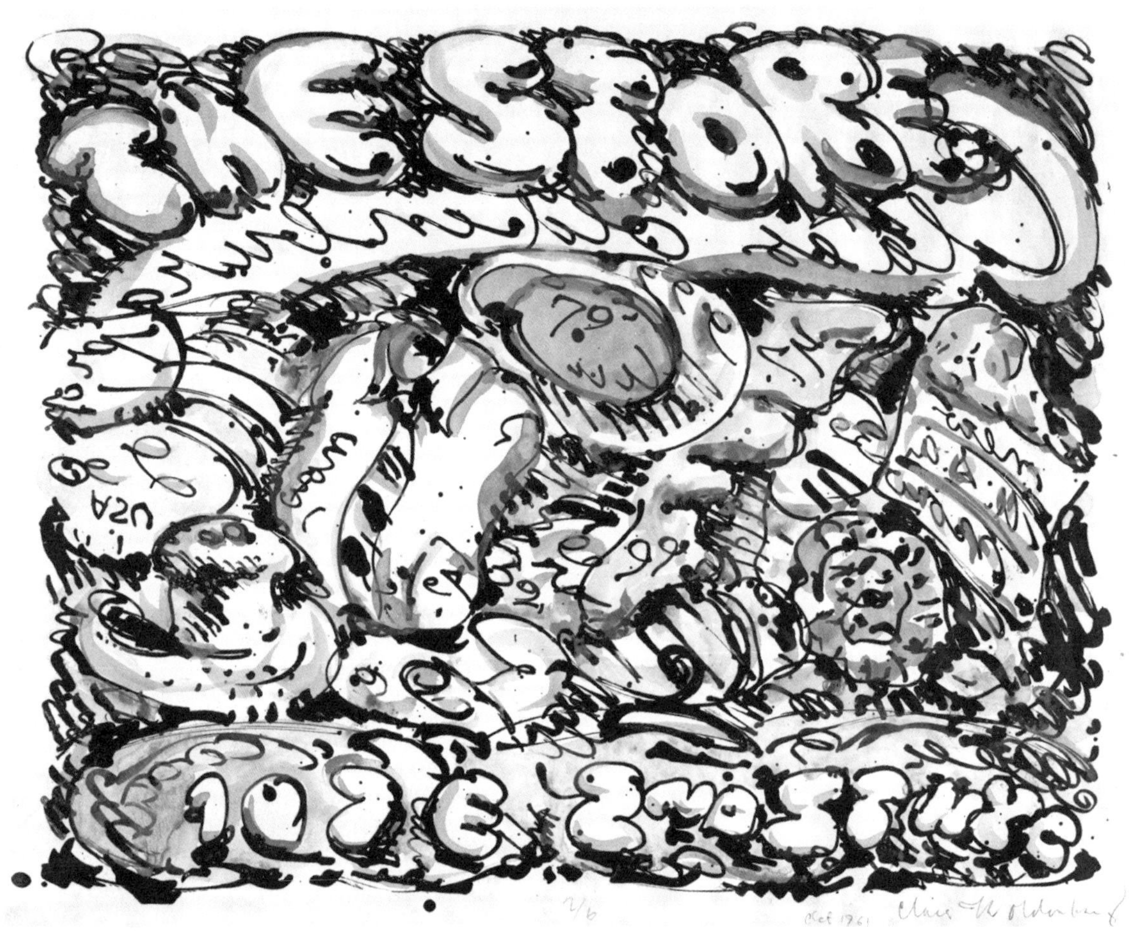

Store Poster, 1961

INVENTORY OF STORE DEC. 1961 (1961)

1. 9.99	free hanging	$ 399.95
2. 39 cents	relief	198.99
3. Store Ray-Gun	free hanging	249.95
4. Success Plant	free standing	249.99
5. "To My Love," Inscription from Cake	relief	149.95
6. Cash Register	free standing	349.99
7. US Flag Fragment	relief	297.95
8. Bunting	relief	149.99
9. Times Square Figure	free standing	149.98
10. Statue of Liberty Souvenir	free standing	169.98
11. Funeral Heart	relief	349.98
12. Store Cross	relief	399.98
13. Wedding Bouquet	free hanging	229.89
14. Bride Manikin	free standing	899.95
15. Injun Souvenir	free standing	124.99
16. Toy Ray Gun	free lying	34.99
17. Manikin with One Leg	free standing	499.98
18. Auto Tire with Fragment of Price	relief	449.69
19. Iron Fragment	relief	449.95
20. Sewing Machine	relief	449.99
21. Rings Fragment	relief	199.98
22. Wrist Watch on Blue	relief	295.98
23. Cigarette and Smoke	free hanging	99.95
24. Girl, Flag, Cigarettes	reliefs on wood	198.99
25. Cigarettes in Pack Fragment	relief	499.99
26. Pepsi-Cola Sign	relief	399.98
27. Oranges	relief	279.89
28. Orange Juice	relief	199.95
29. Plate of Meat	relief	399.98
30. Bacon & Egg	relief	229.95
31. Big Sandwich	relief	149.98
32. Red Pie	relief	399.95
33. Small Yellow Pie	relief	169.99
34. Four Flat Pies in a Row	free standing	149.95
35. Ice Cream Bar	free standing	169.99
36. Ice Cream Cake	relief	169.99
37. Ice Cream Cone and Heel	relief	124.95
38. Red Sausages	relief	199.98
39. Chocolates in Box (Fragment)	relief	399.98

40. Stockinged Thighs Framed by Skirt (Stocking Advertisement Fragment)	relief	299.95
41. Four Flat Panties in a Row	free standing	149.95
42. Blue and Pink Panties	relief	349.99
43. Green Stockings	relief	169.95
44. Blue Legs	relief	299.99
45. Green Legs with Shoes	relief	299.99
46. Black Girdle	relief	249.95
47. Red Tights with Fragment 9	relief	395.99
48. Braselette	relief	299.95
49. Fur Jacket with White Gloves	relief	324.95
50. Small Beauty Parlor Face	relief	49.99
51. Large Beauty Parlor Face	plasterboard on wood plaque	69.98
52. Pink Cap	relief	299.89
53. Two Hats	relief	249.99
54. Dress Jacket	enamel on plaster on paper	49.95
55. Man's Shoe	relief	199.99
56. Mu-Mu	relief	449.19
57. Blouse	projecting relief	299.95
58. Three Ladies' Stockings	free hanging	99.99
59. Black Ladies' Shoe	free mounted	125.95
60. Yellow Girls' Dress	relief	249.99
61. Red Cap	free standing	199.95
62. Man's Sock	free hanging	199.95
63. White Gym Shoes	free standing	129.99
64. Ties	free standing	129.99
65. Blue Shirt, Striped Tie	free standing	149.95
66. Men's Jacket with Shirt and Tie	free hanging	399.95
67. Jacket and Shirt Fragment	relief	249.99
68. Big White Shirt with Blue Tie	free standing	399.95
69. Big Necklace	free hanging	199.95
70. Earrings (Drop Form)	free hanging	44.98
71. Watch in a Red Box	free standing	129.95
72. Two Girls' Dresses	relief	349.99
73. Counter and Plates with Potato & Ham	free standing	279.98
74. Cakes in a Glass Box	free standing	324.98
75. Candy Counter with Candy	free standing	399.97
76. Candy Bar	free lying	49.95
77. Four Pies in a Glass Case		249.99
78. Blonde Pie	free standing	149.95
79. "Vulgar" Pie	free standing	124.95
80. Flat Long Pastry	free standing	169.99
81. Strawberry Shortcake	free standing	84.95

82. Big Chocolate Cake	free standing	149.98
83. Half Cheese Cake	free standing	149.98
84. Cheese Cake	free standing	124.99
85. Striped Cake Slice	free standing	44.95
86. Cherry Pastry	free standing	44.98
87. Shell Cookie	free lying (with plate)	29.95
88. Cube Pastry	free standing	24.98
89. Three Jelly Doughnuts	free lying	99.99
90. Plate of Assorted Pastries	free standing	124.99
91. Two Danish & Turnover	free lying (with plate)	149.95
92. Two Loaves of Bread, One Cut	free standing	349.99
93. Sandwich	free lying	74.98
94. Pile of Toast	free lying	149.89
95. Carrots	free hanging	99.98
96. Liver Sausage & Slices	free lying	149.95
97. Fried Chicken (2)	free lying	99.98
98. Sardine Can with 2 Sardines on Paper Bag	free standing	124.97
99. Roast	free lying or hanging	179.98
100. Fried Egg in Pan	free standing	34.98
101. Roses on a Plate	free lying	49.95
102. Match Cover	free lying	44.98
103. Cigarette Pack	free lying	49.95
104. Air Mail Letter	free lying	74.99
105. Post Card	free lying	39.95
106. Calendar	free hanging	79.89
107. Oval Photograph	free	21.79

A customer enters
Something is bought
Something is returned
It costs too much
A bargain!
Someone is hired. (Someone is fired.)
The founders. How they struggled.
Inventory
Fire sale
Store closed on account of death in family
The night before Christmas
Modeling clothes
A lecture to the salesmen

1. A Customer Enters
The room is dark. A man sits at the table. Two female bodies on the floor. A hand hangs
down from the "attic." The light is very dim. In the slowest possible gesture, the man
lifts the telephone to his ear. The bodies move a little.
   The hand returns to the attic. Sound of the Mickey Mouse banjo.

2. Something Purchased
The lights come on again, dimly. The man is still at the table talking into the phone (not
saying anything). Another man enters very briskly, takes off a heavy winter coat, and hangs
it on a hook, then freezes. Both the man with the phone and the other man are frozen.
   The hand descends to drop a glassful of water.

3. A Bargain!
Sound of the man upstairs reading a paper (i.e., turning the pages). Everyone as they
were. A red paint begins to run down around the walls from the attic. Coughing upstairs.

4. How the Founders Struggled
All as it was.
   The man (woman) from above lowers himself slowly to his waist and hangs there.
The telephone rings time after time. The neighbor begins practicing the trumpet. Bass
drum and tambourine.
   A man enters with a surprised look on his face. He takes off his glasses and freezes.
   The (man) upstairs pulls himself up again.

5. Store Closed on Account of Death in Family

Laughter is heard from upstairs. A number of small objects fall out of cracks and holes from above. A little snow. The man with the phone as slowly as before puts it down, and the man with the coat sinks to the floor in imitation of the gesture.

Snoring from above.

The bodies on the floor wriggle.

One of the women on the floor is pulled slowly up by a rope into the attic so that her underwear shows, upside down. The rope continues to the other girl.

The man at the phone falls slowly forward.

The man with the glasses is slowly covered with a bag.

Saxophone plays.

6. A Lecture to the Salesmen

The head of the (man) in the attic comes down upside down, smoking a cigarette. He is lowered to the floor where he collects in a heap. The girl stands up, very alert, brushes her skirt, puts on gloves.

Rapid counting from upstairs.

Sound of a cash register. Trumpet plays.

The girl pushes the man by the table so that he falls. She sits down and writes a long note.

The covered man with glasses leans more and more forward until he is at a forty-five-degree angle and remains frozen there.

The girl kisses the pieces of paper she is writing on and stuffs them into her dress after writing on each piece and kissing it. She freezes.

A red light, then a yellow light.

(A nose blown.)

A blue light. Long motionlessness.

BUDGET FOR THEATER (1961)

My theater activity in the coming season I would like to be in two manners. The first is
a repertory type of theater, to give short performances at regular intervals, for example,
every two weeks, on Saturdays at 10 p.m. These would be held in My Store, or The
Ray Gun Mfg. Co., 107 East 2nd St., NYC, inside the store or in the courtyard behind
the store, which is quite large. Since these performances would be comparatively brief,
a small amount would be charged for admission, for example, 50¢, and the audience
would have to be rather small. These performances would occur one time only and would
be improvised out of available material and available performers, with no great expense.
There would not need to be any advertising, I think. In fact, advertising might bring too
many people. It is better to be word of mouth. This repertory would be like a workshop
of ideas and possibilities surrounding my concept of personal theater and directed
not so much at the general public as at other artists and connoisseurs interested in
developments along this line. On the basis of one performance every two weeks, starting
in October, there would be about fourteen performances. Assuming about thirty-five
spectators can be accommodated, there would be an income of $17.50 per performance.
A supplementary budget of $25 would be needed for each performance, or for fourteen
performances $350.

Announcement card for the Ray Gun Theater performances at *The Store*, 1962

Room 1: The Bedroom—Jail
Room 2: The Kitchen—Butcher Shop
Room 3: The Living Room—Funeral
Parlor—Whore House

Period 1: A Customer Enters.
Period 2: A Bargain!
Period 3: How The Founders Struggled.

Room 1

Costume: bow tie, jacket, white shirt, pants. Pink feet.

Spirit: coral-pink party dress, $5 Orchard St. or 116th St. style, with paper under to rustle and paper too in the hammock.

Hammock slit and black material, slit correspondingly, hung below.

On walls: pinups, Statue of Liberty, boxers, autos, in the manner of the basement room of the handyman at George Segal's farm.

A bed, very unmade. Dirty sheets, pillow. A bottle or two in bed. Comics. The floor covered with newspapers and clothing, and other debris from the street.

Lighting: bare bulbs frame scene, hurt eyes of spectators. To left a door and a hole, through which things will enter.

A chair, laden with clothes and objects. Pockets of jacket stuffed with various materials. Man unshaven.

Spirit makeup à la Lower East Side school girl, pancake white, white lips, darkened eyes, brows plucked in shape of chunky little birds, hair piled up, etc., or any variations of same.

Position 1

As audience enters, spirit is rocking slowly from above, the paper in her skirts and in the hammock rustling softly. The man sits on the edge of the bed with his socks in his hands. This is the *static tableau* or position number 1. It is held until the audience is settled or until more precisely the end of first subperiod (two minutes).

Period 1: The Sock

The man drops his socks onto the floor. A bell rings. A package is passed to him from the opening in the left wall. He sits down and unwraps it. It is a pair of socks and a book and a can of tomato juice. What does he care? He lets it all drop onto the floor.

He pulls the shade down between Rooms 1 and 2 and lightning is projected onto the shade. Sound of foghorns. He tosses on his bed. The spirit lowers a hand, dangles it. A leg, dangles it. The objects on the floor move. The ceiling sways.

end of period 1

Position 2
Blue bulbs during positioning, always lit. Two minutes of near darkness. The man removes his coat and hangs it on the wall. He lies down and ties himself to the bed with one-inch rope. He lies looking straight up. The hammock continues its gentle undulation.

Period 2: The Shirt
A hard roll full of jam is dropped onto the man's shirt from above. He frees one of his hands and eats it partly. From above and behind him (left wall), a pipe enters. Water runs out of it. He looks up at it. It goes away.
The floor moves (could be a person dressed as the floor). The leg protrudes down again. Milk is poured down around it. The man coughs violently. He ties himself tighter. The unfinished roll falls off his stained shirt. The radio goes on with distant sentimental music.

end of period 2

Position 3
The man takes off his shirt. Stands on the bed.

Period 3: The Shoe
The man kneels. He prays. His mouth moves. A glove is slipped in through the hole. He kisses it. Again he shakes it. He gets onto the floor on his knees, looking for his shoes under the bed. Everywhere.
The spirit drops coins, which fall on the floor . . . feathers . . fruit . . berries . . .
The man crawls under the bed. He emerges, his face covered with shaving cream. He sits down to put on his shoes, which he has found. The pipe returns, pouring water.
The spirit begins sliding down from the hammock through its center slit. Her skirt is caught above, and we see her legs and underwear, then a rough cascade of newspapers, finally herself. She drops limply to the floor in a heap (a slow and beautiful action).
He coughs. He has one shoe on. He limps about looking for the other. He tears some pictures off the wall. He swears softly.

end of period 3 (and *Store Days I*, Room 1)

Room 2

A kitchen-bathroom sink and stove. Tub and shower to right with hose from sink. Table in middle with two chairs and on it an elevatable top with created food. Another top with food under it. Perhaps a third. Stove is not operating. Oven stuffed with newspaper painted brown like fried chicken.

Two persons, man and woman. Woman dressed in T-shirt with a picture on it. The husband in a long-underwear shirt. Woman at the sink. Man at the table. A cutting board to her left, full of vegetables and meat. An alcove full of groceries and meats in bags and structures, which may in some simple way be made to fall down, above the sink. Sink full of dishes.

Above audience in "attic," Operator Two, who is or is not same person as Room 2 spirit, a girl, nude, or so appearing, a cigarette-advertisement type, a girl at the beach. Long hair and cigarette smoking. Her smoke fills the room, hangs like a cloud under the light on the action. Perhaps too, she burns incense or tar. She is made up with rosy cheeks and strong makeup. Long red nails, toes, and fingers.

Position 1

The woman's back to audience at sink full of dirty dishes. Man at table with dead cigar in hand. Spirit holds down a pack of cigarettes from attic, while smoking with other hand.

Period 1: Dishes

The woman turns. Mascara all over her face. However, she has not been crying. She appears jovial. One sees her tits through the T-shirt, and her apron is wet. She wears a skirt with hearts all over it. She smiles in a frozen way, diagonally across the room at no one in particular.

The man sneezes and pushes all the dishes off the table with a swing of his arm. The tablecloth is swept up and out by a wire. The spirit lowers a leg and wiggles her toes. The woman remains, smiling. She takes a large cake from the alcove and pushes it into the man's face.

She bites a capsule in her mouth so that her mouth floods with what appears to be blood, which runs down her chin. The man falls over sideways. A sort of boring, terrible slapstick scene.

end of period 1

Position 2

The man returns to his seat. Sits slumped forward on the table in a plate of cold soup (which to some extent washes off cake). Does not drown. The woman retains same position, smiling.

Period 2: Conversation

The woman comes to life and with fast action frantically begins chopping lettuce and other vegetables. She brings down meat and frantically chops it too. She opens and closes stove, taking out brown newspapers and stuffing in food, taking out and stuffing in . . . Reaching up, she causes a great many things to fall down.

She attaches shower hose, runs to shower, wets herself, washes herself, with clothes on.
Always smiling. The dishes fall off the sink with a great clatter.
Darkness. The spirit's face descends upside down, smoking. Talking silently to someone.
The man snores, sneezes in the soup.

end of period 2

Position 3
The spirit's face swings back and forth in the semidarkness, humming in a high voice.
The man wipes his face and sits up straight, reading a magazine. Talking silently, the
woman pulls down shade over sink and sits down at the table opposite the man.

Period 3: The Argument
For two subperiods, slides are flashed on the screen. The man harrumphs. The woman
whistles and belches.
Lights. She is eating ice cream with chocolate sauce. It drops onto her stockings. She
scrapes it off with her spoon, but it gets away from her.
The pictures continue vaguely above the two.
The woman slams the ice cream down sloppily on the table, spilling what is left out of
the glass, which overturns.
Darkness. More slides. The woman sneezes. She cries and laughs. She falls over backward.
The man puts down magazine. He stands up before window between second and third
room, stretches. He picks up a hammer, then a saw, and saws furiously at a bench.

end of period 3 (and *Store Days I*, Room 2)

Room 3

A longer room. With three separately defined playing areas. The near: a couch
perpendicular to audience and a closet door (door also to "outside"). Above door: a shelf
big enough for a person, about three feet high, four feet wide . . . A "slide" beside the
couch up to or down from the shelf. In center, a painted fireplace and mantelpiece loaded
with objects, above which a mural of simple intention: trees, cows, a pretty girl or two,
as in a bar or a restaurant. Substitute perhaps advertising photos in color, cut out
and pasted.
The room is tangerine color, warm by contrast to the other two rooms, which are black
and white. It is "technicolor." The lighting is very bright but can be toned down to a
simple shaded yellow bulb over a table and a chair in the center. Objects on table are
quite important (as on kitchen table and floor of bedroom—themselves stages for small
actions) . . . a blacked-out Statue of Liberty, a cup, cards . . .

At far end, a square area, which opens to a small hidden room (a toilet).
In this room, Operator 3 and/or hidden figure. From this, a spotlight or bright light can be shot onto wall, illuminating square area.
This is a space for a family plot. To each area: daughter, father, mother. A shelf over the audience faces a mirror, and there is the place of a third spirit, Room 3 spirit, a pinup.

Position 1
Father is playing cards at table under yellow light. Daughter is at closet, pulling out clothes. The shelf above the closet is also full of clothes, all stuffed with paper. Mother is cutting material in the corner. Sound of her scissors in the darkness.

Period 1: Death of Natural Causes
Daughter pulling out clothes, pulling them down, an avalanche of bulging clothing, climbing up slide to reach them and pulling them down frantically. They tumble down over her. One of them, her suitor, either in the closet or down from above. She throws him onto the floor. He too is dressed in a stuffed suit, perhaps in women's clothes. The bottom of the closet is full of jewelry, pots and pans, and other metallic objects, which daughter stirs with her feet. Her heels make a lot of noise. Her long hair swings this way and that. Dance music plays.
Mother laughs violently and walks the length of the mantelpiece and with a deliberate movement pushes down with her arm all the objects there. She stands at end, smiling victoriously. In the square space she's left, an inexplicable creature appears. She walks back, past her husband who is still playing cards. The creature is gone.
The father lays out all manner of peculiar sentimental and ridiculous objects on the table. He picks his nose from time to time.

end of period 1

Position 2
Father the same. Daughter sits down on couch. Mother returns to her corner, sits down at sewing machine on table with her back to the room.

Period 2: Making Love after a Date
The mother knocks over the sewing machine and kicks it. The strange animal enters and goes out again.
The daughter takes off her clothes to her underwear. She pulls at her suitor tumbled among the clothing.
Someone, an apparition, a woman, looks out of the closet door, very beautiful. She is gone. The daughter sits on the couch. She climbs up the slide. The apparition appears again. The suitor stands up and rubs his head ("Where am I?").

The mother is making a large drawing on the wall.
The father has donned a mask and is sitting without moving at all. The lights go out,
leaving him there with his mask on.

end of period 2

Position 3
Daughter on shelf sits dressing herself in another set of clothes. She puts on white
stockings and white gown. She washes off her makeup in a pan of water. Father raises
up a structure and puts himself in it as a sort of body mask. A sphinx? He lies down
on the floor.
Mother onto floor, she puts her ankle into a strap attached to a pulley.

Period 3: The Phone Call
Daughter, finishing her redressing and removing makeup, slides down to the couch.
Suitor is still lying amid debris. She uncovers a box of very greasy machinery and picks
it out, dirtying herself.
A drum roll then begins to play.
The mother is pulled across the floor by the enigma, which secures her above the floor
upside down and then enters. Dance music.
The enigma joins itself to the mask of the father. The apparition appears.
From the shelf above audience . . . a figure lowers itself down into the audience,
dispensing little pats of shaving cream and kisses. Mirrors spin.
The apparition smiles . . . a black tooth.

end of period 3 (and *Store Days I*, Room 3)

NEKROPOLIS II (Script, 1962)

Part One: The Monster

The audience comes in directly, finds places. Meanwhile Lucas is sweeping the floor, which is covered with sand, throwing down new sand and mixing it with this blue dry pigment. The lighting is blue, neurasthenic. Slivers of mirrors hang by string along the wall. Above are forms of stuffed muslin, like sausages or clouds, tied up like garlands. Lucas is dressed as a waiter, in a white costume.

When the table is set, with a plastic flower in a silver bottle in the middle and a blue and white tablecloth, Lucas announces the beginning of the piece rather formally. The names of the parts, the names of the actors and the violinist.

John may enter before or after the announcement. He sits down, facing the large mirror. White face and a baggy suit. He rises to play his interlude.

The three relatives enter, sit down around the table. Lucas serves them. They talk, to themselves, to each other, to Lucas, in different languages. Öyvind—Swedish, Maricla—Portuguese, and Irene—Spanish. Lucas responds from time to time in Greek.

Pat enters into the middle room and makes the bed, which up to now has been covered with a black cloth. The bed is full of talcum. As she shakes the mattress and covers, the dust rises, fills the room. The relatives go on eating and talking. She makes the bed nicely. She wears little-girl pajamas with elephants on them. Having made the bed nicely, she leaves.

An ugly monster, Claes in a burlap costume, enters, swinging its limbs around nervously into the audience, paws at the bed, and finally climbs into it.

Action ceases in all rooms. End of first part.

John, who has been in his chair throughout, rises, plays his interlude, slowly, deliberately, as before. Sits down.

Part Two: The Bride

The relatives resume their eating and talking and business. Maricla takes off her blue stockings and bathes; her feet in a pan on the floor. Öyvind kills a fly or two. Irene tries on flat cardboard masks. Etc.

Milet, dressed as the groom, enters. He fixes his tie and hair in the mirror in front of the violinist, has a few words with him, and then goes into the middle room. He finds the monster sleeping in the bed. Milet pokes the monster. He throws back the covers and pushes the monster out of bed, chases him around the bed. He kicks the monster and chases it out of the room.

He sets the bed straight. He leaves to get his Bride.

He pulls the Bride (Pat) in slowly. She is wrapped in wrapping paper painted white, with a mask under a cowl like a nun, and tied with twine. He pulls her down the corridor into the bedroom. He undoes or cuts the twine with a pocketknife.

Under the paper statue, Pat is dressed in a crepe shift. He takes the bouquet out of her hand, lays her on the bed, and removes the crepe costume, tearing it down the center and laying it aside.

A sort of elation comes over him. He walks rather vaguely into the room of the relatives, stopping to exchange a few words with the violinist and straightens his tie. He takes a bottle of wine and sits down at the table with the relatives. They pay no attention to him. He toasts them and talks to them, in Yugoslavian. They go on about their business.

He gets up and returns to the bedroom, stopping again to talk to the violinist, and straightens his tie. He lifts Pat from the bed and carries her out.

He returns and rather drunkenly stuffs the bed with beer cans painted silver and feathers from a bag hanging over the bed.

He staggers into the relatives' room, again pausing by the violinist to talk, straightens his tie. Sits down, drinks, talks, etc. But the action soon subsides. End of second part.

John rises to play his interlude.

Part Three: The Relatives

A record begins to play (Lucas turns it on) of Hawaiian selections, "The Hawaiian Wedding Song," "Blue Hawaii," "Aloha Oe," a 33 rpm record at 16 rpm, taking about 18 minutes to play through the three pieces.

This is a very long time under the circumstances. After about 10 minutes, the far part of the audience is "released"—the ropes holding them back are removed, and they crowd up to the last room where the slow action goes on.

All the action is in the most intense slow motion. It should take the full time for Lucas to pass the 7 or so feet from offstage to the table and to set down the tray he is carrying onto the table. The objects are fastened to the tray by strings, so that they can only fall a short distance. To keep the objects involved under control, in time, will be the biggest problem.

Lucas already has a mask on, made of aluminum paper sprayed white.

The relatives put on masks made on the spot at the beginning of the part. They crush the aluminum paper into their faces, making rough masks.

Maricla who should be standing, having given her chair to Milet, has a bamboo stick with a crayon in it, with which she draws an outline around her body and arm and hand and fingers. This should take her 18 minutes.

Irene applies makeup, especially lipstick, to her mask. This should take her 18 minutes. Öyvind unfolds a large map of the universe, full of symbols, which eventually covers the whole table. This should take him 18 minutes.

Lucas enters, walks, sets the tray down, bends over it. That takes him 18 minutes.

When the record has played out, the relatives and Milet remain frozen in their positions. From this time to the end, they are as dead, needing only a touch or a shove to fall or break apart.

Lucas leaves the room. John rises to play his interlude.

Part Four: The Bears

Lucas returns, a towel on his arms. He walks on crates, bending over to set one after another in front of him, which raises him high above the table. He drags a large muslin bag and when he reaches the table, he begins to clear it of the many objects that have gathered there.

A commotion in the other end, behind the audience. Pat and Claes in burlap costumes enter struggling. Boxing, wrestling, and rubbing the bottoms of their shoes in the sand on the floor. Shoving the audience, throwing nervous punches in all directions. Gradually, they make their way through the audience and into the last room.

The mirror slivers are set swinging, the large mirror is turned awry. As their fighting approaches and threatens the table, Lucas swats them with his towels. However, the Bears ignore the blows, wrapped up in their fighting.

Inevitably, their fighting intrudes on the table. The relatives are knocked over and the tabletop is tipped off. The chairs fall. Lucas swats at the Bears furiously, finally driving them off, and they run out.

Lucas leaves. The room is a mess. The violinist rises and plays his interlude.

end

Chapter 4
On the Road
1963–1964

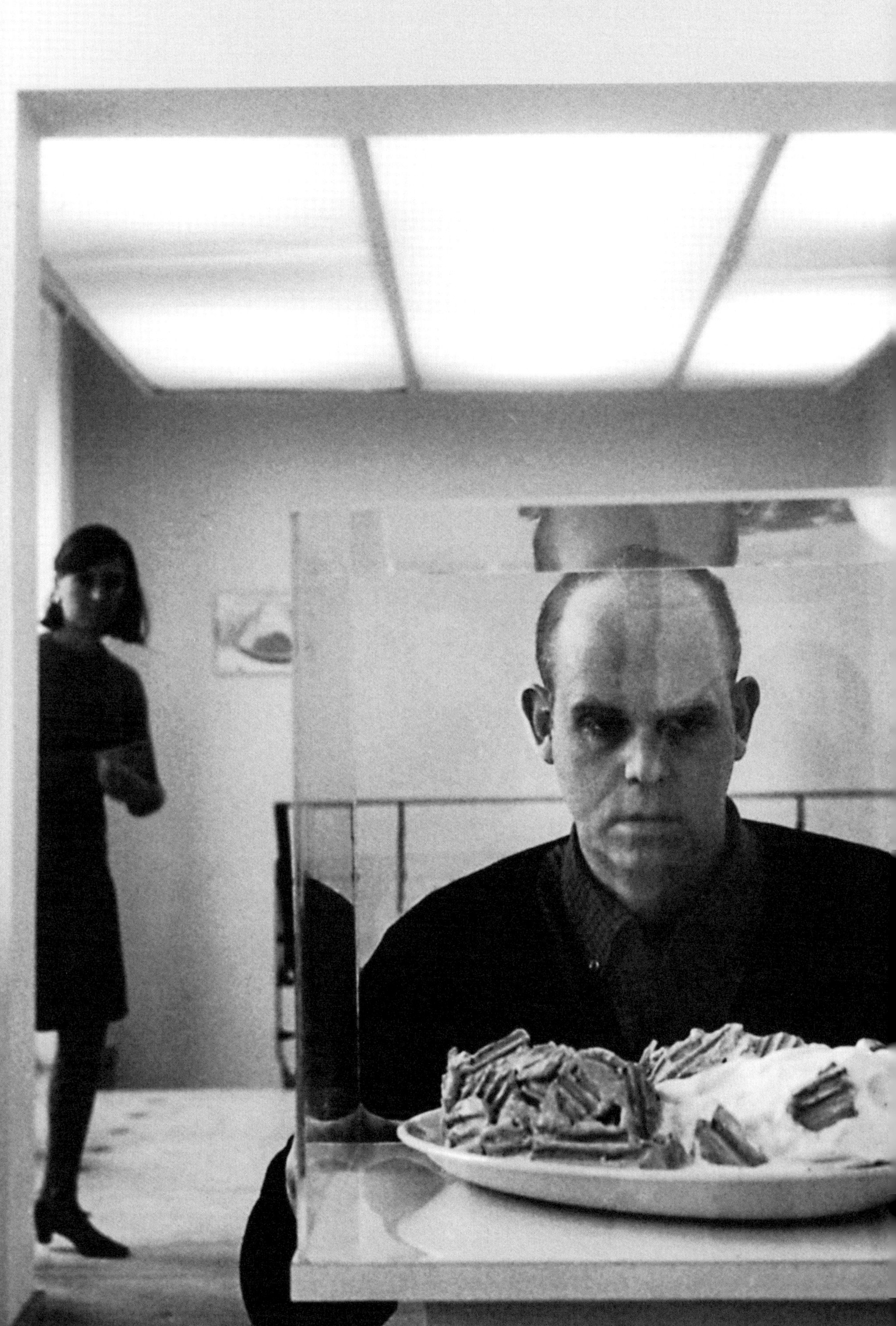

MONDAY, JANUARY 7, 1963

Leave for Chicago. Up early before light. Bus to Hertz, pick up car—a convertible Chevrolet. Return for Pat and to Store for work. Leave New York by 9 a.m. Rain Pennsylvania and icy rain Ohio. Make Angola, Indiana, by 8:30 p.m. or so. Cabins. Drinks at center of town. War statue. The "mysterious forest." Buy postcards.

THURSDAY, JANUARY 10, 1963 OPENING FEIGEN'S

Pat wears plastic dress. Meet Rosenquist. He buys us drinks, talks of Chicago + gallery. Feigen's for Chinese food, late. Persons: Shapiro, Rogers, Yates, et al. Films shown. Punch thereafter. East Inn and up to van der Rohe houses on Diversey, where leave Hunt + others. Home.

SATURDAY, JANUARY 26, 1963 SEW. MACHINE / KAZ PARTY

Drive to Feigen's, give up car. Get sewing machine. Cab back. Again discouraged by lack of material + problems, lack of help. Go from Lexington Hall to party for me + Mischo at Kazimir's. Neumanns—art + his accounts. Champagne. Lymans. Pincus-Witten— calling. WFMT for Polish music. Miss Chippendale.

SUNDAY, JANUARY 27, 1963

Title *Gayety*. Subtitle *A Dull Piece* from burlesque motif. Molly + others imagined in piece.

TUESDAY, FEBRUARY 5, 1963

Drive to Neumann's business + go through novelties and factory. Get suits + other clothing. Woolworth's on Michigan Ave. Buy many things. Get into trouble with old shop ladies.

THURSDAY, FEBRUARY 7, 1963

Final rehearsal. Jim Elliott present. Kaz + friend Sharp film. Piece seems well prepared. Work most of day on script, typing. Interviewed by Philip Weld for *American*. Try motorcycle + create finale. Interview played on WFMT.

SUNDAY, FEBRUARY 10, 1963 3RD

Drive up to Neisner's on Maxwell St. and get Pat hearts for dance. Table too. Lexington at 1 p.m. and film with Vern in p.m. Inspectors on firecracker report. Make chairs neat, each with a paper. Best performance, but Peter does not get light for pot breaking.

SUNDAY, MARCH 10, 1963

Tell Bellamy I want to leave gallery.

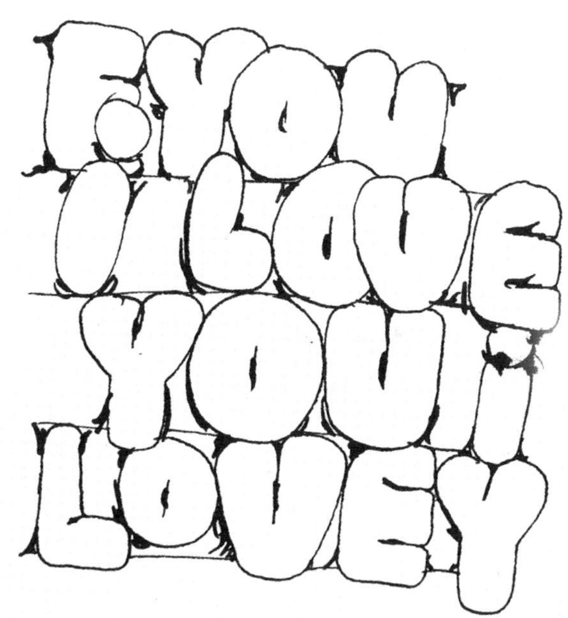

Soft Alphabet, I Love You, 1963

TUESDAY, MARCH 12, 1963
Movies with Pat. *Breakfast at Tiffany's.*
Ultvedt arrives. Meet him.
Working on BLT.

WEDNESDAY, MARCH 13, 1963
Write letter declaring independence. Get high.

FRIDAY, MARCH 15, 1963
Visit Sidney + join his gallery. See tax man. Alan Solomon visits. Pat to rehearsal. I with
Vern to San Francisco films. Leave early. To Sandler's. Alan Solomon again. Seitz, Held,
Yvonne, et al. Pick Pat up at De Maria loft.

THURSDAY, MAY 16, 1963
Buy 8 mm camera + editor.
Film editing—

FRIDAY, MAY 17, 1963
(?) Buy *Glamour* + other magazines, after walk—very restless period.

TUESDAY, MAY 21, 1963
Sleep all day.
Feeling strange and terrified.
Stimulated by magazines.

MONDAY, MAY 27, 1963
Whitman's *Hole, Flower.* Marie Menken showing.
Writing days begin. I am upset about my . . . position . . . life—all things.
Start "novel" around hereabouts and organize notes. Pick up: Pepsi, Sewing Machine,
Bellamy's stuff . . . Breer, Billy, Pontus, et al.

THURSDAY, MAY 30, 1963
Do not go to Chamberlain's picnic—or Red's magazine launch party.
Work in Store on Baked Potato + Hot Dog. First use of Hydrocal.

WEDNESDAY, MAY 13, 1964 SAIL FROM NY
Cloudy day. Call Billy + Olga, shop, pack + sail from NY after traffic jam on pier. Pa,
Ma + Dickie with presents + champagne. Fog outside, harbor sounds in fog, of ship
and planes.
Clog at Ambrose.
First lunch.
Lie around, love.
Martinis with nuts.

Dinner with wine (roast beef).

Falling asleep. Fog all day, all night.

"Concert" in 1st class main lounge. Meet Mrs. Cooke. Crème de menthe. Group plays—horn blows.

Streamers + band playing. Novel incidents, i.e., incidents that have disappeared in history still here. After all suffering + events, Vulcania still here. Sign of V.

TUESDAY, MAY 19, 1964 GRAND DERBY

My ankles are burned and swollen. Also hung over. Beer in bar reading *Black Book*. Spend time mostly in cabin, lying around or trying to finish statement on Happenings. *Bedtime Story*—movie with Marlon Brando.

Martini. Dinner.

Brandies in bar. A concert and then "Grand Derby." Pat wins twice, and I win $2 on her nose.

Dancing floor show.

Ham buffet in bar. With Erik, Jerry David, son + UN man. I reading *After Many a Summer*. I look in vain for Azores.

FRIDAY, MAY 29, 1964 ARRIVAL VENICE

Up early, but no sight of shore. Shore. Ships anchored. Pilot. Russian ship cuts us off. The path through lagoon. Relation of ship to Venice. Right past San Marco Square! Turn around + dock. Customs. Sit in court. Herman approaches. We check bags. Walk to town. Metropole. Orientation. Sit in cafe. Look in book for consulate +/or Barozzi. Look for Hotel Pausania + finally find. With Herman to dock. Porter. Our room with light + painted ceiling: goddess afloat + putti! To consulate: Alan + Alice lunching with Ed. Eat + drink. To Cici to check reserved accommodations. Cancel + return to Pausania. Try to call Panza.

MONDAY, JUNE 15, 1964 LUNCH LIDO / COLOMBA NIGHT

Get up early—at 7 a.m. It is raining a little. Take wash to cleaners. I meet Herman. Wait in St. Barnabas Square thinking of pigeons. Pick up films. Return to dress and take vaporetto to Lido and then bus to meet Sidney in cabana at Excelsior. Fountain + details. See Kasmin. Swim with Sidney. Return to find Maremonts. Father, mother + daughter (shielding eyes). Dress and go to eat. After eating, a motoscafi to consulate. Usual threatening and undecided state of affairs. Sidney helps + we redo room, move case into hall. Alan "no comment." (But this becomes the final arrangement.) Have date to meet Restany at Boston hotel. Find him in San Marco and with him (though we lose him), Pol Bury, Pontus + Belgians to Colomba. Don't speak English + we don't speak Flemish. But Pontus tells stories. Restany creates religion. I build church. To San Marco + then to Toto's for last drinks. Sat with + met Japanese.

TUESDAY, JUNE 16, 1964 PRESS OPENING

We were headed for Lido but to consulate. I mad because my show not ready. Sneak in with help of Torsten Andersson. The pavilion, with additions. Sun on typewriter + people touching it. Want to remove, also to fill out show. Bases have been delivered. Bases are painted. Alan, Alice + Falzoni. I take bath, dress. Set up show at last minute. People arrive rapidly. An enormous crowd + difficult to get drinks. All sandwiches immediately eaten. I watch work, as do Pat + Sidney. Introduced to one person after another. Very warm. People take photos. Leave by motoscafi with Sidney + Georges Marci and Maremonts to Danieli, up to terrace for dinner: chateaubriand + wine in breeze. Move inside and some dancing. Sidney shows how. Out + Sidney on boat to Lido. Marci finds Iolas. We sit down at Florian with Pierre + Greeks. People come and go. More introductions. I admire Greek girl. Continue to Martini's, a dance place. We stay until almost all gone—only Twombly, Janine + friends. Ride home in gondola at sunrise. Pat's dress glitters in night. Applause when we enter.

WEDNESDAY, JUNE 24, 1964 MILAN / VARESE

At 5 a.m., hear car crash. Sleep till 8 a.m. Shave. Call Panza at 9 a.m. Pack + pay. Leave bags, drink tea + take streetcar to Schwarz gallery. Duchamp show. Gallery details. Proposition, inspiring ideas. Lemon soda. Objects on table. Cavalieri. Schwarz too occupied so leave. D'Ariete, Mrs Monti. Pussycat. To zoo, see giraffes, elephants, bears, goats, monkeys, et al. Clouds up. Catch streetcar to restaurant + eat under arch while it rains. An American talks next to us. Silver light. Waiters pack for rain. An umbrella to taxi, to Duomo. Visit to Tresoro. Impatient priest. Silver altar. Elevator to roof. Walk around + to dome. Rain ending. View. Details. I find Torre Velasca. Walk to museum of technology + by *Last Supper* to Pensione Ray. Pay bill + then sit in park. A strange dog. Gets kids' ball. Sit on street corner. All people going home. Back to Ray. In the 1st floor toilet—another rare smell. The sitting room. Old bound magazines of wartime weeklies. Painted ceiling + details. Panza arrives. Load up and drive to Varese, stopping at Pavesi Spider, for pseudo American "hamburger" dinner. Views in cloudy sunset. Check in at Albergo Manzoni. A fine room with bath for price of Ray! Drive to Panza's villa. Collection + inspect pieces. Moon. Garden + stables. Immense. Paint has arrived! Return to hotel + both take baths after unpacking. A fine day.
Buy Panza marzipanza.

SUNDAY, JUNE 28, 1964 STABLE

Sunshine. Make love. To stable by 10 a.m. after tea + brioche. Pat works at hotel until 1 p.m. Eat good lunch at Teatro restaurant. In a.m., work on Pants. In p.m., break out + set table, make some drawings, good, of cheese + Nutella with new materials. A successful day. The plaster, which I had suspected the day before (in low mood), turns out strong and usable. Return to eat at hotel. Type an attempt to supply *Times* with account of Happenings. Feel light + inspired, but I give up the project.
Holidays. Serene—warm, sunny afternoons.

THURSDAY, JULY 2, 1964 DINNER PANZA

Sort of removed poetic state. I do a Nutella sketch in plaster in a.m.

Panza arrives 8:45 p.m., takes us out to dinner north of city. 3 risotto. On road to Ponte Tresa. On return, we have flat. Poor jack. A man stops and helps put it under car. Danger of stopping on "secondary road." Landscape, tree. Return about 11 p.m.+.

THURSDAY, JULY 23, 1964

Set out for Musée des Arts Decoratifs, but it is closed. Walk along shops. To gallery + lunch with Sonnabends and Bianchini, sort of hung over. Hang around gallery + then with Michael to see Christo's place and then to Rue de la Tombe Issoire. We keep the keys and drop Michael off. Return to hotel. Lie around and Emilio calls. Meet him by cab at Coupole. Dinner and sit until 12 a.m. talking and drinking. Drop him off on Saint-Germain and home by 1 a.m. or so.

SATURDAY, JULY 25, 1964

Peach and tea after first night in studio with drips on bad bed. Pincus-Witten delivers message to contact Ileana. I call. Meet them with Alain Jouffroy at Balzar restaurant. First Alain, whose English is bad + none too friendly. He is nervous, talks explosively. Back to gallery. Sonnabends going to London. Get check cashed, see Hahn. Pat + I walk by Galerie J, Galerie Dragon + others, all closed. Back for a drink at café outside gallery. Then cab home. Take laundry + buy vodka + tonic and set up studio. Later, out for dinner at restaurant on Place Victor Basch. Take notes. Return and bed in other cots upstairs.

SUNDAY, JULY 26, 1964

Up about 11 a.m. Hot weather. Write letter. Out to eat about 4 p.m. at restaurant—Café Léger—on Victor Basch. Read of Rochester riot. Steak and dirty watercress. Translate unpublished Restany article. Studio is pleasant but I am in a state of considerable doubt. Lovely sunrises and sunsets. Very quiet. Everything is closed and signs are up announcing August vacations.

New York, January to August 1963

The two hardest things are:
To get into reality—really start making something by accepting it.
To be absolutely certain.

Pizza equals toilet equals plug equals iron equals switch.

Scale equals bread.
Table equals painting (plane).
Floor equals painting.

June 29—When I give interviews, it is not to enlighten anyone but to produce through the factual apparatus of misunderstanding and corruption that is the daily press . . . a poetic effect despite itself . . . a poetic effect, the result of simply reporting incidents and statements.

The physical presence of a thing, the presence of a beautifully organized natural thing, the presence of this *animal* and *fact*, makes it hard to believe that this thing can be disorganized mentally.

The telephone-torso.

Hermaphrodite. Tongue on phone.

Period of inventions, enigmas, jokes.

Potato form nice. Why? So sad.

Gym shoe—Mt. Ste. Victoire.

It is form rather than jokes, of course.

How rococo the subjects are . . .
Cloth pieces: a veritable simplicity of structure, which would be offensive alone, altered by circumstances and movement . . . toward "rococo" effect.

Gravity, my favorite form creator.

Where I use writing, I should like to provoke a physical effect of enunciation, a dance of the lips, somewhat surprising. Certain letters are missing or coil peculiarly. The writing loses its sign character . . .

Physicalize the sign . . . the word. There is a way to do this through the eyes . . . and another way through sounds.

The imagination of horror exceeds the experience of horror or is a disguise for something else (like a nightmare). The representation of horror is not necessarily connected with what is being represented. Horror in reality is too impersonal and the natural body is too quick to protect itself . . .

Imagined horror is absolutely limitless.

The experience of staring into the abyss, the vision of horror, is personal and abstract, like Poe's. Coming when the defenses of the imagination are broken down . . . is an abstraction like music . . .

My room is filled with cigarettes the size of cannons.

Now that rug knows how to communicate!

Bacon—Flag
Ironing board—Washington Monument
Iwo Monument—Battleship—Pie

Anatomy—Ana to my—To My Asshole—Ananas/Pineapple (Swedish)—Tom/Empty (Swedish)—Mot/Against (Swedish)/Om/If (Swedish) OM GUN (Tyler's tool of ass-ass-ination) . . .

The classicism of the Neoclassic Romantics of the early nineteenth century and of the French Revolution—their structures . . .

Candy bars equals lined-up airplanes.
Newspaper equals drawing.
Food equals painting.
Furniture equals sculpture.

But American (it is passionate) commercial art with its distance, while presenting eminently "hot" matter . . . "object pornography" . . . , is in a way a model of the "objective expressionism" I practice . . .

I have found myself during the last two years or so in a specific perverse relation to my surroundings . . . I have combined my unwordly fantasy in a shock wedding to banal aspects of everyday existence . . . so completely . . . the thing is likely to burst either way, as it has arrived at a point where the cohabitation is no longer possible . . . either into banality or the other way into poetry.

Los Angeles, August 1963 to March 1964

Getting cool in Cal(iente).

I wanted to get the feeling of what I was before in NY out of my feelings.

I am as usual hopelessly isolated.

At the time of this writing (August 1963), a shift in theme seems to be occurring with all indications of a new period, a new consistency. The Store is worn out and I am experiencing the lack of interest and desire I remember from fall 1960.

Moon Man's Magazine.

I don't believe in novelty or progress on Planet Earth.

It is home in the impersonal sense.

The impersonal attributes of home . . . the impersonal home . . . the collective dreams . . . through commercial forms.

It is better to begin again than to work on leftover.

My aim is to become an ony mouse. A landscape. An object. A voyeur.
Anony Mouse.
Mickey Mouse.

The Ray Gun image in all is the symbol of the secret image function of the object.

Beans equal film lenses equal cigarettes.

Jet engines, assholes equals ironworks.

Beans equals wallet.

Pat, light, soft. Claes, heavy, hard.

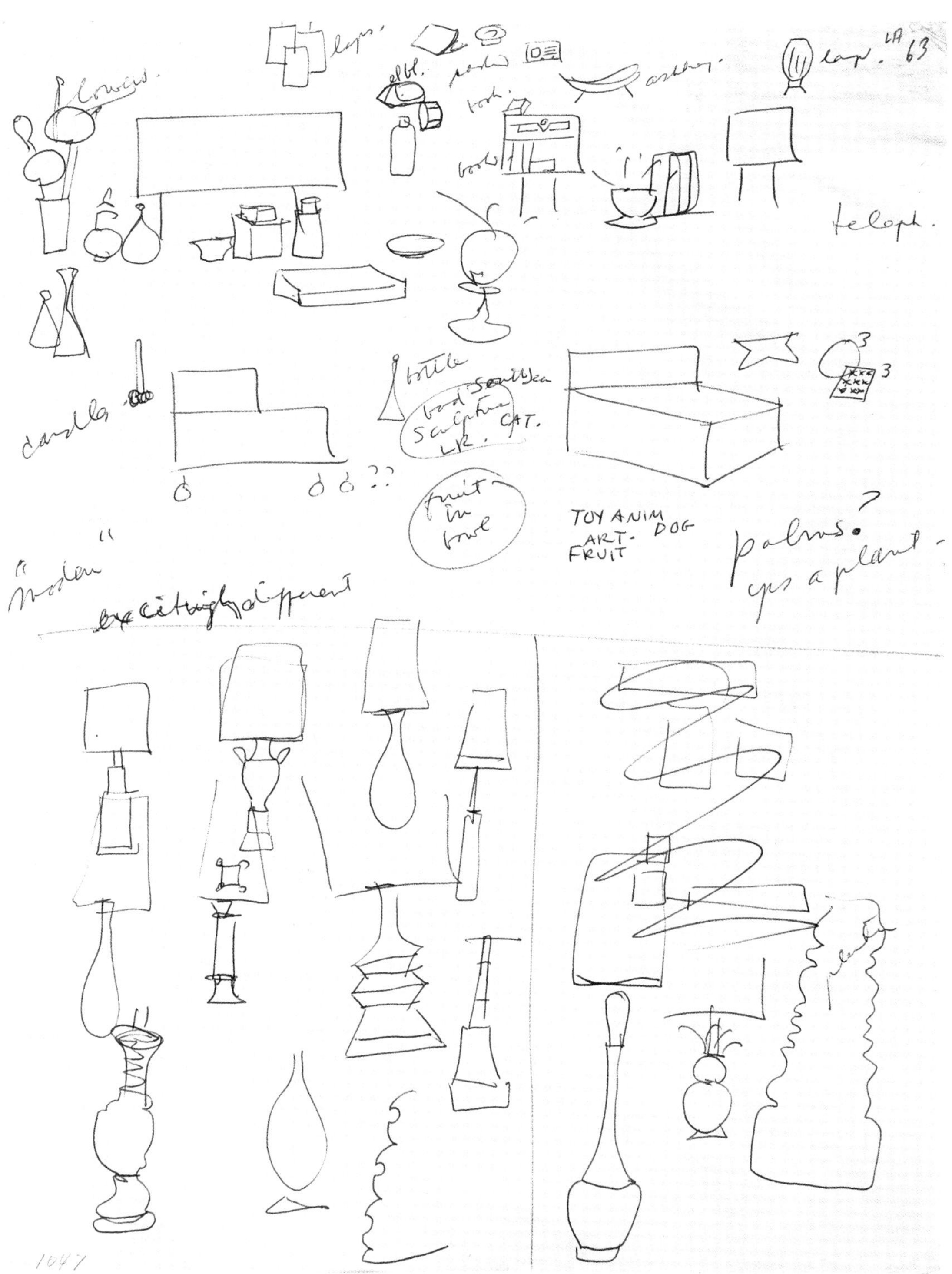

Notebook Page: Studies of Home Objects, 1963

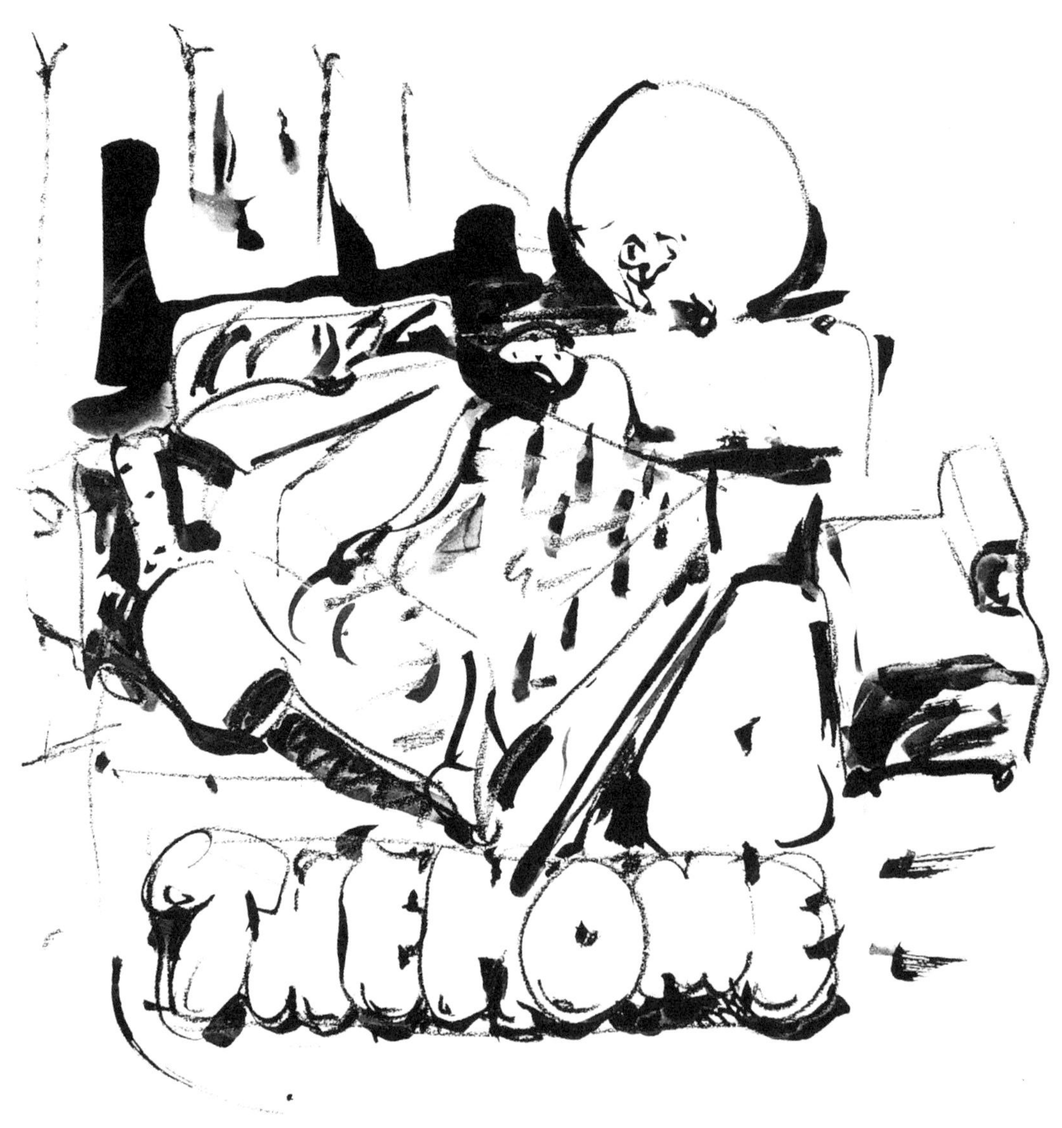

Study for a Poster for "4 Environments," Sidney Janis Gallery—THE HOME, 1963

Lamp bulb. Schmoo. Pop. Formal associations.

Toilet equals Mickey Mouse equals telephone.

California: Sensation, Scale, Mass, Open areas (full and empty), Spreadingness.
In the three-month scheme . . . how I work. Concentration with increasing
productiveness as ideas fall into place. Can work fast because have been thinking so long
about them . . . first month, all thought and painful, f.ex., much drinking. Bad time to
meet me, do business with me.

To use techniques outside art . . . manufacturing techniques.

Black versus white as in ghost/real. Photostats negative/positive.

Paper machines, cross sections.

Guts of machinery.

Machinery equals history.

Toilet upside down. (Finally got it into the right position?)

Light switch equals neoclassic building. Drawing equals Stella.

The theory of the soft sculpture is simple, broad areas in which the material in relation to
the light takes changing and organic forms.

I am concerned more with psychological forces than with economic forces, with
psychological interpretations of history. That is, I am a decadent, a true, practicing,
obstreperous decadent—under my own close scrutiny.

Paris, July to October 1964

All cities have a similar structure and a yellow book. Industry is international in aspect
and organization. Western cities don't differ much, and business habits too tend to be
the same.

Titian's Venus as Vitello Tunato.

Boboli fountain as espresso cup. (Postcards related to drawing.)

Anthropomorphism in the machine, in anything manmade, is a fact. And also in man's

vision. I use it not sentimentally but factually and playfully (promiscuous form).
Painting in Paris 1964.

Imitate wallpaper.

Shrines and religious objects and art—European Pop art.

Paris traffic equals Morris Louis. Kenneth Noland equals Florentine handbags equals
Morrocan effects equals awning.

All these things—out of water, f.ex., hardening form. Form from cast, insides, soft
casts (uterus) are all birth parallels, parodies, paraphrases . . . some form of magic. Use
even to the point of the woman sewing the sack (supplying). The man intruding the
plaster (sperm) in the mouth . . . See appearance of actual process, which should be
photographed . . . then delivery of form from sack . . . repeated. A sympathetic magic.
The pan, the midwife's newspaper . . . the towels, the dashes of red paint (blood), the
alteration of the pigment in the plaster (skin color).

I deliver and deliver . . .

Food as landscape (Europe).

To avoid: Falling slave to and still not avoiding the naturalistic image, as presented by
the photograph, the stylistic image, as presented by art in reaction to the photograph.
The real object, as presented everywhere, but especially the real manufactured object,
created by commercial art, which is so overwhelming.

The only guide is naturally one's own sensibilities and capacity to play one against the
other, and to select one's way to a result. In other words, the method has not changed but
the factors are much more complicated. There is not just the sensibility of the artist and his
skill in the face of a simple nature. There is now a considerable nature of art itself (because
of mass communication and proliferation). There is a false nature, in certain places more
real than real nature . . . and as for motives, both the pro and anti of any question has
been explored to the point of equal validity. The question as always is the putting together,
not the acceptance of confusion, and the only thing to analyze is the result.

Table clock equals roast.

In the desire to maintain contact and play with contact, "Pop" art is conservative . . .
it sees individuality in a general context. I am a conservative, rather than a romantic
individualist, which is what I believe the AbExs were (in theory, but the efforts of the
audience to universalize turned them into beaters of matter). Their universality was
the nonattached abstract vision of nature, which can also be accomplished by spitting

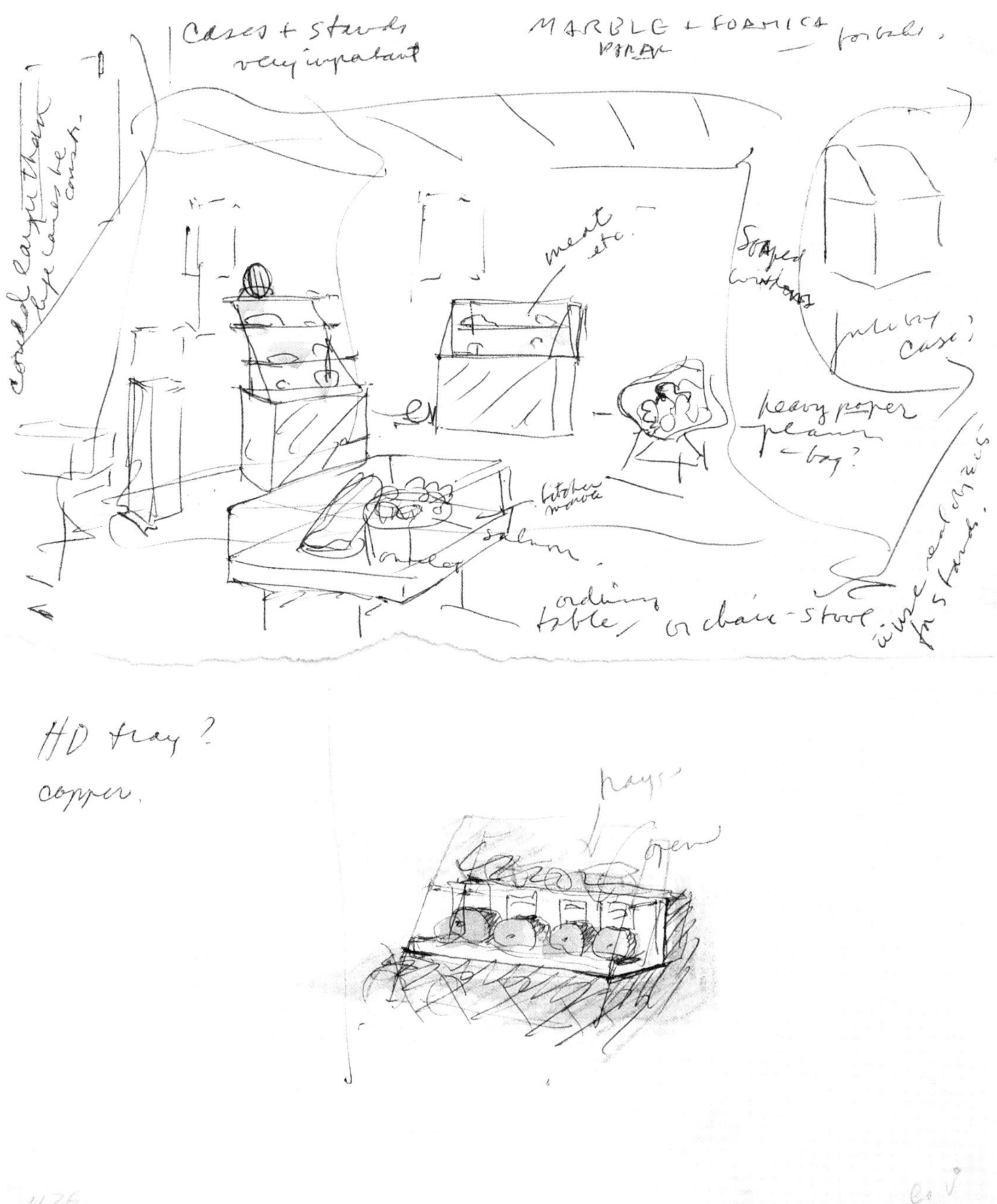

Notebook Page: Study for the Paris Store Installation, 1964

on the sidewalk, so that movement was (as all will be) a failure.
Believe in a defenseless, delicate material easily bruised and destroyed by those who want to.

The more critical the situation, the more delicate the material.

Pop art is antirealist and antisurrealist.

It is neither Zola nor Baudelaire.

In the search for objective procedures—now direct casting.

Some realistic techniques like sausage making or roulade.

An object that is neither readymade nor fabricated readymade. That's the rules.

Studio equals trench equals kitchen equals church.

The erotomystical ritual of mixing plaster and pouring.

Bring back the topic of food as a subject (internal sculpture).

The name of the thing (e.g., omelet) is the key to how you grasp it (mind and hand) or how you might grasp it. There is no reason not to treat the omelet like the moon. It gives you a handle (slang for name), and you can take it or leave it.

The contact of the senses with its surroundings, which is the act of art, is symbolized in an ordinary and concrete way by eating, digesting, and defecating—shitting to you. At the same time, the body images are projected into the surroundings.

All the subjects (the forms chosen) are those that relate the surroundings to the body.

Principle maybe.
When surface texture becomes *relief*. Comparing now the ruts of the surfaces of the rough Paris work with the *painted* texture of the NY or California surfaces . . . The painting of the surface is no longer desirable or functional. At this point, it becomes for the first time possible to recast into bronze or other metals—without having the painting of them in mind. Patina or quality of material is the only paint necessary. This approach is actually demonstrated by the natural peanut and is one of the reasons I have found it a functional subject, which is why the peanuts are a good symbol for a show . . . the peanut, unlike the eclair, does not wish to be form.

My feelings have secretly been to stop clowning around and become a sculptor . . . and the peanuts have led the way.

GAYETY (Script, 1963)

Overture

The overture occurs in the corridor. A subway landscape has been constructed there using many chairs, boxes, newspapers, and smoke. The spectators must pass through the overture to reach the main space.

The main space is laid out like a map of Chicago, such as one sees at the Museum of Science and Industry. There is a center stage (the Loop) a bit north of the center of the area. Bouras welding shop is to the south, steel works, Gary, etc. Two sinks back to back on the right are the lake and also function as the home and the exhibit of stoves (such as in the Edison building opposite of the Art Institute). There is a graveyard for weather (place where noise is made). A blackboard for messages (maps, drawings, menus), stations, and areas for action around the spectators' seats, which are set up to resemble right-angular streets (a diagonal to the loopstage—Milwaukee or Archer Ave., for example). At the southwest side is a large, stuffed airplane, either hanging above (as in the Museum of Science and Industry) or drooping to the floor.

The Happening is for me a personal composition out of elements at hand. It is not a question of chance or random effects.

In *Gayety*, I want to create a civic report on the community of Chicago in the way I see it. After the overture, there are six "combinations" of events, persons, articles, sounds—all the elements of experience in representative situation, either plain or enigmatic, demonstrating such categories as weather, climate, geography, education, culture, poetry, home life, crime, products, food, traffic, heroes, art, entertainment, and so on. This is like the civic projects one did in sixth grade, or I think of O. Henry's or anyone else's municipal reports, sociological studies, etc., but mine is poetic/satiric/symbolic. The enigmatic portions may be taken to be the situation of the spirit in the community, often these have a violent turn.

The relation of the incidents is fortuitous, as is the case in real life. Imagine a map where all that goes on in the city can be seen from above at once, such as the fire charts of the fire department or the multiplicity, simultaneity, of the taxi or police radios. A city is overlay upon overlay of incident. Unfortunately I am limited to typicalities, but the spectator may imagine the numbers.

The piece closes with a finale, an apotheosis, in the form of a destruction, which always seems appropriate, in which the forces of the community are released functionlessly in relieving chaos.

WOPEEDAH

Our Want and Need List

1. Soap and tooth paste.
2. Boys' basketball shoes, sizes 6-10.
3. Sheets and sheeting—twin beds.
4. Army blankets for twin size beds.
5. Bed spreads for twin beds—any color; or material to make them.
6. Toilet paper and paper hand towels, $10 and $4.50 per case respectively.
7. Loose leaf paper, scratch pads, composition books and pencil tablets.
8. Little girls' coats and jackets.
9. Girls' white socks, sizes 6-10.
10. Boys' briefs or shorts, sizes 6-12.
11. Boys' jeans and shirts, all sizes.
12. Boys' socks, sizes 7-12.
13. Little boys' shoes, sizes 13, 1, 2, 3, 4.
14. 4H and 6H drawing pencils.
15. Mechanic and carpenter hand tools.
16. Tools, hammers, saws, paint brushes.
17. Material for dresses and skirts.
18. Sewing machine needles — No. 15x1, size 16.
19. Table cloths, either white or colored 60''x120'', or material to make them.
20. Adhesive tape, all widths.
21. Nash's and Butter-Nut coffee strips.
22. Betty Crocker coupons, Hi-lex coupons, Rawleigh's coupons.
23. Gold Bond coupons.
24. Rakes.
25. T-shirts for grade and high school boys.
26. Basketballs.
27. Shoe Polish—Black, Brown & White.
28. Portable electric tools (Drills, Sanders, etc.)
29. Unbleached muslin for sheets.
30. Toboggan and skis.

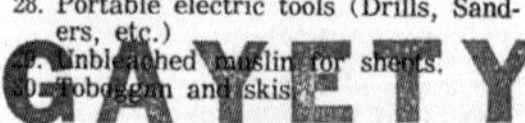

GAYETY

OVERTURE

6 - COMBINATIONS - 6

FINALE

By

CLAES OLDENBURG

February 8, 9, 10
1963
8:30 P. M.

In Lexington Hall, 5835 South University Avenue. $1.50 Per Person. Reservations necessary.
Please call WH 4-6638 9 AM to 6 PM weekdays and BU 8-9682 after 6 PM and Sundays.

Announcement for *Gayety*, 1963

Map of the City

Dantean panorama (diorama)   Parody on civic spectacle

The title *Gayety* comes from the gayety burlesque and has no specific meaning in relation to the events. The Woopedah clip was found on a bus, paper of a Catholic Indian settlement in South Dakota.

I. Combination One: Waves, Maps, Sponges
1. A girl comes in with a bucket and a sponge and colored chalks. Goes to blackboard, cleans it, starts drawing maps of Chicago.
2. Two women dressed in aprons clear tables and wash dishes in the sink. The sound of dishes. Waves in lake. They hum like sirens. (Weather.)
3. Ten or twelve plastic bags filled with colored plastic sponges, desirable and buyable in the light on the loopstage are placed on the loopstage (products). Among them is placed a man covered with newspaper (perhaps wet), tied up with laundry cord. He is trying to free himself.
4. From time to time, the sound of coughing from under the loopstage.

II. Combination Two: Eggs, Meat, Thunder, Sand, Dough
1. In darkness, a projector begins to project live some products in action: an egg blistering and frying, cigarettes slide out of a package, a piece of fine red meat.
2. After some moments of articles-projection, a man in a silver helmet, oversize white asbestos gloves, white fin-feet and in long underwear-putteed calves mounts stage, reads rather quietly a poem made out of Chicago street names.
3. A heavy-built man (butcher) in smock or coveralls, mounts a ladder over the grave with a box of junk, painted red and yellow, and dumps it into the grave (Lake Calumet). Garbage-butcher man. Then another, and so on. Much noise. Weather—Thunder.
4. The tied figure on loopstage is taken off into an open area and unwrapped (found by a passerby). Thanks very much. Dusts self.
5. A bed slides in with a man in it and also filled with sand (park district). The man, in pajamas, gets out of the bed, takes out of it a shovel, and shovels the sand out of the bed. By his bedside is a radio, or tied to his arm with a band, a very small white radio, which plays softly.
6. The poet in the helmet has a heckler (censor), a housewife who shouts to him to shut up, to keep it down, when she is not baking and manipulating dough on the table in front of her. She climbs on a chair to shout.

III. Combination Three: Powder, Mud, Candles, Traffic, Moon over Lake
1. The poet removes his helmet, fins, gloves. He dresses in a shabby suit whose pockets are filled with talcum and which is dusty white. When he pats his pockets the talcum rises out of it. He mounts the white stage (of Graeco-Roman) culture, patting his pockets. He maneuvers around bundles of newspaper (new buildings) and unfolds papers from his pockets. Falls down, raises dust. Mumbles.

2. At the other end of the map, crime and massacre. The butcher-garbage man now starts throwing very fast gobs of mud—red, yellow, and black—which spatter and hit hard the wall.

3. In front of the butcher-garbage man-gangster, there is a clown, coming out when he can, his hands full of cheap candles covered with colored balloons, with a mirror and shaving cream, who sets up the candles on the table, lights them, and then shaves, while avoiding the thrown mud on the one side and only now and then popping a balloon by coming too close to the fire (Bing Crosby).

4. Three figures in burlap bags enter onto loopstage, tie the bags shut, and wriggle and wrestle. From the ceiling, down come bags stuffed with paper, unclear ancient forms (turds, amoebas, beginnings of life), and coiled red sausages. The whole mixing. This is traffic.

5. Figure of a singer in a nice dress. She turns on the moon. She is like the singer in Xian Science church on Sunday but also the singer in O. Henry ballroom (band singer). She has a tape recorder that makes pneumatic sounds. She stirs a tambourine. She has a mike. The words she sings . . .

IV. Combination Four: Ice, Butter, Water, Oranges, Skates

1. A film is shown of a girl in a fur coat and carrying a package, running and falling in the wide field of Washington Park ringed with chimneys. Little Eva. Three minutes about. May be repeated. Memory. History.

2. Two men in aprons writing the daily special, taking turns on the bulletin board. First rule it carefully, put an item on, in big letters, like "Ham and Eggs 75 cents." Erasure. The other puts it on. While one works, the other butters bread and applies drawn pieces of meat. He has a big pile of them. Cuts it. Stirs a smoking pot.

3. A man nails, up the four corners of the loopstage, sticks and ties onto the sticks a Christmas tree light strand so that the loop is ringed (with L). He steps inside, bringing with him a small table, a chair, a pitcher full of water, a glass to drink it out of, and a typewriter. He takes off his shirt, breathes deeply several times, sits down, and types and drinks water, gets up, breathes, and so on. Author, convict, murderer, intellectual, narcissus.

4. A girl sets up a still life of oranges. She is dressed in smock smeared with orange, has an orange paint-filled pot with an orange brush. She paints oranges, squeezing them out of shape, cutting them, eating them. They fall. She gets paint all over herself and the oranges. In her hair. She smashes one with her fist. Rearranges them. Art.

5. A burly guy in his shirtsleeves knocks the dishes off the kitchen table, puts down his cigarette on the sink, and bending over the table chops it up. A girl with ice skates on and a mustache sits watching, still.

V. Combination Five: Feet, Hearts, Buckets, Nuts and Bolts

1. Woman in the kitchen cleans it up after the hatcheting, puts the bottles of beer in a neat row by sink. Her girl wipes off the mustache in the mirror and combs her hair. She takes off the skates and washes her feet in the shower. Mama scrubs the floor with a brush and wipes it with a mop.

2. A girl enters in red costume with two halves of hearts in red oilcloth on sticks, as

illustrated, and with a collection of feathers and other favors pinned on her costume. With a record player and three records, which she sets up on a table next to the loopstage, she dances with the two halfhearts and throws favors at the audience. Entertainment.

3. Spectacle of education: men beat girls, girls beat men. Climbs and terrors. Newspapers, flashlights, buckets, in semidarkness on the south side.

4. The citizen out for a walk with his paper. Reads it, drops it, ties it, and stuffs it wherever he can. Ties it to his legs, stuffs his pockets. Finds thing in the graveyard, collects it. Self-absorbed.

VI. Combination Six: Jackets

1. Another girl follows the first, she with her three records. The first removes her paraphernalia. Dances with stuffed suit jackets, which she takes down from a hanging position.

Finales: Chairs, Sparks

1. Through windows opened to the subway outside, chairs are handed in to men standing on ladders—about a hundred chairs, which fill the room. Also panes of glass, which are dropped in the handling of chairs and glass. Evacuation of school. Fire.

2. A huge plane of stuffed cloth is let down and wrestled with by several persons. Pressed against spectators and maneuvered threateningly.

3. Welding light in Gary sparks and pops. Great crashes from welding room.

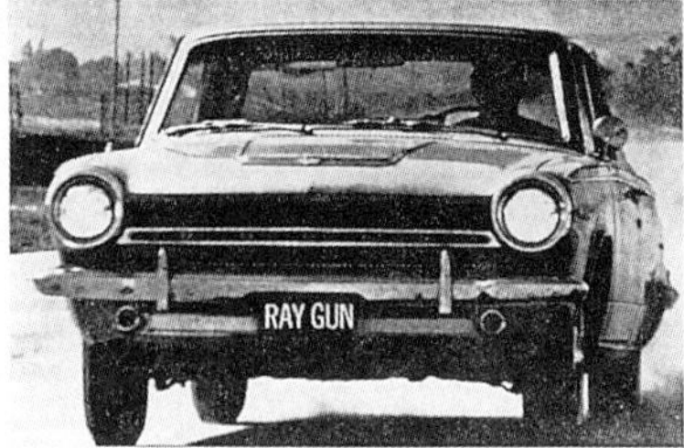

Poster for *Autobodys*, 1963

AUTOBODYS (Script, 1963)

Poem One

Approximate minutes

0   Lloyd drives in from NE
Maneuvers
Stops center facing S
Sits

1–5   Pat enters from NW
Walks to trunk
Opens trunk
Takes out milk bottles

Milk bottles out, Lloyd drives forward
Stops
Sits

Pat leaves field

Bottles isolated

Lloyd backs up to bottles
Pat returns with bucket
Uncaps bottles
Empties milk into bucket
Opens trunk
Puts empty bottles in trunk

Pat walks off field
Spills milk as she walks

Lloyd drives forward
Makes clockwise circle in reverse *twice*
Stops center, facing S
Parks middle S edge on *diagonal* (SE)
Gets out of car

Locks doors on both sides
Walks to center
Returns to car
Opens trunk
Breaks glass in trunk
Closes trunk

Walks off field following milk path (NW)
Smears milk with his shoes

5   Concrete mixer enters from center N
Drives to point marked on field
Stops
Turns on drum

Jim and Tom enter from NE with hoses and brushes
Wash concrete mixer tires on both sides of truck

6   Drum stops
Jim and Tom continue to wash until end of poem

Pat enters from NW

Walks over field to Lloyd's car
Lights traffic flares
Places flares in semicircle around back of car

Johnny drives in sound truck from N beside concrete mixer
Maneuvers, placing sound truck Mercedes close to side of concrete mixer
Stops
Turns on sound track
Sound track remains on for 5 minutes. one past end of poem

7   Lloyd enters from NE
Walks to car
Unlocks car
Leans in and turns on radio (or phonograph)
Locks car
Walks back and off NE

10   Poem One end

Poem Two

Approximate minutes

Sound track plays one minute after end of Poem One

0   When track ends, Santos enters field on motorbike from NE
Circles field slowly twice
Maneuvers to stop S center (leaves room for Dejon), facing S
Kick down
Guns motor
Sits motionless

2–10   Dejon drives convertible on field from NW to N center
Stops car
Fires flashbulbs in car
Works herself out of car without opening doors over back
Fires flashbulbs
Lies down all sides car

Presses against car
Fires flashbulbs under car
etc.

3–9   Ken and Richard enter field from NW
With ice cakes on dollies and creeper
Lift Santos off motorbike
Lay Santos on creeper
Shove Santos on creeper into field

Santos rigid in bike position
Bike continues to run

Ken and Richard shove ice dollies into field
Ice remains to end of *all* poems, melting
Ken and Richard return to NW for sheet of clear plastic and laundry cord
Walk to Lloyd's car
Tie Lloyd's car in plastic

Return from time to time to shove dollies or Santos

9   Carwash manikin brought in by Tony from NE
        Manikin brought to SE corner of concrete mixer, which is turned on by Tony
        Tony returns to NE entrance

        Ken and Richard finish tying up Lloyd's car, replace Santos on motorbike
        Ken and Richard leave by NW

        Santos kick up
        Rides off NE

        Ken and Richard off field, *taking creeper with them*

10   Dejon drives off field to SW corner
        Parks car
        Locks car

        Dejon waits by car

                        Poem Two end

                        Poem Three

20
Approximate minutes

0   Johnny drives Mercedes sound truck forward
        Sound track, for ten minutes

        From all directions players appear.
        NE—Lloyd, Jim, Santos
        NW—Ken, Richard, Pat
        SE—Lori
        SW—Dejon, Rolf, Judy, Nancy

        Walk slowly in individual patterns
        Indifferent to one another
        Diagram of path and tempo in imagination of each one
        Effect of scattered particles. Autobodys

1   Charlie drives station wagon from SE into center through pedestrians
     Slowly with little starts and stops and little honks
     Debby inside
     Debby moves around, showing herself and parts of herself

     Charlie leaves car (joins pedestrians)
     Debby opens doors
     Pedestrians converge on station wagon

     Pedestrians press close to station wagon
     Take out seats
     Walk through station wagon
     All slowly
     Join mass to station wagon mass

5   Johnny gets out of Mercedes sound truck and starts to push it from behind
     Tom enters from NE
     Tom pushes sound truck from front against Johnny
     Continues to end of poem

     Pedestrians resume form of scattered particles
     Debby closes doors
     Locks doors
     Turns on radio (controls station and loudness)
     Smokes much
     Moves around, as before

     Debby honks horn (1st time)
     Pedestrians fall to ground motionless
     Debby honks horn (2nd time)
     Pedestrians change lying positions
     Debby honks horn (3rd time)
     Pedestrians get up. Resume scattered form

     Debby honks horn (4th time)
     Pedestrians converge on locked station wagon
     Rock wagon. From side and from front and back

     Debby honks horn (5th time)
     Pedestrians leave field (return to entrances)

8   Tony enters from NE with bucket of blue suds and yellow sponge
         Walks to wagon and washes it, part by part
         Debby still inside

10   Tony pushes station wagon covered with suds (Debby inside) off field diagonal
         to E middle
         Tony leaves NE with bucket and sponge

                              Poem Three end

                              Poem Four

30
Approximate minutes

0   Dejon on field from SW pushing Rolf as white-bag Santa in wheelchair

         From NW, Howell on field in Dauphine, radio on
         Dauphine aimed at Dejon
         Dejon sidesteps
         Aimed again. Continuing

         Rolf: business
         Dejon: business to end of poem
         (Jim: business)

1   Richard drives Microbus on field from NE, carrying tires, tubes, and Pat
         Turns so that back faces center (diagonal, SW)
         Pat presses out tubes
         Richard unlatches truck and tubes spring out
         Richard gets back in driver seat
         Drives Microbus forward
         Stops

         Pat unloads white and red tires on silver ground
         Richard drives Microbus forward again
         Stops
         Pat jumps off

Richard drives Microbus to NE section
Parks
Richard off NE

Pat builds nativity scene at NW corner of cement mixer

5   Lloyd drives Willys in from SW
        Parks in SE area perpendicular to Charlie's station wagon
        Leaves car. Off SW

        Judy and Nancy from SW with muslin bandages
        Bind up Willys
        Sponge Willys with red
        Climb on top Willys

        Judy: business
        Nancy: business
        Remain on car until end of all poems

6   Concrete mixer drum starts turning
        Turns until covered in Poem Five

10   Pat leaves field (cues end) NW

        Dejon leaves field SW

        Rolf is left tied near W edge (south section) until end of all poems

        Jim parks Dauphine with radio on, diagonal to W edge (north section)
        Jim leaves NW

                        Poem Four end

Poem Five

40
Approximate minutes

0   Ken and Richard on field from NW with black plastic sheets
        Give sheets to Judy and Nancy on top of Willys

        Judy and Nancy unfold sheets

        Ken and Richard return to NW
        Get aluminum ladders, one tall, one short
        Place ladder next to concrete mixer

2   Concrete mixer (drum turning) advances slightly toward center
        Ken and Richard move ladders

        Lori skates in (candy bar and business, bike?)

        Tom and Jim turn water on in hose and wash asphalt of field
        Keep it wet and glistening

        Ken and Richard to Judy and Nancy to get unfolded plastic sheets
        Take to concrete mixer
        Cover mixer, using ladders (and poles)

        Mixer drum stops on being covered
        Cords thrown over and plastic tied on

6   Daggett drives black Cadillac convertible from SE corner, behind parked cars, up
        W lane, behind parked cars and on field via NW
        Into center
        Tom and Jim clear path for Cadillac

        Spectators asked to turn on car radios

        Daggett leaves car. Motor running. Leaves SW
        Bobby leaves car. Off NE

10   Spectators asked to turn off car radios (by Claes)

Jim's Dauphine remains playing radio

Judy and Nancy off SE

Debby out of wagon and off SE

Lori pushes bound Rolf off SW
Walks to concrete mixer
Climbs up on fender
Climbs down from fender
Off NW

                    Poem Five end

What I do as a Happening is part of my general concern at this time, to use more or less altered "real" material. This has to do with *objects*, such as typewriters, Ping-Pong tables, articles of clothing, ice-cream cones, hamburgers, cakes, etc., etc.—whatever I happen to come into contact with. The Happening is one or another method of using *objects in motion*, and this I take to include people, both as themselves and as agents of object motion.

To present this material, I have worked out some structures and techniques that parallel those of the presentation of the static object. I show the static object as one of a number of related objects, in a particular "real" place—itself an object. For example, *The Store*, containing approximately 120 items in a real store (1961, 107 E. 2nd St., New York), or the Home, which I am now developing with items of furniture and appliances, etc., though a real house or apartment has not yet been set up. (*Bedroom Ensemble* [1964] was shown in a room at the Sidney Janis Gallery, New York). I present in a Happening anywhere from thirty to seventy-five events or "happenings" (and many more objects), over a period of time, from a half to one-and-a-half hours, in simple spatial relationships—juxtaposed, superimposed—like those of *The Store*. The event is made simple and clear and is set up either to repeat itself or to proceed very slowly, so that the tendency is always toward a static object.

In some pieces, I tried setting up events in a pattern, a pseudo plot, more associational than logical (Ray Gun Theater, especially after *Store Days II*, March–May 1962, New York). In my first Happening, *Snapshots from the City* (March 1960, New York), the events were fragments of action, immobilized by instantaneous illuminations. Other Happenings have been made from one pattern or another of discrete events: in *Blackouts* (December 1960, New York), the events were illuminated at different stations across a long stage. In *Fotodeath* (February 1961, New York), the events repeated themselves in superimposed lines of movement. In *Gayety* (February 1963, Chicago), the events occurred at stations within and around the spectators. In *Stars* (April 1963, Washington, DC), events moved in and out of sight along a right-angle stage. In *Autobodys* (December 1963, Los Angeles), the audience (in cars) surrounded a rectangle on which widely spaced events occurred.

An individual event may be "realistic," and this may be quite direct, evolving on the spot with a player and certain materials and objects, or a reconstruction (of something I might have observed the day before, read about, or dreamed or of an account that someone else may have brought) or it may be, at an opposite extreme, an enigmatic, fantastic event with altered objects and altered (costumed) persons. I mix realistic and fantastic events, as the imagination does, and I consider the imaginary event as real as the "real" one.

In the process of altering an object or event, I use various methods, some of which are purely whimsical, others having a rationalization, such as the alteration of real (tangible) furniture into its appearance (visual perspective).

The effect of my Happenings will be missed if my specific intention and technique are not understood. Spectators will look for development where none is intended or be bored by the repetition. Or the term *Happening* in its vagueness will raise an expectation unlike the effect encountered; for example, spontaneous effect, an improvisation, or a spectacle of some sort.

My aim is the perfection of the details of the events rather than any composition (except in the later Ray Gun Theater with its "poetic" arrangement of incidents), and the composition is merely a practical structure (usually "real," f.ex., "snapshots," "blackouts," "circus"—a structure that is an object in itself).

The audience is considered an object, and its behavior is considered event, along with the rest. The audience is taken to differ from the players, in that its possibilities are not explored as far as those of the players (whose possibilities are not explored as far as my own). The place of the audience in the structure is determined by seating and by certain simple provocations.

The place in which the piece occurs, this large object, is, as I have indicated, part of the effect, and usually the first and most important factor determining the events (materials at hand being the second and players the third). "Place" may have any extent, a room or a nation, and may have any character whatsoever: old, new, clean, dirty, water, land, or whatever is decided.

There is no limit to what objects or what methods may be used to arrive at events. An account of the "rehearsals" or the making of particular pieces will show the strategies employed to achieve results.

**Chapter 5
Object Consciousness
1965–1967**

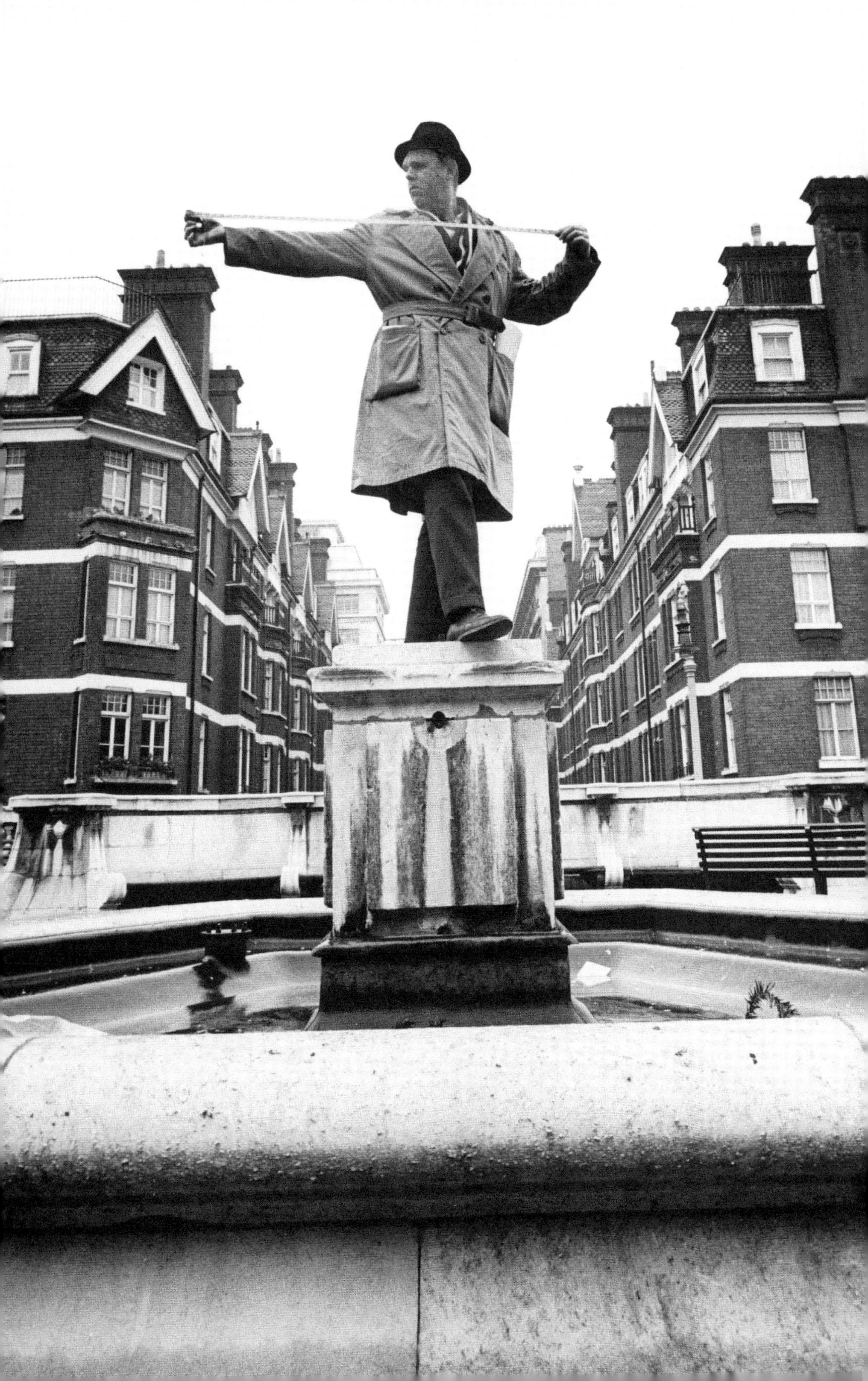

MONDAY, MARCH 29, 1965 MOVED INTO 14TH ST.
Moved into loft in morning from Chelsea Hotel.

SATURDAY, MAY 22, 1965 *WASHES*
Happening *Washes* at Al Roon's. In p.m., with Lucas + Pat working out their "dance."

FRIDAY, JUNE 4, 1965 UP TO RUDY'S TO FILM *BIRTH OF THE FLAG*
Mimi, Lucas, Pat + me in one car with weekend food + all props from Happening. Rudy + Henry + Farbman in his car. Later, Sheldon + Diane Rochlin. In evening, look at slides from *Washes* and supervise Lucas's dance + other business before fireplace.

SUNDAY, AUGUST 29, 1965
199 lbs. Cool, clear. 54°.
Dreams of Garfield the Canary.
Jack Klein and Betty Thomson for breakfast.
Tony Cox paints gray "Bedroom."
Maciunas visits with Fluxus materials.
Work on model of Fan, model of Juicit.
Champagne in evening. Bed 2 a.m.

WEDNESDAY, SEPTEMBER 1, 1965 WORK ON STUDIO / BERKSON PARTY
197 lbs.
Up 11 a.m. with difficulty.
Barrel empty. Continue cleaning. Set up shelf with toys, etc. Fill barrel. Separate nails—paint. Label.
Evening party at Bill Berkson for Ashbery. Frank, Jane, Ashbery, Larry, Andy, et al. Home about 2 a.m.

THURSDAY, SEPTEMBER 2, 1965 SCULL
195 lbs. Very clear. Mild.
Up 12:15 p.m.—phone calls heard distantly, slight carpentry. No dreams.
Buy lights.
Kulicke comes with Potato—paint it.
Abramson—insurance man—brings insurance.
Shigeko—brings sewn Pancakes.
Elaine—marvelous sunset.
Bob Scull—to Parkway East with him for steak dinner. Walk home. 1st Ave., f.ex.—gas logs of iron.
Calls: Rachel, Ma (2), Kulicke, Elaine.

FRIDAY, SEPTEMBER 24, 1965 LIZ STARTS WORK

186 lbs.

Foggy, cloudy, humid day. Last of a set of such.

Pick up Liz at Shandi's. Meet Miles and see my Iron on wall.

Rachel cuts Fan blades and begins painting bedroom.

Vern over. Kulicke over. We talk of Tea Bag. Pat buys vinyl at Leather Guild.

Thunder and rainstorms in late p.m. followed by cooling.

Set on a night's work—starting vinyl Juicit. But Englishman (Jones) + wife visit and get little done, which makes me mad at him.

Up till 2 a.m. correcting Juicit patterns.

187 lbs.

TUESDAY, SEPTEMBER 28, 1965

185½ lbs.—cool (54–56°). Very clear.

Dream of glasses (half), which make you see half-people, half-things.

Evening, clean studio.

WEDNESDAY, DECEMBER 29, 1965 DETROIT TO NY

Buy paper and crayons. To Mr. Breer's for lunch with secretary + Breer. p.m. in garage drawing + photographing + making records of measurements, etc. Then to airport for flight to NY. Northwest Airlines—my ears go out. So strange. Quiet flight. In from airport by bus + home. Then Breer's call! Coincidence. Meet them at Gaslight restaurant. Had champagne. (Was it their anniversary?) Anyway, tell all.

FRIDAY, DECEMBER 31, 1965

With Kienholz + Jones to cemetery. Look at tombs + stones. Film. On return, Ed buys pizza + we drink bourbon. Dallas calls—he is shaving off beard. Jones will film. Dallas brings children + wife + also X + wife. Kusama to see herself on TV. All in bathroom. Pat gets angry + goes to Dickie's. I meet her at John's + then to Dickie's + later home angry.

FRIDAY, APRIL 8, 1966

195 lbs.

Telegram from Pontus. OKs show. Take bath.

Dorothy in.

Pat and I to gallery. Sign pieces + put saddle on Sink. Medicine Cabinet door is wrong. Eat at Cup + Saucer + then take subway home. We follow Groucho Marx on street? Buy beautiful tulip plant in subway.

I draw on Plug. About 11 a.m., go out to Golub's. Artist + writer's protest party, which is being raided. Taxi to police station then march to City Hall. Ad Reinhardt, George Sugarman. Sit on steps. Golub protests to Woody Klein. Return by subway to 14th St. Walk down 3rd Ave. to Andy's. Look in. Then home.

TUESDAY, APRIL 12, 1966

Tired. Anxious. Decide not to drink. Liz in, tells she is moving to Poughkeepsie. Instructions. Pat sews suit, is tired. 3 kids in from Cornell and discuss my Canal St. monument—they are doing paper for architecture course. Alfonse at 4–7 p.m. Discuss film. Larry + Clarice in, leave for country later. Shop at NY Central, see Win Chamberlain. Up by cab to Byron gallery for Marty Edelheit opening. Inspect my preview drawing but too big to carry. Subway back. Steak dinner. Work. I was so dull at opening that I took up drinking again. Beauchamp + Jackie. Work on Tea Bag + stuff Airflow #2.

The clock is set ahead 1 hour. We lie around from 8–10 a.m.—2 hours changing positions, each moving, with a dream or two.

Wake up with clear dreams of unattainable, denied women. Woman takes my palm. Affectionate mornings.

Try to start a "Guide to Work."

THURSDAY, MAY 5, 1966

To Rauschenberg's for meeting between "artists" + Bell Lab technicians. Drink beer, eat "dip." Knut there. Betty on a dirty bed. Technicians demand "motivation." Interesting distance between participants.

SUNDAY, MAY 15, 1966

203 lbs!

Warmer. Sunny later. Up at 1 p.m. Just in time for group from San Francisco, who visit not too long. Work on color for Tea Bag. Alfonse borrows car. I read *Fuck You*. Irving Blum visits with Arnold + Fred. Chinese dinner with Dickie + Lisa. Return to wait for Kasper, who arrives about 9—9 p.m.–1 a.m. Park car. Pat watches TV. Nightmares because so tired.

On the beach in Chicago sleeping. A guy grabs my wounded finger. I say, you jerk. Later he picks up Pat + I threaten him with a paintbrush. On the beach in the surf, an elephant (it turns out to be a horse) on its side.

SUNDAY, MAY 22, 1966

203 lbs. Cloudy, but later in day clears. Warm, nice sunset. Up at 11 a.m. Work on catalogue photos. Clean. Go through notes. Tea Bag label, Bathtub—Pat sews on zipper, cleans. Kasper in evening. 8 p.m.–12 a.m. Cat eats pigeon on roof.

Keeping double diaries the days melt into one, from one year to another.

WEDNESDAY, JUNE 8, 1966

Warm. Pat skating. Petruzelli appears, the trash goes out! Brunch. Work like hell. All a.m. taking down + Moderna Museet picks up. Then second load, all sticks being tied neatly. Pick up corrugated paper to finish Plug and latex shredded to fill Raisin Bread + Baseball Bats.

In evening, dinner party at Feigen's on 67th St. (Irving Penn's apartment) for Powers + wife. Cohens, Laings, Aldrichs, Castro-Cids + others. Marvelous Chinese food. Last to

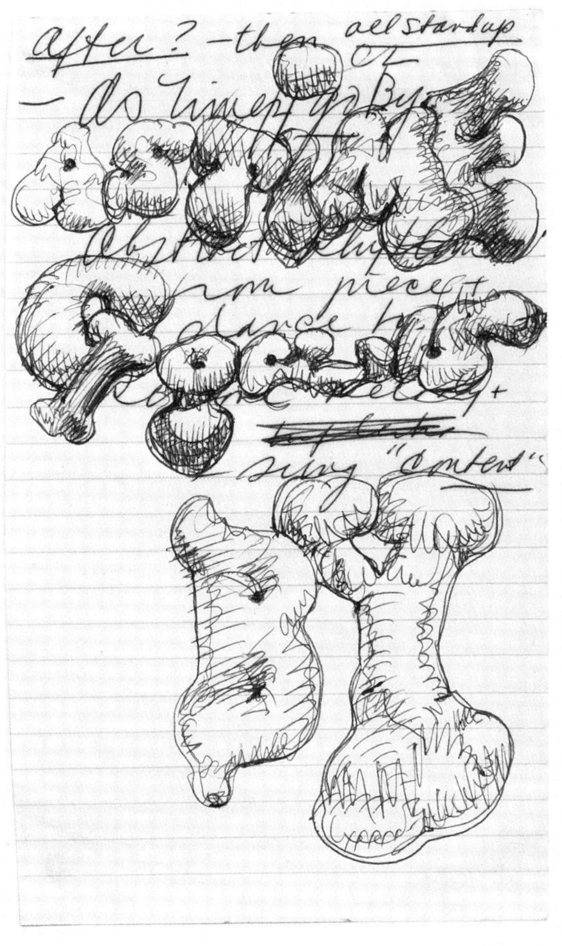

Notebook Page: Doodle: As Time Goes By, 1966

leave, of course. Pat sleeps on couch. When Feigen falls asleep, all decide to leave. Drive back in car.

THURSDAY, JUNE 23, 1966

Very hot.

In a.m., go with Larry to various manikin places and buy $450 worth of manikins, some fake rocks, etc.

To Bell Lab for math lesson. Hot dogs then at Billy + Olga's. Home early.

WEDNESDAY, JULY 6, 1966

Continuing heat but cloudy. Kusama picks up package. Up early, very tired + pick up Fleminger.

Drive to Brooklyn, Fable Toy Co., a sweatshop making stuffed toys, to study stuffing technique. Horrible work conditions—nightmare version of what we do. Return and unable to work. Sit around, drink, lie down. But bugged by voice from upstairs, TV. Arguing, footsteps, etc.

Decide that because of disturbances from upstairs and heat, will return to original plan of leaving early for Sweden. Change ticket reservations, write letters. Decide also to chuck *Playboy* + erotic show + concentrate on Sweden—show + performance.

THURSDAY, JULY 7, 1966

Hot and clear. Go to Michael Kirby's to have my face cast. He does, twice. Afterward buy drawing cabinet + bookcase. In p.m., call Larry + tell him of my disinterest in the manikin piece.

Letty comes by, picks up magazines + Happening costumes for her war on poverty group. Wagstaff for dinner. Talk after, about Raisin Bread multiple. He leaves late. I stay up, writing, or admiring my writing.

SATURDAY, JULY 30, 1966

Cloudy, warm. Pat uptown shopping. I clean studio, working hard + tiring myself out. Bathe + check all last details. Rudy calls, and Sheldon Rochlin (off to Turkey). With our bags to East Side terminal early to airport after taking out insurance. Crowded. Buy four bottles of liquor. Sit in lounge drinking + reading paper. I buy soft monkey + map + a Swedish phrase book. Call folks. Plane leaves on schedule. We fly the length of Long Island—Fire Island, Southampton, Amagansett, all so little. At nightfall, Nova Scotia from high (Tyler's?), its many lakes, then darkness with full moon. Pat has conversation with neighbor who says "draw a line through Paris—all below inspired, all above not." Dinner of capon with champagne. Attempts to sleep. But none too successful. I read from Thoreau *A Week on the Concord* . . .

MONDAY, AUGUST 1, 1966

Cool, clear. Up around 10:30 a.m. Pam-Pam juice, good coffee. Eventually out for razor blades. Fast moving clouds with grays. Tabak shop. Pat buys a comb. I shave. Bus to

Norrmalmstorg. Visit bank. Told check not cleared. Pat goes shopping. I carry my bag over bridge. Karin catches up. At museum, I set up typewriter. From groundskeeper Lundberg borrow tape recorder (as I type I record). Meet Martha, Ulf Linde—who brings in essay for catalogue, talk to Melin. Cable Judd + Ileana. Pat comes by, leaves for more shopping. Waldo Rasmussen appears. Man has heart attack, lies in hall. Pat comes by at 5:30 p.m. We stop at Grand Hotel for drink with Waldo. View from window. Exquisite, clear evening. Silhouettes. Walk to Cattelin restaurant—eat well. Meet Waldo. Cab back home. I go through notes + Pat writes letter to Dickie. Love, and I stay up awhile writing in diary. Hear in Swedish of Austin mass murder.

TUESDAY, AUGUST 23, 1966 1 WEEK CASTLE

I become interested in knäckebröd + set up like Hötorgshus. Also get idea of knäckebröd being eaten for billboards. Work on this idea. Linde + Reuterswürd drop by. Later Carl Fredrik calls and suggests dinner. During day, much inspiration—number of experiences recent. Come together in form of knäckebröd. Associations + connections in rapid order noted on typewriter. In evening, Carl Fredrik comes by with copy of his book *Prix Nobel* + we go to Opera Bar for dinner. Call Melin in Malmö about knäckebröd, etc.

TUESDAY, AUGUST 30, 1966 SECOND WEEK CASTLE

Work on first set of proofs of catalogue with Karin. We start on Switches—I make a drawing of it. Set up also simple 3D sketch of Drainpipe.
I stay on at the museum, draw Knäckebröd Flag + Saw Flag. Göran picks Pat up, then me. Drinks + good dinner on Lidingö. Late (2 a.m.) drives us home showing us this sight + the other in darkness. Previously deluges us with family portraits. Oxfilet + "ice-cream cake." Chocolate sauce? In every way, too much.

SUNDAY, SEPTEMBER 4, 1966

Tired + kind of disgusted with familiarity of scene. Can't face museum. Wait until 10:30 a.m., but Olson does not show up. Walk and sit by water on Skeppsholmen. Have Pommac + grappa at National Museum. Read paper. Pat scratches my head. Water is dirty. Tame ducks. Silence. Chilly. Sun comes now + then but mostly clouds. Stay in museum to get diary. My room frightens me. Last day of *Hon*. Feel like *improvising* the day like a stranger. Instead of going to cemetery, go to Gyldene Freden tomb. Good change to be in a basement restaurant. One can't see Stockholm. Pat: turtle soup, aquavit, beer, chicken, coupe. Me: platter, lox entrecote, aquavit, beer. Walk north up street. Nygatan, Vasagatan. Take cab to see architectural models but closed. Take bus to Stureplan. Return home with soda, etc. Make love + eat potato chips. Sleep. Watch TV—play, Strindberg-like. Bed early.

FRIDAY, SEPTEMBER 30, 1966

Start by planning two possible performances, but find out biology museum not available, so into a piece to be done for the Moderna Museet. Blankets and sausages have been ordered, and in the a.m. I pick up monkey-fur costumes at Karl Gerhard's.

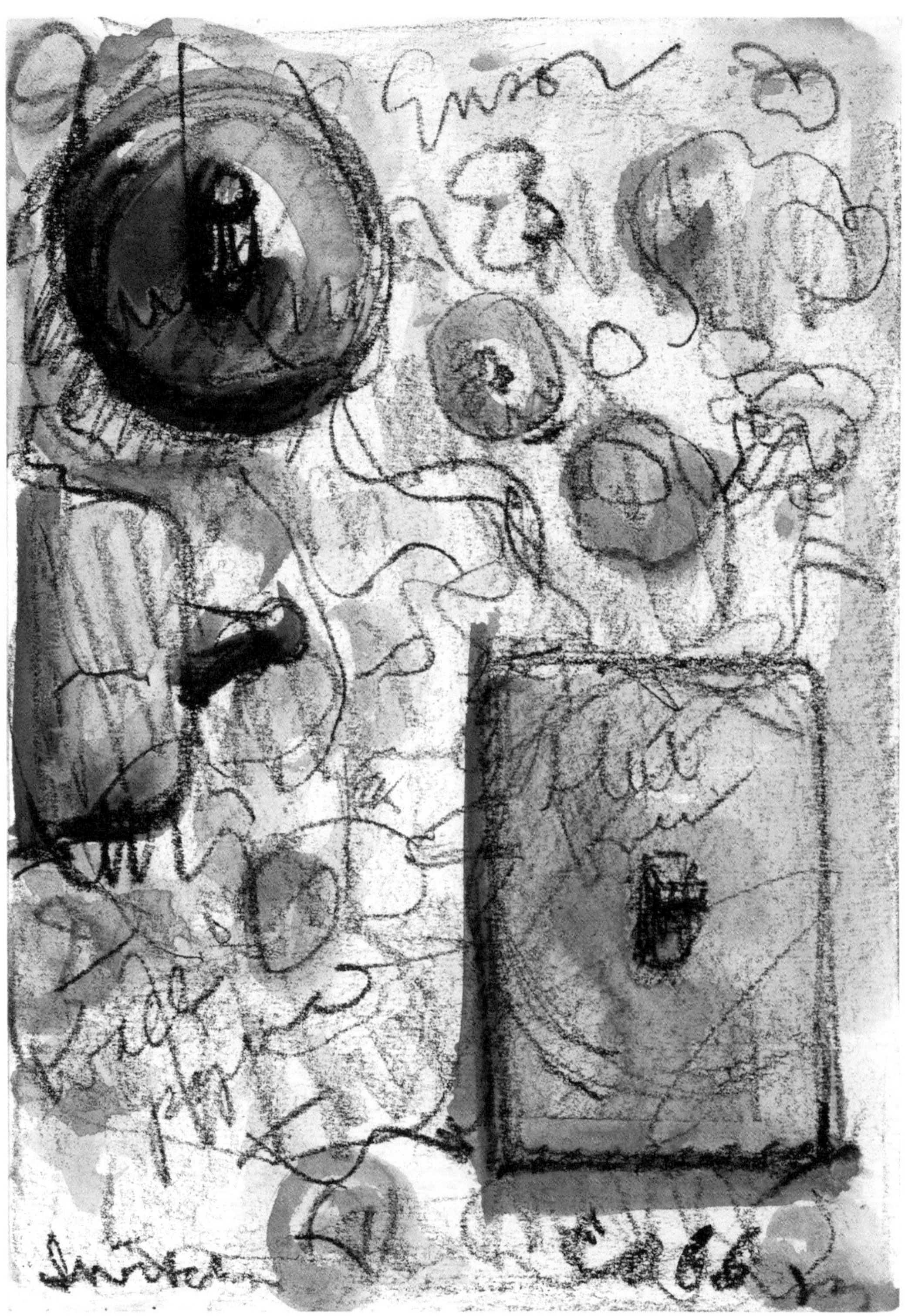

Light Switches, London, 1966

SATURDAY, OCTOBER 1, 1966

Shop for materials—in flag store, boat store, record shop until 1 p.m., when all close. Pat starts making Fried Egg.

First meeting with cast. Show movie of *Washes* rehearsal. Meet later at Carlo's for chicken dinner.

SUNDAY, OCTOBER 16, 1966

Up at 9:30 a.m. I write toward definition of Pop art for me. Thames flickers on ceiling. Pat sleeps. Later watches TV. Takes bath. Lunch around 2 p.m. Continue write + tear up. She brushes my hair. Robert picks us up 4 p.m. Stop by Michael Cooper photography. Drive to Hamilton's north of city. Rita. Tea, music. Look at Guggenheims. Return after dark about 7 p.m. Stop at Robert's. Leave him, he is going on to Blake's. Take cab to King's Road. No room at Alvaro. Eat at cramped + creepy Chinese place (South China). Walk home. I write. Pat watches TV. See scenes from "US" by Brook. Some preacher talks about Nebuchadnezzar.

FRIDAY, NOVEMBER 4, 1966

Sleep late. Michael Broom calls from Alecto. I meet him there at 1 p.m. I continue setting down monument ideas while he climbs about photographing. Michael also photos me in my Sam Spade. Manikin arrives. Study and then plan how to cut the legs with Tony. Eric brings more backs of the knees photos. A busy day. Cab home, where we wait for Robert. Drive to Peter Blake's and Jann Haworth's house. Details. Eat chicken on a rug in dark with Kleenex napkins. Admire collections and works. Leave rather early because Fraser has planned "film program." Christian, two other men, a thin dame in white, and Nigel. Watch Anger's *Pleasure Dome* and Connor's film on the Kennedy assassination. Go home about 2 a.m. rather drunk in cab with Nigel.

SATURDAY, NOVEMBER 12, 1966

Final escape of evil spirits.

A "fever blister" appears on lips, but finally a day when I feel well. I finish letter to Sidney + Toronto. Go to Selfridge's, buy pink spray paint. Spray leg, which is now smooth. Also buy scotch + beer. Cab to Alecto + am there alone. Spray some more. Decide to eliminate collage effect on wallpaper, equate candy with city plans, decide biscuits should be variety of "feels," that the portfolio be monuments only— reproductions of larger monuments; portfolio combining photo engraving, embossing, silkscreen + my drawing. Write silly homage to Lucas. Return about 7 p.m. Go to Europa Hotel, but it puts us off. Meet Robert who suggests "The Guinea." I am looking for a hamburger but none exists—a good one. A narrow place and steaks. Very crowded. Cab to Bridget + Adrian Heath's party for Swedes, Charlotte St. All on top floor at first— a regular cocktail party—people standing around shouting. Hamilton + Rita, A. Jones, Kitaj, Bridget + friend, et al. + the Swedes. Food served, but we ate. Pat talks with Rick. We go home in Riley's wagon. Pat + Bridget in back.

SUNDAY, NOVEMBER 13, 1966

Wake up late, about 12 p.m. Pat milks a cow. Breakfast. Very gloomy day, silent as usual.
Hear parade. Wait for moment of silence. I draw cigarette butt and trim notes. Pat in bed
looking at film on TV about lambs. Pat has stomachache: drank orange juice, milk, 7Up,
coffee. Brushes my hair, eats Scotch broth. Lies and watches *Flying Tigers* with John
Wayne while I write in diary + drink warm gin + tonics.

Later, Kiki + George come. Kiki brings a pair of George's underwear + I lie down to be
drawn + Pat also. Meet Harry Szeemann at Robert's. Have a drink + then drive to very
noisy Alvaro restaurant. Sam Spiegel et al. Celebs. We have hamburgers, which Robert
has ordered for us, having heard of our failure to get them night before. After which,
back to Robert's to see *Scorpio Rising*— the Fraser film society. Szeemann, us, two
young birds with dates. Walk home about 1:30 a.m.—weather surprisingly warm. I am
collecting "fagends."

TUESDAY, NOVEMBER 22, 1966 OPENING

Continue to hang show. Especially basement. Bring Tube from Power's + move
Typewriter down. Robert sends out telegraphed invitations to opening. Crowd of
students early in day. Hans shooting me crossing street. Plate, doilies, Pat makes gelatin
face. Marcia + husband and then crowded opening: Kessell, Cage, McCartney, J. Jones
+ Nibsy, Clarice, Blake, Tilson, Jones, Hamilton, Suzy, et al., et al. Bar set up. Break
away + go to ICA for Kitaj lecture. Details. Crowded + we are late (with Joe Tilson,
Joneses). Details. Separated from Pat, but we meet again + leave. To pub + there are
Caulfield, others, J. Jones, Nibsy—eat salmon on rye, beer. Cab to Spaghetti House for
steak dinner. Afterward pile in bed, watch for me on TV but no, saw instead kids—
runaways—from a utopian project in Mexico, arguing. Fall asleep, rather early after
calling Robert to say we can't make his film program.

FRIDAY, NOVEMBER 25, 1966

Rainy + foggy. Bit tired. Meet Hans at gallery. Walk Tube on Oxford St. Take cab to
Piccadilly Circus. Buy lipstick + shoot there. Then via St. James Sq. to Trafalgar Sq.
Measure bases, etc. + sidewalk stones with pigeons on them. Taxi to Oxford Circus but
no opportunity to photo knees (no manhole). Back to electric plant near gallery + shoot
me as monument. Hans goes on to photo fagends, etc. Many students in. Review in *New
Statesman* by Robert Melville. Kasper + Barbara in to get money—leaving for Münster +
ballooning. I carry on a long conversation with a blonde with outstanding pink ears. Hans
photos installation. To B. Riley, late by cab + forget address. Call Sylvester at Earl's Court
tube stop. To 68 Warwich Road. Environment. Philip King, Francis Moreland, Howard
Hodgkin + wife, New Zealander, Sedgeley. Pleasant. Bridget + I offer to exchange masks.
By Deux Chevaux (New Zealander) to Sylvester's. Raining + dark garden. 3 kids with
bears. Pompeiian relic, strange amplifier. Brown wig, I put on. Demonstration of Alka-
Seltzer effect. Forge, Gowing, Jenny Wolheim, two women, Pamela. Shepherd's pie after a
sort of smörgåsbord. Wine + beer only. Driven back by Forge about 1 a.m.
To Récolte kitchen about making face in pork fat.

MONDAY, DECEMBER 5, 1966

Evening: I lay out *Store Days* book my way (see).

TUESDAY, DECEMBER 13, 1966

Rainy day. Don't leave house.

Big breakfast. Pat in + out shopping. On my suggestion, buys flowery material for foam-rubber cushions for benches.

Cut finger on Dick's drawing.

I am writing in p.m. + having many ideas. Hard to tell if any good. I am in the aftermath of being very stirred up by the making of the book. Clean up studio of the book. Sweep up. Evening. Emmett finishes preliminary dummy + takes it off for Xerox. I seem to be writing well. Though very tired, stay up till 12:30 p.m. Also very hot. Sexed up. Try writing erotic. Bed but can't sleep. Listen to house sounds. Watch sparks from chimney next door. Bandage my finger. Hamburger dinner + watch *Girl from U.N.C.L.E.*

MONDAY, DECEMBER 26, 1966

221 lbs. Set out full of action, but find it is a holiday—everything closed. Work all day on files + call guests for a party. Take bath. About 7 p.m., Roger Davidson + wife with Sam Green, who gives us peanut necklace. To Sign of the Dove for an expensive dinner. Goats in blue light. Cab home. Pat sits up with Xmas tree, listening to music. Falls asleep. I cover her. I continue filing + studying my notes and start again a book: I dream, I live. Bed at 3 a.m.

MONDAY, JANUARY 16, 1967 MD

Up at 10 a.m. 225 lbs! Sunshine. Well rested and full of dreams.

At 2 p.m., to Doc Bergen who informs me needs more tests.

Pat is working on clippings.

Long conversation with Max about Vietnam and after with Jim Elliott. Also Betsy Jones of MoMA about how to hang Abrams's Airflow, about donating Cakes to museum.

Pat visits Clarice + Larry.

Stay up late formulating second possibility of catalogue + show—all "Soft NY" with political implications.

MONDAY, JANUARY 23, 1967 MD / *STORE DAYS*

Very tired. The weather is warm, like spring—just what I said in my letter to Karin. Fussing with the book. Sidney calls me to remind me to work. Calls me a "deadline" fellow. Shave + then to Dr. Bergen by bus. I don't have diabetes—test was wrong. 233 lbs. with shoes. Injects me in butt, prescribes pills. Cab back on FDR drive. Now, though tired, proceed to organize book, making good sense, I think. Pat brings liver + bacon hors d'oeuvres + gin + tonic. We eat veal. Make love. McElroy wakes us. Come to fetch contacts to print extra pix for book. After, watch briefly Dick Powell in *Right Cross*. Bed 12:30 a.m. Immediate deep sleep. Pat rubs my head with grease, gets pills, is nice.

Carpenter comes in a.m.

I call Higgins re: opposition to book.

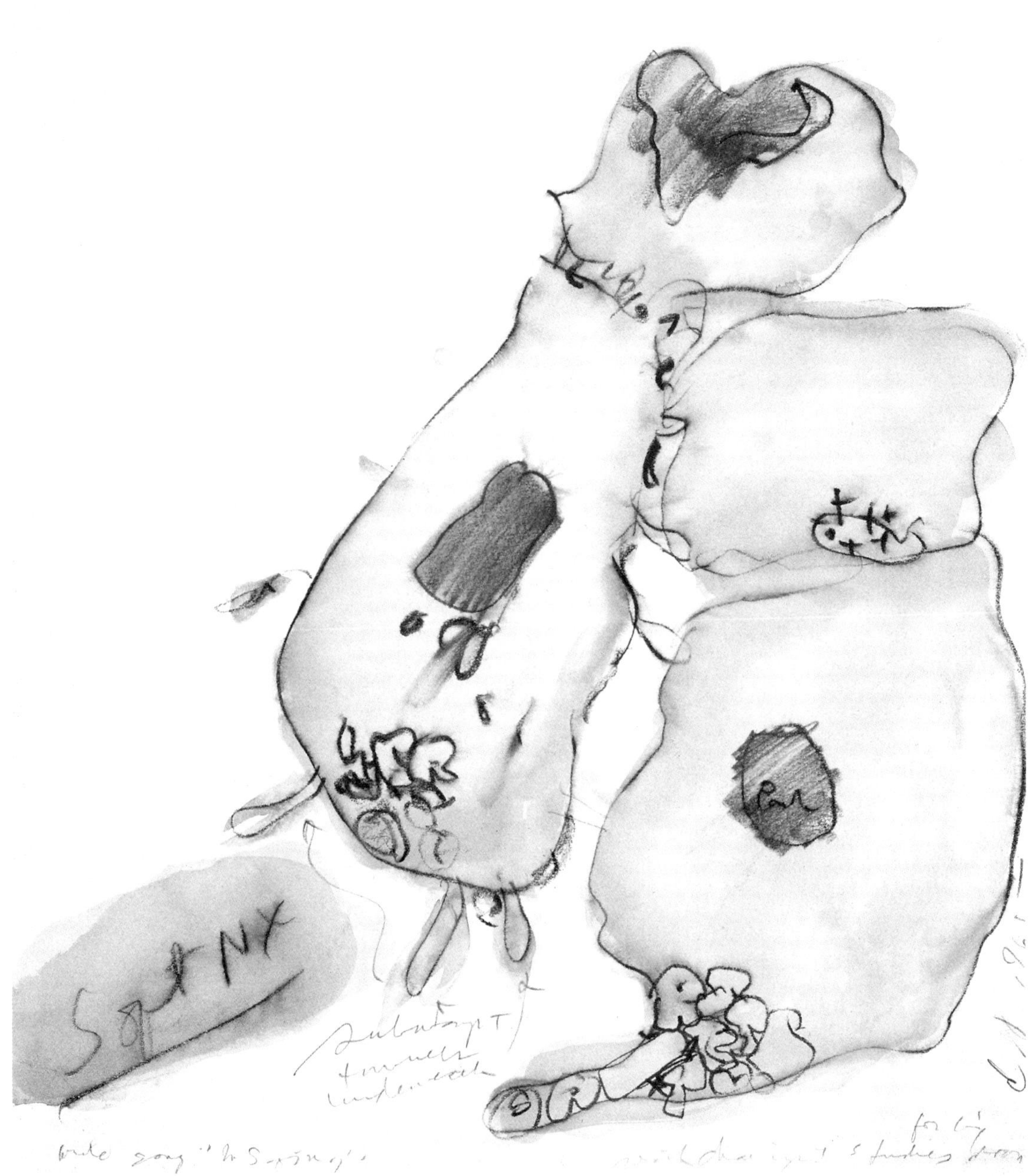

Soft New York, 1965

TUESDAY, JANUARY 31, 1967

227 lbs. Up at 10 a.m. Trying to face facts about party. Call to liquor store. Look up bartenders. In a.m., finish Kostelanetz interview. Feigen calls re: Macrostructures show. I go to work on Skeppsholm model. What a pleasure to work with hands. Pat cleans house thoroughly. Dinner of veal + sour cream. Review Kostelanetz interview, final corrections. Snow. Richard over about 10 p.m. with "Julie" to pick up interview. Work on model, etc., until 2:45 a.m. Am happy to be finished with interview, which has "lasted" since last July. Klein informs us Kawara is not renewing lease. Reading Cage, who now seems easy to understand. Other symptoms—strong gum irritation—start today. Second set pills. Liquor consumption, small scotch, 1 beer, all but 1 inch of quart vodka.
Have headache—rare for me.

SUNDAY, FEBRUARY 5, 1967

Wake up at 2 p.m. Place in terrible mess. Turn on jazz. Weather is pleasant, windows open. Pleasure of picking up. Organization of garbage: 25 glasses at least broken. Windowpane out. Floor covered with spilled wine, ground ashes, lacerated by heels. Walls scuffed. Awful smell of stale cigarettes. Clarice down with beer, talking of necking with someone. Corned beef hash dinner followed by strong Bloody Marys at Dickie's then to Jade Mountain for Chinese dinner with bad wine. Have fun, get stuffed. On way back, meet Tambolini + mistress on way presumably to begin all night flashlight march on Catholic archdiocese. Watch *Man with Golden Arm*. Pat continues loading dishwasher. Bed around midnight. Our cowbell stolen. Many goods left: 2 scarves, 1 hat, coat, jacket, keys, pillows, books, etc.
Pat fills with sadness at wreck of our place, but was also necessary as preparation for work.

TUESDAY, FEBRUARY 7, 1967 BLIZZARD

Blizzard. Can't see out window. Up at 9:30 a.m. to give catalogue to MoMA pickup. Work all day inside, glad of having studio + home the same. Pat sews buttons for Swedish Light Switch, runs out in snow. Sews step for Ladder and sews bottom of small Drainpipe. For dinner, hard meat blintzes. Work on City Island + other pieces until 2 p.m. Snow stops at 6 p.m. Burn incense. Work on Fan.
Blessed isolation.

MONDAY, FEBRUARY 13, 1967

Feeling ill at ease. Compelled to write stupid letter to mayor as a result of request by Paik in defense of Charlotte, who was arrested for playing cello in nude (as usual). Mrs. Varian calls. I write for her a reduced incomprehensible statement, which I deliver over phone. Richard is painting.
Set up studio in back, possible now that Pat sewed curtain over window, which gives lovely daylight effects.
McElroy brings by remaining photos + blowup of kids. It causes me to make some substitutions. I then go on to color sections and this night, staying up late, finally finish off the book as best I can under the circumstances. End pages, for example, store logos

substitute for $ signs—all holes are filled.
222 lbs.

MONDAY, FEBRUARY 20, 1967

221½ lbs. Klein wakes us. I tell him I decide not to take loft below. Guy from Craft Museum. Richard painting + Art Blake to construct styro cutter. Warmer, cloudy, rainy later. Am relieved to have turned down place below—it was escapist—more reasons not to leave house. Wasteful + against change. We must think of getting out of here. It was also conservative, in fear of new tenant?
Thank you drawing from June.

TUESDAY, FEBRUARY 21, 1967

220½ lbs. Put styro on Drainipe, draw up English Plug + others for Emil. Bathe. Higgins calls. Cab to Bergen MD. Injection. Cat's to Wittenborn. To Feigen show of Macros. Subway back. Walk down 14th. Feeling very strange + afraid of people. On subway, girls show their thighs. Have visions of new Park Ave. monument—balls.
In a.m., Sidney proposes postponement of show since deadline for catalogue pix 3 weeks away. Armand Bartos calls to invite us to Aspen July–August. Every day new problems! Contact Basonow. Send Pollock statement, special delivery. Confused post office scene. Many telephone calls in evening. WBAI, Joe Phillips, Hultén, Bill Wilson. My meat grows cold. (Seitz didn't get me.) Breer, Robby Robinson, Brydon Smith, Klüver. Cast tomb sculpture + throw plaster on Drainpipe. Sleep a bit. Glue up Dashboard.
Richard painting.
I give Jim Brody a rock.
Reserve Hollein aircraft carrier.
Thank you poem from Walasse.

WEDNESDAY, FEBRUARY 22, 1967

218 lbs. (Dec. 20 last time before diet). April 18, 1966 I was 195 lbs.
Poopy skating. Quiet as mouse, making up. Rise at 10 a.m. Work on Drainpipe. Morley calls, asks me to see show. Figure out position re: show + catalogue. See Dave in p.m. He promises to do several pieces on his own. Cherry pie + turkey dinner. Use spray gun first time. Pour styro + carve on Drainpipe. Bed 2 a.m.
Talk with Sidney, tell him I must do show as my life is set up for it (couldn't bear the spring without it). He agrees to put out catalogue *after* + poster before! Great. Should have been so every show.
Call Feigen re: model—he wants it to stay in show until March 9th.
Realize the pattern of my shows. They are like the performance preparations: improvised from what is at hand (in the widest sense).
Late at night draw a hat (Stevenson monument.)

THURSDAY, MARCH 2, 1967

Lord Snowdon at 11 a.m. Shoots photos of Pat + me until 2 p.m. Stuff and hang

Swedish Light Switch. As usual when photographers do come, nothing is finished. I glue + shape Thames Ball. Sylvester, who was to show, did not. Crated drawing arrives from Stockholm. Tough to open 260 lbs.—when drawing is only 50 lbs. or so! Richard painting. Tape up Thames Ball. Meet at Lanzas: Pontus, Öyvind + Barbo, Breers, Billy + Olga. Place is lively. Öyvind has been questioned about the dead girl on his doorstep + his name is in paper. All of us have much to talk about but cut short by tickets to *America Hurrah*. But Breer, who arranged it, has to return to babysitter + we don't want to go. Disappointing separation. Goodbye to Pontus. Back to ours with Breers for a drink. They leave at 11 p.m. Give Pat patterns for Drainpipe + she sews until late with music and beer + dreaming of Lord Snowdon. This has disturbed the concentration somewhat on the show by making us self-conscious.
Miss Kaplan party + Rivers/Gaisseau screening. Up late shaping Thames Ball + drawing Drainpipe.

SATURDAY, MARCH 25, 1967
207 lbs.
Drawing late. A girl downstairs sobs. Bed 3 a.m.

THURSDAY, APRIL 6, 1967
Into final period now of my interference: decisions are supposed to be natural, quick + effective, as if these 3 months had been my lifetime profession. Very cloudy + foggy + damp. Santini wakes us at 10 a.m. The usual great tiredness, soon gone, and anxiety. Hung over + super aware until after dinner, a nap. Motivated to rebelliousness by reading Pollock tributes in *Art News*—make radical + peculiar solution to type in poster. Talk to Farland, Ashwell. In a.m., go in rain quite light to Emil + get sample of enlarged type. Cast Bedloe Island model.

MONDAY, APRIL 10, 1967
200 lbs. Busy, wild day. Clear, sunny, warm, cool winds by evening. House is aflutter from west winds. Everything moves. OK poster type brought by Ashwell. Letty sews in p.m. + evening. Eats shrimps with us. I draw madly. Pat works on Fan blades. Allen Jones can't make it. Letty has class in, takes them around studio for 2 hours. Pat skates in a.m., then sleeps. She visits gallery, sees Segal show. Manuel comes to pick up 2nd load drawings + I show him new work. Call Elaine + discover she has rented a real store on 9th St. between Ave. B + Ave. C! Call Peter Moore. Aach visits. Call Dorothy Seiberling about studio show, gallery about drawings. Up late drawing on fallen woman (Ladder) and hanging woman (Fan). Play funny records + watch cynical Academy Awards. Letty says my women all look like Vanessa Redgrave.

TUESDAY, APRIL 11, 1967
200 lbs. Cooler, clear, strong shadows. Private beginning, public day. Gab gab gab. Finally the right side of my lip cracked.

THURSDAY, APRIL 13, 1967

201 lbs. Writing fever over, I hope. Somewhat overstimulated. Add 2 beers to the balloon + come down some.

TUESDAY, APRIL 25, 1967

Pat uptown. Fagends supposed to be picked up by Hague at 4 p.m. They come at 2 p.m.—but they not finished by 4 p.m. either. Fagend base delivered at gallery. I work all day feverishly on Fagends. Scott brings photos + later Grant, his friend, waits to help me, reading in the afternoon light. We load up wagon + get stuck in Passover jam on 1st Ave. Too late for elevator so all meet me on street + grab a Fagend. Show has come together well. Make some corrections in Fan hanging + play at arrangement of Fagends. Except for minor details, show is up. Drive back with Carroll. Eat at Il Faro. Home + I go to work on Cord, Waterfall, etc. But this night, I go to bed.

MONDAY, MAY 1, 1967

196 lbs. To gallery to set up Fagends for rephotograph by Clements. I watch beautiful people watch my work.

SATURDAY, MAY 6, 1967

Teri at 11 a.m. as secretary. Dictate letters off my back, also Smithsonian material, rewrite, she copies. I have gathered material for Sam Edwards, who comes 5:30 p.m. Smoking cigars. Possibilities. I promise to select + organize a paracatalogue possibility around idea of "America: War & Sex, Etc."

SUNDAY, MAY 14, 1967

Turns to rain. Trying to break out of writing + tackle Ketchup Bottle. Up late, very tired. Write several "poems." Read Fiedler. Rudy Wurlitzer by, Charles Henri by—give him drawing of smog mask. Billy, with his EAT package. He is now president. Loose talk. To Chinese restaurant, meet Dickie + Lisa. Dickie has been in East Hampton looking at houses. Home after + have sex, starting in darkroom + moving to bed in front. Then finish stuffing of Ketchup, jam Ketchup into Bottle. Pat sews up. Very tired + to bed about 1 a.m. Wake up around 4 a.m. + sleep poorly after that. Feel I am falling apart physically. Can't breathe, etc. My hands peeling. Almost 200 lbs. at bedtime.

MONDAY, JUNE 5, 1967

193 lbs. 79°. Hot, sunny, wind from south. At gallery in a.m., cab up, shaken by war news. Signing Schmela piece + picking up photos. Lunch at home with Gene Baro, selects some prints for Yugoslavian show. Ileana calls from Paris re: Grassi show.
Go to Cooper student show. 1st time in building since I quit 1961. Strange. A woman recognizes me, drops her earrings, tells me she had a friend who was in love with me, but can't remember where or who. Drawing toward a Chicago monument for newspaper article by Betty Flynn—typewriter for Jackson Park, columns for the lake.

SATURDAY, JUNE 10, 1967

195 lbs. Continuing hot. Up at 11 a.m. Eat lox Pat has bought + left. More work around house: shelving, stencils, etc. I go about 5 p.m. to see Elaine's Store, last day, through Tompkins Sq. throng. "Everybody" there—a sort of party: Michael Kirby, Virginia Dwan, Bob, Jasper, Simone, Leo, Les Levine, et al. Vodka + OJ. I very nervous at first, can hardly bring cup to mouth. By + by relax. Call Pat, who refuses to come. Talk long to Michael. Pieces are strangely effective—but not me at all. Interesting. The paint + plaster a sort of style by itself (Frisco Paint—Lower East Side). Glad I made it. Sign in guest register as Elaine S. Wander back through wild scenes of late p.m. Ave. B. Dinner of veal + salad, not too good, Pat admits, with Rico. Watch *Get Smart*. Rico leaves. I build corner for Pool Balls. Pat works on clippings. Very tired. Bed about 1 a.m. A hot night full of sweat + anxiety—many awful dreams + body convulsions, fear—excretions. Glad to see the sunrise, but no wind. A real heat wave.

Drama Act—love feast.

Realize archive activity has a certain influence of finality—a period seems to have come to a close. '57–'67 or '56–'67. Some initial period of my life. With the future extremely uncertain, if I have the courage to accept it as such.

TUESDAY, JULY 11, 1967

184 lbs. Pat's disease defined as poison oak. A photographer shoots my Drum Set. It is hot and the days continue to glide by with unaccustomed irresponsibility. I drink much fruit juice. I write my poetry. I babble. My body feels strange + I quiver. I wrote poetry in my head as I awakened and was too weary to reach for a pencil. The wet days continue. I bathe + shave.

SATURDAY, JULY 15, 1967

Still tired, of course. But keep on working. Seem to have defined the assignments but change them a bit toward evening—O'Hara's to a static cup + redraw the Drum Pedal for Katz. List piece remains half defined—enough for presentation. More letters. Clean studio. Eat too much all day. Lie down briefly. Pat is home sewing + sleeping + cleaning with radio on. The weather continues very damp + gray with occasional sun + rainstorms. Visit Palardy and see Pool Rack. Very big + grand! In a.m., through rain, get poems, which were statted + arrange them for Higgins + Pat's too (90 of them now). Also to post office to mail letters + receive a 3D heart from D. L. Wigmore in Toronto. In p.m., ribs and then drawing and redrawing in studio. Move bed + go to nice sleep— until 4 a.m. anyway. Season now is over, ending in its customary confusion with a few additional pieces trailing behind. It has been very active.

Talk to Dave who promises Pool Ball boxes for Monday.

190 lbs.

FRIDAY, AUGUST 18, 1967

Very tired. 2nd day of "Aspen weariness" if that's it—anyway—tired. Work slowly, but do things. Reserve tickets, for example. Go to bank, etc. But no idea of my performance.

Al working hard at stairs with Mr. Mystery. Pick up frames and some delivered. Hang my show. Article in morning's *Post* resulting from phone interview about my "chapel" convinces me to use that instead of any other idea, impossible at this late date. Invent costume at home. Pick up Bert at Tippler at 4 p.m. + take him to my studio + set up. Fill glasses with soda + food coloring with help of Dewain kids + Pam + others. Ice was delivered in cardboard, so leaks and drops all over floor. Les's piano working. At 5:45 p.m., hold first "chapel" reading, and am surprised by successful result. Hold three more until I am hoarse and in one of the last my language breaks down into 4-letter words. Brakhages have arrived + are installed. We return home with Steve after reception for a bit of quiet + then to Bartos's house for a dinner—tortillas + stroganoff. Benedetto, Stan's kids. Stan tells Pat how Jane talks to dogs. Dancing after dinner. We leave, not the last. Stan's home later. Rene of Four Seasons summoned + Saturday party arranged. At opening, building was posted as unsafe. Waiting lines were set up to allow 50—then 100 in at a time. Many came but relatively few could see my "chapel" event—the usual. Steve arrived, went to dinner with his parents.

TUESDAY, AUGUST 29, 1967

Sunny, turning to clouds + rain. Walk to studio + draw with interruptions. Interview on radio with Powers and announcer. Stupid questioner. I ramble on, avoiding trouble. Coffee at Epicure with Les + Vicki Barr. Return to draw. Powers asks me to reserve all Drum Pedal drawings. He is with a Texan who asks unanswerable questions about artist's life. Draw more, on Drum Pedal drawings. Shop at bookshop + drugstore. Home by 5 p.m. Drinks with Al. Eat at Austrian restaurant, where I protest darkness + poor service + taste of water. To Toklat to order reindeer sausage. Meet Jon Williams + try to draw softball for him. Home in dark. Watch stars. Reading + bed before 12 a.m. During night, dream I beat up on Mother. Later during night, resolve to be a nice person.
Talk to Ann Wehrer in Ann Arbor.
Buy Emily Dickinson poetry book.
Yvonne R. brings R.M. news clip about panel.
I give John P. the soft bat.
Vicki threatened by a hummingbird.
Took down mean sign.

TUESDAY, SEPTEMBER 26, 1967

190 lbs. Weather warm. A mild fall day, sunny. Up slowly, very tired. Archives man comes. Pat very efficient at sewing early and during day finishes Ghost Snare Drum. I have some good moments and solve Pedal (soft-hard). About 12:30 p.m. I dress up and go to Leather Guild, select material, then up to Liberty + carry out my promise of buying Pat another KLH phonograph. I carry console down in a cab, set it up + cautiously we begin again listening to music. Pat sorts Aspen clips. I pick up material by cab. Lay out material and draw patterns. Eat chicken dinner. Work on patterns and drawings for carpenter, inventory of all Drum Set parts. Very tired. Bed about 12:30 p.m. Pat writing poetry + rinsing her hair brown.

Did not go to Cheetah, Director's party, or get to park to pick dig site. Talked at length
to Kozloff on phone.
192 lbs.

SUNDAY, OCTOBER 1, 1967

186 lbs. Cloudy, clearing, and a beautiful, serene morning with breeze. Cab to Met
Museum 10 a.m.—meet Sam Green and the two grave diggers. Arrange parking for them
(necessitating a call to Hoving), meet a park guard. I find the spot + indicate with tape
measure. The ground is broken. A photographer stands by. An official with a brown +
white dog drops by. The park fills up with people, bicycling, playing ball, picnicking.
A hippie talks to the grave diggers. I ride to Columbus Ave. for film. a.m. scenes there.
Seeing the park first time in a long while. More people + questions. At 5½ feet, strike
big rocks + I halt the digger. The older levels the floor. McDarrah has arrived with his
son Tim who photos standing on Fred's shoulders. Sam + Doris Freedman. The three
of us photographed. A truck loaded with excess dirt + careful raking and information
about care + seeding. By 2 p.m., the event is over. Goodbyes. I ride home with Fred
through Pulaski Day parade traffic. Pat sewing. Write about the event + then interviewed
by *Times* man by phone because grave was mentioned at a press conference. Work on
Drainpipe Falls but eventually reject the new plan. Eat at Tai-Pei—very good. Home +
passing time magazine reading. Bed 12:30 a.m.—sewing machine broke down.

SATURDAY, OCTOBER 21, 1967 CHICAGO / JOHNSON OPENG. / GINZEL'S EVE.

See Alice + Linda + Louis Pearson in dining room.
Pack up and move to Holiday Inn, 22nd floor overlooking lake. To museum to finish
hanging. Pat comes about 12 p.m. Brings me champagne. Opening, members. Big
crowds. Stuff in papers—Pat several times. With Paul Carroll to lunch place, where he
tells his Shapiro story. Clear, cool, quiet day. Pat walks off after for nap. I hang around
crowds talking, meeting, f.ex., the owner of the building next door + we agree I will
design something or choose something for area on wall next to museum. Obscene
photo of agreement, tiny child mounted on our clasped hands. Return to Holiday Inn.
Get Pat + walk to Ray Johnson opening. Meet everyone again + Feigen. From there to
cocktails at van der Marcks'. Then with Meyer Signer + friend + girl, Higginses, Alice
and Doug Davis, first to Red Star, then to Germania renovated tavern for not bad
meal. Walk west on North Ave. into new "Old Town," Pipers Alley, past Crilly Court,
up Lincoln (lose Doug, Alison, Alice) into a ruined, deserted area. Find a cab and
drive to overcrowded party (for Betty Parsons?) at Ginzel's. Mort Neumann + Rose.
Everybody. Sit in a side room most of night with Bellamy, Pat, Jack + Michele Altman,
Lisa Foreman and visitors. A woman opposes my Wiper proposal. Driven home by Ed
Bedno + wife.

WEDNESDAY, OCTOBER 25, 1967 TO PITTSB.

Awake at 10:30 a.m. by radio next door. Had planned to get up early. See Loop from
my room at YMCA and film daylight version. Clean the room, wiping the walls of paint,

picking up paper from floor—a terrible mess in a small place. Collect drawings, mostly overdone, pack, shave, and leave, *not* writing on mirror: "Stop me before I kill another." Cold, slate-colored, windy day. Good grays.

Cab to museum. Repack bag and show proposals for wall to Jan, who is leaving for Minneapolis with Ingeborg. Al photographs me lying on sidewalk. Gets me cab. Goodbye to Lottie and go to O'Hare with talkative driver. Clip final Chicago papers and film on approach. Check in and wait in bar. Meet Pat at TWA counter. Board for Pittsburgh and film on board for first time, the getting out, etc. Limousine to Webster Hall across from Mellon Institute. Through fall colors in a cold limousine. We unpack, order drinks. Later, eat in hotel dining room, spend night in room watching TV, making love. Bed early, 12 a.m. or so, first night without pressure from outside.

WEDNESDAY, NOVEMBER 15, 1967

Roxanne Everett + Don Lippincott come + I show them place + discuss making lipstick for Sidney's Marilyn show, my first concept for metal.

Larry's last day working above my head. He goes to Africa.

TUESDAY, NOVEMBER 21, 1967

Long, sleepless night with recurrent dream of dying. Finally dream of myself very weak, climbing stairs to listen to myself speak on radio in a false theatrical way about religion. Yellow light in a.m. due to stillness of air catching smoke. Too many strange, rich events at once has made me lose grip on my sense of reality. The body quivers, the eyes flicker. I do and say mad things, above all am afraid, anxious. I remember Larry saying things are stranger than I can possibly imagine. John stinks up house with marijuana.

186 lbs. at bedtime.

THURSDAY, NOVEMBER 23, 1967 PARADE

Romantic rain sound after a sense of turning point. Pigeons looking in. A lot of rain. Love, first in some time. Pat: the rain doesn't last long enough. Marge calls + Barbara Rose calls, neither coming. Dress + make coffee. Take camera + ride on lonely bus + subway to 81st St. Raining hard. Walk through National History park, past Green Dome + spy Bullwinkle on back. And others. Take a vantage point at 77th + Central Park West, SW corner, my customary one under my umbrella. Study the preparations, then the departure + raising of first Linus, then Smokey (a new, very good), Dino, Popeye, Donald Duck, Bullwinkle (the last). To drugstore for film (the one I packed ran out) + film along sidewalk 77th St. I encounter George Harris at 79th + CPW watching city workmen trying to film Santa's Collapsed Tree. Santa too is filming. A doorman steals an umbrella I put down. I leave the predicament of Santa Claus. Subway down via D train and Canarsie line. Good luck with subways. Back by 11 a.m. to find Pat in her pink nightgown in our "cave." Have scotch + scrambled eggs. Read about S. Lewis + Pat lies in middle bed reading *The Human Brain*.

Took 3½ films 175 ft.

WEDNESDAY, DECEMBER 6, 1967

Just before going to the Marilyn opening the List Scissors poster solves itself—
spontaneously. I wonder if the awful 2 days that preceded it were necessary to the
gentle natural way the solution came.

FRIDAY, DECEMBER 15, 1967 FAN PICKUP

LeBron appears 10:30 a.m. Fan is wrapped + sent up to MoMA. The Toilet is returned
for cleaning. I am all business. Cold, brisk day. Post a card in Chelsea. Go to Leather
Guild, find just the material being unwrapped. Also take pattern of Fan hanger to Red
for redoing. Pat is shopping. George's Xmas gift arrives—marvelous wood sandwich.
Clean up rooms, rearrange furniture, pin up Fagends, move Ashtray into back studio, lay
out for tubing for Fan cage. Scallops dinner and stay up very late, 6 a.m. or so, drawing,
repairing Skeppsholm monument model, starting Alecto box, and finishing Clothespin
skyscraper. Play music. Larry up late upstairs with his saxophone. We are working in
a curious parallel situation. End of 3 days of resolutely sober attention to obligations,
detail. Having concluded there is so much to do that I can't afford the pleasure of slight
intoxication, and especially the loss of evenings.

FRIDAY, DECEMBER 29, 1967

Up about 11 a.m. Quiet day. Larry's gone to Africa. 186½ lbs. Simone at 12 p.m., who
works on cataloguing publications. Pat finishes pasting clippings and begins taxes. Joyce
essay from Edelheit. I write on Alecto statement. Weather balloon from Jerry Goodman.
Jenny calls re: show. St. Paul, Hamline College, calls I turn down.
Eat cold meat early. Finish up notebooks for November, December. Clarice comes down
for champagne about 11 p.m.+. I read from *My Secret Life*. Pat writes poems and drinks
Cinzano. I find her sleeping on the typewriter + I write a poem about that. To bed in
cave. Heard an auto crash. Some bad dreams. Meyer Signer called from Toronto re:
new "causeway."

New York, January 1965 to July 1966

An irritating pencil.

I have taught myself to do many things at once over a period of time . . . I have trained myself to follow instinct and let the brain-body do its own work without pushing.

An endless train slides by the eye.

An endless . . .

Toilet is a head (pun). Cerebellum, etc. Street Head.

Do diary with tape recorder and instead of taking Polaroids, have Robert McElroy or someone in every two weeks . . .

Daily tape . . . at dinner. Instead of diary.

Toilet equals stove equals Duckwalker!

Some of the most loveful effects have the most aggressive origin. In fact, I could say that almost all my best effects are born out of ugly passions. Being an artist puts you square against your motives, because the emotions are felt both as themselves and as material. To be beastly, to be beastly honestly and yet capitalize, capitalize honestly on being beastly. Not giving an inch either way.

Anti-cat-alogue.

Every show catalogue needs an anticatalogue.

Question is, should there be three-dimensional models of the monuments or should they just be imaginary?

Plug equals Mickey Mouse (Movey House).

The Sport of Forms.

The subject is divided into the interior and exterior, or internal organs (the Store or Home) and external organs (the Street).

Aim: reconstruction of a large mechanical object, exterior and interior, having strong parallels and identification with human anatomy. As compared to a "small object" (???) like the Typewriter or Sewing Machine, of which exterior only was created. A complex object requiring a great effort at selection and simplification for construction in the metamorphic technique of sewing cloth.

The dual nature of the Airflow car: its prehistoric nature is the bird (and certain models do look like fried chicken or a roosting bird). I think I've gotten bird-mad with the pigeon installations all around my loft. Note that in my first meeting with Carl Breer, he opened the trunk of his Chrysler and extracted twenty-four dead ducks.

Several monuments taking opposing positions on a certain subject: f.ex., Privates monument, Sergeants, Lieutenants, Captains, Generals monuments . . . also Victims monuments, Indifferent monuments, Distant monuments, Policy monuments, Man-in-the-street monuments . . . and President-just-before-he-goes-to-bed-glass-of-milk monuments.

Mistake monuments—a subject is commemorated by a monument that was shipped by mistake but, given the ponderousness of monuments, can't be exchanged.

Monuments are made before the purpose is assigned, like gravestones . . . There are a number of applications, f.ex.

The name Airflow suggests the lightness and the pressure possibilities of the soft form. AIR also stands for Artist In Residence . . . i.e., Artist in the form of the Airflow . . . or an object in the shape of the artist.

The car is really an environment, or a show in itself, a gallery, a store . . . many objects in it. A group of related objects, and the car is probably as exhaustible a subject as the Store.

The moving home / movement plus home equals car.

The sink patterns spell CO and so do the toilet-seat patterns.

My favorite event in New York is, of course, the Macy's Thanksgiving Day parade. A true ritual how these enormous inflated phalluses are carried down the path of commerce (the Broad way) to inseminate the Store. All our Gods, Donald Duck, Bullwinkle, Underdog, Popeye, the American Deities as in colossal representation. It is also striking how little they look like what they represent, how the shape is altered by the balloon, so that the sculptures are not at all crass.

Alternative parades:
Parade of Whores
Parade of State Prisoners
Parade of Gangsters
Parade of Indians (real)
Parade in General of Unseen People. On one day a year, these people deserve the right to
see and be seen.
Buffalo Stampede—a thousand buffaloes parade. Pacifist alternative—buffaloes attached
to balloons that float slowly down Broadway, bumping gently at the streets' sides . . .

We are all Teddy Bears, i.e., creatures with the hands chopped off . . .

Thanks for publishing excerpts from my studio notes. In the interest of accuracy you
should have made it clear that I did not select the notes that were published. These were
selected by Max Kozloff. Since the notes are as a whole very contradictory and a sort
of document of the inconsistent wanderings of the mind during creation . . . a choice
of them can point in whichever way the chooser wishes. I agreed not to interfere, and
I am pleased at Max's selection, but something of the nature of the notes (which are
as contradictory as nature) is lost if it is not pointed out that these are not statements
but postures I have taken. The statement that I stand behind and that represents my
judgment is my *work*, which is the sum and resolution of my contradictions.

Zones equals ice cubes equals ice-cream bar.

Summer 1965. Drowning myself in media. Thirty dollars of magazines a week, all
kinds, and leaving TV and radio (three) on all day and also living a daily life of
conversation in the midst. At dinner, eating and talking while reading four different
magazines and watching TV and listening to the radio . . . all senses employed. I also
developed illusion of familiarity with celebrities as a result, sending telegrams and
phone calls to them.

My come-in on films, which I have so much trouble with, is that the flat surface is not
enough. Thus *Moveyhouse* or the film in its space . . . the people, the popcorn, the seats,
the murals, the flying putti, etc. That is . . . side space, the film lengthened or expanded
cinema. I would change to inflated cinema.

Homage to sewing. What is sewing? Sewing is connection.

Sewing is interesting as a technique because there is a constant relation of scheme to
actuality, plan to life, flat to agitated, and in the same material. Cloth (Claes) and flat
to round—I am still working on canvas, that is, still a painter trying to inflate
the plane.

My studio notes are more a way of expelling stupid thoughts, allowing me to continue with my work.

Technological Happening: everything the artist does at the moment is projected onto a huge screen so many can watch.

Strange how soon after starting a concern, the mind begins to assemble material quite unconsciously (to my waking self), like a machine (Machine equals Man)—as if dutiful apprentices throw papers on a big table for the conscious mind's perusal. One must only believe that the material is limitless and that each mind contains Xmas Present, Past, and Future, everything, everyone, everything, supersimultaneousness.

Toilet equals sparkstötting.

The artist is a machine, yes, but a human machine most sensitive. His profession is balance, and he reacts to his surroundings by affirming what is missing. In hard times, he becomes soft, in soft times hard.

Mickey Mouse equals pancakes equals Kasper König.

Softness or softening may represent in itself the fluidity of position I sense as necessary . . . applied to a specific object, usually a traditionally rigid object . . . The clash of attitude is more pointed . . . The audience is especially responsive to the softness directed at mechanical objects . . .

Vibrating sculpture.

I am embarrassed by my public statements because they are attributed to *me* . . . or to a fictional character, "Claes Oldenburg," I'd really prefer to change . . . but who is expected to show consistency.

Change of galleries equals change of roles . . . big-business art finds this incomprehensible. I do nothing for financial or strategic advantage (unless I am playing financier or strategist). I am thoroughly undependable (unless I am playing a dependable person).

If you take New York or any landscape as a toy, you are playing with other people's property, in fact, with other people, since they are contained in the toy. What a strange idea of scale that so much detail can seem to be in the palm of my hand merely by an effort of the imagination . . .

I don't see how people can screw around with the moon the way they do. I thought I made it clear that the moon is *my* property!

Notebook Page: Letterhead MUSEUM OF POPULAR ART N.Y.C., with a Sketch of the Museum Building, New York, 1966

It takes the studio about six months to get into proper condition, but when it is, there is something to do in every square foot. My day is spent floating like a bee from one engagement to another. My walk is irregular, indecisive. I walk back and forth the length of the studio uselessly for such a small thing as a pencil. Along the way, I forget many things. Out of all the meandering issues, perhaps one thing or two. I am indecisive and irresolute and can't concentrate—the variety drives me mad, nuts—I am seduced by too much. Typing is a necessary physical activity.

Birth of the Flag is a metaphor for the birth of painting from the body.

In summer, with its necessary obsession with body and nakedness, fake nature or the city environment becomes especially grotesque. While in winter it is protective, in summer, like clothes, it's a burden.

The works document the attraction for the opposite sex to the point where it is a desire to be the opposite sex. To possess is to be, to enjoy is to be (?).

My position with relation to all my material, and myself included, the contents of my body, my thoughts, and my feelings, f.ex., is that of a manager or a band leader.

Wondering why I had embarked on the succession of monumentalizations (I mean by this isolation from its function and use as adornment, with all the arbitrary freedom of deballed or debased things that this provides) of mechanical objects such as the light switch, the toaster, and now the car . . . I conclude that this is a celebration of their obsolescence and irrelevance, of their passing into history . . . I am thinking as I work of nineteenth-century industrial representations and parodying these.

At this time in the US, everything becomes political.

Studio Rhythm—a musical.

Mickey Mouse in Swedish is Musse Pigg. Museet or Musée or Museum or Muschinski (Pat), MP–PM, or she-who-gets-up-in-the-afternoon (Injun). Mousse (soft). Pigg or Soft Pig (me). Mousse Musée or Musée Mousse.

The lovely, pure, infinitely suggestive thoughts I have on waking up are absolutely useless.

Gaudi died on a bicycle.

Origins of machine drawings: Diderot's dictionary, early nineteenth-century German draftsmen (Runge et al.). The expressionist/classical tradition: Struwwelpeter and Alice. Machine drawings of the nineteenth century (studied in Cooper stacks—Cooper himself). Also General Science drawings for which I won a prize in high school. Erotic drawings in

this style—Sexus ex machina.
Sanding the wooden typewriter keys, I feel like a manicurist.

Fan equals plus sign. Sink controls: two plus signs, one minus.

From 25,000 feet up, the US is the bed, with the Rockies for pillows.

The studio, lying on the same axis, identified with Manhattan Island.

A new police uniform: a clown uniform (I haven't worked out the details). So that the
policeman doesn't scare us so much when he is spying on us.

I am a technological liar.

The original inspiration of the Store was a butcher shop. The Airflow group is like a
butcher shop, too—the parts, the insides.

I had a model of the Airflow, maroon-colored, with lights supplied by batteries, when I
was six years old.

The car as body, flayed, as in an anatomical chart. Cloth as sheets of tissue, rope as muscle.

The power that every one of us has staggers belief: each one of us on waking creates
the whole world, all around (by means of communication brought to us or by what we
solipsistic selves need or want of it). And more, at night each of us creates the whole
reverse world, the things we did not do the other half, the alternate side of the moon.
Magic of symmetry, one half of the globe's dark, one half of the globe's lit. The sun in
its walking.

#1 There's no doubt I need an editor—I want an editor. It is part of my technique.

Store Days is involved with two "styles" of literature.
1. The style of accumulation of the day's material, of fragments, which I arrived
at some years ago. It is a sort of urban Thoreau style with appropriately urban
brutality, fragmentation, and unrest. No walk in the woods but a meandering
through street and studio and through people and drunken events in search of
serenity. This applies to the notes, to the scripts, to the films, and to all my narrative
and poetic material.
2. The second style is Emmett's contribution. For it was he who brought it to my
attention. The Store Documents constitute an accidental poetry, unconscious poetry out
of real matter. This being my unconscious setting down of things, and it has a visual—
concrete—dimension. An objective seismographic record of subject activity.

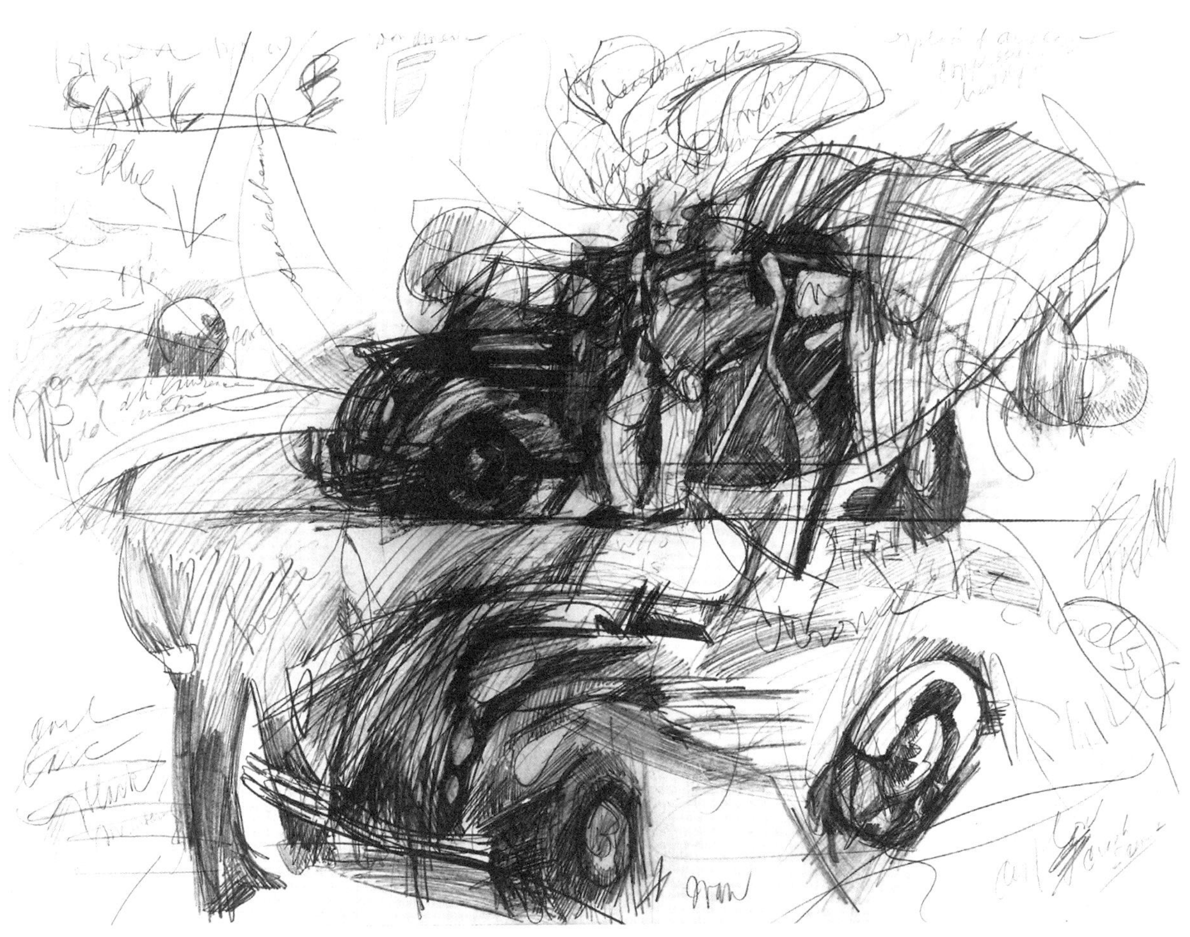

Airflow—"First Sketch," with Figure of Carl Breer, 1965

The Bibles of this theater are (besides the newspaper stylebook) the yellow pages of the telephone directory, Roget's Thesaurus, or any and every form of list and (it so happened) Stekel's *Sexual Aberrations*. I was lucky to have Samaras in my theater to develop the as-yet-undocumented dramatic art of object worship. F.ex., how to spread butter for half an hour on fifty-six pieces of white bread without losing the interest of the audience.

Sitting in a theater I find myself always watching what I am not supposed to watch: the rugs, the walls, the crossing and uncrossing of legs in the audience.

In making clothing, include the flesh that is covered.

Central Park—Claes and Pat.

I need a rest. New York needs a rest. The whole bloody country needs a rest. The damn continents should be put into dry dock, the statesmen soldiers anaesthetized, and the artists and poets left to repair the hulk.

I had completed only one room of the Home, the Bedroom. Originally, I had planned to rent an apartment or house, as I had rented a store, and "furnish" it. Instead the Janis Gallery served as my "apartment." (The expansion of the gallery in 1963 gave it this shape.)

The Bedroom was to have been followed by the Bathroom, which was sketched out in LA (but I had failed to find the typical toilet!).

The shape of the Bedroom Ensemble was the outcome of many factors but its original inspiration was a motel bedroom seen on a trip to the coast in 1947 and was augmented by fantasies around my mother's dressing table (dressing tables, in general). Going back in time (never a sentimentality or a camp, as it is understood by some) is not only the search for modern archetypes but also to find a subject one "knows" enough about emotionally, which one remembers well enough because one feels it and about which sufficient numbers of fantasies hang.

Introduction to catalogue
Into my consciousness crept the dream of California (which for me is a remembered real dream—the Bedroom Ensemble was based partly on a motel bedroom visited in 1947 in Los Angeles).
Summers are always critical. After repeated failure and destruction of work, by August 1963 I felt a total revulsion against my situation and circumstances in New York. It was nothing more than having had enough. New York fills you so fast and so full and you cannot always keep up with it, throwing out the things it gives you.
While everyone was away, we flew the coop, taking Charlie, our cat, with us and leaving few traces.

Los Angeles is the paradise of industrialism, where the object and the home have taken command completely. In New York and Brooklyn, one sees the degradation and terror of production, but one is not aware of that in Los Angeles, only of the finished product, steeped in radiance as on television, a compact and neat result like the frankfurter in its nonremembered distance from the slaughterhouse.

In New York, I had been praising nature for its eating into artificiality, but now I turned for relief to the cultivation of artificial nature, to find a cultivation of the death urge, which generates its own strange heat, the paradoxical heat of refrigerators. Blue became the repeated color, the sensuousness of absence.

It was a pleasure to sink out of sight, though frightening. It became a period of great isolation. I was discovered as an eccentric local artist by the *LA Times* feature reporter. The period was intact on returning there this year (April 1966). I found only a hole in the façade where my studio had been.

We came back to New York by way of Europe and lived at the hotel of exiles, the Chelsea, until we felt the rhythm again. I committed myself to a loft 204 feet long. I was smoking cheap cigars and managed to fall down the stairs and fracture my arm, but by the end of the summer, we were in production. I felt larger, Gulliver-like, whereas before I had been a piece of dust on a truck's fender. Now New York looked small, like an ashtray, and I looked down on it as from an airplane.

Stockholm, August to October 1966

Sweden is highly developed in its billboard advertising. The chief consideration is scale, the intrusion of the artist as personality on a large scale into the surroundings of the city. A project related to the monuments or enlarged object sculpture.

The Gulliver complex. Giant self-portrait. Monuments like dictators.

Sense of my enlargement since a child.

Knäckebrod is a good starting point. Maps. Neubern.

I feel shut in if there is no map on the wall to look at. The natural painting for prison cells would be maps changed periodically.

To Pat
Who patched the clothes and killed the roaches
Who sewed the surroundings and fought off the roaches
To Pat
Who sewed the surroundings
and everyone who bought a seat in my brain
Store Days dedication

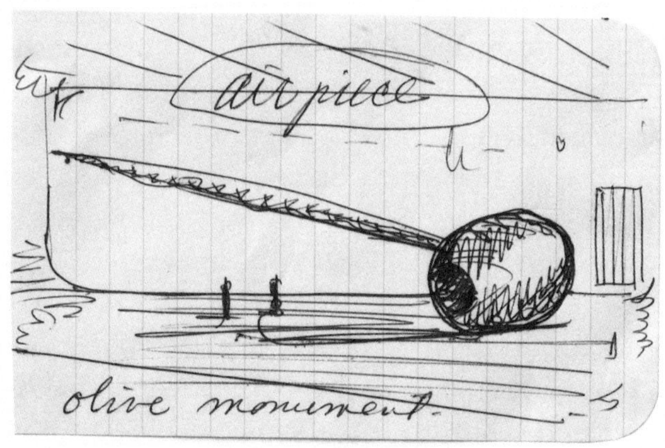

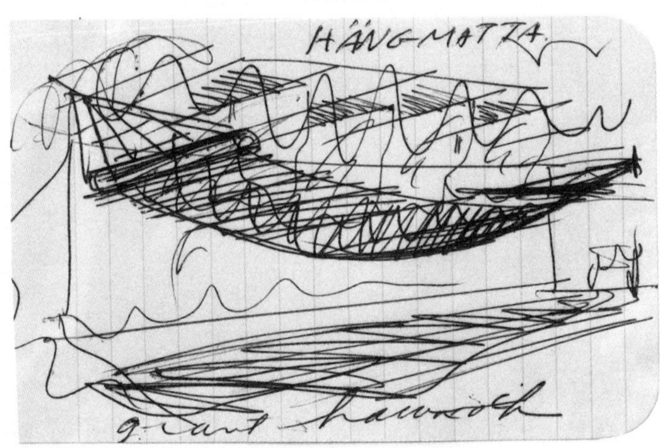

Notebook Page: Proposals for Two Installations at the Moderna Museet: Olive Monument and Giant Hammock, Stockholm, 1966

Use of two similar languages to complicate meaning.

Med smör. Och utan. Smörklick.

Svamp i hängmatta.

Knäckebröd hängmatta.

Why lion like Mickey Mouse?

Nalle puh mania now.

Islands equals pieces of bread crumbs.

In Stockholm, I am looking for contacts, i.e. "kontakter," places to plug in electrical outlets, an outlet for my feelings. They say hook up with the world. The world is electricity.

Knäckebröd—teeth (dream of cracking teeth).

Några projekt til nya moderna monument till Stockholm.

Vanadislunden, blomkål i betong.

Aluminium skulptur i form av ett vanlig sopnedkast läggs på.

Regnränna, i betong eller plast, ensamstående som enmajstång på något.

Badkarskranar i järn eller aluminium, dekorativ effekt till Lidingösidan av nya Lidingöbron.

Bron fortsätter ur bilden till vänster, kanske genom duschslangen.

Modern kyrka i betong i form av jättegrenkontakt, på en höjd.

Mycket enkel bordslampa i målad brons i Kungsträdgården vid Fleminggatan.

På kvällen kastar den ett mjuk ljus.

Claes Oldenburg utställning på moderna museet till 30 okt.

A kind of family of man of industrial objects.

Best sculpture is that in bed, when one feels oneself a sculpture.

London, October to November 1966

Knees also get cold in London.

Backs of knees equals drainpipes.

The subject of Pop art really is style not life. It is the play between art, style, and machine style, not between art and life, because stylization is all—there is no "life."

I can say more firmly than Lucas, whose egotism is perhaps too flawed by honest courtesy and taste, that without Lucas the Happenings I did in New York would not have become the clear and successful thing they were. I was quite aware from the beginning that Lucas was using me, but then wasn't I using him? And my uses of him were always a contest between his ambition and my disinterest in him as an individual (for performance purposes only). Lucas represented (I can use the past tense now that his individuality has been proclaimed and exploited to the point where he can probably never appear in my pieces again) the theatrical direction of the Happening, which fascinated me but which for purposes of definition it was necessary to restrain. Lucas is a great actor. If a man ever had to make a tough choice between careers, it would be Lucas. That he appeared in the performances was both an indication of his compromise and indecision but eventually of his choice. In my Happenings, Lucas the actor had little but to become Lucas the artist—you watched him making his work. I simply gave him the materials, and no words were used. I hope that my performances cured him of acting, and yet the fact that he still fancied himself an actor probably made the performances. He was a bad germ infecting my cast with stage sense, stage fright, hamminess, and theatricality. He was, as Bob said, my purple color. The ambiguity of my Happenings (or anyone's) has always been, is it theater or is it nothing. Only in between these is the form conceivable, and the swing between one and the other makes the form.
Lucas must have asked himself that question many times, as, f.ex., when he was buttering the hundred pieces of bread I gave him. Since Happenings seem to be a form that exists only at the center of contradictions—professional/amateur, real/theatrical, hot/cool—a real battleground, as I always saw it, for tastes and self-realization . . . perhaps Lucas's rather personal problem of what to do with himself was really what Happenings were all about, and we were his agents (as he certainly believed) rather than he ours. I know that Lucas volunteers for nothing he cannot (at least in his imagination) completely possess.
There is certainly a kind of fastidiousness in his choice of which manifestations he will lend himself to, and so, when the history of classical Happenings comes to be written, the subject will be Lucas Samaras, Mr. Pin. Like the impossible prisoner who turns the most degrading task into joy, no amount of degradation (lay up two hundred forms and knives on a table) and absurdity could not be turned by this delicate spirit into small theater and personal gain.

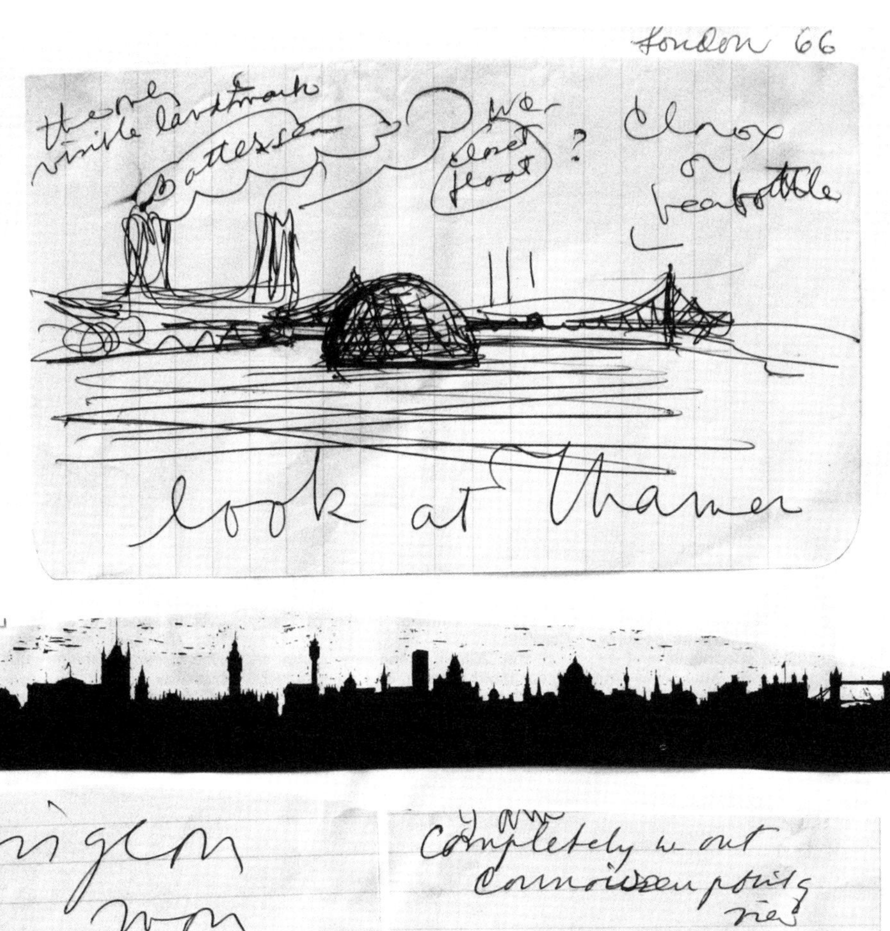

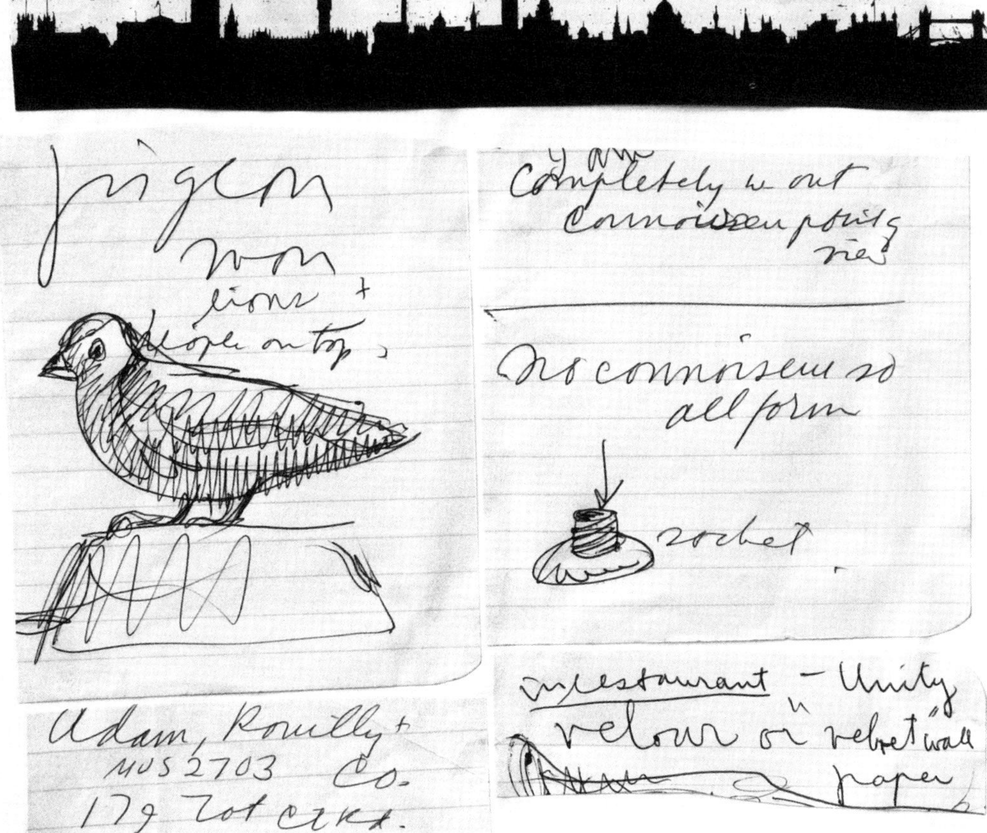

Notebook Page: "Look at Thames" and Study for a Pigeon Monument, 1966

Thames is one big leg.

Pigeon monument. People trip on the pigeons.

Small obstruction monuments.

Peter Pan monument is irresistibly a turd monument.

Drums equals Mickey Mouse.

Fagend, east end, west end.

Drainpipe equals Ray Gun.

Fagends, ends of empire.

We are sitting at a table. John (Cage) calls, says that Jasper feels Billy is wrong about
McLuhan. Brown may be right, but now its up to Bob or Merce, says Jim.

English money
wears your linings out
and weighs
your pants down like
the Dickens

Thames breathes and I've
figured out the Tide
She or is it he wiggles
on my ceiling very
complexly in the a.m.s

While the damp
sucks at my knees

If Paris is a slice of meat
this is a sponge
or Brains

Gigantic mousetrap.

My aim has been to adjust these everyday, small, voluptuous experiences—switching on
the light, flushing the toilet, plugging in the radio, putting on my newly laundered shirt,
eating the industrial bread—to Nelson's victory at Trafalgar . . .

Coughing as basis for London performance.
People wiggle about as the cough comes.

Note: The New Trafalgar (Gearshift) Monument moves at intervals (five minutes)
through the "shifting gear" pattern, flipping with a giant start from first to second to
third, reverse, etc.

New York, December 1966 to July 1967

Hot dog, mechanical Ray Gun.

Fill typewriter with plaster. SHUT IT UP.

What I've been trying to say for days now is that, having laid a base with my insistence on
making my work, a base of analyzed subject transformed, STREET STORE HOME (Legs
Tummy Head), I can now feel free to use any material, not rebuild everything, and that is
a new development: Feeling free. Anxious but free. Too free. Free. Free too to be an Artist.
Like the guy down the street who had a sign saying Studio in his store while I was M-f-g Co.

The body has its own unwritable history, full of changes, full of adventures. A history
with a great deal of logic, no doubt, of proper response, of heroic gestures. A story of
much dignity, nothing at all like the disorder of the mind.

Strange Mickey Mouse equals Death.
Equals Tomb for W. Disney.

Photograph the day-to-day adventures of my garbage can.

Make a show of straight paintings for May?

In this day of superpublication, it seems only fair that every artist should have his own
magazine.

Repeat the same show year after year, sewing new edition every year.

Bed equals Book. "Get off the Title Page."

If USA is TV is Movie is Joke, why is the outcome so not funny?

The time now comes. I am overwhelmed by my imagination of what I would say to an
unpleasant degree.

Mini Mouse—Pat
Meta Mouse—Me
Metamousphic
Mickey Morphic
Mr. Sleep
A modern, white house.
A mushroom on its side.

The sewn objects are prepared carefully, in a long activity in love with itself, of models, stencils, sketches, false tries, etc.

Technology equals blood.

No luxury of ignoring critics, no ivory tower. The ivory tower is full of cockroaches.

Fun, I never have any fun. Most peculiar, actually. People alive seek fun, are supposed to have fun. For some time since the obsessive ambition overcame me . . . 10 years I have sought no fun.

Ah, so Andy is Cézanne. I was wondering who Cézanne was.
Martha Jackson used to say that Jimmy was Cézanne.
Me, I'm Courbet except on Tuesdays when I am Delacroix, coming and going, and also Ingres, or I am a violin playing Cézanne, I mean Ingres.

I always said that, Phil. If you've seen one human, you've seen 'em all.

Why do I use objects instead of abstract forms for my giant sculptures?
1. Why not?

The writing I do is affected by the same emphasis on visual and tactile—the sensuous element that has produced my peculiar kind of theater—of surfaces, of form, of images, of color, and without words. I type because it's the most physical way of writing. I play the typewriter like I used to play the drums. I stand when I type, because that way I feel body, space, and movement. The meaning of my writing is often in the sound rather than the idea, as it would be in the surface of paint rather than in the subject. My literary effects, if any, consist of stringing together images. I analyzed this once because I wanted to become a writer. I found that I was not a writer because I could not proceed horizontally, only spatially. This is probably the trouble when I try to make films too. The writing I do now, scenarios and brief notes in the form of images, is perfectly suited to my limitation. My theater writing is basically a combination of images in single or overlapping structures.

Africa largest Ray Gun.

O. O. Story of O. Openburg. OO. Double Os. LONDON STOCKHOLM OSLO. Triple O. TORONTO. Three Os on their side with a pickle on top.

Filter cigarette. Hard at one end. Soft at the other.

I'm soft in the head.

Fan, in Swedish—Satan.

I don't lie too much
Just a little and
just enough.

Pop means nothing anymore except Here We Are.

My notes are supposed to be inconsistent. If anyone knows how to make sense with language, I wish they'd call me on the phone.

Imagine a situation with innumerable people gesturing, making noises, dancing, and nothing at all really coming across. Be my guest, our world.

Light Switch equals Lipstick and didn't realize that until now, June 23, 1967. Wow. Fantastic.

Sketches on the possibilities of pornography as form.

Buried monument. No marker.

Scream monument.
Each night at 11 p.m., a huge, very loud scream. Use air sirens?

Subway monuments. The sweating, waiting people are surprised when a foolish train arrives. Sound too. Or a car among others to walk through. Each day a different route. Like the midnight maintenance trains. Or a car filled with concrete, nonfunctional.

Hi Bob,
We decided to go west this summer and bought a mountain and are going west to start carving the Airflow out of granite approximately 789 feet long. It will be the world's biggest mountain carved in the shape of a car.
Love,
Claes and Pat

Projected images, sailing images, towed images.

Aspen, August 1967

Have lost myself too much recently in the American optimism.

Exposure in Lenox and Provincetown rid me of my optimistic notions, and so too at Aspen.

Simplicity and view of clouds only.

The Rockies are not sentimental, everyone agrees. They have no legends. They are fact. That is a cloud, that is a rock, that is a bear. May this be caused by their clear light and the generally clear outline of all one can see. One fears only factual elements here, never ghosts (or only in Central City are there ghosts). But the dreams are numerous here and epic. One dream follows another. So many they cannot be recorded or one would sit all day.

Deep prints of the
reeking grass the night
walks hour on hour into
my nostrils

It is a fact that overexcited I produce little compared to my sluggish moods. When moving very slowly I do a lot.

Drum Set equals sunset.

Denver should have sprinkler monument.

I am dominated by my feelings because I choose to be, and I do not always or necessarily think of them as "me" but as a motor that I let run, a professional necessity. Feelings *are* fact.

New York, September to December 1967

CO lossal.

The game of scale is relativity and also symptom of man's loss of importance-sense, of large or small, of hierarchies. Trivial affairs in the news can cost millions.

One hopes that all climaxes will not come at once.

Floating—sleeping.
Surface of water separates dream of waking from dream of sleeping.

Birth.
All half half.
Half water. Half solid.

November in New York is pure.
Is pure inspiration.

Six drawings of object dissolving. Dissolution drawings.

The object thinks
contemplates the world.

Inasfar as I can analyze my monument involvement, it has nothing to do with monument
at all or with actually building anything but is an imaginary importance—i.e., the scale
change that is taking place in thinking.

Words out to fall as stone
(from tender lips)

If you read words as I read words, you tread very slowly and softly, as over mines or
through lovely flower groves; for words are worlds, even the simple street names, names
of loved ones, of cities on maps, all that words are applied to become lovely only because
of the application of the word.

High art is simply elite art, art in love with itself, because of its simple logic of reaction,
rather elementary in its development. Easy, for example, for critics to grasp and to mold,
and therefore the critics perfect art. Self-questioning art is less easy to grasp and may take
years and consist of disguises necessitated by social or socio-art conditions; it fights for its
identity, depends not on critics (they depend on it eventually), and on the whole makes a
more dynamic sixty years of being around. An art not of politics but of strategy, where
the artist is always the aimed at, the out front, developing his tactics as he seesaws across
the timefield, in and out of the ridiculous institutions and personalities presented at any
given present moment, testing his (probably) best friends with the extreme hostility of the
(always) present, a sort of continuous trial by fire (which does not affect him except as a
necessary getting-in-the-way-of his moments of peace, which are his creative moments)—
such an artist sees history in the large, such an artist I wish to be or (hopefully) find
myself. History being a telescope is pretty small because of the repetitiveness of things
in general, which docs not prevent analysis to reveal the extreme dissimilarity in detail
of things. But one may be in as much trouble now, as Rembrandt is represented to have
been for loving his own place. To wish the spiritualizing of the low, so-called, is always
the sign of high spirituality.

The pacifistic implications of the sculpture I accept. The USA needs a good softening.

I certainly would not be pushed either to an emotional or a political statement regarding the awfulness of things, it would be formulated by me in an aesthetic statement, and just as cruel, but I may have had enough of this subterfuge, in face of the awful requirements of history and may become a tyrant, as life with its stupid oppositions requires us to be.

Seen in the subway, a flattened lipstick on an ad, ovalized.

My work is losing its mind.

Did I say: the air view is the greatest unsettler, and no one has taken it into account.

I've said before that callers on the phone, breaking into the consciousness of who-knows-what safe devilry in the hospital/studio/torture chamber, may expect to be hurt regardless of what my outside-studio feelings for them (sweet) may be. The degree to which all of what we do is theatrical and subjective is not understood. Very little of a day's events and statements could be called "real." Who said it and what else is new: all the world's a stage?

Getting drunk is, first fact, fun—even though it may turn to terror if too much. This is a challenge to one's constitution to "hold one's liquor." The ingestion, oral, is an antagonist, a body joiner, to let the devil in one's body. More to me enjoyable than smoke, which is too spiritual, too ghostly, and which kills.

Drink is world identifications through liquid.
There's never any way out but continuing to do.
TAKEOFF

If art mattered,
certainly I'd be
eliminated.

As long as it's preserved as a game
for the irresponsible but enviable
rich we're safe from persecution.
The rich themselves will not move a
finger to disturb our creativeness
or our fearless iconoclastic attitude
toward the matters they hold dear.
They want us to create.

And we want very little more than to be
pleasant and give our supporters what they

desire, which we've prepared for them. They
are tipped off to a good chef. We cake them
deliciously.

We lived our life
selfishly; all the
lovely things we found
and enjoyed we kept to
ourselves and only we
together loved and
enjoyed them.

So time passed with a
faulty respect for fame.
It's factual now we say:
We loved; we won.
Events may do their damnedest and
we shan't be remembered but nevertheless
it may be said now factually
that: we won.

We beat each other to death with
our faults and loves and what muscles
we had (though we lived a lazy life); we
shared numerously, we feared numerously;
we escaped together many times; we slept late
many times; we worked our way wormlike through
the imbecilities of workaday suffering
city structure; we hesitated; we avoided; we were both
cowardly and courageous but always our ideal was our
surviving love. The whole thing wasn't worth a damn.
Were happy to fall asleep but we made the time move.
We made ourselves happy at intervals.
We moved the calendar with action and love. We played
our stupid part
Including our invincible sentimentality.
We bequeathed to surviving generations absolutely nothing.
Because the fact is they will invent their own games and
pleasures to stay alive. Man by the fiat of nature will
continue until he gets fucking tired of the miserable
business of continuity into nothing not even into meat
like the steers and chickens and rabbits.

Inspiration, I learned, comes at odd moments (remembering always that Joyce kept a pad by his bed), and so one trains to always be available to note something down. Most of this is trash, but the few things that count are worth the dross.

I realize now what prints are about; they are about making decisions and, as such, are like posters and have the same sort of neurotic electricity for me surrounding them. A drawing, by contrast, can happen to end in a private and ecstatic and unpredictable moment.

I'm one of those people who can't use paint without spreading it all over everything and myself in a matter of seconds. I use my inexplicable rages. In dreams or in reality, I use them.

The soft metal lipstick is a combination of castrated prick and impotent prick.

Legs now: get dressed.

Faces as composition.
It must be possible to learn a different pattern—periodic, short trips to places without total involvement.

ENLARGED OBJECTS.

Trouble is that inspiration is a result of studio accumulation and away from studio is tough.

Sensational idea for a multiple: My notebooks, diary, etc., all in a bookshelf! Three shelves (the five-foot shelf).

Arrogant Bastard Corp.
Five minutes standing and thinking.

Soft art may be a way of saying Female art, and we are entering, if that is the word, a period of female influence, which is not, as anything is not, to be read as "domination." A leveling of sexual antagonism, pansexuality.

Another sweet idea for a multiple, which is the Telephone multiple or recorded conversations.
Another sweet idea for a multiple, which is the Typewriter multiple programmed to type (my) notes, like a "player piano."
And so on.

Barbara Rose says terrorism will commence next summer to combat American arrogance . . . why next summer? Meanwhile, the police are investing in tanks, etc., and overseas the main weapons are trained on the distracted communities of America.

Stamp—Guillotine.

A museum of diaries, or wastebaskets.

This typewriter is infected with Pat's beautiful poetry and is impossible for me to write my way on. It runs to sentiments and things I have some difficulty comprehending.

The books, lined uncomfortably on the upper shelves, are now attacking, with the aid of gravity. Ouch.

My view of myself has been that of a "perfectly normal" person, excavated, quarried, the walking coal mine, or body museum. Playing with yourself.

CO mmunication.

CO n CO rd

CO mplex Corp.

Body Shop Corp.

There is no end to our lovely sorryforourselves.

The rhyme element in my work is based on the fact that every work is reducible to a simple form or a few simple forms. It is the variation of these forms (by any and all means) that produces the subject. For example:

1. The two disks set side by side are shown as the "ears" of the "Strange Mickey Mouse."

2. If these disks are multiplied in deep space (their paths in time, as in a stroboscopic vision), the result is a cylinder. The cylinder occurs, doubled, in the "Swedish Light Switch" (positive and negative).

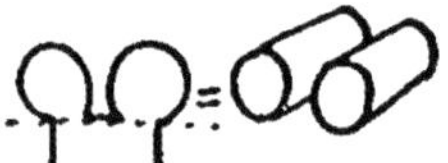

In my daily notes on the typewriter, such a "rhyme" is expressed as "Strange Mickey Mouse"—"Swedish Light Switch" or "Strange Mickey Mouse" *equals* "Swedish Light Switch."

Arriving at a rhyme is not as deliberate as it appears in retrospect. I am usually surprised when I discover it afterward. I am also reassured. It gives me a feeling of certainty and order.

It seems that particular periods, particular circumstances, stimulate the desire to see one form rather than another, and many variations on the preferred form result. Twoness and round forms belong to the time of "The Home," which began in Venice, California. Probably the fact that my studio had at one end a series of arches, of which I was constantly aware, had something to do with it.

The "Swedish Light Switch" was done in Stockholm in 1966, but it was done in the spirit of the Moderna Museet show and was linked up with the earlier obsession.

3. If the disks beside one another, the "ears," are connected in the two-dimensional plane, or filled in, the result is the top of the "toast" in the "Soft Toaster." The top is more important because it is the visible part, but the whole "toast" may be seen as a variation, in a thickened form, of "Strange Mickey Mouse."

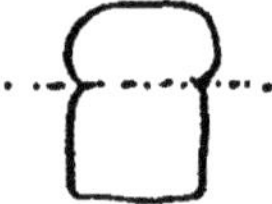

4. In the "toast" occurs also the doubles theme. The "toast" in the holes of the "Toaster" equals the "switches" in their holes. Or the prongs of the "plug"

(here the "toast" is elongated):

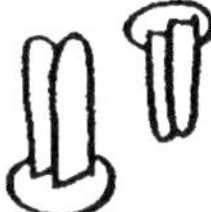

5. If the "Strange Mickey Mouse" is cut in half and the parts moved closer together, the result is a "Ping-Pong paddle":

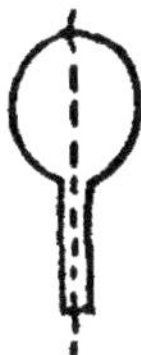

The paddles occur also in two sets of doubles (the name of such a game).

6. If the disk above then is halved, the result is (turning the image on its side)—the "switch."

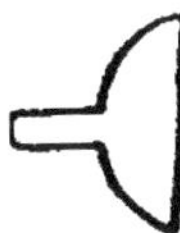

7. If the "Ping-Pong paddle" is "inflated," the result is a balloon, or, more specifically (inverted and extended, as in the effect of a long shadow), the "mixer" part of the "Dormeyer Mixer."

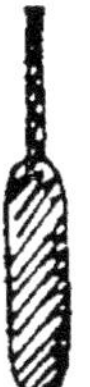

These illustrations give you some idea of what I mean by "rhyming" and "equals." Here are some more, taken from the show at Moderna Museet, and you can probably add more yourself that you see and I don't:

8. "Strange Mickey Mouse" without "ears" and "nose" equals "Switches."

9. "Strange Mickey Mouse," with one "ear" centered (cyclopic) and "face" (rectangle) extended, equals "dressing table."

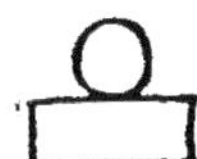

10. "Ping-Pong paddle," its "handle" rounded and "paddle" placed horizontally and extended into a cylinder, equals "bed table lamp."

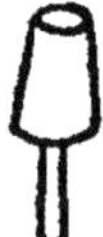

11. "Ears," or disks, continued in space but seen in vanishing-point perspective, equals "Bats" or "Ice-Cream Cone." (Corollary: "Bat" equals "Ice-Cream Cone.")

12. "Ears" or disk, in time path (strobo effect), equals oval "pool" (if two-dimensional).

13. "Pools," another set of two doubles, equals "Ping-Pong Table." Originally, the "Ping-Pong Table" was to have been half a "pool" table (as seen in the side view). "Pool" is an American form of billiards, "pocket billiards." (Note: "pocket pool" is slang for a man scratching or playing with his "balls"—genitals—by using his hand in his pants pocket.) One can buy tables in America that convert from the heavy (serious) table needed for pools to the flimsier (light-hearted, lyric) table of Ping-Pong.

14. If the "car" or disk-in-time-path is three-dimensional, it equals "Hot Dog" or "Ping-Pong ball." The latter is varied by assuming the path is diverted by contact at one point or another:

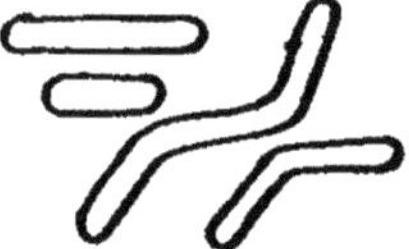

15. "Strange Mickey Mouse" with its "ears" drawn into the rectangle equals "Typewriter":

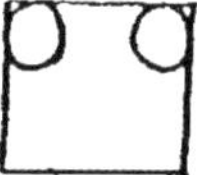

16. The "Wing-Nut" is almost a parody of the hats that used to be given out to members of the "Mickey Mouse Club" on American television. It is more organic, more like a natural mouse, and therefore not "strange" (unnatural) as the very mechanical, geometrical mouse of the show.

Two "Wing-Nuts" (the effect of reflection) equals a handle of the "Washstand":

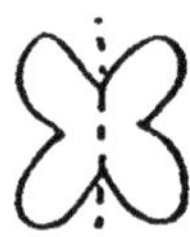

17. Two "paddles" placed beside one another equals a "plug":

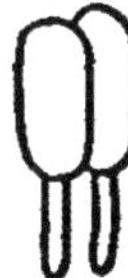

Following are some more complex constructions:

18. The "table" of the "bed table and lamp" may be seen as the "Mouse" rectangle continued in a non-vanishing-point perspective, with the column of the "lamp" the metamorphosis (variation by fantasy) of the nose, and the "shade" of the "lamp" the negative space of the discs (the "ears") continued in time. Therefore: "Strange Mickey Mouse" equals "bed table with lamp."

19. In the "Three Way Plug," the "ear" disk takes the place of the "face" rectangle, so that the "eyes" are contained in the "ears." The result gives the appearance of a pig's nose (*tryn*, in Swedish) and that includes the element of smell.

The show is not entirely "closed"—its forms sometimes refer to earlier ones in my work. One can easily see that:

20. The "Ping-Pong paddle" is a relative of the "Good Humor":

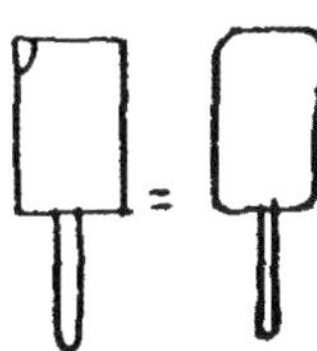

The cutout, or "bite," from the "ice-cream bar" is an abbreviation of what has to be done to convert one to the other—reverse the curve to round the corners.

21. This shape of the rectangle with "tail," which is one of my favorites, recurs in the "Airflow Engine":

22. and in the "Washstand":

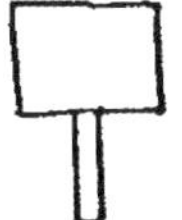

23. and in the "Coupole Lights" (the longer rectangle is partly hidden):

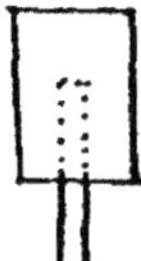

(Note: The "Coupole Lights" are a hanging in the following way—side view:

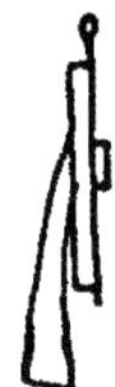

of the effect found in nature—at the restaurant:

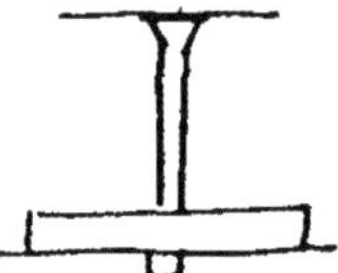

In this way—and through the softening of the form—two viewpoints are combined, which is also true of the "Washstand.")

24. and as the "door handle" in the monument for Skeppsholmen (the longer rectangle, bent but hard):

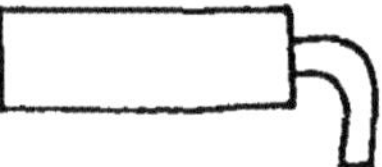

25. and as the "Tube" (the longer rectangle inside and soft—"toothpaste"):

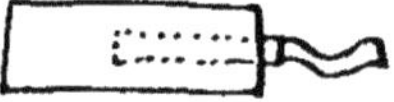

In general, the doubling, the symmetry, refers to the human body, with parallels drawn between the objects represented and parts of the body: ears, eyes, nostrils, limbs, breasts, testicles, etc. The sort of analysis I have done above of the poetic geometry of the works could also be done of their body equivalents. This is why I refer to *The Store* or any collection of my work (of my "objects") as a "butcher shop," a place where the parts of the body are displayed. The body parallels are reinforced by the use of flesh-like material (vinyl, for example) and sculptural "insides"—hard like bone and soft like fat.

Man makes objects in his own image because he doesn't know any other. That the objects resemble parts of him need not mean that he makes them the substitute for his repressed desires. But the reference to sexual parts could be another topic of analysis of the work:

a. The extent to which an object is a male or a female representation—the sex of the object. And which are combinations, double sexed.
b. Which objects refer to "coupling." Plugging in, or establishing contact is a theme—which goes beyond the merely sexual to the contact of the person with his surroundings. Many of the objects also refer to masturbation or forms of touching oneself instead of another: the "Ironing Board," the "Pants Pocket," or the "Vacuum Cleaner."
c. Which objects refer to reproduction. Any doubles, of course, but also more specific references, like that of the "Tea Bag" to the sperm. However, two women have told me they associate the "Tea Bag" with a menstrual tampon and react accordingly. Or the "Toaster" with its capacity, as the result of being plugged in, to pop out "bread."

I should emphasize again that these references come as a surprise to me when they are discovered, and that they are usually discovered by someone else.

I don't mix knowing with doing. If I did, the result would be highly unnatural. As it is, nothing *necessarily* means anything. Which is the way with nature.

Only when someone looks at nature does it mean something. Because my work is naturally nonmeaningful, the meaning found in it will remain doubtful and inconsistent—which is the way it should be.

All that I care about is that, like any *startling* piece of nature, it should be capable of stimulating meaning.

These are the themes of the Bedroom and the Bathroom—the central parts of The Home.

The "Typewriter" is there to remind one that a large part of the show is hidden—is, in fact, *written*.

EGOMESSAGES ABOUT POLLOCK (1967)

1. Following his call to directness got me out of art school and unlocked the use of paint. The school system was to have the student choose a favorite French Impressionist or Post-Impressionist to follow. After a few weeks with Cézanne, I switched to Pollock, i.e., chose the living, which meant trouble. For example, I brought to class a palette of store paints in a cardboard box. I put them on the canvas and they ran off onto the floor, because I didn't know that Pollock painted straight down.

2. Pollock acts in my work as a fiction. I objectify him: American Painter, Painter of Life, Painter of New York. I honor all the stereotypes about him. This extends to the edge of magic procedures of identification, with which the stereotype receiving machinery more or less cooperates (for example, pp. 110–111 in Allan Kaprow's recent book on Happenings). Here I've got the thing down on the floor, though usually I had it on end, and the paint found its own way through gravity.

3. Pollock's paint immediately suggested city subjects, the walls, the stores, the taxicabs. I don't know if he cared about that. In the Happenings, which owe something to him, the world is smeared with paint or its substitutes. I used that kind of paint to entangle the objects in my surroundings. Later I used paint-like material, like water, for dipping people in. The vinyl I now use is still paint, the objects dissolving now in paint. Pollock is a paint legend because, unlike Picasso, he turned the Sapolin loose.

4. His statement in *Possibilities* is the model of truth and unsentimentality, exactly what an artist can say about what he is doing. It seems strange to hear him speak of "my painting," which suggests a small piece of property, or ground, which he is standing on. How hard to stand on other paintings of the time—in fact, his were very large by comparison. The canvas on which I (a post-Pollock painter) now am standing on not only stretches as far as I can see or hear but has layers, roofs, floors, basements, etc. Seeing gold frames around Pollocks now is funny and also hurts.

5. The big symbol energy that vibrates in Pollock's light cords is painful now but also unnecessary. Every simple thing is so engaged in its own vast symbol production that it seems better to switch off. That was a time when no thing spoke for itself and the landscape was full of noisy monuments. But now everything speaks for itself.

6. New York scares the hell out of me. When I ran for death to Los Angeles, I made the Bedroom as a demonstration of my necrophilia. On the walls are pseudo-Pollocks, yard goods from Santa Monica. Whatever else this act suggests, I intended at the time to use Pollock as a symbol of Life, and his reproduction, removal by counterfeit and photography, as the symbol of Death.

Intro

On the bus in from the airport:

Opinion by Soldier One that, all in all, the New York practice (among the kids) of setting fire to the Bowery bums was civically beneficial. Protest by Soldier Two, on the peculiar grounds that "Them poor guys ain't got the means to pay for treatment of their burns."

Competitive discussion between Soldier One and Two: who knows the most wounded man. After several examples, Soldier Two triumphs with a man totally inactivated. He used to be on the football team, now he can only move his mouth.

The young soldiers are in front of me, walking from the bus to the shuttle. A chic woman passes in a miniskirt. "Inch more shed have to shave more than her legs!"

Now that the knee's revealed, the issue's joined. Funny that the eagle's destiny should be decided in the bland valleys of the knee. A battle in the navel naturally would be more vulcanic—or we could have gone to the moon. Disappearance of the garter will separate the men from the boys, create a double standard for Mom: new map of Missouri.

War

These be evil times. What hurt, the work must show it. To use red, suddenly, after so much red denial. This show is about bending, circulating, having yr. fingras cut off (the Fan).

Why must we go thru another hole in the skull?

Vulgar USA civilization now beginning to interfere my art. I only intended a bedwatch with generous drinks from the clock.

Make Useay depend on Canaday. Leave the colonies breathless! Roy explosions, I spots—consequentials fum explosions. In the studio I am quite in sane. Billy Lugosi in his Lab. Ape Man plays Moonlite Sonata. What did you do today? I cut off twentytwo lipsticks.

World is *not* a drawing. Artists the curse of the world. They know how to start things, but not know how to stop them. When Ray Gun shoots, noone dies. Art childs play. Art as life is murder.

Hitler, he erased half of Europe, but the world is *not* a drawing. Flagging of belief in Reality low art to enter life.

There is morality to scale. Drop a bomb violates scale. As the numbers increase, I hug my wife closer. Nature hates us. Every day we eat half of her. Tomorrow she is whole again. Life is—difficult to say—this multiple.

My innocence could have dreadful consequences. Consider too, my backwardspeaking, my mirrorlanguage, my devotion to lies. Bridget—coming always as Joan of Arc—made me again aware of threat from grossness. The sinister elements which may dominate the exhibition.

My work would be terribly misunderstood if it was taken for real. Humanism has its strange passages. Perhaps this whole road leads to immorality. Collecting rocks, that better. But if one is open—symptom too, choice too. I graze, I opencow, chew cud and pass into the metabolikos.

C.O. I gather another identification. Conscientious, which I is. Objectish, which I door. I am Object, or.

The Draft? "C.O., Jail or Canada," Smith says. Flee cool. In studio I really create for me: ideal prison situation. Grant, Gen., Listen, long as youre on your fucking Sleepyship, anchrad in der Mickeymoupsi and watching the arms, noses, fingernails, twats and eyebrows flying by, unwind yr. Cord—Graham in. Bantam, Batnam, Batman, Vat Nam. A Big Big Doctor came Today: he expertly cut the sound out.

Weiss accords the terrorized the dignity of not symbolizing. My imagination too intense (as I told Max). Don't stir me by reminiscinges of firestorms. A little hint of terror give me mos. of fright. I wrestle to turn terror into form.

I have begun to keep, among the notes I turn to, scattered, unpredictably located, faces of the mutilated, or the polaroid of my granduncle at the last living point of death. These throw me off my search. I stumble round the studio as result, forgetting what simple and efficient thing I wanted. We are so poorly educated in Death. We can only dish it out, as they say. Provide Ice Cream. If I hadn't tried out as reporter (out of my love of fire), I might never have acquainted a corpse—or a cunt for that matter. Both these are secrets in USA.

Fuck it, my Time Band slipd. I made Bedloes Island into Boecklin's *Isle of the Dead*.

Fagends equal the P's *Charnel House*. Ball, she bomb. Hbomb-superdrainpipe, Tornado-suckup.

Oh, Injun, thou tired Puritania, Don't Draw on Me!

Exercising drainpipes equal cemetery crosses. The Pipe of Peace too, on his hammer. Reverse (reflected) cross is underground drainpipe. Dirty with the earth, as Plumbing is. Suggest I mount as Butterflys.

Der Schnee now falling all uvver Irish Sea. Also Fallon is Murder. Some fall is good, some fall is bad. Fex: Amonkeriwrenchzekas bumbs hit you, or one of their diabol Low Cals Ize mean Calif. cookies. Dem bust yr. guts and no amt. sewing can, et so on. Ibsey say: No Eat Wily Duck. Dese messyguys dey cum fum New Yawk Hozpitul, Hozpitul fur Westran Wd.

You must realize cops are just you and I in uniform. Now I propose then a uniform which is ridiculous. When they do the thing they do, they learned to do, namely when they do restrain you and they draw the blood—they look ridiculous. As you and I if caught drawing, draining blood.

Kids do the killing—politicians play that like a piano. Why think you the people lean from the windows. War chance to see new wounds, new sewing, new sexual advancements, new aeroplane design. After its poured, styrofoam so called goes up the fagends slowly. It rises like a soda or our famous explosion. All my materials are black and white—what did you expect from Mickey Mouse?

Urethane is Evil. Plaster is Good. After a Urethane feast, the place must be scrupulously cleaned, to avoid contamination. The Studio is the setting for the most horrible crimes: the fagends are pierced with the wire, and twisted. They are then tied to the chairs, twisted again, and the Urethane is poured in. They swell. After a few minutes, all movement ceases. The Ladder—what is that for? I don't know, but then: the hook splits. The Ladder crumples into a rape.

Soon as the show is over, we pick up the pieces. We clean up the house, so there are no traces. Man and wife, we return to peaceful occupations.

Erect a painstakingly accurate replica, Chicago fire, near the end, or San Francisco earthquake.

For Welfare Id., propose a famous park. Disneyland of Death, for Sunday, family visit. Like the War Mouse. Pageantic of the Uceay. Technological contribs to Death: subs in act, planes in strafe, wiggling replics of the Monitor and M. Variety of wounds. Culminate in colossal, concrete Mr. Clean, at the rocky point of the south end, threatening the N. Inside—planetariums, spectacles of the After Life. How Heroes Live Then. But also afterlife of the losers, cowics. Alternating and intermingly—detailed projects for the coming war on Stellar Dust. Also, Soldier Fare Thru the Ages (in the rest.) A Worlds Fair of Death. Now Heart deliciously slips into the cool bottoms, watching the ship depart. Steve whips his horses in the New Jersey highlands. Make up thee mind, Mr. US, thee want wet or hot.

We Promethised Land. We home fire. We Red Man. We run torch to Plato, stumbling angmond za fagends. Lipstick here is bullet. Paint drop here she punching bag.

<h2 style="text-align:center">Sex</h2>

Everything I, great leg fantastico, have wished for, it has all come true. Women All Legs.

Tits have flown to balinesia. No bra spoken here.

Expo fex: All that erecting by the structurers, for mons. That in practise turned to such a simple thing. That what it all about: eyes of the mountin boys zey climb the structures flimsy of the WF, ascend legflesh of ze mountain girls, ascend to the red cheeksies and the coaly hair. The sun hots, the Candenzy jet planes stunt you, the St. Flowrence works. Ships paws, long ships.

Montreal girls are bilingual. That means two tongues, right? Wow!

People are intensifying themselves. I hope we can all stand it. I had a violent desire to go to bed with a painting. I bought a Mondrian dress on 14th street, and made her wear it.

I must not forget the incredible pleasures of typewriting.

My romance with a fan. My romance with a Satanic vinyl fan. I take my appliances to bed with me.

In the Auto Show, women demonstrate. In my drawings too, women demonstrate. Why not, David points out. I imagine myself a woman then, to experience the thing. Men have tough skins, on TV they shave and play baseball.

Me Obvious, you Jane.

Kinetic element in Knees, is time of day.

Aging Clown Exhibits Self

Shows ~~his~~ Oils

do not forget the incredible pleasures of
the flesh
~~wow me what a bore~~   do not forget the incredible
pleasures of typewriting
of typewriting

Oslo - cunt

i sing the bawdy electric

float sleeps in Thames bed

why do you reject   my   monument

one O in asshole right

why do all gods creatures end with an O

Note page for "paracat" of "America: War & Sex, Etc.," 1967

One "O" in asshole, right? Why do all God's creatures end in O?

Oslo is cunt. Why?

I sing the bawdy electric. I sew the Broadway galactic. I slang the body eclectic.

Why do Czechzs sex me up? Why, do you, reject, my monument?

History of the Pool Balls: Somewone suggested swimming but twas cold. My metamorphic nose turned the water to the pool tableaux. Union was "strip pool." When player sunk a ball bearing his number (only he or she know their number) he move his cloz. So this proceed until my wife winning of course, finally only clad one, prolonging the finale among a company of halflit poolplayers (colored by the TV), their balls sunk, standing about with their cues in their hands.

Basically, collectors want nudes. So I have supplied for them, nude cars, nude telephones, nude electric plugs, nude switches, nude fans, nude electrectera and sew on.

Drainpipe inverted: "sheath." Vagina: red, raw, blue. Cool fun.

Pool balls have nothing whatso do with sex. Forget the Loop. Forget oos. The round reflections are breathtaking. Ah, the balls. I spend four days just rolling one of the big balls around my place, seeing myself in it, plastered all over space. The base of the Toronto Mons. should be as if some painful glimps of a forbidden suj.

Drawings, thick and full as knitted sweaters.

This show, it's all about bats and balls and when does the semen start, I hope not April 26.

Roll me on the green, swat me into the Miami sky, pop me in the cup with your amputated wingnut. Let me blast the bottles, bust the dishes. Let me catch the last pin, infloat me with air, hunch me, lemme drift aways. Shoot me down. Now then, gather my data. Touch all the bases.

Mickey M. runs like foam rubber, stumbling thru the situations. The curitas of styrofoam is frightening. I only use white materials. Elmers glue, styrofoam, plaster, and then sperm. Whale and so on. The fundamental material of art is jaculation, confused somehow with New England church spires. A readheaded in the Sunday School showed me her bottoms while we read Mrs. Eddies Matter. Thats where I got the Germy capitals, my platonistic erections.

In fact, I learned to draw fingering and nippletweaking at the DriveIns. Movies were shorter then but chicks did not much care for being treated like art schools. Art did cut once, now it tickles.

What the delirius for musik? Why Frank send his zephyr singing twixt a music lovers strings? Why Henry pianola muff. Or in my private school, why teacher let her pages drop apart, knocking the whole singing football team on the floor?

AGING CLOWN EXHIBITS SELF.

Shows Oils.

The way to the Fig. lies thru geoponography. Starting from body, as I did, descending the coalmine of object by degrees, losing the Fig. in the coal passages of the mind, found my way to mannekins, corpses. Dismembered, as in advertisements. Leg here, Arm there. Invocation of Al Fish, scrotumpuncturer, anusfracturer and backwards hero of Object Art.

Chopd as with food we do. Original assemblyline (*de*-sembly really) was devised to slaughter pigz—this my memory most likely wrong deliver, out of Giedion.

Well, I have taken the Fig. thru all its advertsintitures, not excl. the shit of cannonballs.

Wow was tit shot zat hummer! Mr. Janis was after me to be erotic. Larry 'n I started normal mural of strange practises but got too hot had to shower in Swedenzia.

At 4:35 about, Claudette Colbert gets the torpedo. One sees it coming. Damned fool really for shipping on the Athenia. I fall asleep. Who can watch everything. Art as ecstacy, a tiring occupation.

Where, I wonder, did Bernini find the time to sew all those sculptures?

Images, visions during intercourse. Constructed parallels of the act. The act slowed down. Representations: not photographic, not architectural, not verbal (certainly). What then and how imitate? How abstract a fuck? Why rage to imitate at all? I got off the flesh, I ran into the studio and threw material in the air. I punched twelve holes (by actual count) into the innocent cardboard.

Thing—in Swedish, *sak*, euphemism for Prick.

Dot. Prick, as in Klee. Thats how language cuts us up, makes logs of us.

Fan model parts ought to be hung, like Magreases female body parts.

In *Snaps*, Pat was the first Miniskirt Monster. Women who play objects in my work have that familiar resisting indifferent manner (as you would express).

Bread yes, that has navels, assholes, eyes. Has O's.

"Hot knees"—thats title. Energetically, this would be fact. If the hot one didnt get *red* hot, it would nevertheless give off heat, which you could feel at a distance, say, of four feet, and one could step into the area of its emanations. As in my kitchen there is the feelable presence of my stove, standing next to my frig.

Origin of the Pool Balls: I meet George, on the stairs, sweating. He has just cast pregnant C. He stows her dismembered parts in his red pickup for assembling in NJ. I know Hefners living room because: here we brought women picked up in the Lincoln Park or maybe by the Ambassador, here we buttered them, eating jelly, listening to Eden Abhez, of all places—under sunlamps. That spot is one of my originals: the chairs were big as motor cars.

The pool tableaux? A place to bend down. Green silhouetting the flesh. Some samples come, all colors. Wow flesh—it is so colored! In Lincoln Park vandals separate an arm from one of the goddesses guarding Linné, the namer of all flowers.

Etc.

What part of life gives you authority? It is your childhood. Play S on your mind. One never can have enough S hooks. My April trip to Russia in an English plug. An account of the sights, natives, geography, customs, etc.

The Pinsk was resolutely Magnitogorsk! Language has lost its marbles.

Poopy is my Medium.

If the length of time were not defined, the time game would not be part of the show.

Draw images now that force a certain formation of the spectators mouth, and produce sound. One clear echo note.

Sherwin Williams was right: the world is round, and full of paint. Sherwin Cody had his points too: six Ripleys abreast would march forever.

Openfaced Sanwich tells all. Mr. Openburg. The Store of O.

Anyone who listens to artists should have their eyes examined. Artists are not sportsmen. Imagine Cézanne playing tennis. He didn't even keep his pool filled.

To draw is in fact: to make appear. Only this act is proof of my license to conjure. Also drawing is basically drapery.

Graphite equals nails.

Shrimps have no ears, they *are* ears. I cant eat animals with famous ears: Edw. G. Robinson, Elephants, Mickey Mouse.

What shall we do with all our reproductions? Our cheese sandwiches on the house. The ladder A, why is that a suspicious ladder? The translation mystifies me. Now my Mother is the lather, and my Father is that smug pigeon, three holed, and slipping into a cube tap.

Honestly I try to write straight, along the lines of this machine, but all the Burroughs gives me is misspellings and Jello. Margin releasers and back spacers.

I sailed the seas of Milwaukee like the legendary Gauguin. I came back with a native I bought for packs of gum. To heat me. The drainpipe, aside from introducing itself as Mr. X, is a mechanically simple and supersuggestive form. A thing which has adventures, dramatizes vertical and horizontal. Siamese Ray Gun. Great Books in a nut and bolt.

Rationality is the most aesthetic shape that madness takes.

What is this silly Miltonic opus here I've built—White Fan, Black Fan. Rosycrucian and Friday. Drainpipe, my Injun and his yellow friend, the Ladder.

Only man's need to sleep stands in the way of realizing his dreams.

Not forget that Modern is a strictly western term. The Chinese invented it all, in those mysterious ink centuries near what we call A.D.

When I refer to Brancusis drainpipes (Caros, for that matter and Icaros as well), or to Morrises furniture (forever rearranging), Franks "mattresses"—I mean no harm. Only to assert for me the inescapability of identification, impossibility of a clean, well-lighted mind.

My auto is a hypochondriac. It lies to me, telling me its manifold, or whatever horseshit it can think up, is out of order. I kick it, I say: run you mother, drive, or whatever you call what you do. I can't believe so many parts and details have no sensation. Can't the bloody thing be proud for example of its steering wheel, its carburetor?

Adults Only. Nothing replaces anything. Everything accumulates, binoculars and telescopes. If I slip a magnifier into my beach house, the inhabitants could see Europe. When l draw, as I often do, I try to maintain the simultaneous feel of everything I saw or knew.

If, in dreams, as I have heard, your brain can reproduce any small detail of you were there, since drawing then is sleeping on your feet with lead in your hand, why cannot put on this paper (manual dexterity granted) anything.

Blue drainpipe is Holy Ghost. My left hand is out of business. Queer—my sympathy for things around me start me off, but when I've done my view of them, the originals look ugly. They're, how would I say, runty or puny. I do not expect to squat on that small toilet but in fact, the damn thing fits.

Who is the magician, who the assistant? Who wears the opera hose? Pat and I were once one but I thought it more interesting to have a half running loose, going swimming for example.

Ellen said that "in this small drawing Cézanne is not far off" but I have looked everywhere and cannot find him. Mistah Fuller, he dome. Sevenup—shut up.

Superselfconsciousness turns into white. One is so selfconscious that one dissolves into sky. I am hoping for this. Or slip thru the Mercury. Now as the Uranian dawns, Noah sets forward on his rescued aquarium. I can hardly wait to get to the other side. Burning incense in the snowstorm—it thundered, can you imagine that? I suppose that foreshadowed John's arrival.

The USA, of all places, cultivating fantasy! I read and liked the notion that hallucinogens are secreted naturally in the artists body. Having taught the basic skills, art school supplies 30 years of vision juice. I have to talk to someone and I am the only one who'll listen. If you're tired of me think how *I* must feel.

Do you know what a freedom it is to get up in the middle of the night, take your candle to the office and feel your canvases. The business of absurdity. But Mme. Cézanne clamps her dents on your nightshirt and she hisses: "Switzerland! the Alps!" Keeping a diary informs you: everything returns. Two Ray Guns equal one Winged Victory. I am a Wing Nut. A Nut w. Wings, a cigarette that is no longer manufactured. I am an Avis. I gurgle occasionally in the Tyrrhenian blue.

A foursided face, an English Plug.

Each object, besides being its own flower, is committed somehow, somewhere along the way to War and Sex. Fagends faced the danger of becoming garbage of a torture chamber, also that of coming to rest as the twined limbs and tails of an Ingres orgy, Rubensian asstray. Now I can say with honesty that these are: this, that, the one hand, the other both, but mostly that they are neither. It depends on the weather.

The lipstick did a strong flirt with the bullet. The Fan stayed out all night with the swastika—a terrifying moment. The balls vibrated between testicles and cannons (and or breasts), appearing finally (with the subtle Drainpipes help) in the gorgeous triangular embrace, the rack: pool balls!

The show came out intensely lyric, as it should be. Painting not of pleasure is impossible to imagine. The joy of this show is that 1 assimilated, translated, say maybe transcended my undoubted obscenity but also the twice obscene, twice monstrous infinitely gorgeous horrors of the times. To both I leave myself C.T.O. I am a sausage maker. This is my lyrical sausage factory. Now sweet pinsk, gun nite.

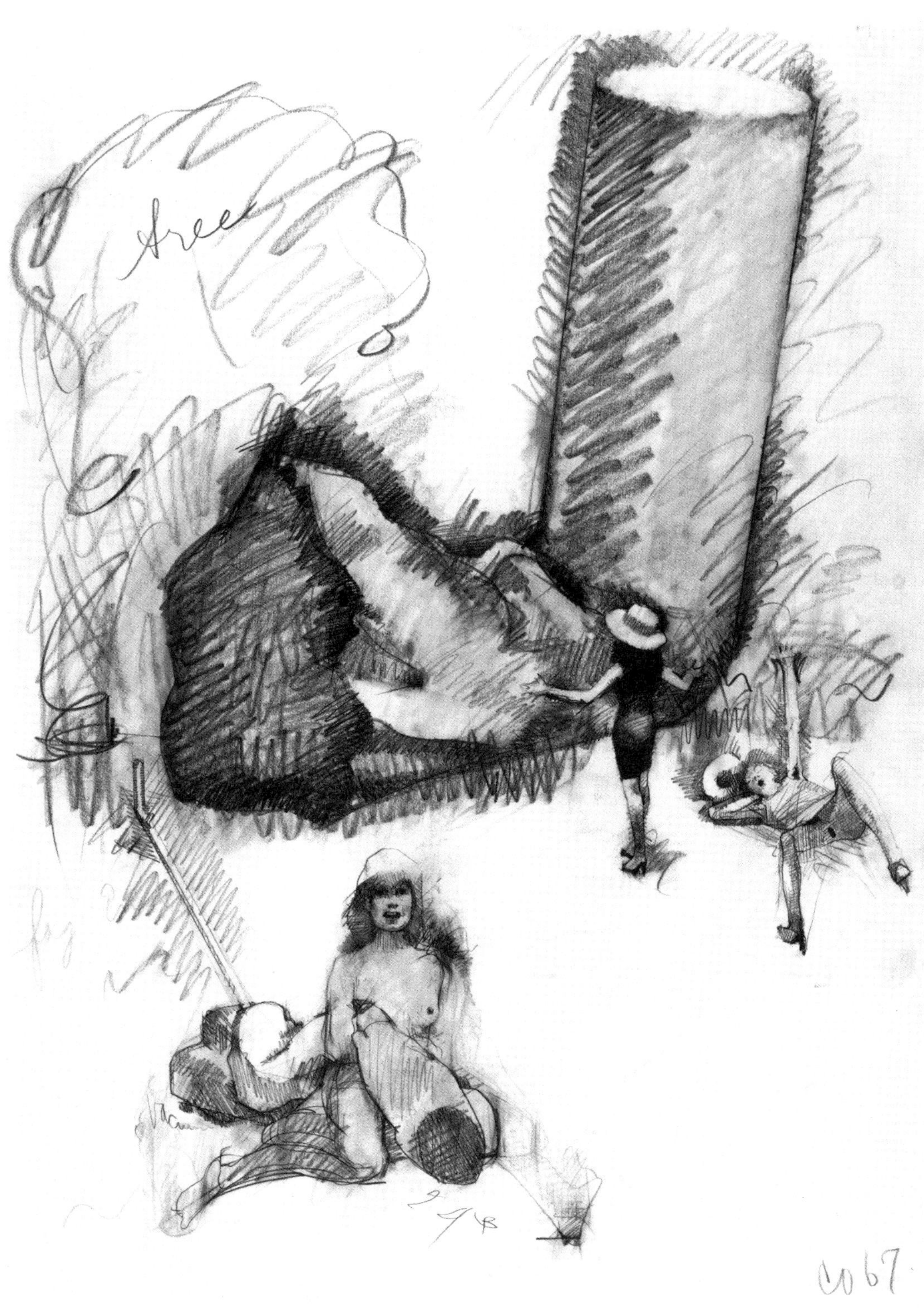

Colossal Fagend—Dream State, 1967

293

PLACID CIVIC MONUMENT (HOLE . . .) (1967)

Placid Civic Monument, October 1, 1967

Location:
Central Park, behind the Metropolitan Museum, northwest of Cleopatra's Needle.
Instructions:
1. A level area of ground, six feet long and three feet wide, is neatly excavated to a depth of six feet.
2. After a short interval—say, a break for lunch—the excavated earth is replaced. The turned earth is neatly raked with attention to clear edges and the ground left unplanted. It may be reseeded at a later date.
Description of the work:
1. 108 cubic feet of Central Park excavated and reinserted.
2. Underground sculpture, consisting of the material in an excavation six feet by three feet and six feet deep, in Central Park . . . , and reinserted.
3. Environmental sculpture, consisting of the material in an excavation . . . , its relationship to its surroundings and all related objects, persons, and events—past, present, and future.
4. An event, consisting of the breaking of Central Park ground and its consequences. From the action of the shovel through the actions of press and bureaucracy.

The work is a gift to the City of New York.

Notes at the Hole opening
Diary of the Hole
Monument for a City Park: The object unidentified (UFO). Burial of an unidentified object. (Pathos of this. City pathos.)
"Some say it was a body."
"Some say a bag full of cats."
"Some say he dropped a dead dog in there."
"I heard it was the corpse of JFK, ghouled up in the middle of the night and brought here," and so on.
A silver ladder
I heard it was a gold bicycle stuffed with hundred-dollar bills.
A toilet
his wife's ears
an icebox full of uranium
Four collectors two alleycats (dead)
Edgar Allan Poe's handkerchief
These be things that were *not* buried, as certified by myself.

(sign)

(seal)

The hopes of a city lie buried here

Winter comes, the monument is ineradicable (only an earthquake).

Central Park land is sacred to the city and expensive, you bet.

Proposal for a monument—shadow only

Grand opening at the cemetery

Winter goes—grass grows (my grass).

If people have not dug it up out of curiosity or greed, for who can believe nothing is buried therein, not to mention the rumors thereof

(Buried Treasure)

Inside the body of the Earth

A tunnel to China

Earthworks

A trap for wild animals (an ocelot came by). Kids said: a trap for kids (for Viet Cong? for Mexicans?).

McDarrah remembered discipline in army "six by six." How long did it take?—as long as it took.

It was virgin ground, the digger commented.

This sacred ground. This poor, grubby, beat-up sacred ground. We freshened it up, we turned it, we put some of the 1967 soot down at the bottom, roughly 1,000,000 years ago, and brought some of those dinosaur tracks up for all to see (or the land softly padded by Injuns).

Down into Earth's time like into tree. Therefore, a sort of time monument (time-space). The diggers were conscientious of the geometry and "loving," as Doris said. True. The rake is subtle.

Dangerous, because the associations attract interpretation as prophecy—coincidence, which leads to the practice of antimagic against one (but my act is a protective magic form), the sort of fooling-the-gods that Steve said the Indians do, lying about having a son, dressing him in women's clothes, cursing "her" and the gods for giving "her," to keep them from taking him away.

The sculpture is placid—it lies down and looks up at the clouds, or it stands and looks at the grass, or it hides its brains like an ostrich.

The event is composed of all its parts, which was steadfastly ignored by spectators.

Including all that is related to the event but which did not happen at the spot of the event.

Discussions, arguments, etc., within the aesthetic bureaucratic structure of the big city.

The setting up of it was the event.

The event has phases in time: preparatory manipulations.

October 1, Pulaski Day, to a.m. Sunday ground broken

Grave dug, 10:30 a.m.–12:30 p.m.

Lunch time (about ½ hour)

Grave filled (Local 65?)

Trimming and cleaning up

Leaving it

And now:

Each day it is visited by the parksman, and some of the dirt that did not fit back in is replaced, because the rain and the weight of the dirt tend to depress the surface.

It is seeded by the parksman (and perhaps by others—some exotic growth).

The artist is communicator, and from experience he knows how difficult it is to communicate the pure sense of being alive. His life is a constant discussion with his audience over some small part of the earth that he has isolated, made, or imagined.

The Central Park Monument is a softened piece of surface.

The grave form was chosen because of its high associational value; thus, the discussion can be more intense because I will, for my artist's part, maintain that the grave association (or pit or trench or tunnel, etc.) is not the point. While admitting it (deliberately) obscures the point, in order to throw my artistic reasons into sharper relief. If I had buried something, that thing would have been the focus of attention (a "sculpture," an object). By not burying a thing, the dirt enters into the concept, and little enough separates the dirt inside the excavation from that outside (a thin line if represented in a drawing), so that the whole park and its connections, in turn, enter into it. Which means that my event is merely the focus for me (on the one hand) of what is sensed, or in the corner of a larger field, if the focus is placed elsewhere as, for example, looking at a ball game or a girl or, in fact, the obelisk Cleo's Needle, which *is* a monument of the concentrated object kind (C.O.'s needle). A monument that I believe was excavated—one explanation given was that we were reburying the needle (in haystack).

This is the spot I played when this high. I repeat, this is the spot where *all* played this high. In Lincoln Park, Chicago, such digging would have uncovered Injun bones or bones from the 1871 fire.

It did.

We visit this spot now for years watching it disappear and become again surface. This thing we broke like a wound on the Sunday a.m., the shovels curving to a point, expertly diving in, turning up (no "probe" had been made so we did not know if rock would be struck, but I had picked a soft-looking "high" spot).

As in buried treasure, the shadow of the tree falls, etc., on such a day at such a time.

There. Dig—X

Monument X

Some wanted to package the dirt in a container of the same proportions and sell it like holy water or Duchamp's Paris air but I did not—hadn't even thought there would be dirt left over, but of course there was; and hadn't even thought that amid the fading green like Lady Macbeth—My God, how red the dirt was!

(Design a Park)

To Doris: when this monument fades, commission a "real" monument aboveground.

Caught a cold back there

In the windy behinds of the Met

Catch your Met of cold

I learned simplicity in the Park in 1957, drawing the cracks in the pavement.

The sound of the shovels, beginning

The jar to the mind and senses of the rupture

The look of the earth coming up from under skin

The shape of the turf's hair

Rocks

Helicopter flies over just this spot. Ball games assemble. "Still digging, eh? How far you gonna go?" "Look, they're digging a hole."

Horse

Dog

Ass in jeans

My tension makes the film jump. The film *is* home movies *is* diary.

Looking into a hole, coming timorously closer, looking for the bottom. A fine diagonal divides a wall of the hole into shadow and light. And behind the mound of the excavated earth, and before, the tools lay like emblems.

The measuring tape included

What is the value of this piece of property; that would be the value of the sculpture (someone says).

Is it art? No, it's an aesthetic event turning the mechanism of the city into aesthetics, i.e., nonfunction (by some read comedy).

Art leads into nonfunction age.

Art event (bring in time)

It is modest because we need modesty. A nice contrast, I thought, to the pomposity that "civic" sculpture always generates.

Japanese

There is no need to build sculptures. We do so, only showing our ambition and proving that we are not enjoying the things that are on this earth.

This is the first clean dirt I've had my hands in in New York, and it took enormous pressure for me to rupture the surface and get my hands clean-dirty with the damp red soil under the soot superstructure.

I'm only sorry I didn't bring my spade for the fine edge work.

Mama says, when you go to Stockholm don't forget to visit the graves, and gives me a map.

Is it a Happening? Yes, defining a Happening as a delimitation of activity (a sort of city or state, i.e., Colorado decreed a Happening).

But call it event, capital E.

Should have been filmed in entirety with unmoving camera

Is there anything in it?

I won't tell. Oh, all right. Yes, there is. What is it?

That, I won't tell.

(It's dirt—shit—gold.)

Someone pointed out when excavation completed, the hard-soft combination, hard hole—soft mound.

Too soon contacted for my rationalizations. Proceed by intuitions. Others believe, of course, I proceed from rationalization rather than toward it, from act.

The main things about the monument are that it's nonvisible, gone underground, removed in the night, and that man has gone and done his modest thing, and now earth enjoy yourself. Man's grave or nongrave.

Or burial is ridiculous (as Fuller says) but moving of earth is beautiful and has an inherent value.

Though only in America (officially) is it a part of the effect.

The entanglement and survival of red tape, important. An antiauthoritarian personal act.

Say, let each person in New York have a plot of ground to do with what they want, make their own garden—such as Central Park.

Kropotkin *Story of an Anarchist*

In our society structure, people are taught to need very little freedom, and they get not even that—give that, and you give a lot.

A store is rented and chairs arranged in bleacher form, and people pay a nickel there per hour to sit and watch the street. And there are binoculars.

Relax, Monument. It is no longer necessary to do, do, do.

Skirts-Raised Day. On this day, women wear what they normally wear but pin their skirts up to their necks, or raise them at, say, 12 noon during the air-raid siren.

The first idea was to bury drawings of "impossible" monuments in a capsule for later times when they would become possible. However, a capsule seemed too object-directed, and instead nothing was buried.

The response by affirmation of fantasy: the invisible or only personally visible monument.

The conceptual monument affirmed. Graphic representation is abandoned completely, and the presentation is simply in prose, a literary form of the monuments. The monuments become focuses for events either imaginary or "real," as in the Central Park case, which involved the whole bureaucracy of the Park Board.

It is still fun to draw, however, and one should never neglect what one likes to do and can do.

One point I did want to make: no one's listening (though everyone's producing).

I must say I have a strange love affair with this city.

We discussed how society methodically assassinates those who try for and might achieve reform. Fred asked me if I knew of any assassinations, past, present, or planned, of artists. But artists are 1) self-destructive and 2) considered ineffectual. I suppose if artists began to interfere with things as they are, they would also become targets.

Grave is a perfect (anti)war monument, like saying no more.

A whole trend of seeing invisible monuments, hallucination monuments like the watcher high at the excavation, supersensing, or a movement of "grave" digging as protest.

People are supposed to use it for their purposes. It offers, as usual, any interpretations, and they will give it a name.

It is nothing in itself.

The buried sculpture reminds one of the "time capsules," so called, which were popular about twenty (?) years ago. Material of the current times was placed in a moisture-proof container like a torpedo, which was inserted vertically into a deep shaft dug into the ground. Visualize a burial of sculpture in a park (Central Park) at a difficult time and under heavy guard so that the thing buried (which will have nothing to do with the time capsule) is never seen. It will be much speculated about, but its true nature will ever be closely guarded.

Invisibility in the most material of the arts. Out of sight but not out of mind. The piece must never be found. Which may not prevent many holes being dug in the park—public sculptures by the public, such as dogs make day and night with hardly any audience.

The film was made because the act of digging and shoveling and the color of the naked earth and its movement—the physical nature and the time quantity of the "sculpture"—were not conveyed by an account of it, or its aftermath.

I felt great excitement at the moment of first incision of the shovel. The first shovelful was surprisingly red and accounted as "virgin" by the diggers.

The film in Super 8 should be projected at five frames per second.

Chapter 6
Self-Portraits
1968–1969

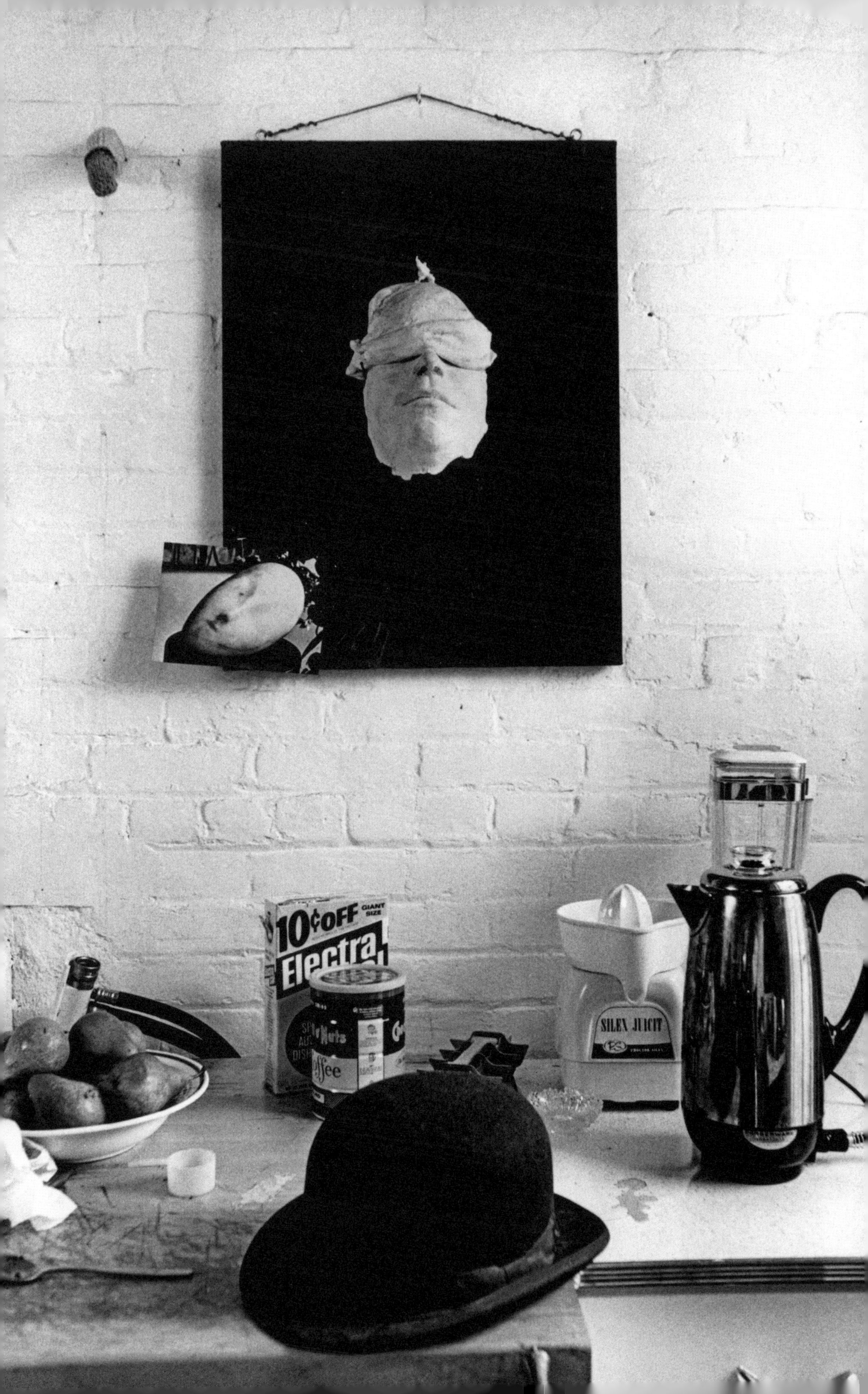

SUNDAY, JANUARY 21, 1968 LEAVE FOR LA

The big bird awaits. I have been up since 2 a.m., writing letters, casting Fagend, painting Ray Gun, packing, etc. Call Roxanne, Higgins. Breakfast with Carroll Janis, instructions to him. Niki and Clarice visit. Clarice gives us cake. Letty doesn't show to pick up Store Ray Gun. We feel late + rush about, get a cab + take the cab directly to airport. I feel faint, can't swallow + am very tired. Afraid to close eyes. At airport, a drink + the short skirts again. Into our 1st class seat for a smooth, lovely flight with lots of food + drink—Pat eventually falls asleep. Monumentally, the earth red through the white snow. Down in a bronze, warm afternoon. Met by Ken, Kay, Stan and his daughter. Ken is efficient—our suite at the Marmont is terrific—large, with a balcony overlooking the city. What luck, or what! Some drinks + then left alone. They return + take us to Shanghai restaurant for "hot" chicken, meet Sid. Afterward, we home + bed early. Very tired. The change is overwhelming.

MONDAY, JANUARY 22, 1968

Up at 10 a.m. or so. Shower, etc. + off to Gemini. There unpack + display all Airflow material, make small studio I'm given into mine. Place is busy turning out Stella prints. See Bob's prints. Ken takes all my requests, delivers them. Pick up car. Work until 2 p.m., when I return to Marmont. Pick up Pat who has been shopping for food, and we drive around looking for place to eat, landing at Canteen for pastrami, lox + margaritas. Return to Gemini until 6 p.m. or so, testing some techniques—monoprint + rapidograph on plate, etc. Pick up Pat + drive fast + windy to Stan Grinstein's. His cousin, kids + later Fred Breer + wife. Learn that Pa Breer was born in LA + many other interesting facts about Breers. Leave with a small radio + copy of Lenny Bruce. Drive fast + straight home, write a sloppy note to Allied Impex, then to bed.
Hear cats in night + imagine burglars.
Got *Vogue* with us in it.
Get typewriter.

THURSDAY, FEBRUARY 1, 1968

Pat plays tennis with Kay + Ann. I write letters, then to Gemini about 1:45 p.m. Spray paint then smoke cigars to overcome the odor. Ken sets up a fan, which has the effect of a barrier physically + by its "drone." Visitors: Danna + Wanda, her dog, Billy Al, Kenny Price + Jeanie Block. Baylis brings photos—I mark up + send out next a.m. for enlarging. Do drawings of Plug + Aspen Drum Set. Ken runs some proofs as experiments. Eat salami sandwich. "Build with color." I work on transfer paper over rough paper with OK but superficial effect. Technique discussions with Ken. Plans for boxes for crayons, rolling table, etc. Ken pushing me into ridiculous requests, unnecessary. I who love to make-do, whose art is built on make-do. Pick Pat up + we go gorge at El Coyote. Return

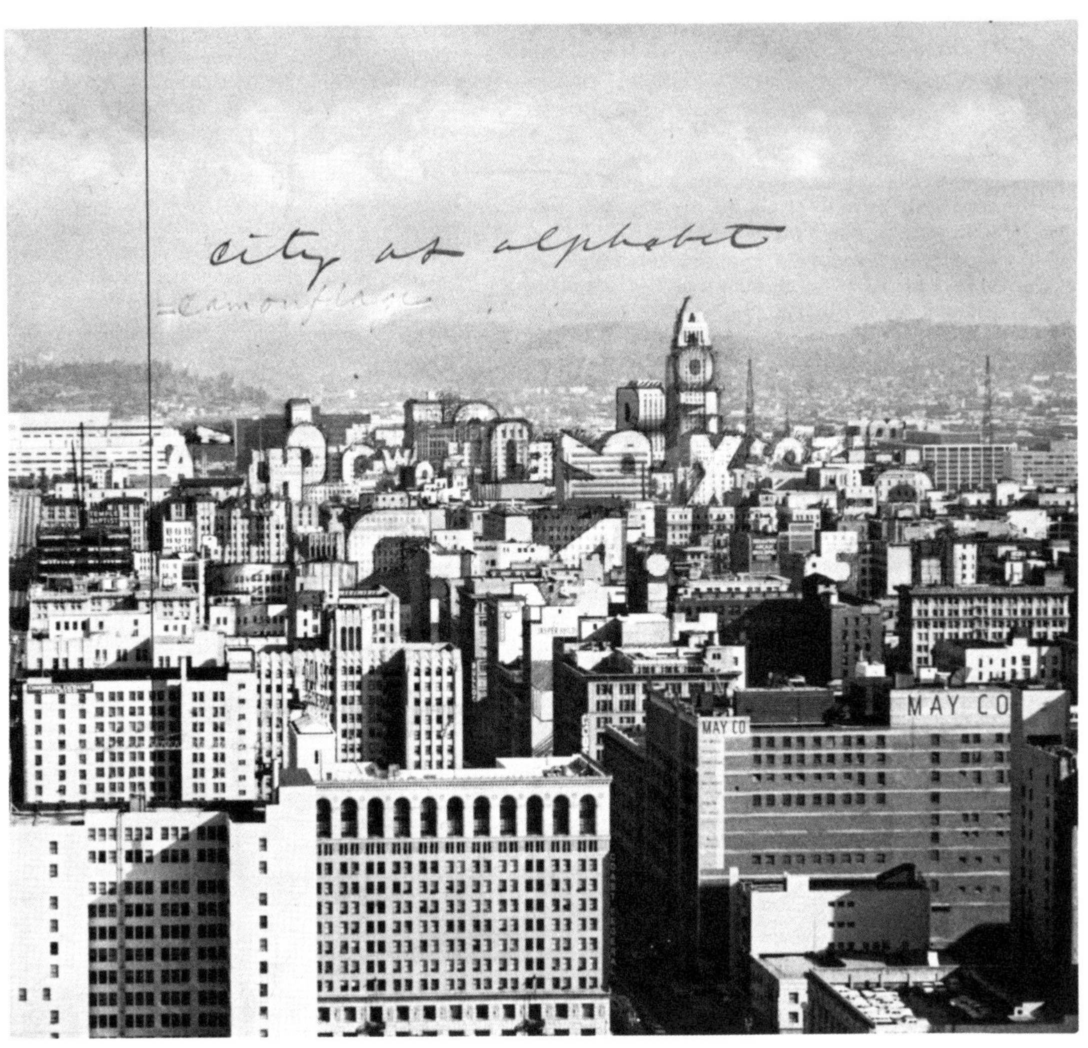

City as Alphabet, 1968

to Gemini, noticing building sags. See prints. Grinsteins + La Monte + Marian visit. Elyse's very blue contact lenses. Discuss drone with La Monte. Eventually home for TV. Reading *The Wild Duck*.

THURSDAY, FEBRUARY 15, 1968
Phone calls while I try sleeping, being afraid: Marian Goodman from NY, telling me my box is ready. Camilla McGrath, Nancy Fish, John Altoon. Cloudy weather. I shower. Gradually I lose my fear of things, walk about. Drive to work in condition of strange blitheness + weariness. Solve the difficulty of the monument prints—pin them up. The shop is active. Move slowly. Eat sausages. At end of day, surprised by how much got done though in a state of slow-moving fatigue. *Sun-Times* article arrives. Show to all. Snapshots. Paste up, select more monuments. Approve this + that. Clarice calls Pat, re: sex life + Kusama, music, etc. Gossip "like six-year-olds." To Frascati's—a passing-out boy in a sheer, blue blouse—a cab is called. Filet + spaghetti. In a comfy room so near strangers. Stop at Liquor Locker for candy, biscuits, brandy, gum. Girls buying cigarette paper. At home, undress, turn on TV. I finish list of recommended works for MoMA. Pat brushes my hair, smokes. Watch Dean Martin, Joe Pyne (incomprehensible cigarette experiment), Les Crane with a "confrontation" between LeRoi + Bart Lytton that is theater. I draw cones + dams. Bed at 2 a.m.

SATURDAY, MARCH 16, 1968
Gloomy, gray day, inert + humid. I recommence Fagends in earnest. But I feel not so good, have stomachache. Pat sews tops + bottoms of Fagends. I buy her a bottle of champagne with a green flower. See Irishman + a marcher in Scot costume. Pat cuts my hair, goes through old love notes. Pummel. Breers take us out to Lanza's for dinner and then home, they being tired. Pat is disappointed—was ready for party but I lost the address. Sit about silently. I put glue on Fagends. Tickle, talk. Bed about 2 a.m. Story suggests itself called the Slug.
Start smoking cigarettes.

THURSDAY, APRIL 11, 1968 LEHRER / BARO
Got up after Pat, who left early for ice skating in Queens. Some writing finishing off notes on sex obsession related to work. Bathed. To Sidney Lehrer + went through tax returns with "Eric." Cab back and continued working on tax. Called B. Rose who was writing article against Greenberg. Ma to say we would be up on Easter Sunday. Gene Baro comes at 7:30 p.m. Drinks + talk about book. Dinner at Faro. Return + talk some more, look at notebook sketches he returned. Watch TV. Too much. Pat and + I fall into a discussion of our relationship, which we end after confessions + tears + whisky somewhere around 3 a.m.

TUESDAY, MAY 7, 1968
Eat at cafeteria and to Gemini by 10 a.m. Enjoying the driving. All my stored stuff in studio—go through it. Confer with Ken, recalling what we were doing. Start drawing

Airflow outline for Dave. At 4 p.m., off to Miramar to compare second draft of *Notes* to what I'd written before. It seems to go well. Eat at Tiki Jo's—shrimp. In p.m., I bought art materials. I start up drawing again, after two months inactivity and produce one or two (among them the Nose for Blum show). Watch TV—populist saga of revenge by a gas-station attendant, also "Ivy." In p.m., I visit Irving, talk to Vivian, meet Irving at café with Don Judd + baby and Larry Bell. Discuss show.
To Home Silk + bank.

WEDNESDAY, MAY 15, 1968 SAY NO TO DOCUMENTA
Sunny weather starts. After breakfast, to Dave Muller about 10 a.m. with Airflow cutouts. Shape those. Watch pussycats. Then to Gemini. Nose finished. Send it to cast-maker + later decide to double it, as punching bag. To Irv's during day, give Vivian a "smoke" to sew. Home Silk, where I am recognized by a lady customer in back. Give Jan first of Scissors to sew. See proof at Irv's of poster. Assembled cardboard Punching Bag. With Sid, Ken + Stan, take me to a "business meeting" at dinner at Italian restaurant in Hollywood. Terms of prints + offer of three-year or more exclusive contract. Dropped at lot + home to Santa Monica. When they talk business, their language changes, becomes nervous + unnatural. I write it all down to think about it.
I awoke early, 6 a.m., very awake and made the decision to skip Documenta, wrote to Leering with copies to Schulhof and Pat.
Pat called saying she is coming the 22nd, going to a La Monte concert.
Watched TV.
Letters from Paul + Pat.
Finish stencils of under view of car.

THURSDAY, JUNE 13, 1968
Barb brings essay, and I read it. Pat shops for car.
Working on drawing catalogue and reading notes. Constructing model of MoMA.

SATURDAY, AUGUST 10, 1968 TO CHI.
70 degrees, first cooler day after a hot spell, wind growing during day, chases clouds, brings sun. Strong wind NE whips waves—a perfect Chicago day! Cab to Carriage House. Overtip cab, who is grateful. Into air-conditioned suite, 21st floor overlooking the black 100-story building and lake—perfect! Call Feigen + Carrolls. Unpack. Watch McGovern enter race on TV. Walk to Feigen + pick up key for Fine Arts building studio—bus there, inspect studio—note from Ellen. Walk down through building. To Art Institute + see my drawings on display (don't like them). Library closed. To Goldblatt's + buy 3 pairs of pants (which turn out to be too small) + a jacket. Bus to Carriage House, try on pants. To Contemporary Museum, see my Iron in Mayer show (don't like that either) and Jan + his secretary for coffee. A Mike Wallace film showing. Back to hotel + check out pool. Then to see Czech film, *Fifth Horseman*. Back to hotel, then to Mme Galli for big + good steak + herring. Walk along shore (also Bellevue Place noting changes—hardly any there), waves high, colors beautiful. Ships, sailboats, rough strong

wind—contrast of gold lower + silver upper clouds moving. Cab to Fullerton + Lincoln
to see *La Chinoise* at 3 Penny. Cab to hotel 11:15 p.m. Call Poopy in East Hampton,
who is playing chess with Letty +. Write in diary.

SUNDAY, AUGUST 25, 1968 SECOND SUNDAY / IN PARK, DRAKE / PUMMELED / POLICE
ACTION BEGINS

Up at 9 a.m. Cool. Metallic sky, changing to patches of strong blue, full of helicopters
(cops' color). Zelle calls. I call. Breakfast at O-I. Reserve for Wednesday on American
Airlines. Wind turning to north. Drive to North Ave. beach and walk out with camera.
Undulation of waves, army helicopters, troops flying in. Film. To Old Town. Buy wine
at drug store + to park, look for tree. Large crowd + in distance, bands. Many police,
contemptuously cruising. Jan + Ingeborg + Ann Zelle. Closer to music. Ginsberg—a.m.
Listener undresses. Gathering trouble after concert. Outlaws. Dress and leave J. at
Mohawk St. To Drake's, parking at Carriage House. A half hour late: Muriel Newman
+ Albert, Bruce Graham + wife, couple from *Time*, another man, Paul + Inara. Drinks,
good dinner, talk. With Paul + Inara to CH + home. On way back, check out Lincoln
Park + drive into Stockton Drive. Get out + walk into police line + am thrown down and
pummeled. Cries. Inara lost. Wandering. Medic scene. Firemen scene. Hands up. Across
Wells St. tough hecklers. McDarrah, Balterman. Walk to car + get in. Drive Paul home
via Mohawk St. Home.

TUESDAY, AUGUST 27, 1968 LERNER / FOLLETT / CONVENTION / SMITH PARTY
Cool weather continues. Very clear day, many in park. To Lerner Newspapers, meet
Lou + receive my press credentials. Downtown, park, to Follet and talk to Carafoli, give
him info. Paul drops in, briefly. To American Airlines, get tickets for Thursday (with
aid of Lerner card). To CH To Near North Guild to buy briefcase, pencils, pads, etc.
Drive downtown on Wabash St. Excited by late p.m. traffic. Park + walk down agitated
Michigan to Hilton. Lobby activity + barriers with hecklers. Find press bus + ride to
Amphitheater through "Daley Country" kids waving flags, "Daley for President" in
windows. Debark and pass security, walk to hall. Inside turmoil, find my seat in balcony.
Anita Bryant sings. Descend twice. No drawing. See Balterman, all details. Leave after
3 hours. Sit in desolate policed zone on Halsted St. for ½ hour waiting for bus, comes,
drops me at Palmer House. I drive north to near State, hear demonstrator shouts at
Ambassador Hotel (marching column). To Farwell Smiths on State St. Paul + Inara,
Chuck + Linda, architect. Discuss situation, of course. On leaving, meet Sandra Feigen,
Paschen + Maria and talk on street. Drive Paul + Inara home. Stop at Park Lane for
drinks + hamburger—busload of cops in dark. 2 guys ask for a jack. Driving home get
tear gas in eyes from park. 2nd night of tear-gas raids.

WEDNESDAY, SEPTEMBER 4, 1968 LUNCH BARB / FEIGEN'S / MORRELLS
Warmer. Smoggy sun. Up at 8:45 a.m. Dreamt of McCarthy headquarters staffed with
women + very spacious. Eat at Tell's. To Russian Tea Room by cab to meet Barb at
1 p.m. Sit at bar composing text for Feigen ad in form of postcard to Lottie. B. ½ hour

late. Meet Ruth Ansel + "Bea." Tartar steak for two, $16!, excluding drinks. B. gives
me manuscript. Leave her at Bendels. By bus up to Feigen's, rather undecided. See
Dick, Robert Mayer, who asks me to donate work to museum! Talk with Dick again of
boycott. I decide not to use postcard. Decide to wait for Julian's photos + leave + cab
downtown.

MONDAY, SEPTEMBER 23, 1968
Warm and humid. Stores closed. Trying to get a ribbon. Ride down to 14th to
Woolworth's, finally get one. Type up *Unattendable Lunches*, which are picked up. Tell's
for breakfast. Resume drawing. Virginia Dwan at 2 p.m. about her Earth show. Kay calls
from Chicago. Contest for Civic Center sculpture. P. Johnson called re: Banana Split.
Jill called, about Alabama exposition. B. R. called. Listened to music, drew, Pat washed
bathroom floor. Bed about 12:30 a.m. Noisy night full of knotty dreams.
Ken called in evening. *Notes* colophon pages lost.
Geoff Hendricks re: a "gun show" at Douglas.
Read on into *Lulu* at dinner.
Called Breer.

FRIDAY, OCTOBER 4, 1968 BREERS' / VIRGINIA'S / MAX'S
Up at 9:30 a.m. Breakfast. The weather shifted during the night to cool. The day is
sunny, cloudless. To parking lot + get Dick's car, drive around corner + then discover
flat—of course! Borrow rod from garage nearby and change tire. Proceed up Hudson,
clear + blue across bridge to Breers'. Bob has made a worm sign (worms ~~10~~ 12¢). Franny
takes me to studio. Ducks. Bob + I dig worms. Wander around garden. 20 worms + sod.
Lamb + wine for lunch. Leave at 2 p.m., return via East River Drive. Wait for Feigen
+ Jacqueline to call, call them. Too late for plaster man appointment. Progress report,
show. Model damaged, being sent back from Jersey. Park car for Dick + walk to pick up
worm box at Poler's, see his house. Bus home. Projector broken. Go through films + tape
ends together. With worms in box + projector with film, set out for Virginia's in cab. Pat
in new pants suit, black satin crepe. On arrival, place worms in tub. Details. Virginia's
apartment. Sol Le Witt, Alicia (at door), Jenny + Ira, Peter Hutchinson, Zwirner +
Hahns, Smithsons, later Andy. Also Glueck, Sieberling, Lippard, et al., et al. With Irv,
Coplans, Shirley, Kay, Ken to Jaeger House. Rather good dinner. Irv + Shirley talk about
having baby. Cab down to Max's, sit around table in back. Drinks (Shirley went home).
Pat sits with Billy Copley, who asks if we are separated, which leads on return home to
long, tearful scene. Cab home, find transcript of erotic art interview on door.
Pat gets a spoon bracelet from Andy, who looks weak, acts "old self." Blum + Coplans
say they want to buy Ketchup Bottle. So does Zwirner.
Talk of Tokyo project. I say no.

FRIDAY, NOVEMBER 22, 1968 DRAKE / GRAHAM / ART INST. / TAVERN / *TRIB.*
Milder weather and clear. I up early—a juice + coffee at Charmet's. Cab to meet Bill
Drake at County Mutual building, where we have coffee, I first, alone. Study site + meet

Sept. 5 1968

Dear Dick and Lottie

The deadline has come and gone on this ad and the reason I
have nothing as yet is that the events in Chicago threw me
into a confusion. In Chicago, I, like so many others, ran
head-on into the model American police state. I was tossed to
the ground by six swearing troopers who kicked me and choked
me and called me a Communist. Fortunately my head wasnt split,
my wrists broken, or my groin gored, but I got the message -
the evil in Chicago (which is considerable) had been mobilized
to destroy the values I came looking for. I was trying to do
the city a favor, but the sore-covered cur would have none of
it. Which is why I am confused: a gentle one-man show about
pleasure seems a bit obscene in the present context. Evil
unsettles me, it doesnt inactivate me, but if evil is the
subject, a show about Chicago requires rethinking. Can you
postpone my show?

Claes.

This Oldenburg exhibition was planned as a
peaceful tribute to Chicago. In its place, from
October 23 to November 23 we will hold a

"RICHARD J. DALEY"

exhibition. Serious artists from everywhere will
be making their statements. The statements will
not impress Daley. But they may impress some
of the people who support him.

RICHARD FEIGEN GALLERY
CHICAGO

Statement postponing the exhibition at the Richard Feigen Gallery, Chicago, in *ArtScene*, 1968

photographer. Then to SOM and see Bruce who takes me to Wabash + Washington to show me crosstown highway project. Cab to Pearson where find Pat puffy-eyed. I am a little tired. Had canceled lunch at Arts Club, and we eat at Eli's in Carriage House + I think of lecture. Back to hotel and down to Art Institute with Fireplug, tape recorder, slides, etc. Students are gathered. Room is dark—we grope down steep stairs to stage. Kurt Heyl from *Gayety* to record. Blond in charge of sound. Set up slides. House more than full. Barb Dickerson. Lecture goes well with quiet period after. Muriel N. says my subject is death. The day, perhaps. Students "adopt" me, but I missed display in café: Welcome Home Oldenburg. After, go for drinks with Mel Johnson, Mary McCarty, W. H., et al. at 77 bar. Then cab to Tavern Club to meet Jan, Ingeborg, Atlanta museum man, Joe, and Maryann + Christo. I meet Jim Gavin + Marie who chides me for my anti-Daley stand. Dinner good + then to *Tribune* to see films at STA. As we leave, we examine souvenir rocks in *Trib.* wall. Jan + Ingeborg home. The rest of us cab to party, which isn't until next night, then to Joe's to see dogs + have a drink, then home, with a beer in bar. A party next door at 4 a.m. I imagine they are discussing my sculpture.

MONDAY, DECEMBER 2, 1968 BAK / B. TELLERS / LEFKOWITZ / SCHMELA ET AL.
Up early, energetic, businesslike. To Metro with stats of "Death" + Picasso stuff. To Sculpture House + reject Fireplugs. Subway up to Dr. Bak, very resistant to the interruption. After subway to Bonwit's, see Plugs there, meet Zwirner and Neuendorf. To Chambers for lunch. Schmela and German + wife join me, they eat meatballs + spaghetti and beer. Down 6th Ave. to Lefkowitz. Talk to Wallin + Simon re: possibilities of business managing my stuff. View from window. Subway down + receive Schmela + pair, show them around. Call Ma, Dickie; Tuchman calls. Watch *Laugh-In*. Celebrating the statement on Chicago + editorial response. Get drunk, draw funny mice, and shout and am bad. Change beds due to creaking of bed upstairs.

TUESDAY, DECEMBER 10, 1968 *ESQUIRE* / WIN / RALPH / PAT SICK
To *Esquire* at 10 a.m. to meet Hedley and Jean, discuss Happening possibility. Tell them of office concept. They show me office upstairs of George Frazier. To Visual Arts and visit with Silas Rhodes, who shows me cubicle I could use on top floor of building. See Dore A. Walk home. Weather very cold. Eat. Surprise Pat by being home too soon. Work on handle for Saw. Win comes, works on catalogue raisonné. I make a lot of phone contacts. Pat's brother Ralph in for a drink. Show place. Jill + friend walk through on way to Chamberlain film showing. Veal dinner with Ralph. After, Kosuth calls, smoke rises from below at showing. I work till 3 a.m. or so on some beginnings, rather hysterical for Happening, and work on catalogue raisonné for Win. No sleep due to noise upstairs. Pat to bed early.
Phone calls:
Frazier's wife re: tea.
Anita re: gallery.
Pace re: Paine.
Jenny re: drawings / Janis—same (Conrad).

Feigen (Joseph) re: Harris.

Lehrer re: returns. Sick. Vague.

Shadbolt re: customs + shipping. Later Glenn Toppings.

Margaret Rose re: book, "I didn't know."

La Monte called re: Wilder show.

Sam Edwards.

Barbara Rose.

Photos arrive for Chicago monument.

SUNDAY, DECEMBER 29, 1968 Colleen din.
218 lbs. Up at 9 a.m. Windy, cloudy. Worked on imaginary Happening + continued to face facts re: coming year. Set up for the MoMA catalogue. Went through notebooks toward Disney business. Sent off Walt Disney contract but realized it is very unfair. Colleen and friend Willie (girl) for pork dinner. Szeemann visited.
Read "Art + Objecthood" by Fried.
Experiments in holding up Soft Picasso.

FRIDAY, OCTOBER 31, 1969 To NH / 13 st. / Abacrome / Load up / M. M. Wrobe. / Budapest / Tel. show
Up at 6:30 a.m. Warmer. Eat at 12th St. + 6th Ave., meet Tovey + "Mimi." Morning liaisons. Get VW bus out of garage. To 14th St. to pack drawings. Phone calls: Rosen et al. Denise at 11 a.m. Packs drawings. To Abacrome, meet Marian and Greenspan. Return to 14th St. Finish packing. Load with Steve's help, give him check (Steve Le Grand). Black dirt at door. Drop off Denise at 5th Ave. Start for New Haven about 5 p.m. Stop in Bronx at Nedick's. Call Chicago with diary message. Arrive at 7:30 p.m. Karl helps me unload. To Budapest restaurant. A cold (catching cold). Return. Work until 4 p.m., finishing base Karl made for Marilyn Monroe Wardrobe, remaking string dresser, writing.
Yucikas called.

SATURDAY, NOVEMBER 1, 1969 NH / Hank deliv. / S. Seas / Shoes
Up at 8 a.m.+. B. R. calls. Call Pat. Hank pick up. Take Marilyn Monroe Wardrobe. Deliver *Time* magazine drawing, Saw Handle, Bedroom Ensemble materials (but not laminates). Start drawing of Eraser. Eat at South Seas restaurant. Make M. M. shoes, write, until 3 a.m.+.

TUESDAY, NOVEMBER 4, 1969 With Maurice to Allied / Banana decision / Letters, Stan, Sidney / LA
Up early, first 6 a.m. then 8 a.m. Cool. Smoggy. Try Chicago but no answer. Glue MDS parts. To County Museum by 9:30 a.m. Look at "Choc Earthquake" model. Then with Gail to Allied R&D, see Tanner + discuss projects. Earthquake changes to Jell-O mold as we discuss + analyze possibilities, then to Banana opening, which pleases all. Return via deli on Fairfax, lox + eggs. Out to buy laundry line + drawing paper,

Today

To Kroftts with Tyler, to see progress of ice bag. Cap built – huge, like Inca sacrificial stone. Model of undulating fabric. Pose in spiral hat among trees with faces. Puppets. Returning to Gemini to see marvelous model of giant screw monument. Talk business, eat hamburgers. Evening with Ed Kienholz on his mountain. Very clear – all can be seen. He presents me with my tombstone, of granite with removable brass letters. Bed 12.

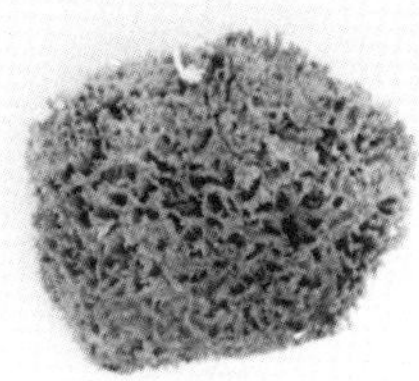

Call-in diary for "Art by Telephone" exhibition at the Museum of Contemporary Art, Chicago, 1969

etc., J. Daniels. Finish MDS parts. Spray. Write letter to Schewel, Janis, Yucikas. Eat at Frascati's. Mood of alienation all p.m. + evening. Film being made at hotel blocks driveway. Answer questionnaire from *Harper's Bazaar* on ideal woman, throw away. Bed 11:30 p.m.
Karl called re: Vacuum Cleaner, etc.

SATURDAY, NOVEMBER 8, 1969 LA / KROFFT'S / GEMINI / KIENHOLZ / MAURICE
Clear weather. Bad stomach.
Tyler picks me up at Marmont + we drive to Valley to Krofft's. Tells me about Airflow developments. Car now being made in his garage. Print sent to Breer in Detroit. At Krofft's see Ice Bag cap, test structures: stretcher of vinyl, "breathing" model. Troy, Malcolm + Crutchfield + wife, photographer from *West*. I pose. Later, Sid. Impressive progress. Bob—man on crane. Return to Gemini. Interview with woman for Italian educational film: Rauschenberg. Business meeting. See *Artforum* article. To lunch with Ken, Jan + daughter Julia, Henry, later Bob + Sid. Back to hotel for nap, wait for Maurice, who picks me up at 5:30 p.m. With him + Blossom to Ed's place. Very clear night. Drink + I see my "tombstone"—Ed's gift. Discuss death + other things on tape. Eat at Auberge. Ed drops me at hotel. Stay up drawing—too much coffee. Agree with Maurice, he is to raise money for model from museum funds rather than going ahead with full-scale Bananas.

TUESDAY, DECEMBER 16, 1969 SCREW MODEL / KROFTT'S / LEAVE LA
Up at 9 a.m. Not hungry. Pack + move out. To Gemini. Discuss Airflow book + material + continue to select same, going through material on hand, again. Coffee, sore in (on) mouth burns. Printing Eraser. See Screw model. Suggestions. New plane tickets. Call Charles to meet us. Call MD Miller. Tells me to drink buttermilk, prescription for pills to chew. I pick up at Major Drug on Fairfax. Andrea + Lloyd mount Airflow print. To Krofft's with Ken chewing gum, driving fast. Smog. Ice Bag has cap on it, looks good. Pleats attached, choose the one with top-stitch, zigzag on dart. Charles, Malcolm shoot. Return to Gemini. Zinc plate has been prepared + draw yellow plate for Eraser. Then into Ken's car + to airport, arriving 5:30 p.m. Good-bye. Meet Stanley Amos, on same plane.

MONDAY, DECEMBER 22, 1969 NH / CAST VACUUM / SCULLY'S, KAREN'S / LIPST.
Cold + raining. Up at 9 a.m.+. Post office and eat Howard Johnson + to studio in slush 9:30 a.m. Karl calls—at Pfluegers. Drive there—mold. Karl out for lumber, to build box to hold model. Receive and make several phone calls. From: Thomas (twice), Alicia re: a show in 1971 of notes!, Holly S. re: a party + a NYC sculpture. Called Scully (accept for cocktail party), Arnold Newman, later Byron. Go to Triton—who are moving. Picked up table for Door Handle monument model—looks good. Return to Pflueger's to see opening of mold. Vacuum head looks good—only 32 lbs.! Take it back to studio. Karl, Dave, others visit. Give + sign books. Good-bye. To HJ and wash/change. Through cold + clearing night to Scully cocktail party at Morse College. Stay briefly, eat shrimp. Then

to Karen + Shelley's on Howe St. for hamburgers on English muffins. Dennis Oppenheim. Medical films. On return, stop + see Lipstick in moonlight. It doesn't look bad, is a bit icy. Bed HJ 12 a.m.+.
Grace Glueck re: New Year.

Drum Set, 1967–1969

As a positive antidote to the emasculated humanism of the Aspen Institute, I turned to Peter Weiss and Marquis de Sade, which caused the metamorphosis of the simple pedal to a guillotine and broken bones and emphasized the essential cruelty of the drum, really an agency for diverting aggression into art, more than any other musical instrument.

Drum—alarm.

Guggenheim Museum equals Drum Set (so appropriate).

It is characteristic of my work that the Drum Set is slightly antique. I always choose an object just passing from use to museum, such as the coin phone or mechanical typewriter. In general, the cemetery of the mechanical world, a series of tombstones in mechanical form. Only antiques present the classical solution to whatever the problem had been, which makes them adaptable to the functionlessness of "art." Only hard originals are taken as subject for softening as a pacifist wish fulfillment (soft car, soft gun). Soft is generous.
The last act of *softening* the thing is like a climax, a deathblow to its functionality and classicism—the object is exorcised and left in a heap. Its soul, one may say, rises to the heaven of things in the "ghost" form, like wrinkled laundry. Amen.

Drum Set equals the Bed. Sleep Set. All gravity, unmade pillows.

My first and only musical instrument was a set of drums (called "traps"), bought when I was fifteen from a pawnshop on Halsted St. in Chicago. My use was not so musical as to get attention. I opened the windows to the street and played as loud as I could.

The large erotic drawing of 1965 is related to the composition of the Drum Set—this kind of composition is also stated in Brueghel. Big fish eat little fish. Both the erotic drawing and the Drum Set are landscapes ("allegorical"?).

The colossal version of the Drum Set is rationalized as a pleasure palace, for concerts, circuses, etc., sited in Battersea Park. The sides (or "hides") of the drums could be rolled up in the summer to let in the weather.

The "hard" version—usually constructed of cardboard—is the mental image one must have in mind to experience the voluptuous, collapsed, soft final result (or victim state).

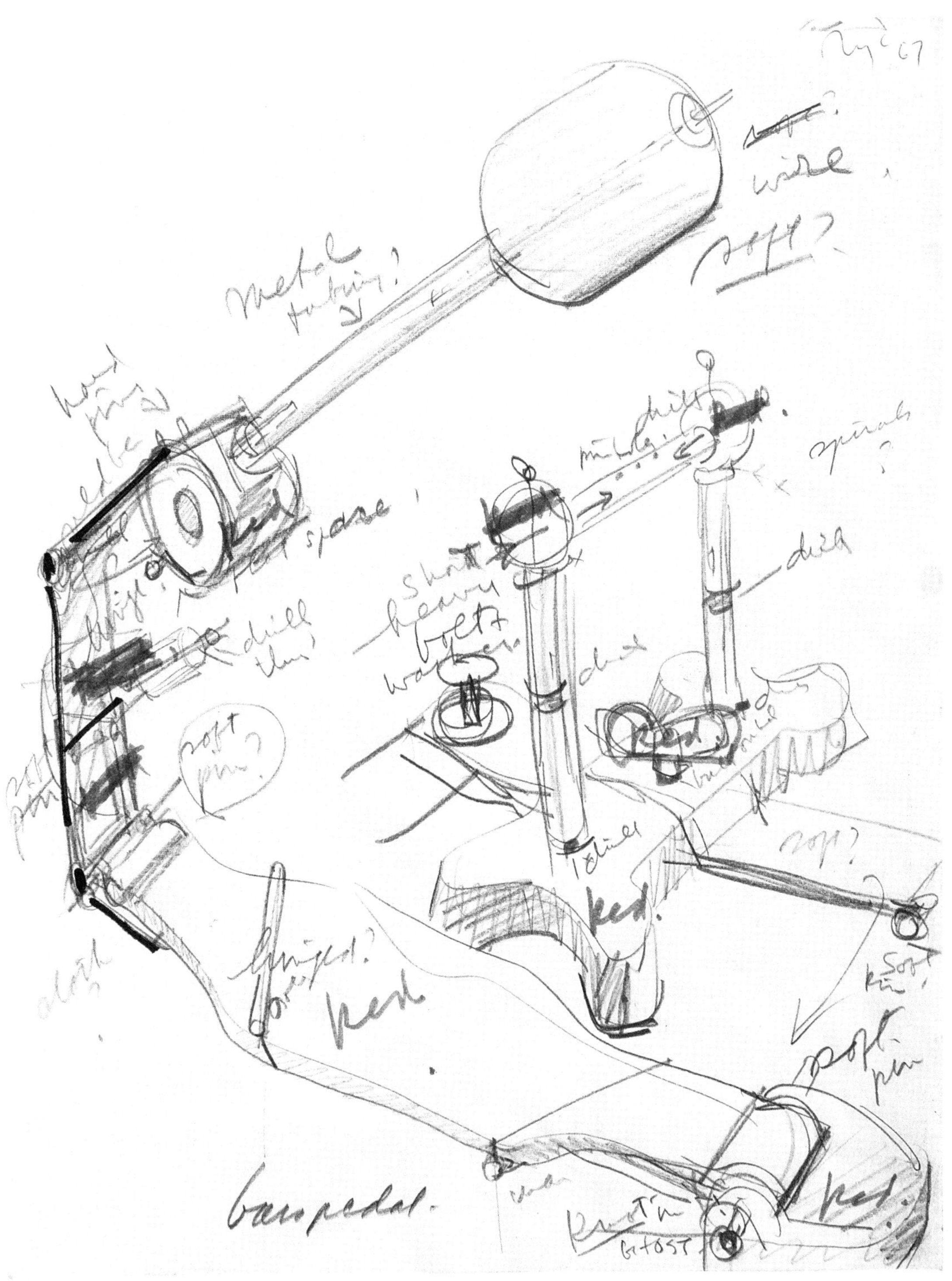

Notebook Page: Study for the Fabrication of the Soft Drum Pedal, 1967

315

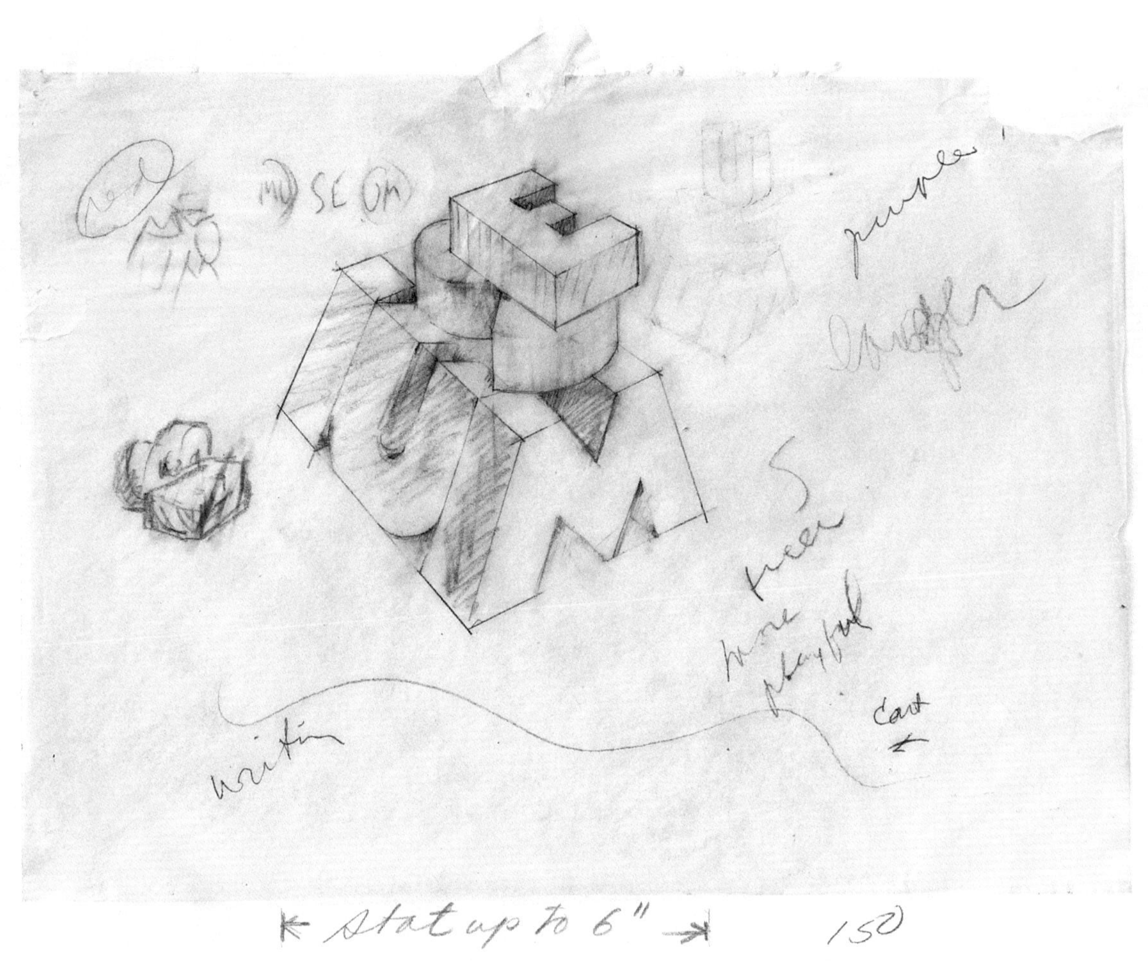

Notebook Page: Museum Made of Letters, 1968

The Drum Pedal is as conspicuous a device on the set as the genitals are on the male
body. The Drum Set is the image of the human body. It is a body of both sexes, a
bisexual subject. Anyone who has traveled with a drum set knows that it must always
be disassembled and assembled, packed in boxes. The organ of the pedal, for example,
the masculine appendage, is detachable, and so are the "breasts" (cymbals), and the bass
(womb) has its own box. The set is like a doll.

I like rim shots. I have always liked edges.

A membrane vibrates, comparable to a drum effect. My model of the ear has a detachable
membrane, rimmed like a drumhead. Sound has a visibility and sound has palpability
(whether or not it is visible). Sound as a force may be considered a sculptural technique.

Well, anyway, I see the Drum Set as a permanent in Aspen, with the front of it facing
eastward like the superimposed images of the setting sun, receiving the light . . . rather
than hammering at the sunset sky.

Los Angeles, January to May 1968

Airflow:
Parodies the profession of inventor. (Today is Tom Edison's b-day.)
Parodies the technique of mass production.
(Parody used personally with the stress on *para*, beside, or a song besides—art being
the song. The comic is implicit but not the main point. The main point is lyrical, is
celebration.)

Printmaking, like car making, is an analytical activity, a matter of separation of elements
in order to put them back together again, in a condition of mass production.

The subject of the Airflow in the largest sense is its invention and production, not its
lingering as an antique or the sentimentality connected with that.

New York, September to December 1968

Fantastic how many things have changed or fallen through this year.

True, I don't talk to the typewriter as much anymore.

I have always needed a collaborator, an in-between, between my "alienated" me and the
world. Also I'm lazy.

Cease one-man shows and concentrate on projects, single, such as the outdoor piece for MoMA—except for small one-mans, possibly.

Pat no longer the collaborator?

I think the revolutionary or rebellious aspect is overemphasized. I would speak more of ironic accommodation. I am not rejecting present society. I do emphasize the ridiculousness of life even under the best of circumstances—its variance with our hopes and ideals.

Given the exposure in communication, the looking eye, almost anything today is a "film"—a sham, a bit standing for the whole, an intimation, a suggestion, a flash of reality rather than nature, a piece of scenery (the rest doesn't exist). I have tried to live with this, while continuing to create something more private and intrinsic, valuable, whole, and substantial (rather than its reflection).

I am doing something different from a show just now and have been for about a year— it's just I haven't rationalized it as a show. As a result, it seems as though I have not been doing anything. What I am doing is making pieces *here and there*: books, prints, multiples—pieces, instead of all in one place (studio) and for showing all in one place. And making them with different collaborators.

The room. The room. Each morning as I flicker awake in this room and look around it, I ask myself spontaneously, this room, is it the destiny of human beings (I represent) to find themselves in such a room? After all their structures, there are yet so many rooms of this sort and so many waking in them. At such a moment as this (recalled) there are probably statistically thousands of persons in this enclave (city) waking now to such a room, a room where I am an exile, as I am in all places, near all things, an exile, an eye in a dingy room now (looking at clock), some minutes past seven.

Telephone.

Organize traveling show pix.

A unity of stylistic interruptions.

I am going through a period of great instability (again) (again), trying to face my problems (*Wild Duck*) rather than use them.

The monuments are becoming literary and unrealizable.

The fireplug is also the grinder.

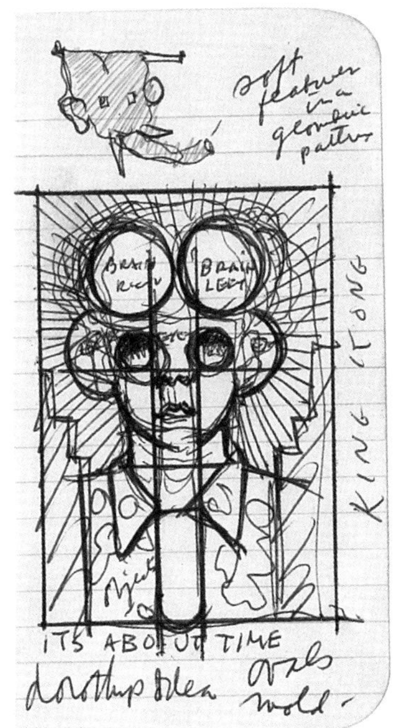

Notebook Page: Self-Portrait as Mystical Mouse, 1969

Interviews are always dreadful—always.

The fact is that Sidney Janis is no longer acting effectively for me as a business representative because my interests are different than simply producing property for shows every other season. There are prints, commissions, lectures, books, etc., projects initiated by me, needing business advice. One must look for another type of agent or manager—manager really—since procuring projects seems no problem.

The circulation of work in shows, damages, etc., and pix distribution remains a service of the gallery agent but could as well be done from an office of the artist's by a secretary.

One knows always, I think, when things have ceased to be useful to one's particular needs.

Some symptoms:
sorry for myself
sense of failure
false modesty
low opinion of myself
fear of details
anxiety about time

To have an MD office, like the store, with waiting rooms and an organization of my material—notes, drawings, my "research" available on appointment.

What is art—always asked. Art is memorialization, attaching significance to memories. Everything experienced is past.

Art is a cemetery.

Art is fantasy.

An old profession.

It takes some time to sense just how, but being a known artist results in a new kind of schedule and new activities (unless one hides away).

My "lectures" are based on the principle of informality and the unpredictable, which I expect to use, whatever comes. So just a bit of priming, which I have been doing in the notes and writing, then confrontation with the situation on an informal basis. The informal is stylistic with me. No funny stories. Agony. What's to see? Just me, there, deprived of my instruments. On view.

Recollect both the dream of being unprepared before a large audience and the palmist's promise that when the moment comes I will always be ready.

Chicago Picasso equals fan equals angel.

Oh, I see what's wrong—it's just that I'm *lonely* (that's why I was attracted to Thomas Wolfe in high school.) That's why I invented art, to share myself with others. That's why I'm so aggressive to strangers—they won't love me. If you work, you don't think.

Soft art is paradoxically cruel art.

It's important not to take on a lot of small things.

Drinking accelerates time, produces a condition that is an activity in itself.

"Happy hour."
Bell rings—free drinks.

Chicago, February to April 1969

The real art here is architecture, or anything really that stands up, making a perpendicular to the magnificent horizontal. Any chimney, any tree, any object (any fireplug), and any of the least significant and most harassed of the citizen slaves "makes" architecture here. I love all the visible verticals, like a huge cemetery. A beautiful city of the dead. I like the halving of space into water and sky, wave and cloud, heavy and floating—for all its heaviness, the city, constructed on the shifting foundation of a swamp, is light as a bird. I can never say enough for its nature—I am a connoisseur of days in Chicago and certain kinds of storms.

Monumentality is really a profession in Chicago—or could be. The space exists for it, history could provide the subjects. My view of "monuments" becomes that conventional here—that "aristocratic." I am seen hanging around the fancy tombs at Graceland Cemetery or making pilgrimages to battered Sullivan houses.

I am a monument drummer now, with a bag full of the latest designs, a traveling salesman in the territories looking for sites.

Sculpture in the air (form in the air) is one thing, sculpture in the earth is another. A third may be sculpture in the water (form in the water). We've watched very little solids in the water element, and I'm thinking of them as sculpture: boats, buoys, swimmers. The police in Chicago call the corpses floaters, and kick them down the river or along the shore into other districts, because of the extreme fullness and subtlety of a drowned man's skin. On a boat on the lake in the summer, one sees small floating forms: a dead cat, a Clorox bottle, a newspaper, cigarettes, orange peels and lemon peels, a Dixie cup. There are stages in such sculpture in water of decomposition and floatability. Kids playing along the canals watch sewage and especially condoms (circa 1944—they are not so common anymore), all things that float—an in-between—and that will be known to sink. Pick them out, they drip, drop them back.

A floating monument may be seen from all sides.

Above the water—waking dream.
Below the water—sleeping dress.

Navy Pier rises like a hinge—monument emerging from water.

Tear Off a Piece Monument.

The Great Lakes are my bathroom, the sink is Superior, the tub is Huron, and the toilet Michigan. Standing by the lake, I seem to be standing in my bathroom by the toilet.

Chicago could not for me be as neutral a framework or subject as London had been or Toronto, or even New York, Oslo, and Stockholm.

C.O.—Chicago
C.O. Ill.—Claes Oldenburg Illustrated

February 14, 1969—The frozen lake outside my window, its glacial look, does suggest the hole in the middle of things here—the Big Empty. Chicago forces you to develop an aesthetic of ennui. Nothing put in the hole is convincing. Only the hole itself, the emptiness, is true art here. I developed my love of emptiness on Sundays, wandering along the lake or taking the El back and forth over the West Side.

February 1969—My Chicago is not about people, past or present, or about objects. It is, like all my work, about conditions. People play a role in the work as fabricators of condition—which my organism responds to, registers, records. My work is about Chicago as nature, as forces, but these include (realistically) all forces, human as well as nonhuman, animate and inanimate, visible and invisible, imaginary as well as palpable— at a given time. The "monuments," like the drawings (and the monuments *are* graphs like the drawings on a grand scale—city as material as surface), are the condensed (record) of condition—totems (?) of condition. I am always seeking my way back to magic. From the very beginning, events are situated in "large" time, and the monuments resulting are not expected to exhaust themselves after the event but to contain the attitude toward either the event that follows the event or the representation of things past as well as present.

Returning now to Chicago in its glacial condition (today: "like spring"—over-hopeful)
so far from the openness, heat, and freedom of last summer. The place distracted by new
events (new outrages). Events as memories frozen lake solid.

New Haven, May to December 1969

The office I want is to store my ideas, my brain, automated somewhat, with files,
recordings, films, etc. A place for me to visit for ideas, and a place for others to visit who
are curious. Then there has to be a large room with tables around the wall for work
current, file material in process of study or use.

Playing office.

I should *not* interfere in business.

I should locate near industries.

Idea art accelerates the competition (because nothing has to be constructed.)

Notable how many ideas have come from magazine and newspaper ads.

A true catalogue raisonné of all solid work is in the future beyond the MoMA show. For
this, we assume that what is not remembered at this moment is not needed.

Isn't it terrible to have sculpture littering the landscape, unremovable?

The studio at 14 St. is now:
A museum.
A storage place.
A place for restoration or finishing what never got finished.
A place of past time and spaces and subjects.
Someday maybe a playhouse too.

All the "catalogues" then are autobiographical, fictional, and for use and not
ostentatious accountings of a life and work . . . (one hopes).

But these are changes positively established, now:
Not drinking.
The studio a museum.
A change in weight.

Curator of my own museum and of past attitudes.

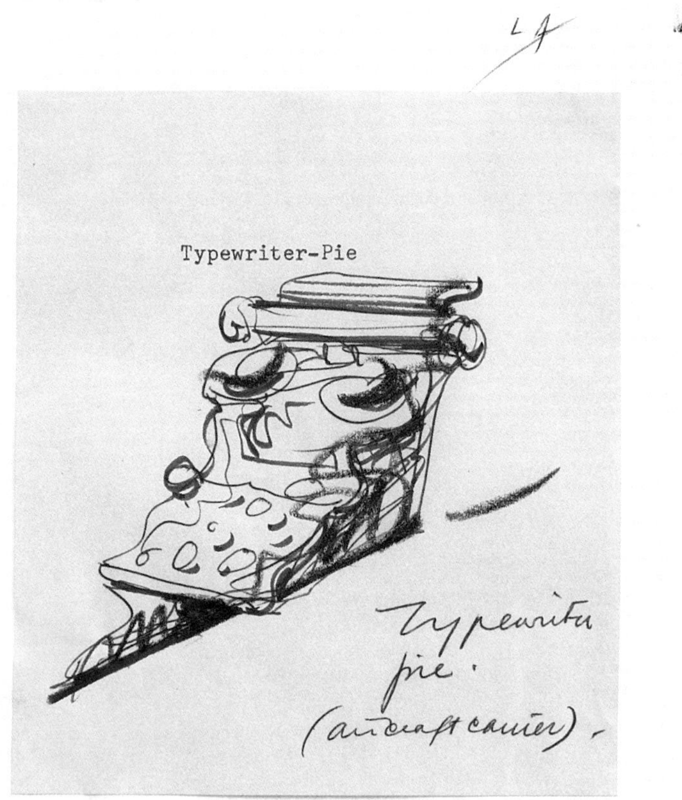

Notebook Page: Typewriter Combined with Pie, Los Angeles, 1969

Changes
In the work: to a public site, in a fiction of a public personality. Not closet work, yet not a public pleaser, not an official fake (not a Vigeland). But problems publicly worked out on site, as sculpture. This may be challenging enough.

Aim to be a public sculptor seems a frontier on my terms. All public sculpture. Even "modern" is for the public an academic style, which no one wants (that's the irony). I mean to make functional items whose "beauty" is yet in doubt and which do not set out to litter the landscape, like the studio turned inside out, forcing beauty on the public in small doses attacked by traffic or gestures for approval by corporations.

The large objects waiting for a purpose in the world of real space.
Waiting or asked for.

Now that I am in a situation of having to make money to please my business agents—of course, in my bad boy way, I will try not to. Would I be able to do *nothing*?

Stop all income-realizing projects at this point. That's the crux of "me-as-industry." The assumption is that I couldn't do that.

The streets where revolutions usually have taken place and where monuments have usually stood or stood to be taken down by Courbet, for example, interestingly enough are not the new battleground, which is in the university.

Protest or not, I think monuments are better for universities (and newspapers) than for streets and corporations.

Things colored red:
Red shirt
Firemen visit
Pat's nose
Exit sign bulb
Bought *Redbook*
Collaged lipstick
Fireplug patterns

Coming to realize my theme for the last two years has been my notes, or myself, or my facing up to self as intellectual and getting out of disguise as baker, etc. The subject has been my own thought processes, my notes. Theme only becomes apparent now . . .
Publish notebooks.

I must do some drawings (after seeing de Kooning show) or paintings.

Painting is such a wonderful solution, clearing the floor and focusing attention, making the statement portable and all.

Every time I see a painting show I marvel at the *sophistication* of it!

In Constructive Times
These days when things go well along, I walk into the studio with a deep breath, calming myself, and begin by sorting out the notes of the day.

The notes were never written for publication in the sense of to an audience but for my own guidance and for the guidance of any writers about my work.
Now I present them at the edges of my work, and more and more each area of work or each complex piece comes equipped with its "text," and I am not so shy about presenting them. If I have a literary form, this is it, interspersed with images, clipped, drawn, or the works themselves (for reference).

Cardboard, so satisfying to cut, to feel.

Cardboard is both soft and hard. Pulpy.

COME RUBBER FACTORIES, I NEED YOU.

Me, the innocent, used for business.
Corrupted by my egotism.

The diary is necessary to still anxiety.

Part of the madness to do one's own art history, long before it's wanted or even if it's not wanted.

Use figures in new drawings for new scale relationships.

I make an issue of the tech contract because I'm *interested* in these possibilities of industry, *use*. All dem little industries waiting for me around New Haven—that's what excites me.

The Yale monument must have "sufficient ridiculousness" and must bridge the age gap, be foolish in regard to its immediate function and yet art—an older value of older people.

Smoking is a symbol of taking in the environment—forcefully, that desire.

Plans in the mind that don't work out in reality.

Moods each hour.

It's just my luck that everything comes out like a prick.

Fireplug—Lipstick Monument (moving).

Sort of a soft and motorized Barney Newman Obelisk.

This has been a metal study time (also other materials: rubber, concrete, gunite). Each item made in the simple means of cardboard and canvas I have been translating in my mind to large scale and different materials. As searching a time as when trying to find form for the Store vision in late '60 or form for the "monument" vision in spring '65.

Empire. The artist's vast, comic ambition. Kosuth said he is having fourteen shows in the next three months all over the world.

Actually the past two weeks (now trying to placate my anxiety by rationalizing) *were* productive. Plunge into material again via cardboard—the Plug and the Yale monument (finished under much pressure). And the little drawings, beginning the feel for drawing again.

A coffee cup may be the universe.

Technique is not just machinery in the limited sense but techniques of thought and vision.

No more decadent funk based on the blues.

Industry—Pat.

Factors were/are a matter of replacement of interest in industry for home work. The move to New Haven is much about that, and Pat did not want to endure another beginning.

New Haven
Problems of artist reborning. Care for beginnings. Repeated nature of locations.
On eve of retrospective, departing for new.
Past achievements.
No jealousy.

The New Haven studio happens to be just where I want to be, in an interpenetration of industry and nature.
Also—the pleasure of privacy, occasional visitors, and removal from New York social life and tear.

I'm in the cab of the locomotive.

Screw—cone.
Soft Screw—smoke.

Studio situation with air conditioning and isolation—reenactment of moon landing, space travel.

Representation of moon aspirations—Screw monument.

Supermultiplessimultaneously sensitive.

Recapturing "lost innocence" as principle.

Strange how what really matters drops out of mind. In all my interviews with Barbara Rose over influences, I never mentioned John Chamberlain, who, of course, was a big influence on the plaster reliefs. I wanted a material that could take its own free shape—yet resemble metal. Imitation of metal is so important in all the work.

Already I am off into the area of feasible monuments. It excites me far more to practice writing, too. And architecture. Film.

Of course, there is such a thing as expressionism and the expressionist way of life, which is not good for health and also does not aim at health for oneself or for others . . . Lately I am surrounded by those who want to be (want me to be) . . . healthy . . . which is different from younger days. That must be the difference, age.

Now what do I want? A simple but spacious life (since I live in my head)—house and option to travel anywhere at any time. Basically isolation, basic form of life (Crusoe) but option to open whenever to others.

The informal, really, is a strong love of mine, or the formal that appears as informal.

The subject of the notes is really the subject of inspiration, which I intended.

1. *The Thames Ball*
The Thames Ball is a giant copper ball based on the form of a toilet float, which is connected by a long rod to the center of one of the bridges in the Thames. The Ball rises and falls with the going out and coming in of the tide (approximately sixteen feet). It may be that the ball will not sink down enough at low tide to make the movement significant, in which case a deflatable bottom could be constructed—or the ball could look like a ball but have a flat bottom.

2. *The Fagends Monuments*
Giant Fagends to be scattered like columns of ancient temples in a park in London, either Hyde Park or a more hilly park like Hampstead Heath.

3. *Monument for Oslo*
Constructed on a hill outside of the city and visible from the Vigeland Monument. On top of this hill, at the present time, is a ski jump. The Oslo monument replaces that with the saucer-shaped front of a penis set on end like a radar receiver. In the center is an oval hole through which the sky is visible and at the bottom of the hill an enormous tear-shaped form, so large that when you are close to it you have no idea of what it might be. At a distance, say from the position of the drawing, it would seem to be a drop of sperm at the bottom of the hill. The drop is made of glass. Inside the drop, there are skating tournaments, etc.—a sports palace.

4. *Ear Monument (for Thames Estuary)*
The Ear Monument is set up nearer the sea where the river widens. It is half submerged so that as the water moves in and out, it washes into the canal of the ear and runs down forms of the ear in a waterfall effect.

5. *Taxi Ear*
I was interested in ears, and in Stockholm part of the film we made was of Pat manipulating my ear. She had a caress for my ear in Stockholm that she did not use in London or New York. My interest in making a very small, intimate monument for London led me to imagine a monument inside a taxicab, where you spend so much of your time in London. There is an oval light to your left above the door, and that would seem to be a good spot for the substitution of a plastic ear, reddish, which could be touched from time to time and which would light up.

6. *The Knees Monument*
The Knees Monument is a set of knees to be erected on the Victoria Embankment. Of course, one is very much aware of the naked knee in summer in London. As I was flying

into London I saw some kind of kiln—they rise up from the ground in a column that broadens at the bottom. I saw two of them together. They are a transition between the Swedish Light Switches and the Knees of London. The Knees Monument stands on the edge of the river; it would be very high, higher than Saint Paul's, and it would be interesting to see the effect of the sun on it—the different colors. One could tell time by the Knees. The up-and-down movement impressed me so much in London—the rising and falling of the Thames. There really is no sun—the river takes the place of the sun going up-and-down. The Lipstick Monument for Piccadilly Circus, in place of the statue of Eros, moves up and down also with the rising and falling of the tide.

7. *The Fallen Hat Monument*

Another minimonument. It would be a small obstacle on the street. The first thought was a shoe, the second was a pigeon, which would add an element of surprise—you would approach the pigeon and expect it to fly away, and of course it wouldn't, and you would fall on your face. This led into the modest monument for Stevenson who fell near Grosvenor Square. The London streets have twenty-four-inch rectangular stones. The Fallen Hat is set into such a rectangle. It could be a modest monument for anyone who died on the street. I was thinking of a very good friend, an older man, who died earlier in 1966. He went out for a walk as he always did in the evening, and he had a heart attack and died on the street.

8. *The Lipstick Monument for Piccadilly Circus*

The color red is prominent in London; the buses are very red; the cars in the tube (or underground) are red. The diagrams of the tubes under construction (posted everywhere) are also red. Red is not a very prominent color in New York—the colors tend to be black, gray, and green. This presence of red has worked its way into the Drainpipe. I rarely use red. These things are related: the Lipstick, the Drainpipe, the drawings of the tube system.

9. *Drainpipe for Toronto's Coronation Park*

The original Drainpipe comes from an advertisement in a Swedish paper, which struck me because it was a picture of a hard object—a drainpipe—in what looked like a kind of soft twisting way. It looked like it was twisting, and at that time I was working on a frontispiece drawing for the Toronto catalogue, and the "T" of Toronto appealed to me, perhaps because my middle name begins with "T." I use the initials "C" and "O," but less frequently the "T" in the middle. I thought I would start using the "T" to see what kind of luck that would bring me. Toronto, very much a "T" word, has three "Os" in it, which appealed to me also. On the drawing, you see that it has a "T" and two "Cs" at the top and an "O" at the bottom. I sent the drawing off to Toronto, and I got a request back asking that I sign the drawing, and I pointed out that it *was* a signature.
Teri: London has two "Os."
Claes: London has two "Os," right.
Teri: And Stockholm has two "Os."

Claes: Stockholm has two "Os."

Teri: And Oslo has two "Os."

Claes: Yes.

Teri: New York has no "Os," . . .

When they called me from Toronto to question me about my Hamburger that had been sold there, I pointed out to them that the Hamburger has three "Os," and that it was very appropriate for it to be in Toronto and that the only other town I could think of in a hurry with three "Os" was Oconto, Wisconsin.

When we went to Toronto in January, I sketched the Drainpipe in a waterfront situation that had suggested itself when we came flying in. Coronation Park, I later gathered from the map. The monument has taken a civic center turn. It would have a waterfall in the front. There would be water inside the Drainpipe like the sub tower in New London, Connecticut. I also envisage a plastic top on the Drainpipe where helicopters will land and, underneath that, a giant swimming pool, which might have a plastic bottom so that people could look down at Toronto from under water, eighty-five feet *up*.

10. *Underground Drainpipe*

The Underground Drainpipe is one of my invisible or inside monuments. From above ground, it is a large rectangular area about a mile long, planted with intensely green grass that is kept always well cultivated. In the center is a little hole, almost unnoticeable, like a golf hole. If you lie on your stomach on the grass and look down into the hole, you look down about eight hundred feet to the bottom of the underground monument. The inside is lit by workmen who are constantly engaged in riding up und down the walls and polishing them. It would never be seen from the outside. The Underground Drainpipe was conceived as a tomb. I fancied it originally in the shape of a public figure. His body, plastic encased, would be suspended in the middle, and in a pendulum effect, would move slightly with the movement of the earth.

11. *The Central Park Balls* and *The Park Avenue Balls*—imagining pool balls colossal and then finding uses for them in the city

a. *The Central Park Balls*

Loose, they roll around and bump against the trees and the buildings at the side of the park. A more realistic thought would be to have them motorized like the gigantic cranes they have at Cape Kennedy. They could shift under control, so that every day, as you got up in your apartment that overlooked the park, the Balls would be in a different position. They would be crawling all the time—all over Central Park. The effect is, of course, a pool table. The Balls would be different colors but not numbered. They would be hollow inside and could be used for housing or civic business—a whole Washington could be built this way. Your position would change constantly. It would be fun to have a constant movement of such houseballs across the whole USA.

b. *The Park Avenue Balls*

Park Ave. has always seemed to me an especially violent street, partly because of the obstacles placed in the middle of the street, sometimes flowers in armored urns (south of

34th St.). Accidents occur because of the view being blocked by these flowers. Looking down Park Ave. from 96th St., I realized there was a gentle slope all the way down to the Grand Central building. Looking from Grand Central up, I saw the stoplights in a row: red, green, and yellow. That translated itself into the idea of balls rolling down the center of Park Ave. They would roll down into a large portal arch in the Grand Central building (certainly that grouping of buildings is one of the most violent and frightening in the world), then would be carried back underground via the railroad—an enlargement of the tunnels—to 96th St. again—the peak of the slope, and from there start down again—a constant flow of balls. They would be very large—ten, twelve stories high—in yellow, red, and green like the traffic lights. Perhaps they should be chrome so that they would reflect the city as they roll. They would *not* stop at intersections—they would keep rolling, and you would have to try to make it through the intersection (with them bearing down on you). This would intensify the terror of Park Ave. The traffic would continue to flow as things do in New York, no matter what happens; it would be just another obstacle in New York. No mercy, of course. You'd have to calculate the frequency and speed, etc., and there would be experts on that and betting, I suppose.

12. *Lunch Box for the Islands of the Upper Bay*
I use threes quite a bit—for example, the Toilet, the Bathtub, and the Sink, also the Ice-Cream Cone, the Hamburger, and the Cake Slice, which are counterparts. In this case, the Lunch Box is simplified to three, and you get the Banana, the Thermos Bottle, and the Sandwich. Papa, Mama, offspring—identifications seem to vary. These three islands of the Upper Bay are quite different.

13. *The Giant Fan for Bedloe's Island*
The Banana Monument for Times Square leads into the Fan. The Banana standing on my refrigerator demonstrates this: the transition was accomplished through an earlier design of Fan; it was a more modern Fan that had sort of a banana end. When you peel the banana, you get the four wings of the Fan (leaves). The Fan replaces the Statue of Liberty. This is to make you *feel* the large version of the object—i.e., *feel* the Fan the way one feels the Statue of Liberty. It's that heavy, that tall. (There is a resemblance: the base of the Statue of Liberty is somewhat like a fan base; and she has this spiked ornament.)

You can also think of the Fan as sort of a substitute image of America. The suggestion is possibly there, but I haven't drawn a conclusion. The Giant Fan is going to hang in the US Pavilion in Montreal, which may make it a representative object. Fan means Satan in Swedish—there is that area to explore. There is a black fan and a white one—a working of the theme of opposites in the context of superstition. I have a shiny black fan and a dry white fan—like the two angels, those winged victories that walk beside you—the white angel and the black angel. One day, the other night, if you turn to the left, etc.—Pat would know more about this. If people want to find things, they are probably there.

I recently discovered that the windmill is the logo of New York City. There were once many, many fans on the hills around the bay.

That the Drainpipe, our native, giant Christ, our T, or the phallusfaucet of my three initials, between the testicular C&O, should land in Toronto, is not an accident. One starts then, there, with such a personal-geographical location. Landscape is Figure Painting, as McSomeone said, but as the rules of coincidence and obsession uncurl, one motors far more nationally. This is also done by others. Your personal and geographical needs are my objectivity. What do I mean by that? Why, that a whole city rises to explain, knocking over benches and their trash baskets. Humans can always explain.

Toronto receives the Colossal Drainpipe, and civic mindedly puts it to use. Some suggestiveness has already come in, pro and con. The upper part, the horizontal, may be used as a heliport (what surface of any magnitude cannot be so applied these days?) but also as an enclosed swimming pool. The water fills the horizontal Trough, which is as deep as a small but geometrical lake and full of fish. The sides are of transparent Plexiglas, red, and of a thickness to sustain the water's pressure. As citizens swim, they may put their heads down and dimly see—a full 850 feet down—the switching of freight cars or citizens strolling in Coronation Park. Truly adventurous citizens, of course, in aqualungs, soar to an almost unbearable depth and make contact with the shining bottom and discover that—if the day be clear—they may clearly see the creeping beer deliveries at Dow and Co. or those annual, but increasingly dangerous, air races. The less adventurous citizens at the surface may disport, too, by staring upward through the glass, interesting themselves in the passengers from Toronto Jetport debarking on their heads. Serenely floating, they may want to assess the color, style, and quantity, if any, of the underwear of visiting women. However, I half-believe they will be all too sensualized by their unexpected nearness to the sun, and the strange odors of the heated plastic. These citizens will simply float. Imagine, too, some days the city itself will be wrapped in fog and thoroughly invisible.

At the center of the Trough, there is a great Dam. The Trough collects water, by a system too unmentionable and complex to enter into, and when the Trough is full, the water is passed down through the Drain in whatever ingenious way will produce the most power. Now Niagara becomes obsolete and the subject of dull attempts to recreate forgotten thrills. Honest Ed, below, will still attempt to move his Niagaras in thin porcelain, but on the whole, very few will want to buy them. Instead there is much interest every Saturday in the new and cheaper reproductions of the Giant Drainpipe. Hong Kong, of course, has taken the trouble. By its surprising, accidental conjunction with the cruciform (the horizontal-vertical of all our activities), the Giant Drainpipe is gathering respect and admiration in the Catholicly dominated provinces. One sees replicas here and there, a new note across the beds and bureaus. I have seen a quite well-made one in an igloo. Honest Ed is increasingly embarrassed by the accumulation of the unreal, unsellable Waterfall.

Finally the Drain emerges as an up-to-date target of worship, a thing-in-itself, thoroughly defended and licensed by the new metropolis of the north. The modern city revels in the possession of it. Not only does the city swim in it, it draws its power from it to heat its TVs, watch its toasters, wash its Christmas trees. Canada erects! The sight of the Great Drainpipe from across the water, from Buffalo, for example, or from distant places like Rochester and Irondequoit, creates vivid and actually dangerous jealousy.

Every day, the colossal fall of water from the Swimming Pool to the monumental, triple-molded, firmed, heavily insured, and reinforced oval Arch creates immense resources. The exit of water is an event comparable to the timely squirts of Yellowstone's geysers. Niagara by now is really a thing of the past, even the well-known pyramids near Cairo are seriously menaced with erasure. As a direct result, under this monument, Toronto turns into the first modern glutination of Istanbul, Stockholm, Calcutta, Saint Petersburg, Magnitogorsk, and Peking. There had been for some time a tendency, as a result of indifference, toward a certain fatal centrifugality and failure to produce sufficient technicians to meet the demand for superimposition. But by the Pipe, the world is saved. It is futile of me then, at some later date, to explain that originally the motive was egocentric. But I will live with what I know.

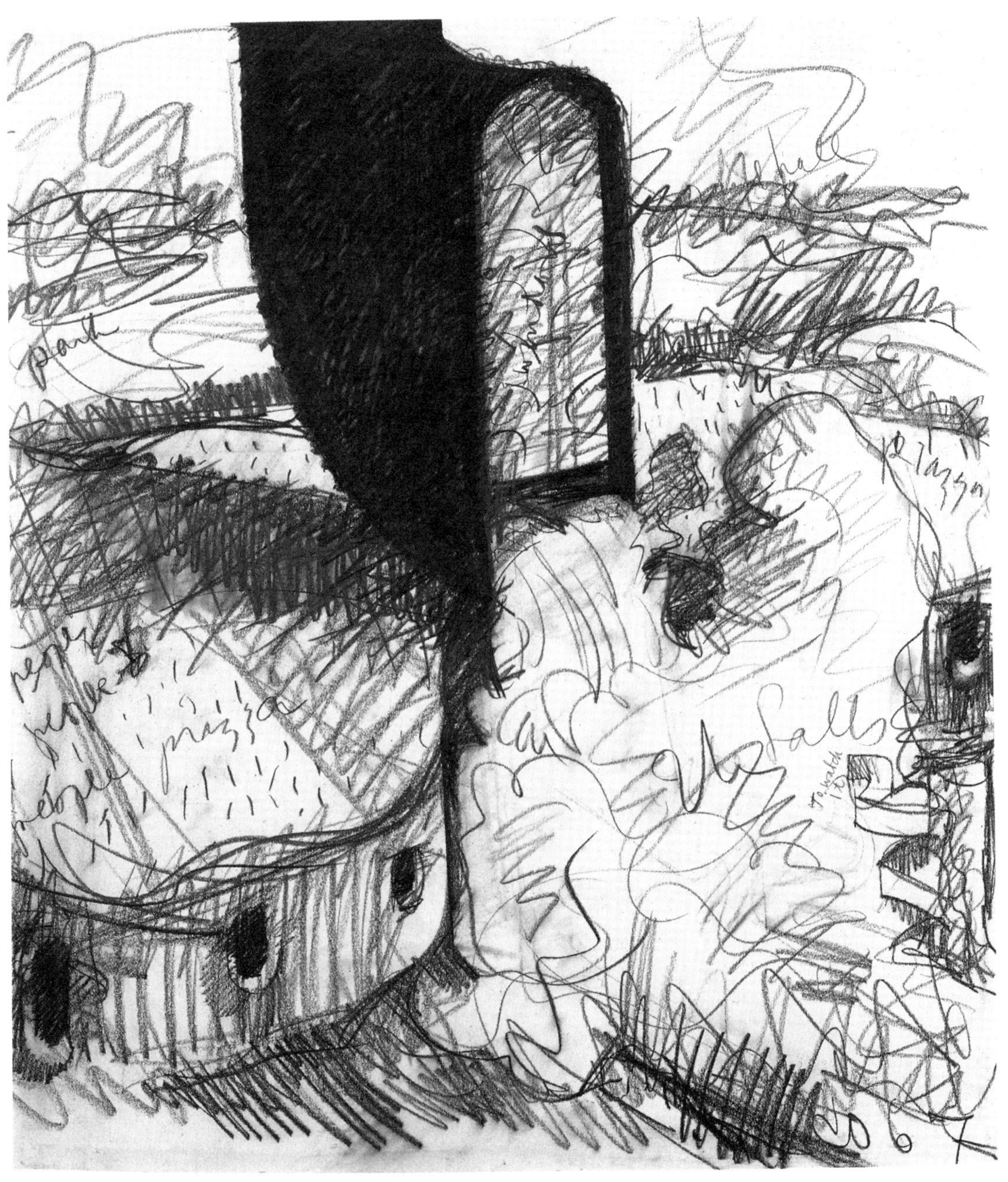

Base of Colossal Drainpipe Monument, Toronto, with Waterfall, 1967

Sounds of the Office, for "The Typewriter," *Esquire*, May 1969

THE TYPEWRITER*
AN ANTIVISUAL THEATRE PIECE (1968)

*First, spend four minutes looking at the words to the left of this column. These are the sounds you should hear as you read the scenario. Now go ahead and read.

Site

A large, square room with a high ceiling—an accounting office. An office of maximum desolation austerely functional and penny pinching. Minimal, gray metal desks, on a hard floor covered with black-and-white-marbled linoleum.

The walls painted a moribund green. A soundproofed ceiling with rows of fluorescent lights.

The desks are placed close to one another in the center of the room. The desks are cleared, except of telephones. Office chairs and smaller tables with office machinery—typewriters, accounting machines, etc., which are under covers—clutter the aisles. Around the room—several wall fans, rotating and turning.

The office selected must be without windows, or it must be possible to mask the windows completely. Proper execution of the piece requires absolute darkness.

The size of the audience will depend on the number of desks: one member of the audience to each desk.

Preparations

Twelve identical hat trees are placed at regular intervals near the walls around the room. On each tree is hung a small, portable tape recorder fitted with a belt, so that it can be fastened to a body around the waist. Each apparatus is provided with a previously recorded tape, ready to play, of a mixture of the following sounds:
1. Sounds of office machinery, typing, adding, dialing, etc.
2. Sounds of the body in the office, sneezing, scratching, yawning, etc.
3. Sounds of object activity in the office, stamping, crumbling, clicking, etc.

Tape recorders with the same material are also fastened under each desktop or placed in a drawer of each desk. These are turned on just before the audience enters the office. Ten minutes are needed to tie the members of the audience to the tops of the desks. Therefore the first ten minutes of these tapes are blank.

An amplifier capable of very loud sound is placed in the office space at whatever spot is determined to be the most effective. When the audience enters the office, taped musical arrangements, such as those heard in lobbies and elevators of office buildings, are playing through the amplifier. After ten minutes, the tape changes to a recording of the typewriting of *this scenario*.

The sound of this scenario being typed continues for twenty minutes and should end simultaneously with the sounds of the portable tape recorders and those concealed in the desks. But, unlike the other recorded sounds, the sound of the typing increases gradually in volume. After fifteen minutes, the sound of typing is *extremely loud*, and this volume is maintained for five minutes, which will seem a very long time.

The office space will resound like a battlefield. The contact of a character with paper will sound like the bursting of a shell. The little pauses for thought while writing the scenario become huge spaces charged with tense anticipation of the next crash.

When sound becomes too loud, the body tends to fall asleep.

Each member of the audience is given two large objects to hold—a giant pencil and a giant typewriter eraser. As many as are needed are reproduced from originals made by the author. A set is placed on the top of each desk, along with 1) a brown army blanket and 2) a length of thick rope or a giant version of a rubber band, before the audience enters the office.

Cast and Costume

The following assistants will be needed to perform the piece:
1. Twelve "Secretaries," six male and six female.
2. Two pairs of "Floorwashers," male.
3. Several uncostumed assistants, to handle lighting and sound production through the amplifier.

All the Secretaries, regardless of size and sex, wear the same costume—a pair of black men's pants with black suspenders, a white shirt, and a black-and-white polka-dot tie. They wear nothing underneath. The garments are all of the same size. The pants are thirty inches long in the leg and thirty-six inches around at the waist. The shirts are thirty-five inches long in the sleeve and sixteen inches around the neck.

These are the author's sizes.

The pockets of the pants are to be filled with small change.

The Floorwashers wear gray coveralls. They carry big mops and huge buckets of hot, smoking water containing a large dose of strong-smelling disinfectant.

All the assistants wear gym shoes.

Action

The audience is kept in a waiting room or a corridor outside the office until preparations are complete. When the first member of the audience enters the office, timing of the piece begins. The office is brightly lit. Soft music is playing. The needed objects are in place on the desks. Each Secretary has chosen a hat tree and stands by his (her) tree, giving the audience a courteous smile.

The Floorwashers are aggressively wetting the linoleum. Their action with the mops and water should be directed at the fine shoes of the entering audience members, with the objective of encouraging them to protect themselves by climbing on the desks. Their doing so will be suggested by the twelve Secretaries, who begin first to demonstrate and then to situate the members of the audience on the desktops. Each audience member is covered with the army blanket and tied with rope or a giant rubber band around the whole desk. Once tied, they are given the giant pencil and typewriter eraser to hold in their hands.

The audience is told (not by announcement but quite intimately by each Secretary) that the giant objects are very fragile and are not to be released. Releasing them would cause them to fall to the floor, to become wet, to be trampled, or to be shattered. The audience members can determine with their fingers that the giant objects are indeed very fragile.

There is no alternative for a decent person, and, in the total darkness of the performance, the holding on to the objects may reduce anxiety. The details of the objects may be explored by the fingers as a pastime.

The office door is shut. The wall fans spread the stench of heated disinfectant.

When all the members of the audience are tied in place, the Floorwashers depart with their equipment, not bothering to wipe up any pools of water they have made.

The Secretaries return to their posts by the trees.

The fluorescent lamps flicker off, one row after another, leaving the office invisible.

The soft music that played during the positioning of the audience continues for a brief while, then stops abruptly.

At this moment, the sounds taped on the recorders hidden in the desks should begin, and also the sound of typing carried by the amplifier. At this moment, too, the Secretaries switch on the tape recorders hanging on the hat trees. The Secretaries remove the office costumes, hang them on the trees, and strap the operative recorders around their naked waists. They then begin a blind journey through the maze of desks and office equipment, using their hands and feet and other parts of the body to find their way to a hat tree on the opposite side of the office. The trip should take fifteen minutes.

At the end of the period of large-scale typing sound (fifteen minutes after the lights go out), each Secretary should have found another tree and another costume hanging on the tree. During the five-minute period of silence that follows, the Secretaries unstrap the recorders, hang them up, and dress again.

The absolute darkness continues but without recorded sound. Members of the audience, adjusting their ears to the new condition, begin to hear the small, real sounds in the space. They hear the breathing and coughing and the sounds of the others turning and twisting in their uncomfortable positions. They hear the sound of small change in the pockets of the Secretaries' pants as they dress. If suffering from aural overstimulation, they may imagine hearing normally unbearable, miniature sounds, such as the dipping of a tea bag into hot water or the sliding of a metal clip on paper.

The five-minute period of silence ends suddenly with the relighting of the fluorescent lamps. They quiver on; the members of the audience rub their eyes.

The music resumes where it ended, recalling the moment when a landing plane recontacts the soothing, sentimental sound that covers the surface of the continent like a natural element. The Secretaries release the audience. The piece is over.

THE COLOSSAL KEEPSAKE CORP.
THE COLOSSAL KEEPSAKE CORP.

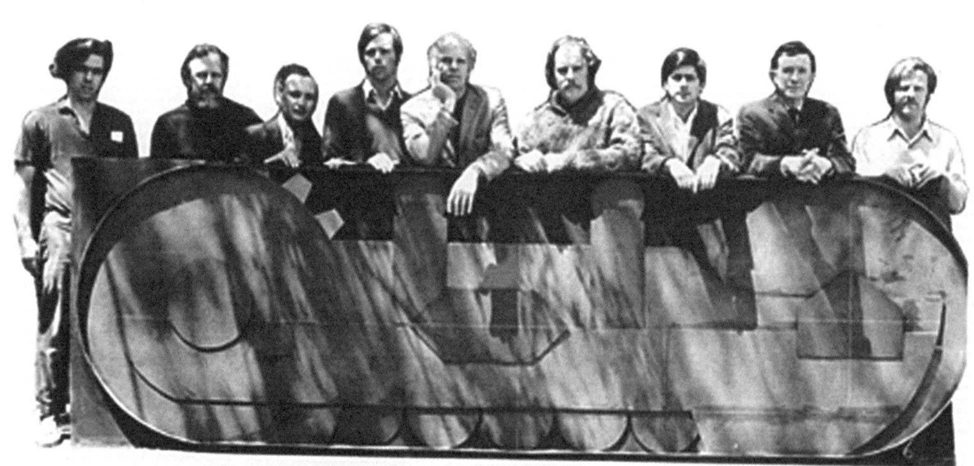

Directors of THE COLOSSAL KEEPSAKE CORP. From left to right:
Gordon Thorne,Charles Brewer, Bob Coombs, John Allen, Claes
Oldenburg(V. Pres.), Danny Goodrich(Sec.), Stuart Wrede(Pres.)
Vincent Scully, Sam Callaway (Treas.) Missing: Peter Almond.

The Colossal Keepsake Corporation is a non profit Corporation dedicated to the
construction and donation of colossal monuments to Educational and Charitable
institutions.

Monument fabricated by Lippincott Inc. at cost Treads built by Gordon
Thorne Vinyl lipstick sewn by Lee Allen, Birgitta Callaway,
Elizabeth Greenberg, and Lee Lee Thorne.

Detail from "Colossal Monument" poster, special issue of *Novum Organum*, May 1969

The Lipstick sculpture is the first realization of a subject that has interested me since 1966, when I proposed a Lipstick on a grand scale to replace the Fountain of Eros in Piccadilly Circus. It is mounted on a movable base. The concept of movable outdoor sculpture was stimulated by watching road equipment and trucks near my new studio in New Haven. The use of treads is also a result, in part, of my use of corrugated cardboard in building monument models—corrugated cardboard translates easily into caterpillar (or tank) treads.

I have designated this piece a "feasible" monument to distinguish it (and others in this scale to follow—I hope) from the impossible, so-called "colossal" proposals of the last few years.

The limited mobility of the Lipstick—moving up and down on a closed track—a caged or small possibility of motion interests me as does the combination of hard and soft material. An earlier version of the Lipstick, in 1967, made entirely of steel, in a flat form showed the point of the stick bent like melting wax, tracing a crescent of red. This too was made at Lippincott's. I have recently realized that the first syllable of the fabricator made (for my obsessional fantasy) the subject a necessity. I think that the combination of soft and hard in outdoor sculpture will expand this rather stiff medium. The right weatherproof material for the soft part has not yet been found. The soft part could also be replaceable, after a pattern.

The subject is not just erotic. A motor car, which it resembles, is equally erotic. It also suggests an Ionic column (upside down), a Chicago fireplug, a drainpipe, or the famous tower of Tatlin for Red Square—the model of which I recently saw set up in the parking lot of Houston's Rice University.

In its changes, rising, the Lipstick imitates the male and the female sex organs—it is a bisexual object. The caterpillar track need not be read as a reference to war machinery— the piece was originally conceived to crawl its way downstairs to its site. The track and the machinery was later translated to a formal, static conception, based on studies from a Caterpillar catalogue. Now the base only gives a suggestion of being able to move.

It remains to be seen at this time of writing just how the piece, the real piece, will look—the finished piece I find is usually surprising, and the interpretations must wait for the presence of the thing itself.

When I investigated possible sites on the campus earlier this year, I found that nothing would do but the central showplace—the Plaza. The piece was suggested too by a long, orange balloon I found fluttering from the antenna of a parked car as I stood contemplating the site. The balloon seemed huge, bouncing against the paternal classical and Egyptian edifices. Just what the place needs, I thought. The students who subscribed to the piece chose between two proposals—one the Lipstick showing three stages of erection (now on exhibit at the Sidney Janis Gallery in New York City), and the other a toothpaste being stepped on. Possibly the Lipstick recalls the tower of the New Fraternity mail I used to receive as an undergraduate from Alumnus Gundelfinger, which always brightened the day. I remembered also the day the Colgate Company mailed free samples of toothpaste to every student, tubes that were fired across the campus by laying them in rows on windowsills and slamming the window down.

The piece is offered as a gift, less out of sentimentality for any abstract version of the university than a response to the opportunity provided by the students to erect my first "feasible" monument. I am grateful and happy to have given my time to do it.

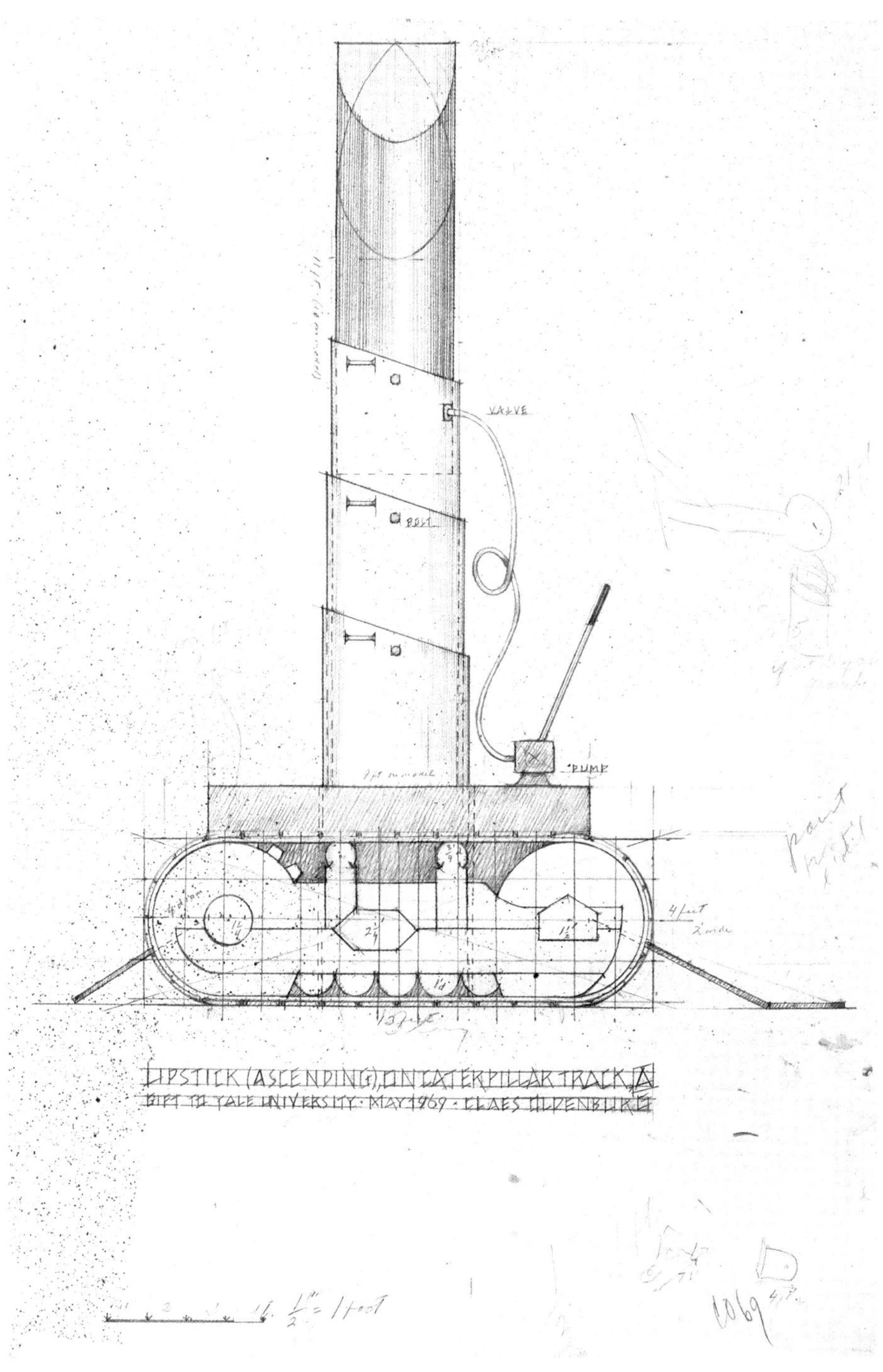

Study for Feasible Monument: Lipstick, Yale, 1969

POSTCARD 8/23/69 (1969)

Here I am in a desolate place called New Haven. I'm in a long factory, high in the ceiling—a marvelous structure, like an ark—pity it dropped here when the waters drained.

The overwhelming sensation of the city is metallic. It is the car-crushing capital of New England. From my windows, I see heaps of ruined autobodies. The back of the studio is only a few feet from the Penn Central yards. All night, the boxcars rearrange, screech, and hop in their orbits, accompanied by mysterious instructions over loudspeakers. It's like a recurrent bad dream. The night sky is lit by burning piles of wrecks, and here in New Haven are found the most avant-garde methods of dicing and reducing the material complexes of the automobile. Large ships arrive from Naples to load, and I presume the cars return as olive cans.

From my control room, right front in the studio-locomotive, I seem hurtling at an unnoticeable rate toward Snake Rock and the cut-rate Soldiers' and Sailors' Monument, which crowns the red hill—ancient rock, seemingly dropped out of Arizona. The old mound is New Haven's only magnificence. From the top, one has a good view of the Sleeping Giant, another mound to the north, which in profile does indeed give the impression that gave rise to the name. This isn't often the case—Great Stone Face, for example. Institutions near the site take its name, acquiring both grandeur and wit: Sleeping Giant Motel, Sleeping Giant Drive-In, etc. I would put commas after the first word. In my search for scale, I suppose the Giant's presence was a factor in locating here and certainly inspired the title of the corporation formed with the help of Yale students to protect our placement of the Lipstick—Colossal Keepsake Corporation, Inc.

As usual, I think only of art, and it is now sixteen years since I decided to do so, rather than drop into the waves of Lake Michigan. Happily, I am graduated now—age sixteen in an increasingly decrepit body, and my notes less and less discuss the subject of art, at least the academics of it. I am ready now for the politics of propagating art, which is why I have gone outdoors, leaving the analysis of art in the salon, and why my interests have shifted to more permanent materials—metal especially.

For some years I have been defeating metal (so I have imagined) by translating it to fabric, but now I doubt that this antagonist metal is bothered by the tactic X. Metal goes on with impunity, forcing art to conform to its limitations, stifling development in style, filling the landscape with monuments to its own authority. As Bernini disposed of the authority of stone, I would like to dispose of the authority of metal, but I haven't any idea of how to do this. John Chamberlain has been on the front lines for years. With his innate love of softness, he can't bear the sight of metal undisturbed—a great inspiration. Inhaling steel here and dodging trucks is just a preliminary.

The Hats Monument is a possibility—unlike some of my "monument" proposals. It is suggested for a city square in Chicago or some other large city in the USA Midwest, to present a concept of twisting inner and outer spaces. The dark interiors of the Hats would serve as shelters from wind and rain, concert spaces, or spaces in which films could be shown in broad daylight. I thought of the many unlit spaces that go walking at noon—inside our bodies, for example. Scale of the monument is given by the representation of citizens as little nails.

SELF-PORTRAIT . . . (1971)

The face is a cutout, like a mask, which is pasted on the diagram of the objects. The ice bag is also a cutout of different paper, pasted on. The face is divided in half vertically. One side shows the kindly aspect of the artist; the other, his brutal one. The body is introduced in the image of the face via the representation of the body's juices—the tongue (bringing out the insides), which doubles as a heart and foot. The stare is partly the result of the working conditions of making a self-portrait—one hangs up a mirror and stares into it—but also emphasizes the artist's reliance on the eyes. The "3½" on the forehead is left on as a reminder of my concern at the time with measurements of patterns. The Ice Bag on the head signifies that subject was on my mind. It doubles as a beret—attribute of the artist.

The objects are shown in the order in which they were made, reading left to right from the Good Humor Bar of 1963 through the Geometric Mouse of 1969. They circulate about the artist's head like the representation of unconsciousness in the comics or the astrological signs on the hat of Merlin the Magician—deflated to an Ice Bag.

I alternated between the image of a magician and that of a clown, trying to make a combination of the two. Two clown representations, I recall, which contributed are the "Joker" from the *Batman* comic strip and the laughing face that used to be on Tilyou's amusement park, "The Funny Place," at Coney Island. I remembered, also, the self-portraits (in agony) of Messerschmidt, which were analyzed by Ernst Kris.

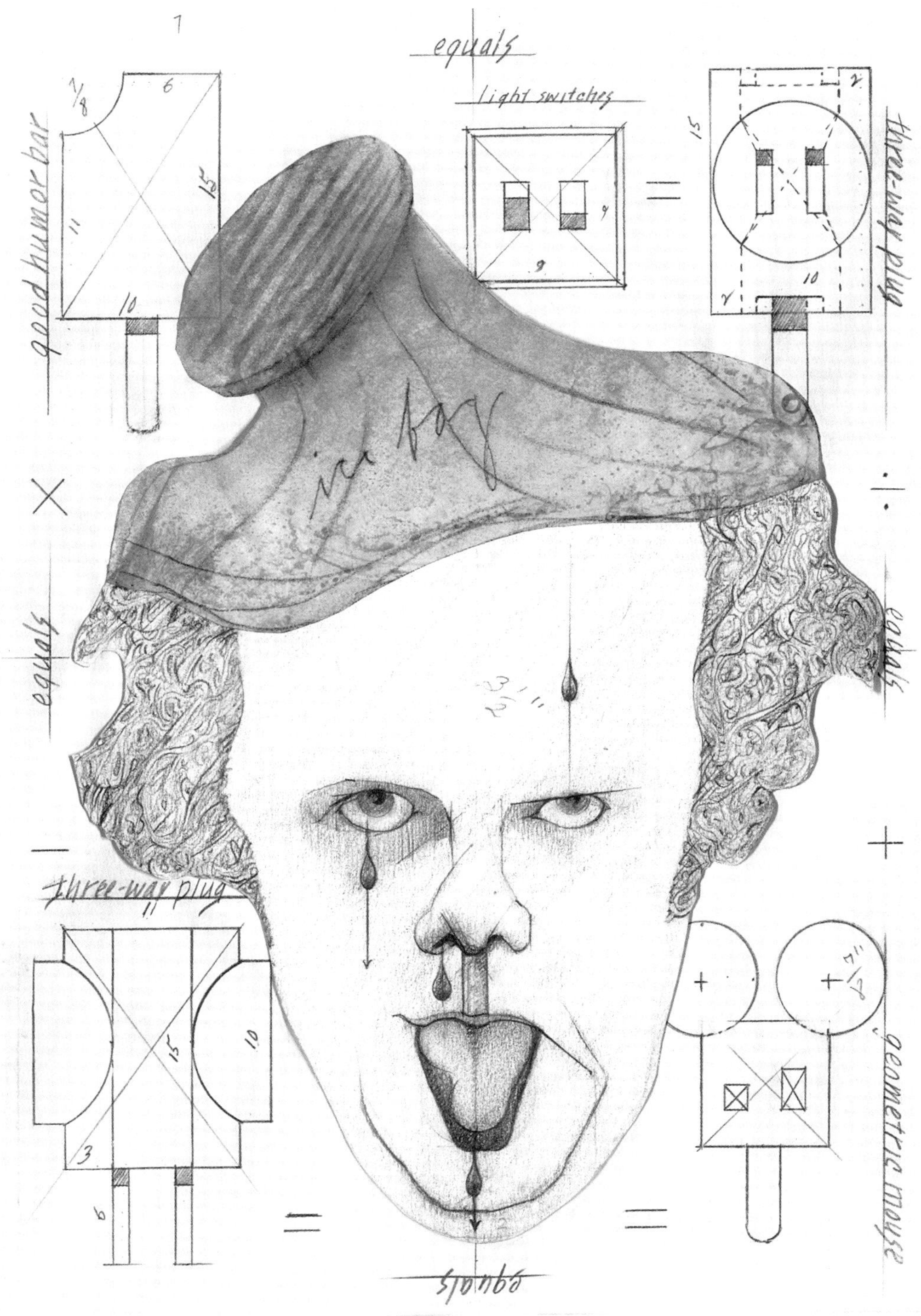

Symbolic Self-Portrait with Equals, 1969

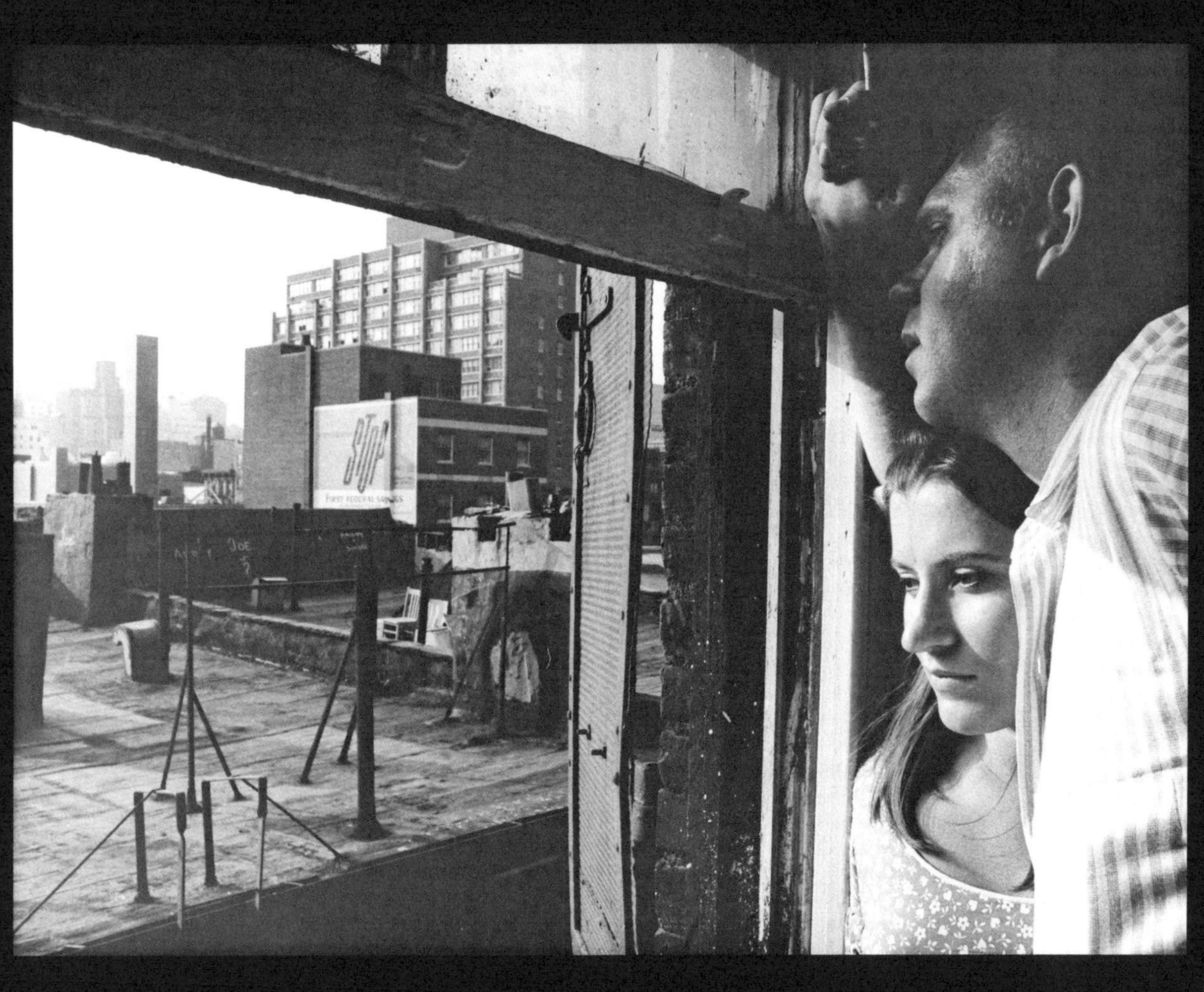

AFTERWORD
Maartje Oldenburg

Before Claes Oldenburg decided to become an artist, he wanted to be a writer—which was the word he used then "to mean a creator, a maker." Although he quit his post-college job as an apprentice reporter at Chicago's City News Bureau to focus on his art education, Oldenburg never stopped writing. For this collection, covering the formative years from 1956 to 1969, Oldenburg proposed the title *Writing on the Side* to capture the dual nature of the relationship between his verbal and visual practices. On the one hand, his voluminous diaries, notes, poems, scripts, and other writings "are complete in themselves," created independent of his artwork as "a world of their own." On the other, his parallel practices undoubtedly inform and animate each other, resulting in organic correspondences, such as shared stylistic fascinations with, among other things, fragmentation and satire, as well as express ones, including his iconic equivalents (for example, "Drums equals Mickey Mouse" or "Drainpipe equals Ray Gun") and, perhaps less known, street graffiti transcribed twofold as typewritten poem and drawing rendered in pen and ink. Befitting both senses of "writing on the side," Oldenburg kept a 1926 typewriter raised on a makeshift stand so that he could readily walk over and type a few lines during studio activities.

Upon moving to New York City in May 1956 to pursue a career as an artist, Oldenburg adopted a daily writing regimen, with notes and diaries as its cornerstones, which he maintained, more or less, through 1969. Although the nature of his writing changed significantly during this period, his commitment to the act of writing remained near subliminal compulsion, moving from a psychoanalytically oriented search for source material, principally "'ikons' of consciousness," in the late 1950s

to an intensifying interest in the visual and performative aspects of writing in the 1960s. Likening his notes to "stupid thoughts expelled," Oldenburg envisioned a multiple in the form of a "typewriter . . . programmed to type (my) notes, like a 'player piano'"; the logic of obsession situates meaning in process as much as end. Notwithstanding his prolific output, Oldenburg's assessment of his own writing is typically ambivalent, subject to the same contradictory positions he frequently assumes therein. He characterizes his notes, for instance, as a record of "the inconsistent wanderings of the mind during creation": "these are not statements but postures I have taken. The statement that I stand behind and that represents my judgment is my *work*, which is the sum and resolution of my contradictions."

And yet, Oldenburg's obvious concern with the status of his writing in relation to his artwork belies an easy hierarchy. Taken here as a whole, his writings coalesce into an equal narrative about artistic and personal development in which a constant problematic is advanced through evolving modes of expression. Presented at the outset of this project with an overflow of unpublished material, housed in Daily Reminders and copious black binders, in addition to material published in artist's books, exhibition catalogues, and art magazines, we quickly recognized the opportunity to tell, through careful selection and respectful editing, Oldenburg's story in his own voice. For this reason, we reserved our comments for an afterword, choosing to open and close the story proper with bookend texts written by Oldenburg in the early 1970s; near enough in time to be born of the events recounted, these self-reflective texts nonetheless strike a distinctly retrospective note in marking the end of a period of successive crises and breakthroughs, or what Oldenburg calls "growing up." Our chapters conform to six "stylistic interruptions" identified by Oldenburg and, internally, to his established writing categories. Diaries, notes, poems, scripts, statements, and, eventually, case histories appear clearly differentiated in order also to underscore their centripetal pull into a narrative arc approximately spanning heady expressionistic beginnings to large-scale imaginative maturity: "I was fortunate enough to have my emergence as an artist inside this very creative period begin with a free personal expression. It culminated paradoxically in a monumental factory-executed form of sculpture." Our reliance, to the maximum extent possible, on first-hand material became instrumental, moreover, to apprehending the metaplot of how Oldenburg actually *uses* his writing to effectuate the search for "resolution," of which all his creative expressions are "a physical result."

A habitual editor and bookmaker, Oldenburg ceaselessly revisits his conscientiously preserved body of written work, well attested by references in his diary and notes to repeated "selecting," "arranging," "rewriting," "filing," and "destroying." Diary entries occasionally betray that they were written after the fact, as when Oldenburg questions the date an event took place, and that they were reread. (The keeping of a double diary—two years in one Daily Reminder—naturally facilitated and encouraged comparison.) Oldenburg recently explained that to this day he keeps a daily record of how much he weighs and what he ate and where he went and who he saw in order "to assure myself I exist." Going further, summarizing headers and sentences that begin, "This is a period of," suggest that Oldenburg's motive, basically and however contrarily, is to assure himself that he exists *and* makes sense. The dialectic structure of his notes, in which multiple Oldenburgs assume attitudes, ranging from private confessional to art-historical criticism to etymological exposition, likewise underpins the engagement of central questions about existing and existing to produce art.

Implicating our second understanding of "writing on the side," Oldenburg

contemplated compiling a "paracatalogue" for each exhibition catalogue: "there will be notes toward every show, verbal and visual. These may be published with the show—if there is time—or afterward." The result of a collaboration with the poet Emmett Williams, *Store Days*, most inimitably, is *of* the Store without being exclusively at its service; exceeding catalogue, this lyrical collection of notes, poems, scripts, sketches, and photographs comprises another expression of the Store theme. More often, paracatalogue and catalogue were combined, and the "collaged" pages of cut and pasted notes mixed in among the virgin during catalogue preparation for the Moderna Museet survey, for example, confirm the importance of Oldenburg's writing, as infinite quarry, to the active development of his thinking. Stylistically, fragmentation lends itself best to this kind of process, so that notes and other writings, regardless of their specific manifestation, read not disjointedly but as a kaleidoscopic whole.

Mindful to balance the potentially competing demands of historic record against living document, we assemble here writing in situ with the ultimate intention of safeguarding the vitality that renders these texts as relevant, poignant, and daring today as when Oldenburg first set pen to paper or finger to key. Culled from over four thousand pages, our selection of notes preserves their overall structure by proceeding chronologically with groupings based on place of writing and, occasionally, theme, as well as their character by interspersing single-line thoughts among lengthier passages. On principle and as the organizing principle, we chose material originating in our time period and limited our editorial intervention to the correction of obvious typographical, grammatical, and punctuation errors; ellipses represent Oldenburg's omissions, not our own.

We begin our account on May 31, 1956, the day Oldenburg left Chicago for New York, and conclude at the end of 1969 with his relocation to New Haven, Connecticut, capturing his transition over the decade plus from painting to sculpture to "feasible" monument. "Begun in earnest" after arriving in New York, Oldenburg's early writings, comprising diary, notes, and poems, all portray his ardent search for source material in the pursuit of a personal style. Oldenburg conducts the "running discussion with [him]self" freely, first associating the stream of his consciousness with the sensory vulgarity of his urban environment then casting both as "life force." On the other hand, the care with which he separates his writing practice into, basically, diary (designated for facts) and notes (designated for ideas) evinces a project of almost empirical self-study in which distancing and ordering are first steps toward achieving form. Isolation spawned poems, in which Oldenburg strives to make influences his own, whether adopted from external surroundings, as in "Observed Fragments," or from self-directed studies of French Surrealist poets, as in his *Violent Landscapes* series. Already, fragmentation and the objectification of emotional expression stand out as motifs, perhaps most clearly in poems about "parts of people."

From 1959, the pacing and density of Oldenburg's writing start building up to the eventual culmination of first searchings in *The Street* and later *The Store*. The notes introduce Oldenburg's alter ego Ray Gun (later succeeded by the Geometric Mouse) as catchall for the dialectical forces invoked for expression, summarized succinctly in the aphorism "when Ray Gun shoots, no one dies." In the diary, tensions surface as conflicting desires to cultivate and reject success. Toward the end of February 1962, the entries break off as, presumably, events outpace their recording; the poems, increasingly visual and alliterative in intent, take on "sculptural" qualities and are eventually subsumed into the notes; the performance scripts evolve from the grouping of sketches and notes that comprise *Snapshots from the City* into the more fully formed Ray

Gun Theater scripts later published in *Store Days*; and the notes, while retaining their status as forum for internal debate and elaboration, are also established as repository for the "dross" from art-making activities.

With Pop art's breakthrough moment in 1963 came an interval of travel, initiated by performance commissions and invitations to show first at Dwan Gallery in Los Angeles then at the Venice Biennale and Galerie Ileana Sonnabend in Paris. Relatively few notes from this period still exist, and Oldenburg kept a sporadic diary, due in part, perhaps, to the demands of life on the road and the intensification of commitments to produce work. Not surprisingly, site-specific performance scripts and a statement on the Happenings round out this chapter. To accommodate the realities of working with a larger cast of mostly first-time acquaintances, Oldenburg grew less freely associative and more instructional in the composition of his scripts. Still, the return to European shores precipitated a brief but fervent episode of travel writing reminiscent of the "urban Thoreau" occasioned by Oldenburg's summers in Lenox and Provincetown. Recorded in his diary almost uniformly in an atypically tight and comely script, these pastoral intermissions confirm, after all, that removing himself from familiar surroundings inspired writing much like it inspired visual work.

Oldenburg frequently describes his diary as "brief facts of the day," but of course these entries cumulatively do much more. Oldenburg resumed a constant diary practice in 1965 with list-like records of daily events, such as "Shigeko—brings sewn Pancakes" or "Kulicke comes with Potato—paint it." Recalling the "Inventory of Store Dec. 1961," verbally and visually, these "lists"—like "glasses (half) which make you see half-people, half-things"— similarly problematize and actualize the relationship between form (fact) and sculpture in the form of (symbol): "Reverberations, beginning in a simple thing and extending from that through all things," is achieved in poetry "through words; in sculpture and painting through form and color. These reverberations, in time as well as space, I call 'metamorphoses or correspondences.'" Playing with scale reveals these metamorphoses or correspondences by shattering context, elevating the ordinary to the monumental—Oldenburg's next move. His writings in the accelerated period of artistic production from 1965 to 1967 are reverberations of increasing volume and sweep, not unlike the recording of Oldenburg typing louder and louder in his final performance *Massage*. Stimulated by preparations for his first retrospective at Stockholm's Moderna Museet in 1966, as well as for successive gallery shows and commissions, his notes ring more confident with positions clearly defined and style nearing the epic of his proposed colossal monuments. Concomitant to the frenetic rate of production are cracks, physical and emotional. Breaking with his own precedent, Oldenburg forewent editing and published his wild statement on the social upheaval of the sixties, "America: War & Sex, Etc.," with typographical, grammatical, and punctuation mistakes intact, thereby underscoring a critical juncture for artist and nation. Again, Oldenburg's writings advance the problematic, too, with first intimations of the systematization of "ikons" and the unification of Oldenburg's fragmentary vision in single object monuments.

Missing from our final chapter, Oldenburg's diary for the first half of 1969 was stolen in a car burglary; the remaining materials, mildly melancholic and somewhat uncertain about the future, place him squarely at another "frontier:" "On eve of retrospective, departing for new." The sobering advent of technology radically altered Oldenburg's method of production: quick to adopt advanced lithographic techniques and drawn to fabrication in metal, he necessarily encountered a rationalization of process and a division of labor that outmoded his private studio practice and made him manager in addition to creator. Diary entries

evidence a slightly tongue-in-cheek concern with "businesslike" activities and are populated with a new cast of supporting characters, such as Gemini G.E.L. and Lippincott Environmental Arts, as well as accountants and lawyers; Oldenburg even situated "The Typewriter," a script not intended for performance, in an office in midtown Manhattan. Resulting, to some extent, from Oldenburg's expansion into public sculpture, the notes bifurcate, one thread conversely inward looking and retrospective, the other continuing to this day in the form of case histories. Crystallized from notes, these concise histories about individual works of art reference his concern with psychoanalysis, and their literary interest derives, in part, from the uncanny taint attendant to hyperrealism, whereby "Giant Fagends to be scattered like columns of ancient temples in a park in London" or "ten, twelve stories high" "balls rolling down the center of Park Ave." become perfectly normal. Ultimately, these histories exhibit the same unifying impulse driving the feasible monuments, in which archetypal conflicts—of theme, form, color, and more—are at once in play and in equilibrium.

Since the early 1970s, Oldenburg intended to gather his writings from the 1960s into a book, and of course, there are many ways to shape the narrative, different selections producing different emphases. We hope with this offering to have done justice to the intelligence, complexity, and humanity of Claes Oldenburg in his glorious multitudes. We extend to him our most heartfelt gratitude—for bravely opening his archive to us, for his generous input, and for giving us a story told with exceptional honesty, curiosity, and literary ingenuity.

All quotations by Claes Oldenburg are from this volume or from recent conversations with the editors of this book.

REFERENCES

Diary: All entries are selected and transcribed from Oldenburg's handwritten diary.

Notes: Unless otherwise specified, notes are selected and transcribed from Oldenburg's handwritten and typed note pages.

Unless otherwise specified, texts in this volume have not been previously published.

pp. 6–7: "Introduction: Notes for an Autobiography" comprises excerpts from drafts for an introduction to an autobiography Oldenburg planned to write in the early 1970s.

Chapter 1: Fear of New York, 1956–1958

pp. 28–44: A selection of poems, including some that are reproduced here, were published as "Fear of New York," in *Notre Dame Review*, no. 9 (Winter 2000), pp. 9–15.

pp. 45–47: "Observed Fragments" was originally published in *Notre Dame Review*, no. 9 (Winter 2000), pp. 4–8.

pp. 32, 36–39: Poems are from a group titled *Violent Landscapes*.

Chapter 2: Guises of Ray Gun: The Street, 1959–1960

pp. 116–25: "Notes for Snapshots from the City" is a selection of notes written in advance of the performance *Snapshots from the City*.

pp. 126–27: "Bulletin Board Notes from Ray Gun Show," transcribed by journalist

Anne Holister in a letter to Alex Eliot, March 3, 1960, comprises a selection of typed notes (or "communications") Oldenburg had posted to a bulletin board during "Ray Gun Show."

p. 129: "Advance Description of the Reuben Gallery Show" was selected from Oldenburg's notes for publication in Ellen H. Johnson, *Claes Oldenburg* (Baltimore: Penguin Books, 1971), p. 16.

pp. 130–31: "Provincetown Souvenirs in the Form of Flags (Postcards)" was originally published as "Introduction to Some Souvenirs in the Form of Flags (Postcards)," in Barbara Rose, *Claes Oldenburg* (New York: Museum of Modern Art, New York, 1970), pp. 191–92.

p. 132: "P......g" was originally published in Rose, *Claes Oldenburg*, p. 191.

pp. 133–35: "Two Scenarios from an Incomplete Pageant of America" was originally published in Claes Oldenburg, *Injun and Other Histories (1960)* (New York: Something Else Press, 1966), pp. 3–5, and 13.

Chapter 3: Guises of Ray Gun: The Store, 1961–1962

pp. 167–70: "Fotodeath," the script for the second part of the performance *Circus (Ironworks/Fotodeath)*, was originally published in *Tulane Drama Review* 10, no. 2 (Winter 1965), pp. 85–93.

pp. 174–76: "I Am For . . . " was first published in its full version in Claes Oldenburg and Emmett Williams, *Store Days* (New York: Something Else Press, 1967), pp. 39–42.

p. 178: "Enter Papa Nosedrop" was originally published in *Store Days*, p. 1.

p. 179: "The Store Described and Budget for the Store" was originally published in *Store Days*, p. 16.

pp. 181–83: "Inventory of Store Dec. 1961" was originally published in *Store Days*, pp. 31–34.

pp. 184–85: "13 Incidents at the Store" was originally published in *Store Days*, pp. 19–25.

p. 186: "Budget for Theater" was originally published in *Store Days*, p. 79.

pp. 188–93: "Store Days I, First Draft," was originally published in *Store Days*, pp. 68–74.

pp. 194–96: "Nekropolis II," was originally published in *Store Days*, pp. 146–48.

Chapter 4: On the Road, 1963–1964

pp. 215–19: "Gayety" was originally published in *Happenings: An Illustrated Anthology*, ed. Michael Kirby (New York: E. P. Dutton, 1965), pp. 234–40.

pp. 221–29: "Autobodys" was originally published in *Happenings*, pp. 262–71.

pp. 230–31: "A Statement" was originally published in *Happenings*, pp. 200–3.

Chapter 5: Object Consciousness, 1965–1967

pp. 278–83: "Afterthoughts" was first published in Swedish as "Eftertankar," in *Konstrevy*, nos. 5–6 (November–December 1966), pp. 214–20, concurrent with Oldenburg's solo exhibition at the Moderna Museet, Stockholm. The text was originally published in English in Rose, *Claes Oldenburg*, pp. 195–98.

p. 284: "Egomessages about Pollock" was originally published in *Art News* 66, no. 3 (May 1967), pp. 27, 66–67, as part of "Jackson Pollock: An Artist's Symposium, Part 2," a series of statements by artists on the repercussions of Pollock's art and career.

pp. 285–92: "America: War & Sex, Etc." was originally published in *Arts Magazine* 41, no. 8 (Summer 1967), pp. 32–38.

pp. 294–99: "Placid Civic Monument (Hole . . .)" was originally published in Barbara Haskell, *Claes Oldenburg: Object into Monument* (Los Angeles: Ward Ritchie Press, in association with Pasadena Art Museum, 1971), pp. 60–62.

Chapter 6: Self-Portraits, 1968–1969

pp. 329–32: "Some Program Notes about Monuments, Mainly" was originally published in *Chelsea*, nos. 22–23 (June 1968), pp. 87–92.

pp. 333–34: "About the Famous Toronto Drainpipe" was originally published in *Artscanada*, 25, no. 3 (August 1968), pp. 40–41.

pp. 337–39: "The Typewriter: An Antivisual Theatre Piece" was originally published as "My Very Last Happening" in *Esquire*, May 1969, pp. 154–57.

pp. 341–42: "Notes on the Lipstick Monument" was originally published on the back of the special poster issue "Colossal Monument" of *Novum Organum*, no. 7 (May 15, 1969), np.

pp. 344–45: "Postcard 8/23/69" was originally published in *Art Now: New York*, no. 8 (October 1969), np.

p. 346: "Self-Portrait . . ." was originally published in *Claes Oldenburg: Object into Monument*, pp. 130–31.

1929–1955
Born on January 28, 1929, in Stockholm, Sweden, Claes Oldenburg lives in New York City and Oslo, Norway, before moving to Chicago in 1936, where he attends the Latin School of Chicago. After graduating in 1946, he enrolls at Yale University and majors in English literature. In 1951, he studies at the Art Institute of Chicago, while working as an apprentice reporter for the City News Bureau. In March 1953, Oldenburg exhibits drawings of street characters in his first group show with Robert E. Clark (a.k.a. Robert Indiana) and George Yelich at Chicago's Club St. Elmo. He attends the Oxbow Summer School of Painting in Saugatuck, Michigan, where he meets his future wife, Patty Mucha (then Pat Muschinski). He is naturalized as a United States citizen in December. In 1954, he encounters H. C. Westermann and younger artists Robert Natkin, Irving Petlin, and Marjorie Oplatka in a painting class taught by Paul Wieghardt at the Art Institute of Chicago. In 1955, he establishes a studio on the Near North Side and befriends the printmaker and self-styled alchemist Richard O. (Dickie) Tyler and his wife, the painter Dorothea Baer, and meets the artists George Cohen, Seymour Rosofsky, and June Leaf, as well as the poet Paul Carroll. Frank Ryan Contemporary Furnishings features Oldenburg's drawings and paintings in November.

1956
After participating in the group show "Exhibition Momentum 1956," Oldenburg moves in May to New York City, where he secures a part-time job at the Cooper Union Museum of Decorative Arts Library.

1957
Oldenburg composes poems and makes collages and assemblages from debris found on the street. In September, he relocates to an apartment large enough to function as a studio at 330 East Fourth Street, where Tyler is superintendent. He produces his first experimental constructions, including *Elephant Mask* (completed 1959), using newspaper strips dipped in wheat paste and laid over chicken wire. He reads Sigmund Freud, Carl Jung, and Wilhelm Stekel. Alan Whitney, a reporter friend, gives Oldenburg a 1926 typewriter.

1958
Oldenburg reverts to painting portraits and figures in oil. During a May Day party at George Segal's farm in New Brunswick, New Jersey, Oldenburg meets Allan Kaprow and other artists represented by the Hansa Gallery. Exhibiting in New York for the first time, Oldenburg contributes drawings to a group show at Red Grooms's City Gallery in December.

1959
Reconnecting in New York, Oldenburg and Mucha begin living together at his East Fourth Street apartment. In March, Oldenburg shows figure drawings of Mucha in a one-man show at the Cooper Union Art School Library. Marc Ratliff and Tom Wesselmann approach Oldenburg about a spring show at the gallery they are starting in the basement of the Judson Memorial Church. Opening in May, Oldenburg's first public one-man show in New York introduces metamorphic paper, wood, and wire constructions in combination with black-and-white drawings and poems. Hired for the summer as director of the Lenox Art Gallery (sponsored by the resort and art school Festival House) in Lenox, Massachusetts, Oldenburg returns to landscape drawing and figure painting for the last time. Back in New York, he resumes the style of his Judson exhibition in ink and pencil drawings on street life. He

attends Kaprow's *18 Happenings in 6 Parts* at the Reuben Gallery and sees Grooms's *Burning Building* several times. For the two-man show "Dine-Oldenburg" at the Judson Gallery in November, Oldenburg exhibits drawings and constructions including *"Empire" ("Papa") Ray Gun, Street Head I*, and *C-E-L-I-N-E, Backwards*, made after reading *Death on the Installment Plan* by Louis-Ferdinand Céline. He also makes a monoprint poster to announce the exhibition. In December, Oldenburg joins Jim Dine, Lester Johnson, and Kaprow on the panel "New Uses of the Human Image in Painting" at the Judson Gallery and appears in the Judson's Christmas group show. With *Street Ray Guns*, a wooden box containing eight right-angle objects of assorted found materials, Oldenburg initiates his practice of collecting "Ray Guns." At the end of the year, several works from "Dine-Oldenburg" are exhibited in the group show "Below Zero" at the Reuben Gallery.

1960

In January, Oldenburg appears in Kaprow's Happening *The Big Laugh* at the Reuben Gallery; *Girl with Furpiece (Portrait of Pat)*, included in a group show at the Reuben later that month, is Oldenburg's final figure painting. He turns next to "Ray Gun Show," which opens at the Judson Gallery on January 30; the exhibition comprises two environments, *The Street* and *The House*, by Oldenburg and Dine respectively. "Ray Gun Spex," a series of performances, takes place in late February at the Judson Memorial Church. The series opens with Oldenburg's first performance, *Snapshots from the City*, in the environment of *The Street*. Happenings by Dine, Al Hansen, Robert Whitman, and Dick Higgins follow. Kaprow concludes the event with *Coca Cola, Shirley Cannonball?*, in which giant objects, including a cloth telephone booth with Oldenburg inside, hop around the gym. On April 13, Oldenburg and Mucha marry at City Hall in Staten Island. For a solo show at the Reuben Gallery in May, Oldenburg produces more paper, cardboard,

and burlap constructions, including *Street Chick* and *The Big Man*. In June, the cardboard construction *Mug* is included in "New Media—New Forms I," at the uptown Martha Jackson Gallery for which Oldenburg makes the poster and catalogue cover. Oldenburg and Mucha spend the summer in Provincetown, Massachusetts, where Oldenburg works part-time as a dishwasher. He produces American flags and "postcards" from driftwood, which are shown with related ink drawings at the local Sun Gallery. Returning to New York's Lower East Side in the fall, Oldenburg begins drawings and watercolors of store goods and windows, as well as plaster reliefs of common objects in tempera. In December, *C-E-L-I-N-E, Backwards* appears in the Christmas group show at Richard Bellamy's Green Gallery on Fifty-Seventh Street. Oldenburg makes monoprint posters announcing his four-part performance *Blackouts* for "Christmas Varieties" at the Reuben Gallery.

1961

In January, Oldenburg designs athletic wear–like costumes and the poster for an Aileen Passloff Dance Company concert. The following month, he stages the two-part *Circus (Ironworks/Fotodeath)* at the Reuben Gallery. Oldenburg leaves the Cooper Union Museum Library and focuses on developing the Store theme. He begins to apply enamel to his plaster reliefs, using seven colors that he never mixes. He installs the new plaster reliefs in a mural configuration for the group show "Environments, Situations, Spaces" with George Brecht, Dine, Walter Gaudnek, Kaprow, and Whitman at the Martha Jackson Gallery in late spring; for the catalogue, he composes his statement "I Am For . . ." In June, Oldenburg relocates his studio to a storefront space at 107 East Second Street. He posts the name Ray Gun Mfg. Co. on the door and prints stationery and business cards. That summer, Oldenburg develops a close friendship with the Swedish engineer Billy Klüver, who introduces him to the works of Jean Tinguely and other European

New Realists, such as Arman, Yves Klein, and
Daniel Spoerri. In September, *Big Man* and
Street Head I are included in a group show
with Jean Follett, Charles Ginnever, Lucas
Samaras, and Mark Di Suvero at the Green
Gallery; Oldenburg contributes the poster to
the show. On December 1, Oldenburg opens
The Store at 107 East Second Street and for
two months displays almost sixty new pieces
in addition to the reliefs from the Martha
Jackson Gallery show.

1962

In January, Oldenburg again designs costumes
and the poster, as well as two-dimensional
canvas representations of objects, such as an
airplane and an ice-cream cone, for an Aileen
Passloff Dance Company concert. Next he
develops the Ray Gun Theater in scripts
and notebook drawings. With Oldenburg,
Mucha, and Samaras forming the basic cast,
ten performances are held at *The Store* twice a
night on Fridays and Saturdays from February
through May: *Store Days I* and *II*; *Nekropolis
I* and *II*; *Injun I* and *II*; *Voyages I* and *II*; and
World's Fair I and *II*. Performances evolve
from material on hand, including newspapers,
burlap, and a large box of costumes bought
at Lower East Side thrift shops. The series is
interrupted by the show "1961" at the Dallas
Museum for Contemporary Arts, which
features the entire contents of *The Store*.
Oldenburg stages *Injun*, commissioned by the
Dallas Museum, in an abandoned house on
museum property; the performance is restaged
as *Injun I* on Oldenburg's return to New York.
In June, he collaborates with Robert Breer
on *Pat's Birthday*, a film shot with the Ray
Gun Theater cast in Palisades, New York. At
Bellamy's invitation, Oldenburg turns the Green
Gallery into a summer studio and produces
large-scale soft canvas pieces sewn by Mucha,
while he continues plaster and enamel pieces
and drawings at *The Store* studio. The first
large-scale soft sculptures—such as *Floor
Burger*, *Floor Cake*, and *Floor Cone*—as well

as new *Store* pieces, such as *Breakfast Table*
and *Pastry Case I* and *II*, are exhibited in the
one-man Green Gallery show in September.
Sports, commissioned by the producers of
the film series "Mondo Cane," is performed
by Oldenburg, Mucha, and Samaras in the
setting of the exhibition. In November, *Lingerie
Counter*, *Assorted Food on a Stove*, and *Pastry
Case II* are shown in "New Realists" at the
Sidney Janis Gallery. "My Country 'Tis of
Thee" at the Dwan Gallery in Los Angeles also
includes work by Oldenburg.

1963

In January, Oldenburg participates in the
group show "Three Young Americans" with
Joan Mitchell and Robert Rauschenberg at
the Allen Memorial Art Museum in Oberlin,
Ohio. *Breakfast Table*, *Shirt with Objects
on Chair*, and *Soft Calendar for the Month
of August* appear in the sixty-sixth annual
exhibition of American painting and sculpture
at the Art Institute of Chicago. To coincide with
the exhibition's closing, *Gayety* is staged at
Lexington Hall at the University of Chicago. In
addition, a Pop art show at the Richard Feigen
Gallery in Chicago features a large number
of Oldenburg's works. Back in New York,
Oldenburg makes his first vinyl piece, *Giant
BLT (Bacon, Lettuce and Tomato Sandwich)*.
In April, *Bride Mannikin* and *Bacon, Lettuce
and Tomato Sandwich* are shown in "The
Popular Image" at the Washington Gallery
of Modern Art. *Stars: A Farce for Objects* is
performed in the gallery as part of the Pop
Art Festival, organized by Alan Solomon.
Oldenburg's work appears in "Popular Art" at
the William Rockhill Nelson Gallery of Art—
Atkins Museum of Fine Arts in Kansas City,
Missouri, and in a group show of "American
New Realists" at Galerie Ileana Sonnabend
in Paris. *Tray Meal* is exhibited in "Recent
Acquisitions" at the Rose Art Museum at
Brandeis University in Waltham, Massachusetts,
and eleven pieces are included in "Americans
1963" at the Museum of Modern Art in New

York. In March, Oldenburg joins the Sidney Janis Gallery. He continues producing vinyl pieces, typically starting with a "hard version" in cardboard, from which he draws patterns that Mucha then uses to sew a practice "ghost version" in muslin. Offered a show in Los Angeles by Virginia Dwan, Oldenburg and Mucha decide to vacate their East Fourth Street apartment and *The Store* studio and relocate to a bungalow in Venice, California, in September. He rents a former bank building nearby to use as a studio and focuses on making large-scale works toward a solo show at the Dwan Gallery. He also makes studies for a poster that use the mouse subject for the first time. Opening in October, the Dwan Gallery show features work such as *Baked Potato I*, *Giant Good Humor Bar*, *Giant Blue Shirt with Brown Tie*, and, introducing leopard-print vinyl, *Leopard Chair*. Throughout the fall, Oldenburg's work appears in "The Popular Image" at the Institute of Contemporary Arts in London; "The Harvest of Plenty" at the Wadsworth Atheneum in Hartford, Connecticut; and "Mixed Media and Pop Art" at the Albright-Knox Art Gallery in Buffalo, New York. Oldenburg pursues the Los Angeles–inspired theme of the Home and develops *Bedroom Ensemble* in drawings and models for the group show "Four Environments by Four New Realists" with Dine, James Rosenquist, and Segal at the Sidney Janis Gallery. The performance *Autobodys*, in which performers mix with automobiles, is held at night on December 9 and 10 in the parking lot of the American Institute of Aeronautics and Astronautics in Los Angeles.

1964

From January to March, Oldenburg works in Los Angeles toward a solo show at the Sidney Janis Gallery, developing the Home theme in technical and free-style drawings. *Bride Mannikin* and other *Store* pieces travel in the exhibition "Amerikansk pop-konst," organized by Pontus Hultén, director of the Moderna Museet in Stockholm. In March,

Oldenburg and Mucha move back to New York; they live at the Chelsea Hotel and work out of a loft at 48 Howard Street. *French Fries and Ketchup*, *Soft Pay Telephone*, *Soft Typewriter*, *Giant Toothpaste Tube*, and *Soft Light Switches* are shown at the Sidney Janis Gallery in April. Selected by Alan Solomon as one of eight American artists to represent the United States at the Thirty-Second Venice Biennale, Oldenburg sails with Mucha for Venice on May 13 on the Italian liner Vulcania. He spends August to October in Paris at Ileana Sonnabend's invitation, working in a borrowed studio on sculptures in the form of food. Made from plaster of Paris poured into cardboard or canvas forms and painted in tempera and casein, the finished sculptures rest on plates in vitrines and on display counters typical of Parisian shops. The sculptures and related drawings are exhibited in October at the Galerie Ileana Sonnabend in Paris. On November 22, Oldenburg and Mucha return to the Chelsea Hotel and the Howard Street studio.

1965

In March, Oldenburg and Mucha move into a block-long studio in a loft building at 404 East Fourteenth Street; on a set of shelves stenciled "museum of popular art, n.y.c.," he places unaltered, altered, and studio objects accumulated while moving from studio to studio. Oldenburg makes his first Proposed Colossal Monuments, comprising drawings of outsize objects placed in New York settings. The group show "Recent Work" at the Sidney Janis Gallery features proposals for an ironing board stationed above the Lower East Side and a cement pat of butter blocking the intersection of Broadway and Canal Street. In May, *Washes* is performed in the swimming pool of Al Roon's Health Club as part of the First New York Theater Rally, organized by Alan Solomon. On July 4, the *Washes* cast, including Samaras and Henry Geldzahler, as well as volunteers such as Carolee Schneemann visit the brook-side estate of the novelist and screenwriter Rudy Wurlitzer in upstate New York to make the film *Birth of the Flag*, photographed by Stan VanDerBeek and Sheldon and Diane Rochlin. Throughout August, Oldenburg produces watercolors of Proposed Colossal Monuments, which are later featured in *Domus* magazine in an article by Pierre Restany; subjects include a teddy bear for Central Park, a fan for Staten Island, and a banana for Times Square. Oldenburg creates his first multiple editions, *Baked Potato* for Tanglewood Press and the vacuum-formed *Tea Bag* for Multiples, Inc. That fall, Oldenburg revives his drawings of female figures in a series of erotic fantasies rendered in ballpoint pen. Concurrently, he works toward his second solo show at the Sidney Janis Gallery, continuing the Home theme in drawings and sculptures in the form of bathroom fixtures and kitchen appliances, such as a toilet, a washstand, a medicine cabinet, a bathtub, a scale, a Silex Juicit, and a Dormeyer mixer. The sculptures are realized in white, blue, orange, silver, and black vinyl obtained from California. In December, Oldenburg stages *Moveyhouse* at Film-Makers' Cinematheque in New York; performers don mouse masks that resemble the profile of a movie projector.

1966

In January, Oldenburg initiates the Airflow project by visiting Robert Breer's father, the inventor Carl Breer, in Detroit to research the first streamlined automobile, the Chrysler Airflow. He creates components of the car's "anatomy," such as the motor, the radiator, the tires, and the horn, in canvas impressed with enamel sprayed on corrugated cardboard panels; he also experiments with smaller versions of the whole car in vinyl. In March, sculptures on the theme of the Airflow and in the form of bathroom fixtures and kitchen appliances are exhibited in the show "New Work by Claes Oldenburg" at the Sidney Janis Gallery. The show also includes three-dimensional canvas maps of Manhattan postal zones and the New York City subway system, as well as Proposed

Colossal Monuments for New York sites. At intervals, Oldenburg continues his erotic drawings in pencil, combining female figures with objects in large scale. In August, he travels to Stockholm to prepare a survey of sculpture and drawing from 1963 to 1966, organized by Kasper König at the Moderna Museet. In studio space provided by director Pontus Hultén in the museum, Oldenburg produces additional work, including drawings and models of Proposed Colossal Monuments for Stockholm, such as a giant wing nut slowly rotating above a traffic circle. He makes a cast-iron multiple of knäckebröd (Swedish crispbread) and creates a large-scale soft sculpture in the form of a circular Swedish light switch. Banners in the shape of a saw using the colors of the Swedish flag, yellow and blue, hang outside the museum for the opening. At König's suggestion, the Geometric Mouse appears on the letterhead of stationery Oldenburg prints for exhibition correspondence. Based on the *Moveyhouse* mask, the Geometric Mouse consists of a square and two circles, with an organic appendage identified as "the nose." Colored Jell-O is prepared in *Life Mask*—a ceramic mold of Oldenburg's face made by the ceramicist Signe Persson-Melin from a plaster cast taken by the author and performance artist Michael Kirby— and served during the show. Oldenburg makes an amplified recording of himself typing louder and louder for his final performance, *Massage*, at the Moderna Museet on October 3, 4, 6, and 7. From October to November, Oldenburg utilizes a studio in London arranged by the Robert Fraser Gallery. He produces London-sited drawings, including *Proposed Colossal Monument for Battersea Park, London: Drum Set*, *Proposed Colossal Monument to Replace Nelson Column in Trafalgar Square: Gearstick in Motion*, and *Proposed Colossal Monument: Fagends in Hyde Park*. Oldenburg develops the theme of London Knees, relating them to the columns of the city's architecture; he proposes a colossal version for the Victoria Embankment at the edge of the Thames River. The ensuing multiple, *London Knees*, made in latex the color of the Elgin Marbles, comes in gray felt bags in a box filled with related materials, such as photographs from a knee contest at the local art school and drawings that compare knees to outsize fagends scattered in Hyde Park. At the end of November, the London drawings are shown together with a selection from the Moderna Museet survey in a solo show at the Robert Fraser Gallery. On his return to New York, Oldenburg collaborates with the poet Emmett Williams on a book about *The Store* and the Ray Gun Theater. A collection of notes, poems, scripts, sketches, and photographs, *Store Days* is published by Dick Higgins's Something Else Press the following spring.

1967

In January, Oldenburg travels to Toronto to attend the opening of "Dine, Oldenburg, Segal" at the Art Gallery of Ontario. He spends the winter working on constructions and drawings toward a solo show at the Sidney Janis Gallery in April that includes *Giant Soft Fan—Ghost Version*, *Giant Pool Balls*, and *Giant Fagends*, as well as drawings of Proposed Colossal Monuments elaborating on variations of cigarette butts and drainpipes. Selected by Alan Solomon for Expo '67, the black vinyl counterpart of *Giant Soft Fan— Ghost Version* is hung in the dome-shaped U.S. Pavilion, designed by Buckminster Fuller. At the beginning of the summer, Oldenburg makes a drawing of a composite image of a teapot, an elephant, and a Buddha for the Frank O'Hara memorial volume, *In Memory of My Feelings*. In August, Oldenburg and Mucha travel to Aspen, Colorado, to take part in Culture-In, an artist-in-residence program at the Aspen Institute for Humanistic Studies. He designs parts for a soft drum set and makes soft bats for a baseball game between resident artists and musicians. *Bedroom Ensemble* is the official selection of the United States at the Ninth Bienal do Museu de Arte Moderna in São Paulo, Brazil, that fall. Asked to take part

in "Sculpture in Environment," sponsored in October by the New York City Administration of Recreation and Cultural Affairs and Parks Department, Oldenburg directs city grave diggers to dig and then to refill a hole in Central Park near the obelisk behind the Metropolitan Museum of Art; he titles the event *Placid Civic Monument (Hole . . .)*. *Giant Soft Drum Set* is completed for the 1967 Guggenheim International Exhibition, "Sculpture from 20 Nations." "Projects for Monuments," a survey of Proposed Colossal Monument drawings, marks the inauguration of the Museum of Contemporary Art in Chicago; included are drawings proposing the Geometric Mouse as a facade for the new museum. *Pop-Tart*, a mural commissioned by the museum for the exterior wall of an adjoining building, is executed by the Arrow Sign Company after a clipping selected by Oldenburg. For a portfolio commemorating the opening of the National Collection of Fine Arts at the Smithsonian Institution in Washington, D.C., Oldenburg produces the lithographs *Scissors as Monument* and *Scissors to Cut Out* at the Mourlot workshop in New York; a reproduction of the *Scissors as Monument* lithograph serves as the poster for the Smithsonian commemoration. He also creates the lithograph *Double Punching Bag* to benefit the Foundation for Contemporary Performing Arts. In December, "Homage to Marilyn Monroe" at the Sidney Janis Gallery features Oldenburg's first metal sculpture, *Lipstick with Stroke Attached (for M. M.)*, fabricated at Lippincott Environmental Arts in North Haven, Connecticut. Also on view, *Ghost Wardrobe for M. M.* renders in string three signature items of clothing worn by Marilyn Monroe, removing all but the seams.

1968

From January to March, Oldenburg resides temporarily in Los Angeles to produce *Notes* with Kenneth Tyler at Gemini G.E.L. *Notes* consist of lithographic equivalents of notebook-page drawings of Colossal

Monuments, including images of the Geometric Mouse in Los Angeles settings. Returning to the subject of the Chrysler Airflow, Oldenburg also makes an aqua-green cast-polyurethane relief of the car's profile laid over a two-color lithograph. In May, Oldenburg returns to Los Angeles to write the text accompaniment to *Notes* and to prepare a solo show at the Irving Blum Gallery. Opening in June, the show includes monument drawings for Los Angeles using letters, such as *City as Alphabet* and *Design for a Police Building Using the Word "POLICE."* A proposal for a new museum in Pasadena in the form of a cigarette package is also exhibited along with constructions in the form of soft scissors and a punching bag. In August, Oldenburg procures a press pass and attends the Democratic National Convention in Chicago. To protest the use of violence by the Chicago police during the convention, he designs a multiple based on a typical Chicago fireplug for a group show at the Richard Feigen Gallery. Oldenburg also proposes a colossal sculpture for Grant Park in the form of Mayor Daley's head resting on a platter. Approached by *Esquire* magazine in December, he writes "My Very Last Happening" ("The Typewriter").

1969
Oldenburg travels frequently to Los Angeles during the first half of the year. He builds a second *Bedroom Ensemble* for "Pop Art Redefined," an exhibition at the Hayward Gallery in London. At curator Maurice Tuchman's invitation, Oldenburg participates in the Art and Technology program sponsored by the Los Angeles County Museum of Art. Assigned through the program to the theme-park division of Walt Disney Enterprises, he proposes *Giant Ice Bag*, which is subsequently completed at Krofft Enterprises with assistance from Gemini G.E.L. to become his first motorized construction. A commission by the artist and collector Bill Copley's Letter Edged in Black Press results in Oldenburg's *Soft Version of the Maquette for a Monument Donated to*

Chicago by Pablo Picasso, a copy of the Picasso sculpture in Chicago's Civic Center made to challenge the city's unlawful appropriation of the sculpture's copyright. *Saw—Hard Version*, commissioned by the Vancouver Art Gallery, is exhibited in the group show "New York 13." "Constructions, Models, and Drawings," a solo show at the Richard Feigen Gallery, features Chicago-themed work based on Oldenburg's recollections; a skyscraper in the form of a fireplug appears on the catalogue cover. *Frayed Wire*, a comment on the sociopolitical tension of the late sixties, replaces *Pop-Tart* and its successor *Emerald Pills* on the wall adjoining Chicago's Museum of Contemporary Art. In May, Oldenburg and Mucha agree to separate. Oldenburg rents a warehouse in North Haven, Connecticut, and establishes a studio close to Lippincott to develop large-scale outdoor sculptures. The first "feasible" monument, *Lipstick (Ascending) on Caterpillar Tracks*, is commissioned by a group of Yale architecture students led by Stuart Wrede. The Colossal Keepsake Corporation is formed, subscribed by alumni, students, and faculty. Fabricated at Lippincott, *Lipstick* stands on a platform visualized by Oldenburg as a podium from which to speak on the issues of the day. The sculpture is carried by students and installed without university approval in Beinecke Plaza. "Claes Oldenburg," a comprehensive survey of sculpture and drawings from 1954 to 1969, organized by Alicia Legg, opens at the Museum of Modern Art in New York on September 25. A week later, the black *Geometric Mouse— Scale A*, the first large-scale Geometric Mouse fabricated in steel at Lippincott, is installed in MoMA's sculpture garden. *Giant Pool Balls* is exhibited in "New York Painting and Sculpture: 1940–1970," curated by Henry Geldzahler at the Metropolitan Museum of Art. In the fall, *Claes Oldenburg: Proposals for Monuments and Buildings, 1965–1969*, with an interview by Paul Carroll, and *Claes Oldenburg: Drawings and Prints*, with text by Gene Baro, are published.

SELECTED BIBLIOGRAPHY

Books by Claes Oldenburg

Injun and Other Histories (1960). New York:
Something Else Press, 1966.
Store Days. Edited by Claes Oldenburg
and Emmett Williams. New York: Something
Else Press, 1967.
Notes. Los Angeles: Gemini G.E.L., 1968.
Claes Oldenburg: Notes in Hand. New York:
E. P. Dutton; London: Petersburg Press,
1971.
More Ray Gun Poems 1960. Philadelphia:
Moore College of Art, 1973.
Raw Notes. Edited by Kasper König. Halifax:
Press of the Nova Scotia College of Art and
Design, 1973.

Articles and Statements by Claes Oldenburg

Texts accompanying Fred McDarrah's
photographs of the performance *Snapshots
from the City*, p. 33. In *Beat Coast East: An
Anthology of Rebellion*. Edited by Stanley
Fisher. New York: Excelsior Press, 1960.
"Portfolio and Three Poems." *Exodus* 3
(Spring–Summer 1960), pp. 73–80.
"New Talent USA." *Art in America* 50, no. 1
(January 1962), p. 33.
"The Artists Say: Claes Oldenburg." *Art Voices*
4, no. 3 (Summer 1965), pp. 62–63.
"Fotodeath/Washes." *Tulane Drama Review*
10, no. 2 (Winter 1965), pp. 85–93, 108–18.
"A Statement," pp. 200–3; "Injun: The Script,"
pp. 204–6; "World's Fair II: The Script," pp.
220–22; "Gayety: The Script," pp. 234–40;
"Autobodys: The Script," pp. 262–71.
In *Happenings: An Illustrated Anthology*.
Edited by Michael Kirby. New York: E. P.
Dutton, 1965.
"Extracts from the Studio Notes (1962–64)."

Edited by Max Kozloff. *Artforum* 4, no. 5
(January 1966), pp. 32–33.
"The Airflow—Top and Bottom, Front, Back
and Sides, with Silhouette of the Inventor; to
Be Folded into a Box." *Art News* 64, no. 10
(February 1966), cover.
"Eftertankar," *Konstrevy*, nos. 5–6
(November–December 1966), pp. 214–20.
"Portfolio: 4 Sculptors." *Perspecta*, no. 11
(1967), pp. 44–53.
"Egomessages about Pollock." In "Jackson
Pollock: An Artist's Symposium, Part 2." *Art
News* 66, no. 3 (May 1967), p. 27, 66–67.
"America: War & Sex, Etc." *Arts Magazine* 41,
no. 8 (Summer 1967), cover, pp. 32–38.
"Statement." In "Homage to the Square."
Edited by Lucy Lippard. *Art in America* 55,
no. 4 (July–August 1967), pp. 50–57.
"Some Program Notes about Monuments,
Mainly." *Chelsea*, nos. 22–23 (June 1968),
pp. 87–92.
"About the Famous Toronto Drainpipe."
Artscanada 25, no. 3 (August 1968),
pp. 40–41.
"Claes Oldenburg: Fireplugs." *Design
Quarterly*, no. 74–75 (1969), np.
"Statement." In *Dubuffet and the Anticulture*,
p. 13. New York: Richard L. Feigen, 1969.
"My Very Last Happening." *Esquire*, May
1969, pp. 154–57.
"Notes on the Lipstick Monument." *Novum
Organum*, no. 7 (May 15, 1969), np.
"Bedroom Ensemble, Replica I." *Studio
International* 178, no. 913 (July–August
1969), pp. 2–3.
"Claes Oldenburg: Postcard 8/23/69." *Art
Now: New York* 1, no. 8 (October 1969), np.
"Chronology of Drawings." *Studio
International* 179, no. 923 (June 1970),
pp. 249–53.
"Letter to Maurice Tuchman, Jan. 27,
1969." In "An Introduction to 'Art and
Technology.'" Edited by Maurice Tuchman.
Studio International 181, no. 932 (April
1971), pp. 176–77.

Pincus-Witten, Robert. "The Transformation of Daddy Warbucks: An Interview with Claes Oldenburg." *Chicago Scene* 4, no. 4 (April 1964), pp. 34–38.

McDevitt, Jan. "Object: Still Life, Interviews with the New Object Makers, Richard Artschwager and Claes Oldenburg, on Craftsmanship, Art, and Function." *Craft Horizons* 25, no. 5 (September 1965), pp. 28–32, 55–56.

"Waldorf Panel 2" (discussion between Isamu Noguchi, Claes Oldenburg, Phillip Pavia, George Segal, George Sugarman, and James Wines). *It Is* (Fall 1965), pp. 77–80, 110–13.

Schilling, Alfons. "Bau Interview with Claes Oldenburg." *Bau* 4 (1966), pp. 83–87.

Glaser, Bruce. "Oldenburg, Lichtenstein, Warhol: A Discussion." *Artforum* 4, no. 6 (February 1966), pp. 20–24.

Baro, Gene. "Oldenburg's Monuments." *Art and Artists* 1, no. 9 (December 1966), pp. 28–31.

Fraser, Robert. "London: Male City." *International Times*, December 12, 1966.

Gablik, Suzi. "Take a Cigarette Butt and Make It Heroic." *Art News* 66, no. 3 (May 1967), pp. 30–31, 77.

Kostelanetz, Richard. "Interview with Claes Oldenburg." In *The Theater of Mixed Means*. New York: Dial, 1968.

Coplans, John. "The Artist Speaks: Claes Oldenburg." *Art in America* 57, no. 2 (March 1969), pp. 68–75.

Siegel, Jeanne. "How to Keep Sculpture Alive In and Out of a Museum: An Interview with Claes Oldenburg on His Retrospective Exhibition at the Museum of Modern Art." *Arts Magazine* 44, no. 1 (September–October 1969), pp. 24–28.

Claes Oldenburg: Skulpturer och teckningar. Stockholm: Moderna Museet, 1966. With texts by Öyvind Fahlström, Ulf Linde, and Claes Oldenburg.

New Work by Oldenburg. New York: Sidney Janis Gallery, 1966. With a text by Claes Oldenburg.

Baro, Gene. *Claes Oldenburg: Drawings and Prints*. Lausanne: Publications I.R.L.; London: Chelsea House Publishers, 1969. With texts by Gene Baro and Claes Oldenburg.

Claes Oldenburg: Constructions, Models, and Drawings. Chicago: Richard Feigen Gallery, 1969. With a text by Claes Oldenburg.

Claes Oldenburg: Proposals for Monuments and Buildings, 1965–1969. Chicago: Big Table, 1969. With an interview by Paul Carroll.

Claes Oldenburg. New York: Museum of Modern Art, 1970. With texts by Claes Oldenburg and Barbara Rose.

Claes Oldenburg: Object into Monument. Los Angeles: Ward Ritchie Press, in association with Pasadena Art Museum, 1971. With texts by Barbara Haskell and Claes Oldenburg.

ACKNOWLEDGMENTS

Claes Oldenburg: Writing on the Side 1956–1969 celebrates the artist's long-standing engagement with the medium of the written word. This volume is the product of many intense months of collaboration between the artist and the editors, sifting through a seeming infinity of raw material in order to create a book that strikes an appropriate balance between the many facets of Oldenburg's writing activity. Using only the products of the artist's own pen and typewriter, this volume chronicles the invention and evolution of a modern artist, at the same time as it reveals for the first time the remarkable breadth and depth of this realm of Oldenburg's work.

The Museum of Modern Art is honored to publish this book on the occasion of the exhibition "Claes Oldenburg: The Street and The Store (1960–1962), Mouse Museum and Ray Gun Wing (1972–1977)." This exhibition developed from "Claes Oldenburg: The Sixties," organized by the Museum moderner Kunst Stiftung Ludwig Wien. In conjunction with the preparation of these exhibitions, the artist has devoted much of the past few years to thinking about his life and work half a century ago. To complete that retrospection with a publication of his extraordinary writings from that time seemed not only natural but essential. This book is a fitting successor to the catalogue that accompanied the exhibition "Claes Oldenburg" at The Museum of Modern Art in 1969, written by Barbara Rose, which included an invaluable selection of the artist's writings.

Ann Temkin, The Marie-Josée and Henry Kravis Chief Curator of Painting and Sculpture, a close partner in this ambitious project, joins me in extending gratitude to all those involved in its realization. The volume's editors, Achim Hochdörfer, Maartje Oldenburg, and Barbara Schröder, brought great skill and tireless devotion to a task that was nothing short of herculean. Joseph Logan has collaborated with the editors and the artist to create a design that brings the material into clear and inviting form. Karen Kelly provided a keen and sensitive editorial eye to all of the texts. Alexandra Lane and Carey Ascenzo in Claes Oldenburg's studio offered instrumental support on a daily basis.

Christopher Hudson, Charles Kim, David Frankel, and Marc Sapir in The Museum of Modern Art's Department of Publications expertly guided this project along its way from the outset. With warm and inspiring generosity, Anna Marie and Robert Shapiro provided the funding necessary to enable a publication as rich and complex as the artist and the editors envisaged.

Finally of course, it is to Claes Oldenburg that we extend our deep admiration and immense gratitude. It is a joy to reveal within these pages his splendid accomplishment as a writer, no less brilliant for being "on the side."

Glenn D. Lowry, Director,
The Museum of Modern Art

Published in conjunction with the exhibition of
"Claes Oldenburg: The Street and The Store and
Claes Oldenburg: Mouse Museum/Ray Gun Wing,"
organized by the Museum moderner Kunst Stiftung
Ludwig Wien, Vienna, and The Museum of Modern
Art, New York. On view at The Museum of Modern Art,
New York, April 14–August 5, 2013. Organized by
Achim Hochdörfer, Curator, Museum moderner Kunst
Stiftung Ludwig Wien; and Ann Temkin, The Marie-Josée
and Henry Kravis Chief Curator, and Paulina Pobocha,
Assistant Curator, Department of Painting and Sculpture,
The Museum of Modern Art.

Major support for the MoMA presentation is provided
by The Dana Foundation, Donald B. Marron, The
International Council of The Museum of Modern
Art, Marie-Josée and Henry Kravis, Sue and Edgar
Wachenheim III, The Contemporary Arts Council of The
Museum of Modern Art, and The Junior Associates of
The Museum of Modern Art.

Support for the publication *Claes Oldenburg: Writing on
the Side 1956–1969* is provided by Anna Marie and
Robert F. Shapiro.

Produced by the Department of Publications,
The Museum of Modern Art, New York

Edited by Karen Kelly
Designed by Joseph Logan, assisted by Rachel Hudson
Production by Marc Sapir
Printed and bound by Brizzolis, S. A., Madrid

This book is typeset in Sabon and Futura. The paper is
115 gsm Lessebo Smooth White.

Published by The Museum of Modern Art,
11 W. 53 Street, New York, New York 10019

© 2013 Claes Oldenburg. All rights reserved

Library of Congress Control Number: 2013935423
ISBN: 978-0-87070-870-1

Distributed in the United States and Canada by
ARTBOOK | D.A.P., New York
155 Sixth Avenue, 2nd floor, New York, NY 10013
www.artbook.com

Distributed outside the United States and Canada by
Thames & Hudson Ltd.
181A High Holborn, London WC1V 7QX
www.thamesandhudson.com

All images of works by Claes Oldenburg © 2013
Claes Oldenburg.

Unless otherwise noted below, all writings by
Claes Oldenburg © Claes Oldenburg.

"Egomessages about Pollock," p. 284: © 1967 ARTnews,
LLC, May, and Claes Oldenburg
"Placid Civic Monument (Hole . . .)," pp. 294–99,
and "Self-Portrait," p. 346: © Norton Simon Museum
Archives, Pasadena, California, and Claes Oldenburg

Unless otherwise noted below, all images collection and
courtesy the Oldenburg van Bruggen Studio.

Page 104, Collection Milly and Arne Glimcher; p. 109,
Collection Ad Petersen, Amsterdam; p. 166, The Menil
Collection, Houston, Tex., Gift of Claes Oldenburg and
Coosje van Bruggen, 2010; p. 180, Collection The
Museum of Modern Art, New York, The Associates Fund;
p. 210, Collection H. Gael Neeson, Chicago; p. 240,
Collection Maurice Payne, London; p. 244, unknown
collection; p. 258, The Menil Collection, Houston, Tex.,
anonymous promised gift; p. 261, unknown collection;
p. 293, Collection The Museum of Modern Art, New
York, Gift of Lily Auchincloss, Charles B. Benenson,
Ronald S. Lauder, and Purchase; p. 335, Collection
Whitney Museum of American Art, New York, Gift
of the American Contemporary Art Foundation, Leonard
Lauder, President; p. 343, Collection Whitney Museum
of American Art, New York, Purchase, with funds
from Evelyn and Leonard A. Lauder, President; p. 347,
Collection Moderna Museet, Stockholm, photo:
Moderna Museet-Stockholm/Åsa Lundén.

Cover, typewriter in Claes Oldenburg's 14th Street studio,
c. 1965, photo: unknown photographer; back cover,
Oldenburg in 14th Street studio, 1967, photo: Charles
Moore, © Charles Moore/Black Star; p. 2, Oldenburg
in the Moderna Museet, Stockholm, 1966, photo: Hans
Hammarskiöld; p. 9, Claes Oldenburg, *Self-Portrait*,
1956; p. 49, Oldenburg dismantling the set of *Snapshots
from the City*, Judson Gallery, 1960, photo: unknown
photographer; p. 141, Oldenburg speaking to the
audience before a performance of the Ray Gun Theater
at *The Store*, 1962, photo: Robert R. McElroy, © Robert
R. McElroy/Licensed by VAGA, New York, N.Y.; p. 199,
Oldenburg and Patty Mucha at Galerie Ileana Sonnabend
in Paris, 1966, photo: Shunk-Kender, © Roy Lichtenstein
Foundation; p. 233, Oldenburg in London, 1966, photo:
Hans Hammarskiöld; p. 301, kitchen in 14th Street studio,
1968, photo: Ugo Mulas, © Ugo Mulas Heirs, all rights
reserved; p. 311, photo: unknown photographer; p. 349,
Oldenburg and Patty Mucha in 14th Street studio, 1964,
photo: Ugo Mulas, © Ugo Mulas Heirs, all rights reserved;
p. 368, Oldenburg in 14th Street studio, 1968, photo:
Arnold Newman, © Arnold Newman–Getty Images

Printed in Spain

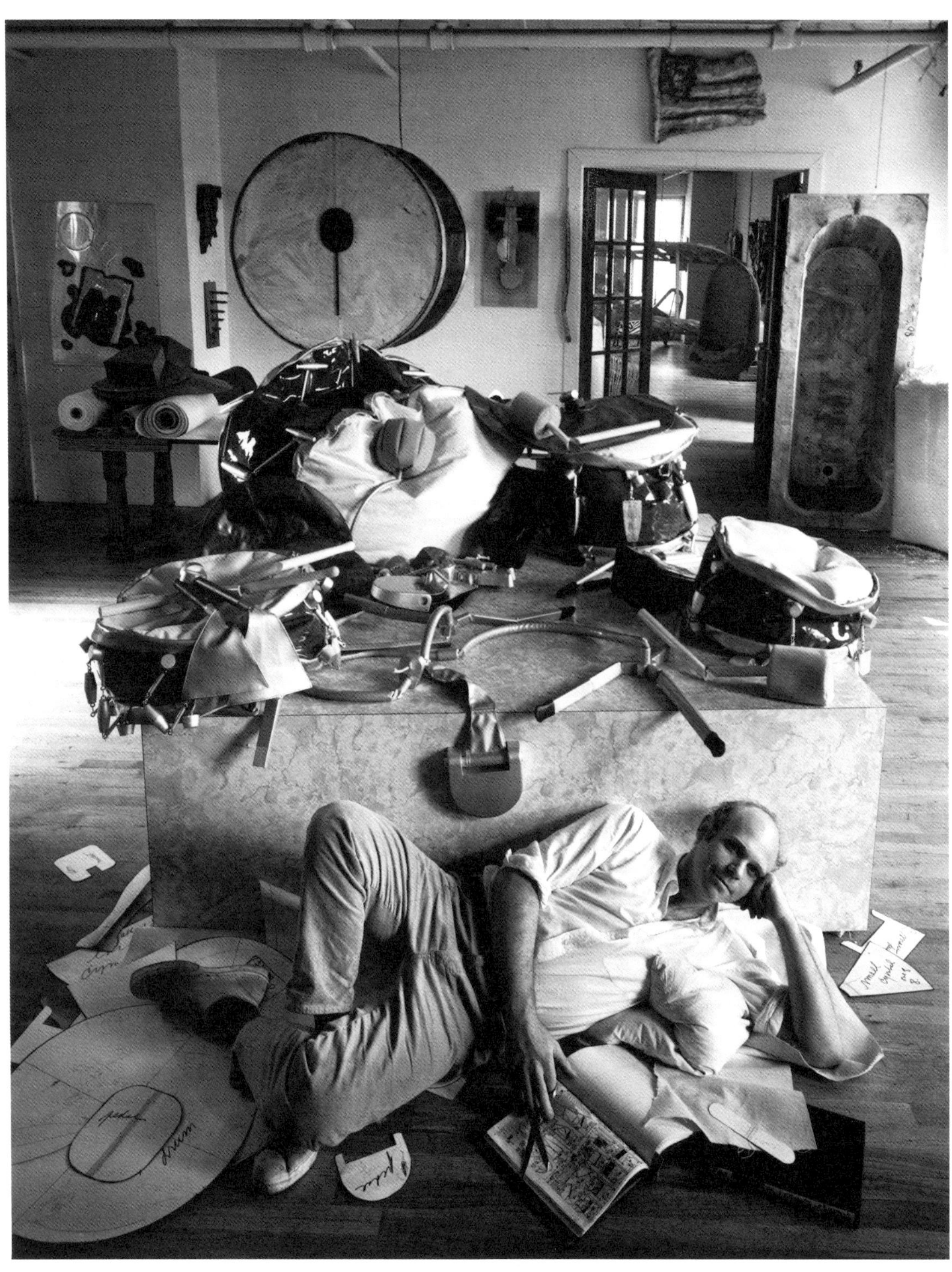